Jeremiah Smith, Ovid Butler, Thomas Wiley

Is Slavery Sinful?

Jeremiah Smith, Ovid Butler, Thomas Wiley

Is Slavery Sinful?

ISBN/EAN: 9783337412739

Printed in Europe, USA, Canada, Australia, Japan

Cover: Foto ©Suzi / pixelio.de

More available books at **www.hansebooks.com**

IS SLAVERY SINFUL?

BEING PARTIAL DISCUSSIONS OF THE PROPOSITION,

SLAVERY IS SINFUL,

BETWEEN OVID BUTLER, ESQ., A BISHOP OF THE CHRISTIAN CHURCH, AT INDIANAPOLIS, IND., AND JEREMIAH SMITH, ESQ., LATE JUDGE OF THE 11TH AND 13TH JUDICIAL CIRCUITS, IND.; AND BETWEEN ELDER THOMAS WILEY, LATE PASTOR OF THE CHRISTIAN CHURCH, AT UNION CITY, IND., AND JEREMIAH SMITH, LATE JUDGE OF THE 11TH AND 13TH JUDICIAL CIRCUITS, INDIANA; WITH AN INTRODUCTION, EPISODE, AND CONCLUSION OF THE DISCUSSION.

BY JEREMIAH SMITH.

INDIANAPOLIS:
H. H. DODD & CO., PRINTERS AND BOOK BINDERS.
1863.

DEDICATION.

To all who love the truth; to all who are willing to "obey the truth;" to all who are willing to "do nothing against the truth, but for the truth;" to all who love their country, their fellow-citizens, their neighbors, themselves, and their posterity, this work is respectfully dedicated,

BY THE AUTHOR.

ERRATA.

Page 58, line 12 from bottom, for *given* read *giving*.
Page 113, line 18 from bottom, insert *the* before *fanaticism*.
Page 154, line 10 from top, insert *the* before *servant*.
Page 168, line 17 from bottom, insert *that he* before *gave*.
Page 171, line 15 from bottom, for *had* read *has*.
Page 177, line 13 from top, for *auswer* read *answers*.
Page 258, line 10 from bottom, insert *shall* before *have produced*.
Page 268, line 6 from top, for *inventors* read *inventor*.
Page 338, line 18 from top, for *set* read *sit*.

There are other errors merely orthographical, which do not affect the sense, and hence are not noted.

PREFACE.

Our country is in a terrible condition. There is a cause, or causes, for its being so. All who love their country themselves and their posterity, should endeavor to ascertain the cause or causes of our present unhappy condition as a people, that by removing the cause of our troubles, we may restore the public health, vigor and prosperity.

It is alleged by the dominant party, that *the sin of slavery* is the cause of our calamities. If, however, slavery is not sinful, this is a false allegation. Hence, it behoves us all to examine the proposition, and ascertain *correctly* and *satisfactorily*, whether it is true or false, that slavery is sinful. For, if the proposition is false, as the powers that be, the men who control the destinies of this great people, base their action upon the assumed truth of the proposition, they are shedding rivers of blood, and wasting millions of treasure, and making thousands of widows and orphans, carrying devastation, fire and sword throughout the land, and sweeping with the besom of destruction the fairest and hitherto the most blest and prosperous portion of God's foot-stool, upon a falsehood. If this is the true state of affairs, how great and how dreadful is the responsibility upon us as a nation and people! and how incumbent it is upon us to drop the falsehood, seek the truth, and pursue it!

I am clearly satisfied that the proposition is false. The

object of this book is to show that it is false. It is my duty not only to ascertain the truth upon the subject to govern my own action by, but it is my duty to lend my humble aid to my fellow-citizens in ascertaining the truth also, that they may govern their conduct by it. And this is the more so, inasmuch as it is so persistently iterated and reiterated that the proposition is true, by " the power behind the throne greater than the throne," that now unfortunately controls the public affairs of this people. They, forsooth, will hardly brook the thought that the truth of the proposition should be doubted, denied, or controverted. But all who love the truth for truth's sake, are willing to examine and re-examine propositions, particularly when they are cardinal ones as this one is, to see if they are true or not. Truth never fears fair, candid investigation. And although clamor and detraction may decry her out of countenance for a time, yet eventually she will rise again, and shine the brighter for the ill-treatment she has received.

> "Truth crushed to earth will rise again,
> The eternal years of God are hers:
> While error wounded writhes in pain,
> And dies among her worshippers."

All that I ask of the reader is a careful, faithful, honest reading of the book; and a re-reading of it, if necessary to a full understanding and comprehension of the proofs adduced in it. If, after he shall have so read it, he still thinks the proposition true, let him do so. That is with him, and between him and his God and his country. We all have to answer for ourselves, and not for others.

I have written the book, or rather my portion of it, under great disadvantages, growing out of pressure of business and other affairs, including a protracted sickness which I had whilst it was being written. In the writing and preparation of it for the press, my thoughts were bestowed upon the matter—upon the proofs adduced—and not upon the manner, except to try to state the proofs so that they could be understood by all. Diction, style, and fine rounding of periods, I paid no attention to. My thoughts were otherwise engaged. So the critics need not trouble themselves as to those matters. Should the public demand a second edition, I may, in the preparation of that, devote some attention to style and diction. But the fact, the truth of my position, and the proofs adduced, I am ready for the critics to go to work at, if they really want to come to the knowledge of the truth. If they do not, and want only to throw dust in the eyes of the public to prevent the people from reading the book, or considering the proofs, they will be unworthy of consideration or regard by me, or of answer from me.

All of which is respectfully submitted: and I now give the book to the public, for its examination and consideration.

JER. SMITH.

Winchester, Ind., Oct. 1st., 1863.

INTRODUCTION.

Unfortunately for our country and people, slavery has been used as a subject of agitation and declamation, for a long series of years.

Agitate! agitate!! agitate!!! was the exclamation publicly made to his followers, by Mr. John Q. Adams, many years ago. Alas! they too faithfully followed his advice.

Agitation is not a means of acquiring either truth or knowledge. Examination, investigation, comparison, induction, &c., are the means of ascertaining truth, and thereby storing the mind with knowledge. This is true in all departments of truth and knowledge, whether moral, mental, physical, scientific, or historical. Agitation is only a perturbation, a disturbance of the thoughts; it excites the passions and prevents reason, reflection, and comparison. The agitator infuriates a nation, and makes it cry, even of the Lord of Life, crucify him! crucify him!! or pours millions of infatuated Europeans into Asia, as did Peter the hermit.

Hence, nought else could be expected from the continued agitation of the subject of slavery, but the terrible calamities with which our beloved country is now overwhelmed.

The great JEFFERSON, saw the danger at the beginning. "This momentuous question," said he in his letter of April 22d, 1820, to John Holmes, of Missouri, " like a fire bell in the night, awakened and filled me with terror. I considered it at once as the knell of the Union. * * * * * I regret that I am now to die in the belief, that the useless sacrifice of themselves by the generation of 1776, to acquire self-government and happiness, to their country, is to be thrown away by the unwise and unworthy passions of their sons, and that my only consolation is to be, that I live not to weep over it."[1]

---

(1) Jefferson's Works, vol. vii, pp. 159–60.

INTRODUCTION.

The *National Intelligencer*, then the leading political paper of the Union, in its issue of August 16th, 1825, said:

"We will inform the editor of the Boston *Sentinel* that we are neither the champions nor the apologists of slavery; and that we lament its existence with as much sincerity as any of those humane gentlemen who daily fulminate their anathemas against it, and the only effect of whose writings, if they have any, on the foul blot which they rail at, is to excite insurrection and consequent blood-shed."

Even Mr. Horace Greely, who for twenty years last past, has been so great an agitator of the subject of slavery, some twenty-seven or twenty-eight years ago, in his *New Yorker*, the first paper, I believe, that he ever edited and published, said:

"To a philosophical observer, the existance of domestic servitude in one portion of the Union, while it is forbidden and condemned in another, would seem, indeed, to afford no plausible pretext for variance or alienation. The Union was formed with a perfect knowledge on the one hand that slavery existed at the South, and on the other that it was utterly disapproved and discountenanced at the North. But the framers of the Constitution saw no reason for distrust and dissension in this circumstance. Wisely avoiding all discussion of a subject so delicate and exciting, they proceeded to the formation of a more perfect Union, which, leaving each section the possession of its undoubted right of regulating its own internal Government and enjoying its own speculative opinions, provided only for the common benefit and mutual well being of the whole. And why should not this arrangement be satisfactory and perfect? Why should not even the existing evils of one section be left to the correction of its own wisdom and virtue, when pointed out by the finger of experience?"

Had a prophet of God then met Mr. Greely and told him that he would do the evil to the government and people of the United States that he has since done and is still doing, would Mr. Greely have replied to him as Hazael did to Elisha, "But what! is thy servant a dog that he should do this great thing?"[1]

Mr. Jefferson, the *National Intelligencer*, and Mr. Greely, looked on it, and spoke of it, in its political aspect, as a political question. That is what it is. Slavery is an institution of civil society, or civil government. Its adoption or rejection in any State or nation, is a political question; a question to be decided by the kingdoms of this world, which all civil governments are, as contra-distinguished from the kingdom or government of our Lord and Savior Jesus Christ.

Hence its consideration, as an institution to be adopted or rejected originally where it does not exist, or to be continued or abolished where it does exist, is purely and truly, a political question, to be determined by the laws of political economy.

In our form of civil government in the United States, it

---

(1) 2 Kings, viii, 11-13.

belongs exclusively to each State to determine, for herself, whether or not she will have the institution. The right to interfere with her in her choice to adopt or reject the institution, or to inter-meddle with it, or with her in her management and enjoyment of it if she adopts or has it, is not granted by her in the Constitution of the United States, to the Federal Government, nor to the people of other States, but is expressly reserved, by her, in that instrument, to herself and her people.[1]

Viewed in that, its true aspect, there have been and are differences of opinion among the States and people of this Union. Some States and their people choose to have the institution; some because according to their views of political economy, as to their soil, climate, production, and social and domestic habits, think it proper for them; and some because the institution existed among them when they became independent States, and when the present generation was born and came into existence, and they can see no proper and safe mode, consistent with humanity, of getting rid of it. On the other hand, some States and their people, now constituting a majority of the States and people of the Union, choose not to have the institution. Some of the States that were originally slave States, have by systems of emancipation devised and carried out by themselves, each within herself, rid themselves of the institution. They disapprove of it politically as a domestic institution, and hence have decided and still decide not to have it.

My own views, I believe, concur with those of the mass of the people of the free States. I am satisfied that they do with the mass of the people of Northwestern States, where I reside. I think it proper, in the out-set, to prevent misapprehension and misrepresentation, to state my views as to the institution.

I am opposed to the institution, and prefer to live in a community where it does not exist, for various reasons, some of which are: 1st. I prefer not to live in a community where negroes are, either slave or free. God, by his fiat, has placed a broad and marked line of distinction between that race and ours, and I prefer, in my political and social relations, to regard that distinction, and not to mingle

---

(1) Art. X, Amendments to the Constitution.

with them in political and social relations, either of equality, or of servility on their part, and mastery on mine; and much more, of servility on my part and mastery on theirs. 2d. My political principles being democratic, I prefer to live in a community where all can have equal political privileges; and as negroes can not enjoy those privileges among the American people, either as slaves or free, I separated myself from them thirty six years ago, as Abram did from Lot, by coming from a slave State to wooden, wet, cold Indiana, and want myself and my posterity to remain separate and apart from them for all time to come. 3d. As a question of political economy, I am of opinion that the institution of slavery is injurious both to the country and people where it exists.

For these reasons, I am opposed both to the institution of slavery, and to living in contact with the negro race. And in coming to this conclusion, it is not necessary for me to settle the captious question sprung by abolitionists, whether it is because I am better or worse than the negroes, that I decline to stand in political and social contact with them. God has placed a broad and palpable line of demarkation between the races; and that is enough for me to know or answer, in determining whether as a political question, it is proper to keep the races separated, or to commingle them, without determining the question whether the races are equal, or the one is superior to the other. I have however, my views, and am well established in them, as to the question of equality of the two races, and of the inferiority or superiority of one race to the other.

The two races are here, and were here when this government was formed. It was formed by the white race, and not by the negroes. They did not participate in, nor have any hand whatever, in forming the Constitution and the Union. The Constitution was formed by the white race, to secure the blessings of liberty to THEMSELVES and THEIR POSTERITY,[1] and not to secure those blessings to the negroes. The *status* of the negroes was left as it was, subject to the action of each State within herself and for herself. And,

(1) Preamble to the Constitution of the United States. They had a perfect legal and moral right to confine the objects of the Constitution to those stated. They were as much legally and morally bound to undertake, by the Constitution, to secure the blessings of liberty to the down-trodden of Europe and Asia, as they were to secure them to the servile race in the several States. And even abolitionists do not contend that the object of the Constitution was to secure liberty to the subjects of despotical or monarchical governments.

as Mr. Greely pertinently asked in the extract above given, *Why should not this arrangement be satisfactory and perfect?* It was *satisfactory* to all who were willing to obey the Constitution in its letter and spirit, and while so obeyed, the system was *perfect*. Its failure has been brought about by a failure to live up to the rule, and not because the system was imperfect. The system of christianity is a perfect system to unite all the human family in harmony and brotherly kindness. It has hitherto failed to do so, not because of the imperfection of the system, but because its requirements are not lived up to. So of the federal system devised by the Constitution; its failure is not because of its imperfection, but because its letter and spirit have not been lived up to—because the people have harkened to, and acted upon the false theory of an "irrepressible conflict."

Mr. JEFFERSON, with the political sagacity that he possessed so thoroughly, gave the true reason why the arrangement made by the founders of the government, was not satisfactory. He said that the slavery agitation was a mere party trick. That "the leaders of federalism, defeated in the schemes of obtaining power by rallying partizans to the principles of monarchism, a principal of personal not of local division, have changed their tack, and thrown out another barrel to the whale. They are taking advantage of the virtuous feelings of the people to effect a division of parties by a geographical line; they expect that this will insure them, on local principles, the majority they could never obtain on principles of federalism;" but he thought that they would fail in the effort.[1] He was right in that; for they failed as long as they agitated the question on mere political grounds. The rights and duties of the people of the several States on that subject, were too clearly laid down in the Constitution, and the patriotic hearts of the people too firmly fixed in the determination to observe and respect all its rights and guaranties, to be drawn off by this federal trick, so long as the effort was made to operate upon them merely on political grounds.

This made it necessary for the "leaders of federalism" to devise another and more deeply laid "party trick." As religious feeling is the strongest sentiment of the human

---

(1) Jefferson's Works, vol. vii, p. 180, letter to Mr. Pinckney, of Sept. 30th, 1820.

heart, their trick was to attack the institution of slavery on moral grounds, declare it a sin, and get up a religious phrenzy and furor against it, and induce political action upon a "higher law" than the Constitution, with a total disregard of its injunctions as to the rights and duties of the several States and the people thereof. This they did after Mr. Jefferson had gone the way of all the earth. And after years of incessant "agitation," they have succeeded in "obtaining power," but at the fearful cost of a dissolution of the Union, and of a gigantic civil war!

In their denunciation of slavery as a sin, they had peculiar advantages in misleading the public mind, and working it up to religious phrenzy. They operated in the free States, and in them alone. In those States, the politicians and political press opposed to abolitionism, confined their discussion of the question, to constitutional and political duty and obligation, and did not touch the moral phaze of the question, because that was a question of theology, and hence not legitimately within the pale of political discussion. For a cardinal maxim of our theory and form of government, is, that church and State should be kept distinct and separate. Whether slavery was sinful or not, they did not inquire into nor discuss, because we, in the free States, did not have the institution, and were all agreed not to have it; and, whether sinful or not, we had to discharge our constitutional duties and obligations to the States and people that had the institution. This and this only, was urged by the political press and orators opposed to abolitionism.

The clergy of the free States who were not abolitionized, did not enter into the discussion of the question in their pulpits, for the very good and sufficient reason, that slavery was a political institution, and questions relating to it were political questions, and hence improper themes for the pulpit. The same reason operated upon the religious press not abolitionized, and kept it from the discussion of the question.

Those not politicians in the free States, being opposed to slavery as a political institution of their civil society or government, did not care to examine the question whether the institution was sinful or not, and felt wholly indifferent to it, as they and their States did not have the institution. While those that had examined the question and ascertained that the institution was not sinful, were deterred from combatting the abolition rant upon the subject, lest they should be placed in the false position before the community of being advocates of the institution, when they really were opposed to it as an institution of civil society, on political grounds. I was of this class for some years. Some ten years ago, I investigated the subject for myself, and became satisfied that slavery was not sinful, and that the abolition denunciation of it as a sin, was all false clamor. But I was, and had been for thirty years, opposed to the institution, and still continue to be, and expect to remain so. Had I combatted the abolition dogma that slavery is sinful, the whole brood would have poured their denunciations upon my devoted head, that I was the advocate of slavery—a pro-slavery man—a slave-holder in sentiment, &c. A principal means of operation used by abolitionists, is, and has been for years, to overwhelm with misrepresentation, vituperation, and slang, all who attempted any opposition to their wild vagaries. Hence I, in common with thousands of others, who desire " to lead a quiet and peaceable life in all godliness and honesty,"[1] refrained from combatting the abolition dogma that slavery is sinful. But when I saw the fearful calamities that were being brought upon our otherwise happy country and people, by the uncontradicted assertion and re-assertion of the dogma, I felt that duty to myself and my children, required that I should no longer refrain. Friends whose opinions were entitled to my most profound respect, advised me still to desist. The most prominent among our Christian brotherhood, wrote to me— " Still in the present state of affairs, I would let the matter rest, at least, for the *present*. They will put you in a *false issue* continually, and make you *the advocate of slavery*." Yet I have yielded to what I felt it to be my duty to do, and have entered the arena to cast in my humble mite to disabuse the public mind upon the subject, and roll back the torrent of misrepresentation, declamation, and sophistry, that abolitionists have been surfeiting the public mind with, for years. And for this I have already received a considerable amount of vituperation and slander, and shall doubtless receive much more hereafter. But having put my hand to

---

(1) 1 Tim., ii, 2.

the plow, I shall fearlessly advocate THE TRUTH, and leave the event with God. As the abolition dogma that slavery is sinful, is the cardinal tenet of their theory, and the main lever with which they have wrought the present great mischief to our country and people, it is absolutely necessary that its fallacy be shown, to restore to our unhappy and distracted country, the blessings of which she has been bereft by the belief of the dogma. This restoration I earnestly desire to see before I am called hence; for I can not bear the thought that the political blessings I inherited from my ancestors, I can not transmit to my posterity, because they perished in my keeping. And this is the reason why I have engaged in this work.

The reason why the people of the slave States did not combat this abolition dogma, was correctly stated by a presbyterian gentleman, a citizen of Kentucky, in a conversation I had with him last fall. He said: " That is a question I will not debate with them, [the abolitionists]; for if it is a sin it is my sin, and not theirs, and they are not accountable for it." This, I have no doubt, is the sentiment of the entire southern people, and is the reason why they did not enter into the discussion of the question with the abolitionists.

Hence, the abolitionists had a clear field. The politicians did not combat their dogma that slavery is a sin, because that was a theological question; the clergy of the free States not abolitionized, did not combat it, because slavery was a political institution, and not a proper subject for pulpit discussion; the citizens of the free States not politicians, did not discuss it, because they were indifferent to the question, as they had not the institution; and the citizens of the slave States did not discuss it with the abolitionists, because they were satisfied it was not a sin, but if it was a sin, it was not the sin of the abolitionists, and hence their intermeddling with it was sheer impertinence.

In addition to these advantages that the abolitionists had to mislead the public mind, the religious periodicals that first took the ground that slavery was sinful, closed their columns against those who wished to meet and refute their dogma.[1]

---

(1) Pulpit Politics, pp. 75 and 78, and proofs there cited.

How they proceeded in the various churches and ecclesiastical bodies to effect their objects, is well and fully shown by Professor CHRISTIE in his PULPIT POLITICS, a work that all should read who desire to ascertain the facts bearing on the subject. I shall omit giving here, even a summary of their action. They severed the churches one after another with their dogma that slavery is a sin. All sound-thinking men saw that these were but steps foreshadowing and leading to the final severance of the Union.

I shall close this branch of the subject by copying the views of the great statesman and patriot, HENRY CLAY, as reported by Dr. Hill, editor of *The Presbyterian Herald*, of Louisville, Ky. He says:

"Concerning the greatest source of danger to the country. A few weeks prior to the death of Hon. Henry Clay, when he passed through our city on his way to Washington, at the request of a Methodist minister from one of the Northern States, who had never seen the great statesman, we called with him to see him. He was quite feeble, and spoke of his death as a probable event within a few months. He said that nothing but a deep and abiding conviction that the Union of the States was in imminent peril, could have induced him, in his state of health, to leave the quiet of his own home, and go back to the Senate, the seat of so many of his struggles and great achievements. The opinion was expressed by one or both of us, that the danger of disunion was greatly overestimated; that if it ever came to the test, it would be found that there were very few who would be mad enough to rush into disunion, either North or South. He shook his head ominously, and replied: 'Gentlemen, if I have studied anything, it is the genius and spirit of the American people, both in the North and in the South; and I tell you, there is danger. There is a spirit rising up in both sections of this republic, which, if not speedily quelled, will bring about a severance of the Union of these States, not into two, but into half a dozen little petty republics, or despotisms, as the case may be.' It was replied that on several former occasions, the North and the South had been arrayed against each other in bitter hostility, but that the hostility had died away, and the parties restored to more than their former friendly relations. 'Ah!' said he, '*that was before the rise of modern Abolitionism. Fanaticism can not be controlled, and especially religious fanaticism. The churches of the country then stood together, and in their great national assemblies they drew the bond of Union and of brotherhood together. Now most of them have been rent asunder, and they are acting as dividers, rather than to bind the country.*' Said he: '*Gentlemen, you are both ministers of the gospel, and I tell you that this sundering of the religious ties which have hitherto bound our people together, I consider the greatest source of danger to the country. If our religious men can not live together in peace, what can be expected of us politicians, very few of whom profess to be governed by the great principles of love. If all the churches divide on the subject of slavery, there will be nothing left to bind the people together but trade and commerce.* That' said he, 'is a very powerful bond, I admit; but when the people of these States become thoroughly alienated from each other, and get their passions aroused, they are not apt to stop to consider what is to their interest. It is against the interest of both parties in every contest, to go to war, but nations constantly do it, notwithstanding the fact. It is against the interterest of men to fight duels, but they often do it, when they know that ruin, both to themselves and families, stares them full in the face. So,' said he, 'men will fight, if they consider their rights trampled upon, even if you show them that ruin to themselves and families will be the probable result. Besides, in times of high party excitement, the violent men on both sides get the control of matters, and moderate men are thrown into the background, and their councils go unheeded.' Finding that the venerable statesman had exhausted his strength in talking, we arose to bid him adieu, as we thought, for the last time on earth. He shook the hands of both of us, and said, '*If you preachers will only keep the churches from running into excesses and fanaticism, I think the politicians can control the masses. But,*' added he, '*yours is the hardest task, and if you do not perform it, we will not be able to do our part. That I consider the greatest source of danger to our country.*'"

The preachers did not perform their task of keeping the churches from running into excesses and fanaticism, and hence the politicians were not able to do their part; and demagogues devoid of statesmanship, taking advantage of the excitement of the times, violent men on both sides got control of matters, and moderate men possessed of statesmanship and patriotism, were thrown into the back-ground, and their counsels went unheeded. And the result is a dissolution of the Union and civil war, as foreseen by Mr. Clay.

The various religious denominations that were severed, had in their polity, ecclesiastical bodies called General Assemblies, Synods, General Conferences, &c., which had power to prescribe rules, ordinances, tenets, and tests of membership, for their several denominations, and through them the abolitionists operated by procuring the adoption of rules, ordinances, tenets, and tests of membership upon the subject of slavery. But the body called Disciples of Christ, or Christians, or Campellites, have no such authoritative ecclesiastical body. They acknowledge no creed, or rule of faith and practice, or test of membership, but the New Testament. They do not acknowledge the authority of any ecclesiastical body or court of judicature, to adjudicate for, speak for, or bind the whole body of their brotherhood. They acknowledge only the Lord Jesus Christ as their King and Law-giver, and the Apostles as his only Judges, who were set by Him on twelve thrones to judge or give laws to the church, the body of Christ; and that their judgments and laws are written out in the New Testament, to govern the church or body of Christ, for all time to come; and that they did their work fully and completely, and have no successors to add to or subtract from their adjudications there written out and left for us. And that each congregation of christians, through their presbytery, or eldership of bishops and deacons, have simply to administer or apply the adjudications and laws, so written out and left in the New Testament, to their respective congregations and the members thereof. Or in other words, that the Head of their body is the Lord himself, and their General Assembly, Synod or Conference, is the College of Apostles, which fully did its work and left recorded in the New Testament, all adjudications and laws necessary and proper for the body of Christ. Hence the few abolitionists among them could not work schism and division among them in the manner that abolitionists did among other bodies of professed christians. But the abolitionists among them were seized and possessed of the same restless and contentious spirit (peculiar to all abolitionists) that had wrought schism and division among the other denominations. But as there was no authoritative ecclesiastical body to resort to now on earth, the Apostles having long since left it, they resorted to the press to effect their work. When they found that they could not divert the standard periodicals of the brotherhood, from their proper vocation of being christian periodicals, and convert them into organs of abolition agitation, they got up periodicals to advocate and disseminate their views. They thus started a Weekly paper in Cincinnati, called *The Christian Luminary*, notwithstanding THE AMERICAN CHRISTIAN REVIEW was then published in that city, and ably conducted by ELDER BENJAMIN FRANKLIN, to the satisfaction of the entire brotherhood except the few infected with abolitionism. The *Luminary* was edited by brother John Boggs, and efforts were made to scatter it broadcast among the brotherhood of the North-West. Specimen papers were sent to me with a request that I should aid in its circulation and dessemination. I was anxious that our brotherhood should not be divided and dissolved as the other religious denominations had been, and that our dissolving civil government, should be saved if possible. Hence I wrote to the editor, which led to a correspondence, part of which was published in his paper, but all of which I think proper to insert here; it will speak for itself.

WINCHESTER, IND., JAN. 26TH, 1861.

Bro. John Boggs, editor Christian Luminary:

DEAR SIR :—I have received your paper of the 10th and 17th instant, with a special notice enclosed, requesting me to become a subscriber, and ask my neighbors to do likewise.

I can not become a subscriber for two reasons. 1st. I am taking as many of our religious periodicals, as I think it proper to expend money for. This is sufficient, and I might stop here; but I think it proper to give the other reason. 2d. A principal, if not *the* principal subject treated of by the paper, is the institution of slavery; an institution of *civil society* existing in a portion of the States of this Union. Now though that institution existed in a worse form in all the society that the Lord and the Apostles labored in during their ministry, than it does in any State of this Union, yet they never discussed the rightfulness or propriety of it, nor denounced it as sinful, but gave explicit directions to both masters and slaves, as to their conduct towards each other, without directing or even reccommending a severance of the relation existing between them. Therefore the discussion of the rightfulness or propriety of that institution, or the denunciation of it as sinful, is no part of christianity, nor of the work of a christian. Hence the *Luminary's* course is outside of christianity, and in the political field. Professing to be christian when it is political, it is, for that reason, anti-christian. Making schisms and divisions among christians about matters not pertaining to christianity, it is heretical—making a sect—and is therefore denounced by the divine law. In violation of the divine law, it is, under a pretence of being free, "using its liberty for a cloak of maliciousness" against the brethren in Christ who are slaveholders, as well as against fellow-citizens of the best civil government ever given by God to man, instead of using its liberty "as the servants of God; honoring all men; loving the brotherhood; fearing God; honoring the king," or the civil authority and its institutions existing in our nation and States.[1] The course of the *Luminary*, as well as that of those brethren who think and act with it on this subject, is sinful, and is doing the cause of Christ much harm. I can not therefore, take the paper, nor encourage others to do it; and I should be much gratified if you, and those who act with you as to that subject, could see the error of your ways, and abandon them. Your opinions on that subject, no one would object to your having and entertaining, so long as you kept them as private property, or mere political opinions as they are; but when you teach and insist on them, you become heretical, schismatical, anti-christian.

O! that we all would come to the *knowledge* of the Lord, that is, come to the *knowledge* that the Lord has imparted to our fallen race in the scriptures given by inspiration.

---

(1) 1 Pet., ii, 16, 17.

The divine injunction to us is, to "grow in favor and the knowledge of our Lord and Savior Jesus Christ."[1] If we continue in, or keep, or observe his word, we shall know the truth,[2] that is, come to the knowledge of the Lord; but if we set up our own vain philosophizings, and continue in, or keep them, we become "proud, knowing nothing," &c.[3]   Affectionately yours,
JER. SMITH.

[From the Christian Luminary, of Feb. 7th, 1861.]

NO NEUTRAL GROUND.

There is *philosophy*, as well as divine wisdom, in the assertion of the Savior, recorded by Matthew, "He that is not with me is against me; and he that gathereth not with me, scatereth." No christian man can occupy neutral ground on any of the great moral questions of the day. If we do not take a stand *against* sin, we will before we are aware, be apologizing for it, and then there is only one step left to make us its open advocates. Practically every professor of christianity is either *for* or *against* every moral question. If we are careful about our words, our *influence* will all the time be telling for weal or for woe, in the community having cognizance of our lives.

A short time ago we sent a specimen copy of the *Luminary* to a prominent member of the Christian Church, living in Indiana—a man who *politically* takes strong Republican ground. Appended was a note politely requesting him to become a subscriber, and to use his influence to induce others to do likewise. To show the reader where some of our brethren, even in the non-slave-holding States, stand on the slavery question, *even* where they are identified with the Republican party, we make the following extract from a letter we have just received from him:

"A principal, if not the principal subject treated of by the paper, is the institution of slavery; an institution of *civil society*, existing in a portion of the States of this Union. Now, though that institution existed in a worse form in all the society that the Lord and

(1) 2 Pet., iii, 18.   (2) John, viii, 31, 32.   (3) 1 Tim., vi, 4.

the apostles labored in during their ministry, than it does in any State of this Union, yet they never discussed the rightfulness or propriety of it, nor denounced it as sinful, but gave explicit directions to both masters and slaves, as to their conduct towards each other, without directing, or even reccommending a severance of the relation existing between them. Therefore the discussion of the rightfulness or propriety of that institution, or the denunciation of it as sinful, is no part of Christianity, or of the work of a Christian. Hence the *Luminary's* course is outside of Christianity, and in the political field. Professing to be Christian when it is political, it is for that reason anti-christian. Making schisms and divisons among Christians about matters not pertaining to Christianity, it is heretical—making a sect—and is therefore denounced by the divine law. In violation of the divine law, it is under pretence of being free, "using its liberty for a cloak of maliciousness" against brethren in Christ who are slave-holders, as well as against fellow-citizens of the best civil government ever given by God to man, instead of using its liberty "as the servants of God; honoring all men; loving the brotherhood; fearing God; honoring the king" or the civil authority and its institutions existing in our nation and States. (1) The course of the *Luminary*, as well as that of those brethren who think and act with it on this subject, is sinful, and is doing the cause of Christ much harm. I can not therefore take the paper, nor encourage others to do so; and I should be much gratified if you, and those who act with you as to that subject, could see the error of your ways and abandon them."

The foregoing is, the reader will observe, written in a kind spirit, and is only hard because the writer actually feels that he is doing God service in opposing the *Luminary*, and all the brethren who are in any way laboring to divorce the church of Christ from the sin of slavery. He does not manifest any dislike to any of us as men or brethren, but looks upon us as engaged in a heretical work. He occupies about the same position to the anti-slavery movement in the church, that Saul of Tarsus, did to the church, when he "verily thought that he ought to do many things contrary to the name of Jesus of Nazareth." We have no doubt but the writer of the aforesaid letter is just as *sincere* in his opposition to the *Luminary*, as was Saul when he consented to the death of Stephen, and held the tunics of those who stoned him. We award to him then, the credit of sincerity. There is just one question to settle on the whole question of slavery, morally considered, and that is, *whether it is a sin in the sight of God*. That question once satisfactorily settled, there must be an end of the controvesy so far as *Christians* are concerned. If slave-holding is a violation of the great law of love, under which all the disciples of Jesus are brought, then those who are laboring to *abolish* it, as far at least, as the church is concerned, are not " heretical," as our correspondent is pleased to style us. PURITY is a law of heaven, and also a law of the church. " First *pure*, then peaceable," is the apostolic order. If, therefore, there is any *impurity* about the institution of slavery, it is the duty of all Christians to labor for its removal from the church. With the

---

[1] 1 Pet., ii. 16, 17.

stereotyped sophism that, "Christ and his apostles never discussed the rightfulness of slavery," we shall not at present stop to hold any argument. It has been exploded time and again, and could be used with just as much propriety in justification of gambling, horse-racing, dancing, *polygamy*, and many other immoralities as slavery. The question covering the whole ground is: "Is American slavery sinful?" We take the *affirmative*, and our correspondent and all others who occupy his ground, must, to be consistent, take the negative. We are not going to elaborate our affirmation at this time, but stand pledged to do so whenever the writer of the foregoing extract, or any other *respectable* member of the Christian church, is ready to take the other side. Suffice it to say at this writing, that the very act of chattelizing a man is a sin, and every thing connected with slavery, from the beginning to the end of it is evil, only evil, and that continually. American slavery can not exist without oppression, cruelty, covetousness and the total violation of all the relations of husband and wife, parent and child, brother and sister, and the systematic exclusion of all education from the slave. Is it "heretical" then, to oppose such an institution? We hold that Christians are bound to oppose it.

It is seen by the foregoing, that Mr. Boggs stated what is the truth; that the proposition *Slavery is sinful*, is the gist of abolitionism. Hence if it is untrue, abolitionism falls.

[From the Luminary, of March, 7th, 1861.]

PRELIMINARY CORRESPONDENCE.

BRO. JOHN BOGGS.—*Editor Christian Luminary:* I see from your paper of the 7th instant, which you were so kind as to send me, that you published a part of my letter of the 26th ult., declining to subscribe for your paper, and giving two reasons why I declined.

As I understand your remarks upon it, you are willing "to elaborate" your position on the slavery question, and "stand pledged to do so, whenever" I "or any other *respectable* member of the Christian church, is ready to take the other side."

I am much engaged in other business, and am not certain that I can find time to investigate the subject properly; yet, believing as I do, and as I stated in my former letter to you, that the course of the *Luminary*, as well as that of those brethren who think and act with it in the slavery agitation, now pervading our whole community, both religious and political, "is sinful, and is doing the cause of Christ much harm," I do not feel myself at liberty to decline the investigation with you, but feel constrained to contribute my humble mite, to enable us all to "grow in grace, and in the knowledge of our Lord and Savior Jesus Christ,"[1] and to come to the knowledge of the truth, as it is in Jesus,[2] so "that we all speak the same things, and that there be no divisions among us; but that we be perfectly joined together in the same mind, and in the same judgment,"[3] and "live in peace."[4] Hence, I now propose to investigate the subject with you in the columns of the *Luminary*, not for a mere polemic victory on either side, but that we may all ascertain where the truth is, and having ascertained it, to do as all lovers of truth do, follow it, let it lead where it may, notwithstanding our previous opinions, and our previous conduct resulting from those opinions.

You seem to think, that the question covering the whole ground, is, "Is American slavery sinful?" I respectfully submit, that that is *a principal* question, rather than one "covering the whole ground." I frankly admit that it is *the principal* one, in your theory, or view of the premises; but to fully canvass and understand the law of the Lord, and our duty as Christians in the premises, I respectfully submit that there are three other questions proper to be considered. Hence I propose the following, as the questions for consideration:

I. Slavery is an institution of civil society, or civil government. Jer. Smith affirms.

II. Slavery is sinful. J. Boggs affirms; Jer. Smith denies.

III. Christian preachers should preach against slavery,

---

(1) 2 Pet., iii. 18.   (2) Eph., iv. 21.   (3) 1 Cor. i. 10.   (4) 2 Cor. xiii. 11.

both orally and in Christian periodicals. J. Boggs affirms; Jer. Smith denies.

IV. When Christian preachers preach against slavery, either in the pulpit, or through the press, and insist that Christians should free themselves of it, and that those Christians that refuse to do so, should be disowned or dis-fellowshipped, they, that far are heretical, schismatical and anti-Christian. Jer. Smith affirms; J. Boggs denies.

The parties shall have equal space (say two columns to each number) in the *Luminary*, and the numbers to follow consecutively, one after another. The propositions to be discussed in their order, as numbered. The first proposition (if the parties differ upon it) to have three numbers on each side, if the parties desire so many; the second proposition to have six numbers on each side, if the parties desire so many; the third proposition to have four numbers on each side, if the parties desire so many; and the fourth proposition to have five numbers on each side, if the parties desire so many. The party who has the affirmative, to open the discussion on the propositions respectively, and to have a short number, say half a column, extra, in reply to the last number on the other side, but to introduce no new argument or authority in it.

Either party to have the privilege of publishing the discussion in book form after it is closed, if the opposite party shall decline to participate in the publication of it.

If this meets your approbation, you may publish this as introductory; and, if you take the negative of the first proposition, I will proceed to open the discussion of it. If, however, you admit the first proposition, you can say so, and proceed to open the discussion of the second.

My part of the discussion will necessarily be furnished irregularly; but I will be as prompt as I can. If the discussion goes on, I shall want two copies of the papers containing it, sent to me regularly, as they are issued.

    Fraternally yours,   JEREMIAH SMITH.
Winchester, Ind., Feb. 9th, 1861.

P. S.—You are in error, in supposing me "identified with the Republican party."

Bro. Jeremiah Smith, Esq., *Winchester, Ind.*

Dear Sir:—Your favor of 9th inst. came duly to hand, and would have been answered sooner, had not a short absence from home, and other matters, prevented. I am truly gratified to find *one* man in our brotherhood, who is willing to defend his pro-slavery principles—principles entertained by a majority of our whole membership. I also rejoice that I am likely to have so respectable an opponent, as I understand you to be—never having had, I believe, the pleasure of meeting you personally. From the circumstance of your being an old practitioner at the bar, and being at this time, (if I am not mistaken) District Judge in the circuit in which you reside, I have no reason to doubt your entire ability to discuss the subject in the most creditable manner.

I would suggest a few changes, and verbal alterations, in your propositions, which I hope you will accede to. If so, I shall be happy to engage with you in a friendly discussion of the slavery question. The *first* proposition is, as far as it goes, *true*, and it is so interwoven with the whole subject, that its discussion, as a seperate proposition, seems to me entirely unnecessary. I suggest, therefore, that it be stricken from your list of propositions.

Your *second*, I accept, with simply one qualifying word. I want to affirm, that "*American* slavery is sinful." I suggest this amendment, simply to confine the discussion within proper limits. The only slavery with which we have much to do in this country, is American slavery, and I am ready to affirm its sinfulness.

Your *third* proposition, is virtually involved in your *fourth*, and may, therefore, be included in it. Your propositions will then be reduced from four to two. But before accepting your last proposition, I wish to offer an amendment. It is to strike out the words, "and that those Christians that refuse to do so, should be disowned, or dis-fellowshipped." The proposition would then read thus, " When Christian preachers preach against slavery, either in the pulpit, or through the press, and insist that Christians should free themselves of it, they, that far, are heretical, schismatica and anti Christian."

On the first, I affirm, and you deny. On the second, you

affirm, and I deny. I agree with you in the suggestion that "each party shall have equal space (say two columns to each number) in the *Luminary*, and the numbers to follow consecutively." As the propositions will be two instead of four, I suggest that the time be lengthened, so as to allow eight numbers each, on each proposition. I object to the "extra" half column to the affirmant, inasmuch as it is contrary to general usage.

To your stipulations in reference to publishing the discussion in book form, should it be thought necessary, I agree, with the single addition, that if published conjointly, the work shall be done wherever the best terms can be obtained. Now, if you accept my amendments, I will open the discussion upon the proposition, that "American slavery is sinful," at my earliest convenience, after hearing from you.

I am, with kindest regards,
Fraternally yours,
JOHN BOGGS.
Hopewell Home, near Cin., O., Feb. 29, 1861.

[From the Luminary of March 14th, 1861.]

LETTERS THIRD AND FOURTH.

BRO. JOHN BOGGS, *Editor Christian Luminary*.

Dear Sir:—Your letter dated Feb. 29th, was received to-day, but after my note of to-day had gone off in the mail. I haste to reply, that one letter from you may answer both.

I did not suppose that a discussion of the first proposition would be necessary, but was willing to affirm it, if you denied it. As you do not deny it, but admit it, we set it down at the head of our propositions as admitted by both. I prefer to retain it as one of the series.

I disapprove of the qualifying word you propose to insert in the second proposition.

Slavery, as an institution, is, the relation of master and slave existing between two or more persons. Now, if this relation is sinful, it is immaterial whether the parties bearing it to one another, are in America, Europe or Asia. A man and woman not lawfully married together, but one or both of whom are married, that live together as husband and wife, are living in adultry, and bear the relation of adulterer and adultress to each other. Were it proposed to discuss the proposition, *Living in adultery is sinful*, would it be pertinent or proper, to insist on having the proposition modified by placing the adjective *American*, at the commencement of it? Would it aid the inquiry into the sinfulness of it to call it American, European or Asiatic, living in adultry? I apprehend not. If slavery is sinful, it is so without regard to the place where it exists; and in an inquiry as to its sinfulness, it is entirely unnecessary to take into the account the place of its location.

For these reasons, I object to the modification of the second proposition that you propose. But if you must have the word American inserted into it, to enable you to contemplate an institution that is either sinful or not sinful, independant of its locality, why, I will not be strenuous about it, but let you insert the word.

I can not agree to have the third proposition dropped. If one of the two has to be dropped, let the fourth be the one. The third affirms that the practice pursued by you, and by those brethren who think and act with you, is proper and right. I think it is not. It is for you to sustain your action, in the face of the reasons I shall urge against it. I am willing, and offer, *after that is done*, to affirm the fourth proposition; but not to become the attacking party until you have made the effort to sustain your conduct over my objections. The third proposition must be discussed if the discussion goes on. I am willing to drop the fourth, but think that it is necessary to retain it to cover the whole ground that should be examined in the discussion. I am not willing, however, to modify it as you propose. If I affirm the proposition, I shall affirm it in the language in which I framed it; which, in my opinion, describes the evil as it exists among us.

I agree that there may be eight numbers on each side of each proposition, if desired, whether there be two or three propositions discussed, and will not insist on the extra fractional number, though the affirmative having to preponderate the scale, has the close in courts for that reason.

If we publish conjointly, we will have equal voice in arranging details, as a matter of course, and can make no agreement beyond that now.

When the preliminaries are arranged, and before the discussion opens, I wish all the correspondence, commencing with my letter of January 26th, to be laid before the readers of the *Luminary*, as introductory to the discussion.

Fraternally yours, JER. SMITH.
Winchester, Ind., March 4th, 1861.

BRO. JEREMIAH SMITH, *Winchester, Ind.*

Dear Sir:—Your favor of the 4th inst., is before me, to which I hasten to respond. I am greatly surprised that you object to the modifications suggested in my last, as I certainly think they greatly simplify the propositions, while they cover the whole ground of controversy between us. In reference to the third of your series, which you indicate in your last, to be the "*sine qua non*" of the discussion, is, to my mind, wholly included in your fourth, and in precisely the form in which it should come up. You affirm that preachers, and others who preach and write against slavery, are guilty of heresy, schism, faction, etc., and of course I deny the indictment. As a lawyer, you certainly are aware that the accused party is not under obligations to prove himself *not* guilty. But on the contrary, the "*onus probandi*," rests entirely upon the accuser. It is not my business to prove myself innocent of murder, or theft, or arson, or drunkenness, or schism, or heresy, or anything else that I might be charged with. You affirm that my course is schismatical, heretical, and anti-christian. I *deny*, and call for the proof. I affirm that it is anti-christian, and contrary to the morality of the Bible, for the disciples of Christ to hold their fellow human beings as property. You deny. I am ready to adduce the testimony to establish my proposition. I think, therefore, that the two propositions made up of your second and fourth, entirely cover the points in controversy. As to leaving your *first* proposition as one to which we both assent, I object. It would be an unheard of thing to insert in a list of proposition for discussion, one that was assented to by both parties. Besides the proposition can be so worded that I would be willing to take its negative, and should be if retained at all.

You object to the striking out amendment I proposed to your fourth proposition. But you should not, for the proposition without that sentence, expresses the sentiment taught by me, and by the regular contributors to the *Luminary*. I have not yet defined the exact point of forbearance there should be exercised towards slaveholding church members.

The right and duty of preachers and editors, to enlighten the whole brotherhood in reference to the sinfulness of slaveholding, is the point of distinction between the *Luminary* and our other periodicals. We affirm, and they deny. I think our slaveholding brethren are many of them greatly in the dark on the subject, and that it is our duty to give them light. I trust you will see, Bro. Smith, that your objections are not valid, and that your second and fourth propositions as amended by me, cover the true ground of controversy.

I am very anxious to have a friendly, candid discussion with you, and in case you refuse the two propositions as above stated, I will present the four following, as a substitute for the four first proposed by you:

1st. American slavery is wholly a civil institution, and one that no wise concerns the disciples of Christ. You affirm, I deny.

2d. Slaveholding, as legalized and practiced in fifteen of the United States, is sinful in the sight of a just God, and in the light of the Bible. I affirm, you deny.

4th. It is the duty of the church to bear its testimony against the sin of slaveholding, through the press, the pulpit, and every other means legitimately, within its power. I affirm, you deny.

3d. When Christian preachers preach against slavery, either in the pulpit, or through the press, and insist that Christians should free themselves of it, and that those who presistently *refuse* to do so, should be dis-fellowshipped, they are heretical, schismatical, and anti-christian. You affirm, I deny.

If you must have *four* propositions instead of two, I think you can have no reasonable objection to the foregoing, inasmuch as I have incorporated in the third the very expression I wished stricken out of your fourth, in the series presented by you. But, as I said before, I do not want to lose the the opportunity to discuss the whole subject with a christian gentleman, so well qualified to do justice to the cause, as you are reported to be.

I remain with kindest regards,
Fraternally yours,
JOHN BOGGS.
Hopewell Home, near Cin., O., March 9th, 1861.

[From the Luminary of March 21st, 1861.]

LETTERS FIVE AND SIX.

BRO. JOHN BOGGS, *Editor Christian Luminary:*—I have not yet received an answer to my notes of the 4th instant. You were so kind as to send me the *Luminary* of the 7th, in which I found my letter of the 9th of February, and your reply, dated the 29th of February, (printed different in some respects however, from the letter received by me,) and to which my last of the 4th of March was a reply. I have just received the *Luminary* of the 14th instant, in which I find my note of the 4th, with a reply from you. If you sent a reply in manuscript, it has miscarried.

Having stated in my last that *when* the preliminaries were arranged, and *before* the discussion opened, I wished the correspondence commencing with my letter of January 26th, to be laid before the readers of the *Luminary*, as preliminary to the discussion, when I received the *Luminary* of the 7th instant, with my letter of the 9th and yours of the 29th of February, in it, without receiving any reply to mine of the 4th of March, I could but presume that you had accepted the terms, stated in that letter, and that the preliminaries were arranged, and you had commenced the publication of the correspondence, not wishing to give space in one paper for it all. I was disappointed, however, in not finding that the publication of the correspondence commenced with my letter of the 26th of January, as requested. From yours of the 9th of March, it seems that the preliminaries are not yet arranged. This, therefore, is in reply to that.

I respectfully submit and insist, that the first and second propositions have been agreed upon. The first you admitted, but deemed it unnecessary. The second I accepted in your own form, giving reasons however, why you should not insist upon the modification you proposed to it. That acceptance stands, and I will not agree to modify it as you propose in your last.

The first proposition should remain though we both affirm it. It is not necessary that we should take opposite sides upon it, to make it one of our series. For, the institution of slavery and the duty of Christians in relation to it, being the subject we desire to investigate, in order that we may not "strive about the words to no profit, but to the subverting of the hearers,"[1] we should know what the institution of slavery is. Hence I affirm that it is an institution of civil government. If you deny it, say so, and I will undertake to prove it. If you do not, it stands admitted. It must be an institution of civil government, or an institution of the Lord's kingdom; for there are but two; the kingdoms of this world, and the kingdom of our Lord and Savior Jesus Christ. You have admitted it to be an institution of civil government, (kingdoms of this world); hence we agree as to what it is, but still it is an essential proposition to be kept in our series, and used in our further investigations, that we may contemplate and talk about the same thing. Many of the unfortunate dissensions that have existed in the human family have grown up because the persons who got into them, contemplated different things in their dissensions. Clear ideas are essential to correct reasoning and just judgment. Hence we keep the first proposition in the series as a truth admitted by both. I could not affirm the proposition you framed in yours of the 9th of March, be-

---

(1) 2 Tim. ii. 14.

cause the institution does concern both Christian masters and Christian slaves, and places them under the necessity of obeying that part of the law of Christ addressed to them as masters and slaves, and imposes that much more responsibility upon them. The third proposition I will accept as you have it framed in your last; but I respectfully and earnestly solicit you to amend it by substituting the word *Christians* for the words *the church;* and to strike out the words *the sin of.* These amendments, I think, are eminently proper; but if you will not agree to them, let the proposition stand as you have framed it. Three propositions are now agreed to; one admitted by both to be true, and the other two to be discussed.

The fourth proposition, as framed by me, will be retained or stricken out as you may say. I think it should be retained for the reasons given in my last, but I will not insist upon it.

You are the accuser, brother Boggs. You are accusing Christian brethren and sisters who are slaveholders, and Christians who are not, that differ with your views on that subject, and, by your action, you affirm that your conduct is right. I deny it; and as a Christian brother, as I have a right to do, I call upon you to justify your course by the law of the Lord. So far, I am no accuser. I am willing however, and offer, after you shall have answered my call upon you, not to accuse any one, but, to attack such conduct as is described in my fourth proposition. If you are willing to investigate it with me, I will engage in it with you; if you are not, I shall not press it.

We have now two propositions to discuss, and a third if you say so. I promise that the discussion on my part, shall be " friendly and candid." As you are " very anxious to have" it, you will go on with it; and as you " do not want to lose the opportunity to discuss the whole subject," you will consent to have the fourth proposition retained.

In the same paper in which you print this, print the propositions as agreed upon, including the fourth or not as you may elect; and in the following paper, the discussion will be opened—by me, if you deny the first proposition, and by you, if you do not.

I enclose $2,00 to pay for two copies of the *Luminary*,

for eight months; if the discussion shall not be concluded within that time, I will send an additional amount.

Fraternally yours.   JER. SMITH.
Winchester, Ind., March 15th, 1861.

BRO. JEREMIAH SMITH, *Winchester, Ind.*

Dear Sir:—Your kind favor of 15th instant, came duly to hand this morning, to which I hasten to respond. My last reply was written just in time, to have it set up for last week's paper, and I had not leisure to copy it at the time, but intended to send you a proof-slip in advance of the paper. It was, however, overlooked in the press of business bearing upon my mind. For the failure to do so, I feel that I owe you an apology.

Through a mistake of the person making up the form, I see we do not understand each other in reference to the *order* in which the propositions are to stand. The proposition you call the "*third*," is really the fourth of the series, as I have them numbered, although awkwardly placed immediately after the second. I will agree to the amendments you suggested in reference to it, *provided* you agree to the order as numbered by me, and will accept the *first*, still further amended as hereinafter specified. We will then have *four* propositions, and the affirmatives and the negatives will be both alternate and equal. As amended then, the propositions will read and *stand* as follows:

First—American slavery is wholly a *civil* institution, and one that in no wise concerns Christians residing in the non-slaveholding States. You affirm, I deny.

Second—Slavery is sinful. I affirm, you deny.

Third—When Christian preachers preach against slavery, either in the pulpit or through the press, and insist that Christians should free themselves of it; and that those who persistently *refuse* to do so, should be dispelled; they are heretical, schismatical, and anti-Christian. You affirm, I deny.

Fourth—It is the duty of Christians to bear testimony

against slaveholding through the press, the pulpit, and every other lawful means within their reach. I affirm, you deny. The foregoing propositions, I think concede every thing that you can reasonably demand, and I trust will be entirely satisfactory to you. In the first proposition, both your objection and mine are removed. I do not want an undebatable proposition in the series, and indeed *can not* consent to any such arrangement. As now worded, it leaves out the classes of church members to which you alluded in your last. To give you all the ground you possibly ask, I accept the second according to your original draft, notwithstanding you had partially agreed to accept my amendment. The third as it stands, you have accepted, and the fourth is now amended as you suggest in your last. If you accept the series as amended, we will then decide definitely in reference to number of articles allowed on each proposition, and the greatest amount of space to be assigned to each article.

As the present volume of the *Luminary* is so nearly expired, I would prefer commencing the discussion with the first number of the next volume.

I am with kindest regard,
Fraternally yours,
JOHN BOGGS.
Hopewell Home, near Cin., O., March 18th, 1861.

[From the Luminary of April 6th, 1861.]

LETTERS SEVEN AND EIGHT.

BRO. JOHN BOGGS, *Editor Christian Luminary:*—Yours of the 18th of March is just received. SLAVERY is the subject that we, as christians, wish to investigate. The natural and logical order of considering the subject is this: 1st. What is it? 2d. Is it sinful? 3d. What should christians do in relation to it? Then, after these matters are ascertained, an inquiry whether any particular action by a christian, or christians, is wrong, schismatical, or anti-christian, is proper, if any such inquiry is desired; for in making any such inquiry, the three previous ones must be taken into the account, and should be settled before this one is entered upon. To take them up, and consider them in any other order would be illogical.

We should ascertain what slavery is, without coupling with that inquiry any predicate or affirmation of, or concerning it. Yet you insist that to a proposition defining it, shall be added an affirmance of a thing relating to it. We agree to the proposition defining it; and hence there is no need of debate upon it; and because of that, you will not agree to let it stand in our series of propositions. You say "I do not want an undebatable proposition in the series, and indeed, *can not* consent to any such arrangement." Would it not look strange for a mathematician to say that he could not consent to have either definition, postulate or axiom placed at the head of a series of geometrical propositions that were to be demonstrated? that though he admitted the definition to be correct, was willing to grant the postulate, and that the axiom was self-evident; yet as they were "undebatable," they should not occupy a position in the series?

The propositions were placed by me in their logical order. There is no propriety in breaking that order, merely to have affirmatives and negatives to come alternately.

In my letter of the 4th of March, speaking of my fourth proposition, which you number *third*, I said that I was not willing to modify it as you proposed; that if I affirmed the proposition, I should "affirm it *in the language in which I framed it;*" and, in my next and last letter, I said: "The fourth proposition, *as framed by me*, will be retained or stricken out, as you may say;" and yet you say in your last, "The third (my fourth) as it stands, (in your series just above,) *you* (1) *have accepted!*" How you could have fallen into such an error, I am at a loss to conjecture.

As you will not let the first proposition stand at the head of the series, either as a definition, postulate, or axiom, I now here strike it out.

I now place the series as the propositions stand agreed to; the words in brackets I desire left out; but you can retain them if you insist on doing so.

I. [American] Slavery is sinful. J. Boggs affirms; J. Smith denies.

II. It is the duty of christians to bear testimony against

[the sin of] slavery through the press, the pulpit, and every other means legitimately within their power. J. Boggs affirms; J. Smith denies.

III. When christian preachers preach against slavery, either in the pulpit or through the press, and insist that christians should free themselves of it, and that those christians that refuse to do so, should be disowned, or disfellowshipped; they that far, are heretical, schismatical and anti-christian. J. Smith affirms; J. Boggs denies.

The last above proposition you can strike out if you desire it done; if not, it stands as above—not as you modified it.

The first and second propositions above will stand as there, unless the words in brackets are left out with your consent; I desire them out.

There is no need now of any more convassing and discussing this branch of the preliminaries. If you intend to discuss, say so; say what and how much of the above you will discuss. The other preliminaries, I think, are agreed upon as follows:

The parties to have equal space in the *Luminary*, to-wit: two columns to each number.

To be eight numbers on each side of each proposition, if either of the parties desires so many. The numbers to follow consecutively one after another.

The propositions to be discussed in the order in which they stand; the one having the affirmative of a proposition, to open the discussion of it; the other to reply; and so on alternately.

Either party to have the privilege of publishing the discussion in book form, after it is closed, if the opposite party shall decline to participate in the publication of it. If the parties publish conjointly, they are to have equal voice in settling and arranging the details.

I think that your reply to this ought to close the preliminary correspondence. If you want to delay the opening of the discussion until the commencement of the next volume of the *Luminary*, you may do so; but that is no reason why the preliminary correspondence should be protracted till then.

Fraternally yours,
JEREMIAH SMITH.

Winchester, Ind., March 22d, '61.

BRO. JEREMIAH SMITH, *Winchester, Ind.*

Dear Sir:—Your favor of the 22d inst. is before me, and contents noted. I agree with you that "*slavery* is the subject that we, as christians, wish to investigate." But I differ with you in your opinion that your series of propositions is the most "natural and logical" that can be framed.

Your affirmation that "slavery is a civil institution," is true as far as it goes, but it is not the *whole* truth. Therefore, as you have it worded, I can neither affirm nor deny, without doing violence to what I conceive to be the true definition of slavery. But with my amendment, I can deny your affirmation, while you retain only what I suppose you intended by your first affirmation. I am pleased, however, to find that you are willing to dispense with the whole proposition, inasmuch as a full definition of slavery is enjoined upon me, by accepting the affirmative of your second proposition, which I am ready and *anxious* to do. Your allusion to the solution of mathematical problems I consider altogether foreign to the subject under consideration, and, hence, in no wise a parallel case. You say, "If you intend to discuss, say so." I answer, that I intend not to let the present opportunity to discuss the whole slavery question slip, if I can bring you to what I consider fair and honorable terms. But I am not anxious enough for a discussion, to give you any very decided advantage, in the arrangement of the propositions. If they must all be just in your language, and stand in your order, there will be no discussion. If your last two propositions are to be discussed, their order *must* be transposed. I am ready and willing to affirm that "slavery is a sin," whether in or out of America. But I am not willing to affirm a negative, or what amounts to the same thing, undertake to prove myself and others *innocent* of the charges you have so gravely made. I insist upon it, that your *third* proposition should be the second, and your *second*, if discussed at all, should be the third.

If you accept of the transpositions, we are then ready for the discussion, for I agree to take the three propositions as worded by you, rather than have you decline the discussion. The propositions will then stand as follows:

I. Slavery is sinful. I affirm, you deny.

II. When christian preachers preach against slavery in

the pulpit, or through the press, and insist that christians should free themselves of it, and that those christians who refuse to do so, should be disowned or disfellowshipped, they that far, are heretical, schismatical anti-christian. You affirm, I deny.

III. It is the duty of christians to bear testimony against slavery through the press, the pulpit, and every other means legitimately within their power. I affirm, you deny.

To all your other preliminaries, as detailed in your last, I agree. I confess I do not admire the wording of the *second* proposition. It is too long and too complicated, or, in other words, it is *too lawyer-like;* but I will take it as it is, provided that will obvate any further *preliminary* discussion. If you consent to the propositions, as hereinbefore stated, I will publish the propositions and other specifications in consecutive order, and then the way will be clear for the discussion proper.

Fraternally yours,
JOHN BOGGS.
Hopewell Home, near Cin., O., March 27th, '61.

LETTER NINE.

BRO. JOHN BOGGS, *Editor Christian Luminary.*

Dear Sir:—Yours of the 27th of March is just received.

To affirm that it is the duty of christians to bear testimony against slavery through the press, the pulpit, &c., is not "to affirm a negative, or what amounts to the same thing;" and I am at a loss to conceive why you should say so. This whole correspondence, and particularly my last letter, disproves the charge that I have claimed or desired, that the propositions "must be all just in my language, and stand in my order." The propositions, as put down in your last, are not as worded by me; and yet you say that you agree to take them that way rather than have me decline the discussion!

The first and second propositions, as set out in my last, *are agreed upon*, you having the right to retain the words in brackets, or to let them be left out, as I desire them to be. And if you do not want to discuss the third, *after the other two are discussed*, you were directed in my last to say so, and it would be stricken out; if not, it was retained. So we had two propositions to discuss, and a third if you were willing to discuss it; but I have twice expressly said I would not press the discussion of it. It now so stands, and I now, a third time, say, that you can have the third discussed after the other two are discussed, or not, just as you elect and say. I think it should be discussed, *but will not press it*.

In looking over my letters of the 15th and 22d of March, and your replies to them, I begin to apprehend that we shall not have a discussion. I hope otherwise.

The first and second propositions, as set out in my last, are agreed upon, and ready for discussion; and the other preliminaries are agreed upon; the third proposition will be retained where it is, or stricken out entirely, *as you may say*. Why not, then, proceed at once with the discussion? If you are not willing to undertake to justify, by the good word of the Lord, your course and action on the subject of slavery, in the pulpit and through the press, in the face of, and over the objections I shall urge against the proofs you adduce, say so manfully, and do not try to avoid it by saying it is a negative, or by trying to get the investigation of an inquiry *that logically arises after that investigation is had*, thrust in before it.

Fraternally yours,
JER. SMITH.

Winchester, Ind., April 10th, 1861.

This letter, though sent immediately, was suppressed, and not published in the *Luminary*. I can not imagine any reason for its suppression, but that it too plainly exposed his course, and got him up into too tight a place. He had either to undertake to justify his conduct in slavery *agitation*, (not discussion) or to manfully say he could not do it. Agitators can not stand a close logical investigation; and abolition agitators are no exception to the rule. They must have ample sea-room, and when about to be pinned down at any one point, they flee to some other. Had brother Boggs published this letter, he could not have practiced the *ruse* he did upon the public and his readers by suppressing it, not answering it, and in his paper of the 16th of May, 1861, publishing the following article to cover up his retreat:

"OUR DISCUSSION.

As there seems to be considerable difficulty in adjusting the propositions submitted by Bro. Jeremiah Smith, Esq. for a discussion, we propose the following two as a substitute for the whole:

1st. To hold human beings in involuntary servitude, as property, is a sin in the sight of God, and contrary to the teachings of the Holy Scriptures. Boggs affirms; Smith denies.

2d. The agitation of the anti-slavery question in the church, either orally or through the press—teaching the duty of christians to withdraw their fellowship from such as persistently continue to hold slaves, is schismatical and heretical, and consequently a sin in the sight of God, and contrary to the Holy Scriptures. Smith affirms; Boggs denies.

The whole ground is thus covered by two propositions. We have sought no advantage in the wording of them, but rather to express clearly the real sentiments held by us respectively. Bro. Smith thinks it is sinful to make the slavery question a test of fellowship in the church, or to agitate it in the pulpit, or through the press. We think slavery is a sin, and are willing to affirm it; and we presume Bro. Smith is willing to affirm his sentiments. If so, we can have a discussion *right away*. If not, it is hardly worth while to prolong our *preliminary* correspondence. We are satisfied that slavery is contrary to the teaching of the Bible, and are ready to affirm it anywhere, and before any tribunal. We are also willing to defend the whole anti-slavery movement by our brethren, against the charge of schism and sinfulness, made by Bro. Smith and those whom he represents. If he is ready to deny what we affirm, and affirm what we deny, the discussion will commence immediately."

On the reception of this I immediately wrote to the editor. In the *Luminary* of May 30th, my letter appeared, with accompanyings, in matter and form, as follows:

THE DISCUSSION.

In the absence of the editor, the *pro tem* takes the liberty of publishing both of the following communications. They will, no doubt, be intelligible to those readers who have read the preliminary correspondence upon this subject. In the meantime, the absence of the editor for some weeks will be a sufficient apology for any apparent neglect of the subject.

BRO. JOHN BOGGS, *Editor Christian Luminary:*—The *Luminary* of yesterday is just received, containing an article headed "Our Discussion." That of last week was also received, in which nothing is said about our discussion, nor was my last letter to you, of the 10th of April, contained in it.

There is not, and has not been, on my part, any "difficulty" in adjusting the propositions for discussion. I have stricken out the 1st proposition to gratify you; I have agreed that the 2d and 3d may be modified as you propose to modify them; and I have agreed to withdraw the 4th, if you are not willing to let it occupy its logical position in the series. I use the numbers here, as they stood in the propositions as originally proposed by me.

Were I now to accept the two propositions you set out in the *Luminary* of yesterday, as there set out, I still could not rely that the discussion would go on; for two propositions have long since been agreed upon, and yet you do not proceed with the discussion, but say in your paper of yesterday, that "there seems to be considerable difficulty in adjusting the propositions."

I respectfully claim and insist, that my last letter, dated April 10, 1861, and this note, be inserted in the next number of the *Luminary*, and do hope that you will at once proceed to open the discussion. If you do not, and the discussion does not go on, cease to send the *Luminary* to me.

Fraternally yours,
JEREMIAH SMITH.

Winchester, Ind., May 17, '61.

Bro. Boggs:—I have for two years been a reader of the *Luminary*. I like it in the main. But I must take the liberty of protesting against your interminable discussion of the slavery question. I don't wish either to be understood as being opposed to free discussion, but I must be allowed to judge of what will be suitable mental food for my children.

I see by the last number, that you are about to enter the list with a Bro. Smith, upon the subject again. You must suffer me to say, that I can hardly stand it. I don't like to say, "stop my paper."

You don't know, perhaps, that my seven children, whom I love dearer than my own life, belong to the proscribed class. If, instead of discussing the question whether we should be made to work for you white folks without wages, and sold to the highest bidder by the pound, you change the form of it and discuss, "Is it sinful to fatten and barbacue those children?" it would not be quite so repulsive. Perhaps Bro. Smith would accept of it in this form. If he should not, and the discussion must go forward in the old way, please stop my paper.

Yours very truly,
MANA POINTER.

P. S.—Should Bro. Smith consent to the question as above stated, could you not get Bro. Hartzell to undertake with him? He is a much more experienced debater than you. M. P.

Hopedale, O., April, 1861.

This correspondence, and brother Boggs' conduct in relation to it, exhibit a fair specimen of abolition tactics; and I introduce it here as well to show them, as to lay what I said before the reader. After making a great show of willingness and anxiety to undertake to sustain his dogma that slavery is sinful, and to justify his conduct in agitating the slavery question in the pulpit and press, when brought to the point, he backed square out, suppressed the letter that brought him to the point, and after a month's silence, to mislead his readers as to the true state of the correspondence, said, in his paper, that there was "considerable difficulty in adjusting the propositions," when there had not been, as is shown by the correspondence; and finally, when held to his position again by my letter of the 17th of May, he got either a real or fictitious negro to protest against his "interminable discussion of the slavery question," to help him out of his predicament. *Discussion* is what he and Mana Pointer both object to; but *agitation* must go on. Discussion might make bare their folly and impiety; agitation, however, would poison and mislead, if not infuriate, the public mind. The one must be suppressed; the other must be persisted in, in the pulpit, press, and everywhere, except where there is an opponent. And derision and obloquy must be invoked, by having Mana to talk of selling by the pound, and fattening and barbacuing his children! These are abolition tactics, and are practiced and indulged in by men who claim that they are christians, and are doing "the work of the Lord,"[1] in thus acting!

Thus ended the flourish of trumpets with which brother Boggs set out. He kept Mana Pointer on his list of subscribers, and struck me off, but did not return my $2 that I had sent him. His paper, I believe, went down soon after.

Brother ELIJAH GOODWIN, an amiable and excellent brother, who was publishnig a monthly religious periodical at Indianapolis, commenced issuing it in weekly form on the 1st of January, 1862. It soon began to show that the dissemination of abolitionism was its mission, equally with, if not more than, the dissemination of christianity. I speak thus because they are distinctly different things, and lie in different fields, departments and kingdoms. *Abolitionism* is *political*, and belongs to the kingdoms of this world; while *christianity* is *religious*, and belongs to the kingdom of our Lord and Savior Jesus Christ.

Believing, as heretofore stated, that duty required that I should not longer remain silent, as to the abolition assumption, that slavery is sinful, by which (it being uncontroverted) abolitionists had been enabled to do so much harm to our country and people, both religiously and politically, and were still doing harm in that direction, with increased exertions and vigor, and being anxious that our brotherhood should not be rent and torn asunder, as almost all other religious denominations had been by that abolition assumption, I resolved to combat abolitionism in brother GOODWIN'S

---

(1) 1 Cor. xvi, 10.

paper so far as it exhibited itself there, and that it should not go to the brethren who read that paper unanswered and unrebuked.

Brother A. R. BENTON, President of the Faculty of the Northwestern Christian University, at Indianapolis, wrote for brother GOODWIN's paper. His eminent abilities, and deservedly high position, made his teaching upon that subject the more readily accepted as correct by the mass of readers, and pointed him out as a proper person to sustain the abolition dogma that slavery is sinful, if it is sustainable. He was therefore the proper person to pay my respects to, in doing what I thought, and still think, it was my duty to do. An article of his, published in brother GOODWIN's paper, *The Weekly Christian Record*, of April 8th, 1862, made the proper occasion for me to enter the arena; and I dropped a note to brother GOODWIN, to know if I could have space in his paper to reply to the article, and received the following answer:

INDIANAPOLIS, April 12, 1862.

BRO. SMITH:—Yours of yesterday is at hand, and I answer, that you can have space in the *W. C. Record* to reply to BRO. BENTON's article. I suppose you wish to notice that portion which seems to refer to American slavery. I have always been opposed to discussing that question in our paper, not because I thought it should not be discussed, but because I conceived the public mind not to be in a proper state to be profited by the discussion—nor am I sure the time is now fully come, though I think it is approaching. Please write in christian love, and for the good of the cause. Yours in hope,

E. GOODWIN.

I sent an article, which was replied to by brother OVID BUTLER, one of the bishops of the Christian Church at Indianapolis, and President of the Board of Directors of the Northwestern Christian University. For a number of years, he was a prominent member of the bar at Indianapolis, where he deservedly stood high; but he retired from the practice some ten or fifteen years ago. His eminent abilities and position, and the fact that he had long been an abolitionist, and was well grounded and established in his conviction that slavery is sinful, made him a very proper person to discuss that question with. A public correspondence ensued, which resulted in our entering into a regular discussion of the proposition, *Slavery is sinful.* Those preliminary articles, commencing with President BENTON's, I now lay before the reader.

[From the Christian Record, of April 8th, 1862.]

FANATICISM OF ERROR.

It is a most inexcusable wrong to stigmatize as fanatics, men of pure, disinterested and philanthropic aims in life. From this most flagrant injustice, even the religious press, and the pulpit are not altogether free.

As a convenient polemical weapon, it has always been found easier to demolish an opponent by hurling public sentiment against him, than by calmly canvassing his views.

This kind of treatment has been in vogue from ancient times, as for example, the case of Paul at Athens, when he preached to the people of that polite metropolis, Jesus and the Resurrection. When he came to that part of his discourse that treated of the Resurrection, they mocked, or tried to raise a laugh at his expense, as a most incorrigible simpleton and fanatic. Nor was this his only experience of that sort.

While he was expounding the faith in the presence of Agrippa, Festus interrupted the flow of his discourse with this decisive refutation, in a loud voice—the louder the better in such a case—" Paul, thou art beside thyself, much learning doth make thee mad;" or, in modern parlance, you are a fool and fanatic. In calm response, the apostle affirms his perfect sanity, and that he speaks forth " the words of truth and soberness."

In this case, can there be any doubt who was the fanatic, and who the wise and sober man ?

Festus personates the fanatic of error; Paul represents the man with the soundest judgment and life.

Festus was loud-mouthed in calling him by an opprobrious name, without the least propriety in fact; Paul evinces his freedom from all extravagance, by the most civil and courteous response.

As the word fanaticism is somewhat in use now, and indeed all the bad words of our language are in uncommon demand at present, it must be worth a little thought to get the right use of the Satanic vocabulary. If we must use abusive and malign words, let us learn to use them with some propriety, for the sake of scholarship, if not of decency.

I do not pretend to say that the bad words—the abusive epithets of the language—should be altogether dropped, for those are the Dahlgren guns by which some men do the most execution. They are the heavy artillery by which an adversary is sometimes effectually demolished, and great eclat comes to the victor. It is a very convenient proceeding, to send men straight to perdition upon our own judgment and responsibility. It is not enough that we can excommunicate, but we have learned to anathematize and to brandish the most terrifying epithets.

We do not insist, therefore, upon the total relinquishment of prescriptive rights in the use of formidable words, but only that they be used with due, Christian discrimination. Now who is the fanatic?

Is he the man who is a great enthusiast in behalf of the truth? By no means. Paul was a great enthusiast, but no fanatic, in the opprobrious sense of that word.

So enthusiastic was this devoted apostle, that, losing sight of every other interest, he said, " this *one* thing I do," and that in him we applaud. But the man who in the present time devotes himself to some *one* great philanthrophy, is stigmatized as a " man of one idea," a fanatic, and forthwith to be frowned out of respectable society.

Is this decorous, and of Christian charity, or of demoniac malignity?

Many Christian ministers, like Paul at Corinth, have determined to know nothing in their preaching but this *one* thing, " Jesus Christ, and him crucified." Let them rise to the most unwanted pitch of enthusiasm on this unique theme, do they become thereby fanatical? All right minded men will answer, no.

Mere enthusiasm then for any truth is not fanaticism nor reprehensible, but they are obnoxious to this name, whose whole energy is given to the advocacy of wicked institutions and immoral practices.

It is not strange that men of stolid indifference to the efforts made for meliorating the condition of mankind, should brand this philanthropic zeal as extravagance and fanaticism. Nor is it to be wondered at, that wicked men, zealous for the growth of some collossal crime in human society, should strive to bring into reproach, men by whom their craft is endangered. But that men, professing to revere God, and to obey his law, would strive to abate any ardor of Christian philanthropy, no matter in what form exhibited, and to contrive the means for the downfall of men devoted to any special good work, is passing strange.

This fanaticism of wickedness often becomes "exceeding mad" against all forms of goodness, and like Saul of Tarsus, pursues its victims even into strange cities. Fanaticism is never allied to true religion or philanthropy,[1] but is always in league with malignant emotions, and diabolical practices. It is a word derived from "*fanum*," a temple at whose shrine the devotees indulged in the most abominable orgies.

These "*fanatici*" were the patrons and abettors of every detestable practice, and are the prototypes only of those who reverence some idol abomination, which, though ugly, is nevertheless mighty.

St. Dominic, the arch inquisitor, was a famous type of a fanatic, in pursuing, with unflagging zeal, all dissenters from Roman Supremacy, in order to extirpate them utterly.

To burn the body for the good of the soul, was the prime dogma of this class of fanatics. But this is a most malignant type of the evil, re-produced in different forms, from that time until the present, exhausting every form of persecution for opinion's sake; at one time assailing the person, then the property, character, reputation or influence of the object of its hate.

Every string in the whole gamut of persecution has been struck by this pestilential demon of fanaticism.

---

(1) This is true; hence it can not be allied to what pertains to christianity, nor to true philanthropy. And as abolitionism is fanaticism, it is not allied to christianity nor to philanthropy. It is neither.

No earnestness in the cause of truth and right should be stigmatized by an opprobrious name, but he is a desperate fanatic who lends his powers to the devil, in order to make wrong respectable, and to wear the semblance of religion.

No sophistry will ever convince the world that the noble zeal of Howard, Wilberforce,[1] and such as they, was an odious fanaticism; but the record of their philanthropic labors will be pondered with increasing delight, as long as virtue and religion are esteemed among men.

A. R. B.

[From the Christian Record of April 22d, 1862.]

FANATICISM OF ERROR.

My esteemed brother A. R. B. has an article under this caption, in the *Record* of the 8th of April, that I propose to notice briefly.

Fanaticism is defined to be: enthusiasm, religious phrenzy; wild and extravagant notions.

A *fanatic* is defined to be: an enthusiast, a man mad (or monomaniac) with wild notions. See Walker and Webster.

Hence, "men of pure, disinterested and philanthropic aims in life," may enthusiastically endeavor to effect their "aims" by "wild and extravagant notions;" or, their aims,

---

(1) That President Benton, and all others of his school of opinion, may see how far they misapprehend Mr. Wilberforce, and how far they are misled by their abolitionism, I append from the Boston *Courier* the following, copied by it from the London *Times* of March 2d, 1863:

* * * * We now give, from the *Times* of March 2d, a letter of a similar purport, from one of the sons of Wilberforce. Will the newspapers referred to allow their readers to see this?

MR. WILBERFORCE ON A SERVILE INSURRECTION.

To the Editor of the London Times:

SIR—As far as it relates to Sir T. Fowell Buxton, the letter of Mr. Buxton has fully answered your question, "whether the sons of Wilberforce and of Buxton, who have all been brought up in the teaching of their fathers, now share the opinions of the Emancipation Society as to the proclamation of Mr. Lincoln."

Allow me to add my testimony, as far as your question refers to the late William Wilberforce.

The last time I had the happiness of hearing him speak in the House of Commons, he expressed in the strongest terms the same feelings contained in the words quoted by Mr. Buxton from his father's speech. None of his surviving friends need be reminded that he retained them undiminished to his life's end. On that occasion he had avowed in the House his fears that the rejection of Sir T. F. Buxton's motion for the emancipation of the

though they think them philanthropic, may really be misanthropic, utopian, impracticable, or such as they have no right to attempt to effect or carry out; and, if so, they are clearly fanatics.

My brother asks, "Who is the fanatic? Is he the man who is a great enthusiast in behalf of the truth? By no means," says he.

Those who follow the truth are not "great enthusiasts." The Lord's life and teaching is conclusive proof of this. Paul was not an enthusiast, though my brother charges him with being one; and though he did "one thing," to-wit, "press toward the mark for the prize of the high calling of God in Christ,"[1] yet he also became all things to all men,[2] and was not a "one-ideaed man." He pressed toward the mark for the prize of the high calling of God *in Christ*, and not out of him, toward the effecting of some "aim" of his, which *he* thought was philanthropic, but which Christ, by his precepts and example, had taught him not to interfere with at all; though the institution which is made the pretext or occasion for this modern philanthropy, existed then universally in a worse form than it has ever existed in any portion of this Union.

Fanatics always seize hold of some truth, and combine with it some error, either of theory or fact, and become mad, monomaniac or phrenzied, upon their idea, and get into the strange hallucination that their way is the only way to benefit all mankind, and that all must partake of the benefit of their "wild notions."

Witness the Jews when Titus sat down before Jerusalem.

---

slaves might lead to insurrection. The words were received with a cheer, as a concession, by his opponents. I shall never forget the earnestness with which he declared his horror at the thought, and solemnly appealed to Almighty God that it was his daily prayer that nothing of the sort might take place.

It would be impossible that any of my father's sons should have watched, without the deepest interest, the bearing of recent events upon the condition and prospects of the negro race, and I doubt not they have all formed the same conclusions with myself. My own position, as editor of a journal, has imposed upon me the moral responsibility of expressing an opinion, and so compelled me to consider the whole subject. Allow me, then, to say that, if my father's life had been prolonged, I am certain, on the one hand, that his abhorrence for slavery and his zeal for emancipation would not have been lessened; and equally certain, on the other hand, that *he would have considered it a grievous crime to stir up insurrection and servile war;* doubly so, if it were done, not from mistaken benevolence, *but from selfish political purposes.* This, as Mr. Buxton truly says, *is the only meaning of Mr. Lincoln's proclamation,* if it has any meaning at all. * *

I am, sir, your obedient servant,

HENRY WM. WILBERFORCE,

Weekly Register newspaper office, 32 Brydges street, Strand, Feb. 26th, 1863.

(1) Phil. iii, 13, 14.   (2) 1 Cor. ix, 22.

They had the religion given from heaven through Moses, were of the stock of the chosen people of God, and had the holy of holies to guard. See the Saracens. They had the truth that there is but one God, combined with the falsehood that Mahomet was his prophet, and coupled with these they had the "wild notion" that they must eradicate idolatry (in which christendom was then sunken) and extend the benefits of their theory to all mankind. See the Crusaders of the seven crusades. They had the truth that our lives, labors and estates belong to God, and should all be expended in the service of Christ, combined with the falsehood, that reclaiming the tomb of the Savior at Jerusalem was the "one thing" required of them as servant's of Christ.

The Jews' "one idea" was the extermination of the "monster iniquity" of the desecration of the holy city and temple by the Roman "power;" and by that fanaticism, 3,000,000 were destroyed in nine months.

The "one idea" of the Saracens, was the extermination of idolatry, and the extension of "the true faith" over mankind; and that fanaticism, in 150 years, destroyed "the third part of men."[1] The Crusaders had the "one idea" and "philanthrophy" of redeeming the holy sepulcher from the infidels; and, for two hundred years, in their seven crusades, they committed atrocities and injuries to mankind so horrible, that when they were uttered by the seven thunders in the vision given to John, he was forbidden to write them out in the apocalypse.[2]

These are noted instances of fanatics and fanaticisms. And, as history is philosophy teaching by example, those of us who claim to be philosophers, should be taught by these fearful lessons.

My esteemed brother calls the institution a "wicked institution," a "collossal crime in human society;" and regards the utter eradication of it, without looking to our present condition and surroundings, as the "one great philanthropy." *In both of these he is in error.* It is not a crime; nor would the utter and immediate eradication of it be a philanthrophy, but a most woful calamity.[3] But be-

---

(1) Rev. ix, 15.   (2) Rev. x, 4.

(3) What little has actually been done in immediate emancipation of the slaves, up to this time, (March, 1863,) begins to show how great the calamity would be to both the white and black races, if the 4,000,000 slaves of the United States had really been emancipated by Lincoln's proclamation of Jan. 1st, 1863.

yond these, and more potent with christians, the institution is a part of, and belongs to, kingdoms of this world—human governments; and hence is entirely a distinct thing, and separate from the kingdom of the Lord, which is not of this world. The Lord refused to interfere with, or to attempt any philanthropic reformation of any of the kingdoms of this world, or of any of their institutions. His efforts and labors were to reform man, not to reform governments. He uniformly refused to interfere with governments, and governmental matters and business.

Hence, this institution, and the philanthropy of my brother in relation to it, are questions in political economy, and outside of christianity. Christians ought to be careful how they become "zealous," "enthusiastic," about things outside of christianity. All the divisions among christians, and the consequent evils to christianity, from the Arian controversy down to the dreamy theory of soul-sleeping, *have been about matters outside of christianity, and on which revelation is silent.* Hence, christians should learn wisdom from this sad experience, and adhere closely to the high calling of God *in Christ*—in his body—in his kingdom—and not get outside of him, and of matters revealed to us through or by him. May the Lord enable us to do so, that our zeal may be according to knowledge. J. S.
April 15*th*, 1862.

[From the Christian Record, of April 29, 1862.]

FANATICISM OF ERROR.

BRO. GOODWIN:—In the *Record* of the 22d inst. I see an article by J. S. purporting to be a reply to the article entitled "Fanaticism of Error," by A. R. B. published in the Record of the 8th. Apart from some immaterial difference of opinion as to the meaning of the words, fanatic and fanaticism, I see nothing in the article of J. S. which can claim to be either a reply to, or a fair notice of the article of A. R. B. If I am not much mistaken, J. S. in his article affords abundant evidence that, according to his own definition of the term, he himself is a fanatic. A. R. B. says nothing about slavery, and in his whole article neither makes an attack upon that institution, or a defense of abolitionism, unless it be by an implication and construction, which clearly and certainly J. S. is not authorized to make. It is true that he says that "the man who in the present time devotes himself to *one* great philanthropy, is stigmatised as a "man of one idea," a fanatic, and forthwith to be frowned out of respectable society," and again, "nor is it to be wondered at that wicked men, zealous for the growth of some collossal crime in human society, should strive to bring into reproach men, by whom their craft is endangered. But that men professing to revere God, and to obey his law, would strive to abate any ardor of christian philanthropy, no matter in what form exhibited, and to contrive the means for the downfall of men devoted to any special good work, is passing strange." Believing, as I do, that the institution of slavery is a collossal crime, and that the effort to eradicate it is a great philanthropy, I might, perhaps, be justified in applying the language of A. R. B. to that institution, and to the efforts which are being made to effect its overthrow. But there is nothing in the article itself, to warrant my asserting that such ideas were in the mind of the writer,[1] and I could only venture that inference from my own deep convictions, that in that sense, the language is true. On account of these convictions, J. S. would call me a fanatic, and yet he must admit that they are *his convictions*, to justify his construction of the language of A. R. B.

Apprised, as I have long been, that J. S. rejected the idea that slavery was a collossal crime, but that, on'the contrary, he professed to believe that it was no evil, and that, instead of regarding the efforts for its removal as a great philanthropy, he entertained, and often expressed the opinion, that the agitation of the subject was criminal, and ought to be suppressed, I confess to a little astonishment at his readiness and quickness in construing the language of A. R. B. as referring to that subject. It proves, however, very clearly and conclusively, either that his convictions are at war with his professions, or that he is really and tru-

---

(1) Yet Bro. Goodwin understood it as referring to slavery. See his letter, page 45.

ly the wildest fanatic—a monomaniac upon the subject of slavery. He has been long engaged, both in religion and politics, in efforts to exorcise the ghost of the slavery question; still it haunts him. Is a collossal crime spoken of—the ghost of slavery is presented vividly to his imagination. Talk of a great philanthropy—and his teeming brain is alive with a whole army of abolition fanatics. If this be not fanaticism, and if he be not a fanatic, I confess that I do not understand the meaning of the terms, and it will be necessary for me to get a new dictionary to learn what they mean. I might, perhaps, get the right kind of one "down south," but as it might not be quite safe for me to go there just now, and as I could not hope that my order would be honored at Charleston or New Orleans, I must request J. S. to get me one from the printing establishment of De Bow. That, of course, would be all right.

But there is evidence of progress in this production of J. S. I know him to have been opposed, bitterly opposed, to the agitation of the question of slavery. Neither in church or State—in religion or in politics, would he admit it to have a place. As a politician, he would suppress the discussion everywhere, "either in or out of Congress." As a religionist, he contended, as it seems he still contends, that "the institution is a part of, and belongs to the kingdom of this world—human governments, and hence, entirely a distinct thing, and separate from the kingdom of the Lord, which is not of this world;" and that "it is a question of political economy and outside of christianity." This citizenship in the two kingdoms has been quite convenient to J. S. It has enabled him in either kingdom to evade the discussion of the question of slavery, by putting in a plea to the jurisdiction. But this article of J. S.'s affords some evidence that he is getting ashamed of the dodge. He ventures beyond the line of his defenses, to meet and refute, in the moral field, the proposition which he himself has constructed out of the material furnished him by A. R. B.

He says, "My esteemed brother calls the institution a 'wicked institution,' a 'collossal crime in human society,' and regards the utter eradication of it, without looking to our present condition and surroundings, as the one great philanthropy." This involves a proposition, which, although not to be found in the article of A. R. B., J. S. has framed for the purpose of meeting and refuting it. In thus attempting to refute the proposition, he has entered the field of controversy, which he so much deprecates, but in thus crossing the Rubicon, he has used the precaution to throw across it a pontoon bridge, not only to assist him in crossing, but to facilitate his retreat, in case he should deem it prudent to retire. He enters the field under protest to the jurisdiction, and still says that the matters in controversy, "are questions of political economy, *and outside of christianity.*" In other words, that the christian's Lord has no jurisdiction over them, and here is his whole argument, in refutation of the proposition above named. He says, in reference to his "esteemed brother," and to his supposed proposition, "*In both of these he is in error.*" "It," (the institution) "is not a crime, nor would the utter and immediate eradication of it, be a philanthropy, but a most woeful calamity." This is a bold and brief argument, and is final and conclusive, if we accept the opinions of J. S. as unerring and infallible. In one respect, if in no other, it resembles the teachings of the Master, for J. S., speaks "as one having authority." If we admit the authority, there is an end of all controversy upon the subject. But upon this point of authority, I hesitate, and I suppose that others may be reluctant to allow the claim.

But there is hope for J. S. His position is in advance of his former one. He is willing that the question of slavery should be discussed, at least on one side of it, and that is yielding half of his objections to its agitation. I suspect that he will yield farther soon, and relying upon his own powers of assertion and argument, he may perhaps offer a full discussion of the question, provided he can have the privilege of shaping the propositions to his own liking.[1] *But it is too late. The question is no longer a debateable one.* The logic of the schools has been exhausted upon it, and so far as the argument of words is concerned, the question is settled. The glorious gospel of a common brotherhood in humanity—of man's equality before God and before the law, has been preached to every willing ear thorughout the

---

[1] This satisfies my mind that brother BUTLER had a hand in shaping the course that brother BOGGS took in the preceding correspondence.

land. Those who have rejected it, have done so obstinately and willfully, and no human argument can reach them.

Our God, the Father of all, has assumed, and is now conducting this great controversy. "He doeth according to His will in the army of Heaven, and among the inhabitants of the earth." By the stern and terrible logic of events, He is developing this argument, and working in the hearts of the unwilling, a conviction of the great truth that "God is no respecter of persons." I have strong faith that the doom of slavery is the inevitable result of the present fearful conflict,[1] and I pray to God that in the effort to save it from utter destruction, our Government and our Union may not be borne down and perish with it. O. B.

[From the Christian Record of May 6th, 1862.]

FANATICISM OF ERROR.

My dear brother O. B., in the last *Record*, has a very heated article on the brief notice of (not reply to) the article of my esteemed brother A. R. B. under this caption.

I said nothing about slavery, if A. R. B. did not. Slavery is not found in my article any more than it is in his. Neither of the words *slavery* nor *abolitionism* is found in my article. But it is clear that A. R. B.'s article referred to slavery as the "collossal crime in human society," and abolitionism as the "*one* great philanthrophy," for which he complained that they were stigmatized as men "of one idea," though he did not use the terms. I did the same in noticing his article, though I would just as soon have spoken out, and used the terms direct.

If others choose to sow their poison in the public mind, under covert means, by using indirect terms, that when called to account for it, they may deny and say, "that was not what I meant," I choose to beat the bush, and drive them from their covert, by assuming the same flimsy garb,

---

(1) This shows that abolitionists, from the beginning of the present unfortunate civil war, regarded it as a war for the abolition of slavery.

that they may have assumed; and, so far as my dear brother
O. B. is concerned, it seems that I have succeeded admirably in this case.

Fanaticism was the subject under the consideration of my esteemed brother A. R. B. and myself. After my dear brother O. B. says, "*it is too late*" to doubt that the institution of slavery is sinful, that "*the question is no longer a debatable one*," it is not hard to find where the fanaticism is, in this unfortunate and dire controversy that is upon us in all its horrors. But if added to that, we look through the paragraph in which this is found, and the succeeding one, demonstration clear as noon-day bursts upon us.

Slavery is an institution of civil government; it is a part of the kingdoms of this world. In the United States, it always has been, and still is, a State institution. Hence, citizens of the States where it exists, are the only ones that have any constitutional right to take any political action in relation to it, or to discuss any political action in relation to it; and if others do it, they are "busy-bodies," so far as political action is concerned.

But it has been harped so long, that thousands of excellent people have got to believe that it is true, THAT IT IS A SIN; and hence, as they desire to eradicate all sin from the earth, they have entered into crusades against it, increasing in intensity and vigor, till our present woful condition exists. And now it is too late to question that it is a sin! "The question is no longer debatable"! What further proof need any sober, rational man have, of the fanaticism of the crusades, and of the dire situation we are in, our public affairs being in the hands of men of that notion?

The institution of slavery is not sinful. If it were, however, as it is a governmental sin, christians, as such, have nothing to do with it; for they labor in a kingdom not of this world. But if it were sinful, and christians might interfere with governmental sins, as it does not exist in the free States, we of the free States, as christians, have no more right, and are no more bound in christian duty, to interfere with it, than we have right, or are bound to interfere with the Cuban, English, French or Austrian governmental sins.

These are my positions, and show the reasons why I say that christians should not allow themselves to be divided

5

and distracted by matters pertaining to the kingdoms of this world; and though I do not desire to debate, yet, with the truth of God's revelation of his will to us, I hold myself amply able to sustain them upon all proper occasions.

J. S.

April 30*th*, 1862.

The following note was appended to A. R. B.'s article in the *Record* of May 6th, 1862:

NOTE TO J. S.

My respect for Br. S. would not permit his remarks on my article entitled "Fanaticism of Error," to pass without notice, and therefore I prepared another article on that subject for the *Record* of this week; but as another brother has seen fit to make some strictures upon Bro. S.'s communication, I have thought it unnecessary to publish what I had written before the article of Bro. O. B. came under my notice. A. R. B.

And the following appeared as editorial in the *Record* of May 6th, 1862:

"FANATICISM OF ERROR."

Our readers have noticed a few articles in our paper under the above title. They are well written and breathe the right spirit; but we think those who have written the last papers are given the subject a turn that the author of the first article did not anticipate. How much farther these brethren may desire to carry the matter, we know not; but we wish it distinctly understood, that we publish an independent sheet, and that both sides to any question that may be introduced into our columns shall be heard, as long as the writers discuss the merits of the question at issue, avoid personal invectives, and treat each other as christians. Any matter of a moral character, upon which honest men may have different views, may legitimately be discussed in our religious papers. Purely political questions we prefer, however, to keep out of the *Record;* but the moral phase of questions that only exist by the protection of the civil law, may be investigated, without considering its political bearings. Should these brethren continue this subject, we hope they will look at it only as a moral question.

[From the Christian Record of May 20th, 1862.]

COMMUNICATION.

Bro. Goodwin:—I suppose that J. S. will expect me to notice his article, published in the *Record* of the 6th inst., and I desire to do so briefly. He calls my former communication a very "heated article." If it deserves that epithet, I was not aware of it. I leave the readers of the *Record* to judge whether the epithet is rightly applied.

He says, that "neither the word *slavery* or *abolitionism*, is found in" his article, and intimates that it was as free of the ideas represented by these words, as was the article of A. R. B. He seems to suppose that I had not noticed the absence of these words in his article, and had been as hasty in my construction of it, as I had charged that he was, in his construction of the language of A. R. B. I certainly had not failed to notice that neither the word slavery or abolitionism was used by him, and if I made an erroneous or even hasty construction of his article—if his language be fairly or even possibly capable of any construction, other than that I gave it, I am properly subject to his criticism. Of this, too, the readers of the *Record* can judge.

But a graver matter is the insinuation of J. S. that the article of A. R. B. was an effort to "sow poison in the public mind under covert means, by using indirect terms," and that these covert means and direct terms were employed by A. R. B. to enable him to deny their real meaning "*when called to account for it.*" This charge[1] against A. R. B. is

---

(1) It was not a charge against A. R. B. particularly, but a general proposition that fits the action of abolitionists generally; and my application of it to O. B., that I had thereby brought him to use direct terms, shows that I used the expression in the general sense, and not as a charge individually against brother Benton.

most unjust, and might be construed to involve a threat, which it is possible J. S. might not have the power to execute. I need only to refer the reader to the article of A. R. B. to show that the language used by him has no concealed or covert meaning, and that no indirect terms are employed by him. The words objected to by J. S. have as clear and certain meaning as any words in the English language. It is not probable that A. R. B. will think it necessary either to confess or deny, or to give any explanation of his language, either to help or to hinder the construction which J. S. has put upon it, even if "called to account for it."

Under the apprehension that something offensive to him was hidden under the language of A. R. B., J. S. says that he "chose to beat the bush, and drive them from their covert," and he felicitates himself, that, so far as I am concerned, he has "succeeded admirably." If it is a bush he has been beating, I was not under its covert, and hence he can not claim to have driven me out. I had nothing to do with the article of A. R. B.—was not consulted in reference to it—and had no knowledge or intimation of its existence, until I saw it in print.

It is, I think, evident, that J. S. wishes to have a discussion upon the subject of slavery, and is somewhat disturbed at my remark, "that the question is no longer a debatable one." Indeed, he seems to regard the disposition to consider the question settled, and the debate upon it closed, as of at least as baneful a character, and as pernicious a tendency, as he has hitherto regarded, and still seems to consider the disposition to discuss it. According to his logic, the harping upon—the agitation of this subject—has brought us to "our present woful condition." And now, if it be proposed to cease agitation, to terminate the debate, and regard the question as settled, he discovers fanaticism in the proffered silence, and talks of "the dire situation we are in," on account of "public affairs being in the hands of men of that notion." There is apparent inconsistency in these views of J. S., but perhaps he thinks that our community is affected with a species of hydrophobia, from the bite of that rabid animal, called agitation, and concludes, perhaps wisely, to apply the well recommended remedy of "the hair of the dog to cure the bite."

However that may be, J. S. has presented and crowded together rather confusedly three propositions, which he seems not unwilling to debate. He thus states them:
"The institution of slavery is not sinful. If it were, however, it is a govermental sin; christians, as such, have nothing to do with it, for they labor in a kingdom not of this world. But if it were sinful, and christians might interfere with governmental sins, as it does not exist in the free States, we of the free States, as christians, have no more right, and are no more bound, in christian duty, to interfere with it, than we have, or are, to interfere with the Cuban, English, French, or Austrian governmental sins."

These J. S. calls his positions, and, in reference to them, he says, "and though I do not desire to debate, yet with the truth of God's revelation of his will to us, I hold myself amply able to sustain them upon all proper occasions."

Were I to undertake to discuss the subject of slavery with J. S., I should not choose to do so upon his propositions, in the form he has given them. They are all negatives, and by negation, is the worst and most unusual form for stating a proposition for discussion. The second and third propositions are stated hypothetically, and are, I doubt not, simply intended as a double line of defense, around the first or main proposition. The third proposition raises an immaterial question, for it may be that it is our right and our duty to denounce sin, in both a sister State and a foreign jurisdiction, and that the extent of the right, and the measure of the duty, in either case, would depend upon our means and facilities for doing so effectually. The proposition presents no issue of sufficient importance to invite discussion. Indeed, I regard the language of all the propositions as inapt and indefinite.

But all this is immaterial, as I am not disposed to undertake a set debate, or a formal discussion of the subject. Neither health nor time will permit me to promise so much now. I will, however, suggest a proposition, which I think would cover the whole field of argument. It is this:

American slavery, as established, recognized, or permitted by the laws of the slaveholding States, and exemplified in the condition, character and conduct of both masters and slaves, is sin against God, and against humanity.

This proposition is, I think, broad enough to embrace the

whole subject, and definite enough to invite a full discussion of all its details.

Although, for the reasons above stated, I can not promise to attempt a formal discussion of it, yet if J. S. thinks proper to assume the negative, and the editor of the *Record* consents to give us room in his columns, I will endeavor to furnish some articles, from time to time, to sustain the proposition, and to meet, as best I may, and so far as I may think necessary to a proper understanding of the subject, such arguments as J. S. may offer against the proposition.

If, however, J. S. is not satisfied with this proposition, or if he prefers another course of proceeding, it is possible to present the question in a form, and to proceed with the debate, in a manner which I presume is quite familiar to him, much more so, indeed, than they are now to me. I would propose that, upon an agreed case in *the Court of Conscience, Jesus the Lord presiding as sole Judge*, Legree be considered as arraigned, upon an indictment for the enslavement, oppression, and murder of Uncle Tom, the facts charged in the indictment to be such, and only such acts of ownership, control, use and treatment of Uncle Tom, by Legree, as by the laws of slaveholding States, are regarded as the lawful, justified, or permitted acts of the master, in reference to his slave. If J. S. thinks that the laws of the State of Louisiana, or of any other slaveholding State, will constitute a good defense, he can make them available, by pleading them in abatement to the jurisdiction of the Court. Upon a demurrer to such a plea, the whole question would come up for argument in a form with which J. S. is undoubtedly familiar, for, if I mistake not, he has long practiced before, and presided in courts of justice, in some, or at least one of the "kingdoms of this world." It would be an aspersion of his character as a christian, to suppose that he was not also familiar with the practice in the "*Court of Conscience*," which is a *high Court, in the "kingdom which is not of this world."* The law which would govern the case, would be "*God's revelation of his will to us,*" which is the supreme law and sole authority in that Court, in which *Jesus the Lord presides as Judge*. Although the Judge might be suspected of pity and sympathy for the poor, degraded, down-trodden, and oppressed of humanity, yet, as J. S. affirms that he "refused to interfere with, or attempt any philanthropic reformation of any of the kingdoms of this world, or of any of their institutions," I suppose he would be willing that the case be tried in this Court. I submit these suggestions for the consideration of J. S., and wish to know his further pleasure in the premises.

O. B.

[From the Christian Record, of May 27th, 1862.]

FANATICISM OF ERROR.

An article from Bro. O. B., in the *Record* of the 20th of May, requires some notice from me.

I spoke of "the dire situation we are in, our public affairs being in the hands of men" who set it down as a foregone conclusion, that slavery is sinful, and that that proposition is no longer disputable. This my language clearly indicates, and not that they are in the hands of men who agitate (not discuss) the slavery question, as Bro. O. B. says I say.

Slavery is either sinful or it is not sinful. Brother O. B. and those who have been and are acting with him—"agitating"—constantly denounce it in such phrases as "the sin of slavery," "the sum of all villianies," "the monster iniquity," "the colossal crime," &c. And yet my dear brother O. B. will not undertake to affirm directly that it is sinful, and attempt to sustain his affirmation by the good word of the Lord, written in God's revelation of his will to us! But in lieu thereof, he proposes this wordy verbosity—not to discuss it in form—but to "furnish some articles from time to time, to sustain" it.

"American slavery as established, recognized or permitted by the laws of the slaveholding States, and exemplified in the condition, character and conduct of both masters and slaves, is sin against God, and against humanity."

Slavery and marriage are both institutions of civil government, and relations existing in human society. Had it been constantly "harped" and "agitated" for thirty years past, that marriage is sinful, using constantly such set phrases in speaking of it, as "the sin of marriage," "the sum of all villainies," "the monster iniquity," "the colossal crime," until society was upturned, and civil war of most gigantic proportions was inaugurated; and then, when it was proposed to examine and see whether there was not an error in the grand, cardinal proposition, by which the storm had been fanned into existence, those who had been so constantly "harping" and "agitating," instead of meeting the question squarely, and affirming directly that marriage is sinful, as they had been doing all the time, propose to furnish some articles, from time to time, to sustain the proposition that "American marriage, as established, recognized or permitted by the laws of (some or all) the States, and exemplified in the condition, character and conduct of both husbands and wives, is sin against God and against humanity"! would not all see that it was an evasion, and an attempt to avoid the discussion of the question whether marriage is sinful or not, and to get off into a logomachy about the laws of States, and the conduct of husbands and wives, in discharging their respective duties pertaining to the marriage relations? I think there can be no doubt but that all would so see it. Can not we now look equally dispassionately and sanely upon the question, whether slavery is sinful or not? and upon the conduct of those who have been so long asserting that it is sinful?

The inquiry is, Is the relation of master and slave a sinful relation? Is it sinful for men to hold that relation to each other? It is not whether a master or a slave sins by improperly discharging the duties required of him by that relation. Many husbands and wives commit many sins, by failing to discharge the duties required of them by the marital relation; but that only proves *them sinners*, and does not prove *marriage sinful.* So many masters and slaves commit many sins, by failing to discharge the duties required of them by the relation existing between them; but that only proves *them sinners*, and not that *slavery is sinful.*

Brother O. B., not only thus goes away from the question at once, but gravely proposes to me to go into trial in a "court of conscience," of Legree and Uncle Tom, as set forth in the fiction called Uncle Tom's Cabin! The revealed will of God to him and me is, to "think of whatsoever things are true,"[1] and not to think of, or contemplate, much less to enter into a grave discussion in a public, religious paper, of fictions that never existed, except in the imaginations of persons whose conduct in bruiting abroad such fictions, whether intended by them or not, produce "hatred," "variance," "wrath," "strife," and "sedition," all of which are denounced by the good word of the Lord, as being works of the flesh, and sinful.[2] I shall abstain from either discussing or circulating such fictions. Bro. O. B. and those who agree with him, will, of course, act as they see proper in the premises. They and I have each to account for himself, and not for the rest of us.

The Lord has not erected a "court of conscience," nor made it a "high court" in his kingdom. Our own consciences are witnesses for ourselves, not courts in which to try either ourselves or our brethren, much less such a fictitious person as Legree.

The fanaticism of the error into which my brother O. B. and those who think and act with him, have fallen, is now apparent. They assume that slavery is sinful. They repeat it till they believe it to be not only so, but indisputably so. When their proposition is denied, and they respectfully asked to prove by the word of God that slavery is sinful, they "enthusiastically" say that American slavery, as it exists, by the laws of the slave States, and exemplified in the character and conduct of the masters and slaves, is sin; that is, the conduct of the masters and slaves is sinful, and they have a bad character, therefore, the slave laws of the States are bad; therefore, American slavery is a sin against God and humanity, and............slavery itself is sinful, but we will not undertake to prove it to be so by the word of God; and then propose their "wild notion" that we go into the high court of conscience, created by the Lord, when he never created such a court, and there try a fictitious being, taking fictions for facts, and thus settle the question![3]

---

(1) Phil. iv, 8.   (2) Gal. v, 19-21.

(3) That the reader may see the difference between the *fiction* of Uncle Tom's Cabin, and the *fact* of Uncle Tom himself, I insert the following from the the Frankfork Kentucky *Commonwealth* of December, 1862:

UNCLE TOM'S CABIN.—Some time after Mrs. Beecher Stowe had her Abolition production, called "Uncle Tom's Cabin," published, and it had taken a run, such as works of fiction

May we all grow in the *knowledge* of the *truth*, and thus be cured of our errors, as well as be relieved of the fanaticisms of them, is my prayer. J. S.

P. S.—If O. B., or A. R. B., or any of that school of opinion, will undertake to prove by the Scriptures that slavery is sinful, I will discuss the question with them in the *Record*, on equal terms. If they do not, I hope that they will quit denouncing it as a sin, and thus misleading the brethren, and fanning up strife and civil war for its extermination, and the destruction of us as a nation and people.

[From the Christian Record of June 3d, 1862.]

COMMUNICATION.

BRO. GOODWIN:—Passing by some remarks in the recent article of J. S., as unnecessary to notice here, I desire to notice his assertion that I will not undertake to affirm directly that slavery is sinful, and attempt to sustain the

---

often do, without any one being able to account for the morbid appetite that craves such books, we saw it stated in a newspaper that Henry Ward Beecher had represented, in a puplic lecture he was delivering, that there was such a personage as Uncle Tom—a real character, on whose history his sister founded her book; that Uncle Tom lived in a cabin near Indianapolis, Indiana, at the time he himself resided there, and, in connection with his account of Uncle Tom, he spoke in very feeling terms of his own early trials in beginning his ministry at Indianapolis, and the words of encouragement received by him from the then Governor, N. Noble, of that State, under whose protection Uncle Tom then lived.   *   *   *   *   *   *   *   *   *   *

We have sometimes thought that we had done wrong in not making known the facts about Uncle Tom, as we have since found many Abolition brothers and sisters, and other weak-minded, story loving readers, who believed firmly that there was not only such a personage as Uncle Tom, but that his life and history were truthfully given by Mrs. Beecher Stowe, and that all of her other characters were drawn from life.

In one thing she gave Uucle Tom's character correctly. He was a noble man by nature, and a Christian by practice—what used to be called an old fashioned Virginia gentleman—a man of mark wherever he went. For, though a negro, and a full blooded one, his personal appearance was commanding, and his open, gentle, manly countenance made him warm friends of all persons, white and black, who became acquainted with him. He lived to be, as was believed, over one hundred years of age, and, whilst a slave, never was out of the family to which he belonged. He was born and raised in the family of Nobles, of Virginia ; came to Kentucky, the property of Dr. Thomas Noble, who lived, when he first came to Kentucky, back of Covington, then Campbell, now Kenton county, about ten miles, at a place which was afterward the farm of Major Winston, and on which he lived many years. Dr. Noble afterwards moved to Boon county, at a place afterwards called Bellevue, and there lived many years, and was there buried.

Dr. Noble was a man of the old school, the compeer of Major Thomas Martin, Col. John Grant and his brother, Squire Grant, Gen. James Taylor, George Gordon, and many other early settlers, who were old men when we were a boy, men full of that jollity and

affirmative by the good word of the Lord, written in God's revelation of his will to us, but in lieu thereof, I propose a "wordy verbosity," &c.

The proposition which I suggested, and to prove which I offered, in case it should be denied, to submit some arguments, is as clear, as definite, and as positive an affirmation, that " American slavery is sin," as it is possible for me to make it. I limited the affirmation to American slavery; for whatever may be our opinion of the moral character of Jewish servitude, or Roman slavery, these opinions are merely speculative, and have no practical importance at the present day. I decline any discussion of them any further than they may be legitimately introduced as arguments, either for or against American slavery. My proposition embraced a definition of American slavery, or, in other

---

good nature so common among the early settlers of, Kentucky: who took a part in their time, and a goodly part of it, too, to the cultivation of the social graces; who loved each other as sparsely-settled people, in a new country, always do, and did not make the gain of dollars and cents the only or chief object of life.

After Dr. Noble's death, Uncle Tom continued on the farm and managed the same, under the direction of his mistress, until she died, when, under some arrangement among the heirs, Thomas and Sarah, his wife, were permitted to go free.

During the period that Uncle Tom was chief overseer for Mrs. Noble, our first recollection of him began. We were a small boy, and being on a visit to kindred were playing with an uncle, also a boy about our age, in the vicinity of Mrs. Noble's barn, when we heard the sound of stripes being pretty well laid on some person, who was begging earnestly to be let off; on looking through a crack in the side of the barn we saw old man Thomas administering upon a young negro man pretty severely.

The cause, we learned, was that the young negro had failed to worm a piece of tobacco which Thomas had directed, when leaving home a day or two before, and which his experienced eye detected to have been greatly slighted by the young negro.

Young as we were we could but express our astonishment at the young man submitting to be whipped, when Thomas remarked, "He knew he deserved it, my son, for disobedience of my orders, and for telling a story by saying he had killed all the worms, when the plants showed the contrary."

Uncle Tom believed that the negroes were, in the general, better off with good masters than to be left to themselves. That white people never would recognize them as equals, nor consent to their having equality with them, in church or State.

His own history verified his belief. When Mrs. Noble died, Thomas, who had never thought of leaving her whilst she lived, was advised to go to Cincinnati and live; that he would there find many of his race free, and have their society, and be where he could have church advantages. He spent some days amongst the free negroes of Cincinnati, and returned to the house of one of his advisers with this answer:

"Miss M———I can't live with the people I have seen in Cincinnati. They would not suit me to live with. But few of them work, and nearly all are worthless. I am going to get master N——— to buy me some ground near Lawrenceburg, where master L——— N——— and Miss L——— V——— live, and Sarah and I will live near them, and we know they will see we are not imposed on."

They lived at Lawrenceburg until L——— N——— and L——— V——— left there, and then becoming dissatisfied, Noah Noble moved the old people to his land, near Indianapolis, where they both remained until they died.

Thomas and Sarah were never separated for a week in their lives. Never belonged to any one but Dr. Thos. Noble and his wife, and the heirs of Dr. Noble, and, when they were permitted go free, they clung to the family; knowing this fact, there was not one of them who would not care for them and provide for their wants.

The mock sensibility, which so often wept over Uncle Tom's fate, has lost its tears over a fiction. We have ourself seen men and women making a great to do over the negroes, who would let the poor white women and children perish with hunger and cold. * *

Three of the Noble family yet live, who can correct us if we have not stated Uncle Tom's history aright. L. T.

words, simply expressed what I mean by those terms. It is, I suppose, on this account that J. S. calls it a "wordy verbosity." The objection shows clearly the necessity for defining, in the proposition itself, what is meant by the use of the terms American slavery.

American slavery is not simply an abstract idea—a legal fiction, or a naked theory. It is also the necessary incidents, results and consequences of these, as developed in the condition, character and conduct of both masters and slaves. Slavery exists both in theory and in practice, both in law and in fact. It is not simply in the abstract, but in the concrete, that I desire to consider it, if I make it the subject of discussion. I would not undertake to prove Satan a sinner, if limited solely to the consideration of his personal being, and precluded from any and all reference to his sensations, volitions, and actions, nor am I disposed to attempt to prove that the theory—the institution or system of slavery—is a sin, separate from, and independent of its effects and consequences, in and upon the condition, character, and conduct of masters and slaves. The whole effort to show that slavery—the relation of master and slave—is sinless, has been expended upon the consideration of slavery in the abstract, and in the unwarranted separation of the institution, and the relation from their necessary incidents and qualities. I do not propose to meet the question in that shape. I do not know that it would be profitable to do so. The proposition, as it stands, embraces my definition of American slavery, and expresses my conviction of its moral character. If, in the terms in which it is stated, J. S. admits its truth, there can be no controversy between us about it. Or, if he regards the proposition as immaterial or unimportant, he will, of course, decline to discuss it. But if he considers it false in fact, and pernicious in tendency, he will probably attempt to refute it.

I will here re-state the proposition. It is as follows: American slavery, as established, recognized, or permitted by the laws of the slaveholding States, and exemplified in the condition, character, and conduct of both masters and slaves, is sin against God and against humanity.

The institution of marriage and slavery, J. S. regards as parallel institutions, equally sacred, and equally entitled to the respectful consideration of a christian people. In presenting his views, he thus speaks of them: "Slavery and marriage are both institutions of civil government, and relations existing in human society." He reasons, in effect, that the one is entitled to equal protection and respect with the other. This view is so monstrous, so abhorrent, and so offensive to the moral sense, that I confess I am not yet able to look steadily and calmly at it.

The divine institution of marriage, paralleled and associated with the diabolical institution of chattel slavery, is a thought too revolting for calm consideration. But they are so presented by J. S., and the consideration is thus forced upon me. I remark, then, that marriage is a divine ordinance, existing before and above the institution of marriage by the civil government. The civil institution of marriage is in harmony with, and in furtherance of, the divine purpose in its ordination. For this reason the institution of marriage is rightly regarded as sacred and holy. If there be aught in the civil institution, in contravention of the divine purpose, or in violation of the law of God in reference to it, in just so far is the civil institution sinful. Such are some of the features of the civil institution of marriage in the territory of Utah, and these might, perhaps, justly be paralleled with the institution of slavery in some of its revolting features. But the consideration of the subject of marriage in its relation to slavery, properly belongs to a more advanced stage in the discussion of this question. Should I reach that point in the discussion, I may then give it further consideration.

J. S. seems much shocked at my offer to discuss the question with him, in the form of a legal argument, upon a case to be agreed upon, and referred to a court of conscience. He rebukes me for proposing to use "fictions that never existed," in making up an agreed case for "a grave discussion in a public religious paper," and asserts that "the Lord never erected a court of conscience, nor made it a high court in his kingdom." J. S. is well aware that there are in the civil courts agreed cases, or cases founded upon assumed facts, having no real existence, and that these constitute a large proportion of the cases litigated in such courts. To these J. S. does not object. He is familiar with their use, and aware of the benefits derived from them. But he objects to their use, in "a grave discussion in a public religious paper." On the bench and at the bar, he possibly regards himself as "outside of christianity," and at liberty to use means for the ascertainment of truth, which he thinks are prohibited in the "kingdom of the Lord," and in the investigation of moral questions. The Great Teacher was proverbial for the use of parables, as the means of communicating moral truths, and this fact, as it seems to me, fully justifies the use of fiction to the extent and in the manner I proposed. If J. S. does not like the names of Legree and Uncle Tom, there could be no objection to his selecting such as he might choose, to personate the characters and conduct of masters and slaves.

Civil governments have their courts of conscience so designated because they assume to decide according to right and conscience, unembarrassed by the technicalities of strictly legal proceedings. The highest Court in England is called a court of conscience, and the Lord Chancellor, who presides in it, is called the keeper of the king's conscience. Our own courts of equity, either State or National, are courts of conscience. Writers upon national law recognize the existence of a national conscience, a public moral sense, before and by which public acts, done or contemplated, are tried, and either approved or condemned. There is established in the human heart, by God the Creator, who has so fearfully and wonderfully made man, a court of conscience, which decides upon the moral character of human actions. If Jesus the Lord presides in that court—if the law of the Lord, as revealed to us in his Word, be administered there, its decisions must be just, righteous and irreversable. Is it possible that there can be found a citizen of the kingdom of the Lord Jesus, who denies the existence of such a court in the Lord's kingdom. J. S. does so, and we therefore need not be surprised at his denial of the sinfulness of American slavery.

J. S. expresses the hope, that if I will not discuss the question of slavery with him, in the form he presents it, I will "quit denouncing it as a sin." I decline the discussion in that form; but I hope and trust that, while life lasts, I may not cease to denounce American slavery as a sin. As I regard the subject, to promise to do so would be voluntarily to abjure allegiance to the Lord and Master, and to renounce forever my hope of heaven. O. B.

[From the Record of June 3d.—Editorial.]
THE DISCUSSION BETWEEN O. B., AND J. S.

Our readers have noticed, some with regret, and some with delight, the articles in the Weekly Record, by Breth. O. B., and J. S., out of which, discussion of the vexed subject of Slavery, is likely to grow. This was not anticipated when these articles were commenced, and how far they are to be continued we can not now say. We need not say to these brethren, that we hope they will treat the subject with that dignity and christian forbearance which so grave a subject demands. Whether the bodies and souls of men for whom Jesus died, may be chattelized, and sold on the *auction block*, in common with horses and mules, without incurring the displeasure of the great Father of all, is a question of no small moment. Still, as thousands of our fellow citizens, and even of christians, have been taught from infancy to believe this is all right in the eyes of God, and the light of the Bible, the subject demands serious, scriptural investigation.

We hope, if the discussion is to go on, that Bro. J. S. will cease to even intimate that the north is chargable with all the horrors of the southern rebellion, thus indirectly justifying the south, in their attempt to pull down our glorious temple of liberty. Stick to the text, brethren.

[From the Christian Record of June 10th, 1862.]
FANATICISM OF ERROR.

As further proof of the fanaticism of the error into which my brother O. B. has unfortunately fallen, I will note the following in his last article.

"The institutions of marriage and slavery, J. S. regards as parallel institutions equally entitled to the respectful consideration of a Christian people."

I said no such thing; I meant no such thing; and no such thing is inferable from what I did say. Supposing that he could reflect dispassionately when marriage was the subject of consideration; I used it in lieu of slavery, in stating his course as to slavery, to show his evasion, and attempt to avoid the discussion of the question at issue, whether slavery is sinful or not. I said nothing about the two institutions being " equally" sacred, or " equally" entitled to respect; and nothing of that kind is inferable from what I said.

Again, he says:

" He reasons in effect, that the one is entitled to equal protection and respect with the other;" and confesses that he is "not yet able to look steadily and *calmly* at it."

And again, he says:

"The divine institution of marriage, paralleled and associated with the diabolical institution of chattel slavery is a thought too revolting for *calm* consideration. But they are so presented by J. S."!

An intellect that is so unhinged as to honestly and in good faith, thus misapprehend what is said, and imagine that something entirely different is said, is in a very bad condition to " think on whatsoever things are true."[1] Hence a calm consideration and investigation, in "the words of truth and soberness,"[2] of a subject about which that intellect is so unhinged, I fear is wholly unattainable.

My brother O. B. will not " attempt to prove " that " the institution or system of slavery is sin, separate from and independent of its effects and consequences, in and upon the condition, character and conduct of masters and slaves."

I understand this to be an admission that the institution of slavery is not a sin; that it is not sin to hold the relation of master to a slave; in other words, that it is not sin to own a slave. If this is inferring more than the language of O. B. justifies, let us take it in the language in which he utters it—that he is not disposed *to attempt* to prove that slavery is sin.

But he professes to be willing to attempt to prove it, if we will couple with it, its effects and consequences, in and upon the condition, character and conduct of masters and slaves.

Here it is at once seen, that, if this course should be tak-

---

(1) Phil. iv, 8.   (2) Acts xxvi, 25.

en, our discussion would be, not whether slavery is sinful or not, but what are its effects? its consequences? and what are they in and upon the condition, character and conduct of masters and slaves? Judging from the specimens we have already had of his proneness to deal in fictions instead of facts, that is to deal in fictions instead of dealing in "whatsoever things are true," we should, at once, differ as to what its effects and consequences were, and get into a discussion of that, and not of the question, Is slavery sinful? He would insist that certain gross fictions, that those of his school have been bruiting abroad for years, are facts, and are the effects and consequences of the institution. I should deny that they were facts, and also deny that they were the effects and consequences of the institution, and should call on him to show that they were the effects and consequences of the institution, instead of being what rational men would say they were, that is, that they were the effects and consequences of the proneness to sin, and of the actual sins, of the masters and slaves.

I should insist that the character and conduct of *Christian* masters and slaves were as good as the character and conduct of other *Christians*, even as those of Bro. O. B. or myself; and that the character and conduct of christians do not depend upon their state and condition in life, whether it be that of masters or slaves, or of those who do not hold that relation to any other human being, but upon their "patient continuance in well doing," and "growth in grace, [favor] and in *the knowledge of our Lord* and Savior Jesus Christ," by continuing in, observing, or keeping his word,[1] and require him to show the contrary.

Here, Bro. O. B., if he should be consistent with his former assertions, and with those of his school, would say that one could not be a Christian and a slave-holder; that to be a Christian and guilty of "the sin of slavery," "the sum of all villianies," "the monster iniquity," "the colossal crime," and "associated with the diabolical institution of chattel slavery," it "is a thought too revolting for calm consideration."

This would bring us back to the starting point; that the institution of slavery is a sin. But, Bro. O. B. is not dis-

---

(1) Rom. ii, 7; 2 Peter, iii, 18; John viii, 31, 32.

posed to attempt to prove it to be a sin. The result, then, would be, that slavery is not a sin; but according to O. B., some things that slave-holders do, and which, he says, are the effects and consequences of slavery, are sins.

O. B. can not consider slavery in the abstract, but in the concrete, if he discusses it. There is no abstract or concrete about it. It is neither compound nor complex. It is a simple single relation. If it were proposed to inquire as to the sinfulness of adultery, or drunkenness, how strange would it sound to hear one of those who proposed to discuss it, say, that he could not consider it in the abstract but in the concrete, if he discusses it! and insist upon mixing up effects and consequences, either real or supposed, of adultery or drunkenness, in the discussion of it, so as to confine it (according to his notion,) to "American" adultery, or "American" drunkenness!

The good word of the Lord does not so speak of persons or things. It denounces liars, fornicators, covetous, extortioners, idolators, drunkards, adulterers, whoremongers, effeminate, abusers of themselves with mankind, thieves, and *railers*, as sinners, without any abstraction or concretion about them, or either of them, and does not place slave-holders with them, either abstractly or concretely, notwithstanding, there then were as many slave-holders, when the Lord taught and the apostles wrote, as there were of the classes above enumerated. The good word of the Lord also denounces lying, adultery, fornication, uncleanness, lasciviousness, idolatry, witchcraft, *hatred*, *varience*, emulations, *wrath*, *strife*, *seditions*, heresies, [sects] envyings, murder, drunkenness, revellings, *bitterness*, anger, *clamor*, *evil-speaking*, malice and blasphemy, as sinful, without abstraction or concretion, without designating them as Asiatic, European, or American, and does not place slavery among them, though it was as rife when that word was written, as these vices were, and abounded much more in the human family than it does now. If such a crusade against it as now exists, is so very essential, why was it not necessary for those inspired men to, at least, enumerate it among the vices that the good word of the Lord denounces as sinful? Why did not the apostles make the discovery that Bro. O. B. has, that failing to denounce it as a sin, " would be voluntarily to abjure allegiance to the Lord and Master, and to renounce forever my [their] hope of heaven"? But they did not make the discovery, and did not so denounce it; and yet Peter and Paul put off this tabernacle, not only with the hope, but the full assurance of heaven.

I will here add, also, that the good word of the Lord warns Christians, and enjoins upon them, that they should none of them "suffer as a murderer, or as a thief, or as an evil-doer, or as a busy-body in other men's matters;" but that "if any man suffer as a Christian, let him not be ashamed; but let him glorify God on this behalf."[1] Suffering as a Christian then, is not suffering as a busy-body in other men's matters; and the busy-body in other men's matters, is ranked with murderers and thieves, by the inspired Peter, just before he put off the tabernacle of his body, as the Lord had showed him.[2]

O. B. still insists that there is a court of conscience in the Lord's kingdom. I will be under great obligations to him, if he will cite me to the passage of the New Testament, establishing it; for I confess that I have not seen it, and I think I have seen all that is in the book. There is nothing in the Lord's kingdom that is not mentioned in that book, *that is certain*. If it is not mentioned there, it is not in his kingdom.

A few words to my much esteemed and amiable brother, E. Goodwin, Editor of the *Record*. In noticing our articles, he says:

"Whether the bodies and souls of men for whom Jesus died, may be chattelized, and sold on the *auction block* in common with horses and mules, without incurring the displeasure of the great Father of all, is a question of no small moment. Still, as thousands of our fellow citizens, and even Christians, have been taught from infancy to believe this all right, in the eyes of God and the light of the Bible, the subject demands serious scriptural investigation."

This shows how great the mischief that railing, evil-speaking, and evil-surmising has done among us, when it has produced such an effect upon so amiable and intelligent a brother, as the Editor of the *Record*.

1. The question he states is not involved in the inquiry whether slavery is sinful or not. 2. Nobody has been taught

---

(1) 1 Pet. iv, 15, 16.   (2) 2 Pet. i, 14.

as he states. 3. Christians neither believe nor practice such things.

Again:

1. The question is not involved; for slaves (why could he not use that term instead of the false periphrasis "bodies and souls of men, for whom Jesus died"?) are sold on the auction block only in three cases. 1. When the owner voluntarily puts them up at auction. 2. When they are sold by the sheriff on execution. 3. When sold by executors or administrators. The first, christians do not do, and no others do, except the regular slave dealer; and he only gets the refractory slaves, who have failed to discharge their duty as slaves, as laid down by the apostles in the christian scriptures, and are, I suppose, in the providence of God, thus punished for their sin in that failure.

The 2d and 3d can not take place where the christian law to "owe no man anything"[1] is kept by the master. In that case, there will be no sheriff's sale of his property; and his executors or administrators will deliver his slaves over to his heirs, and not put them on the auction stand. So, it is the sin of the slave, or of the master, that puts slaves on the auction block, and not the institution of slavery.

Bro. Goodwin, like Bro. O. B., puts something that he supposes to be the effect and consequence of slavery, for slavery, and denounces that, saying it is a question of no small moment, when it is really not the question involved.

2. 3. Such things are not taught in the slave-holding communities; and christians living in those communities, neither believe nor practice such things.

Bro. Goodwin further says:

"We hope, if the discussion is to go on, that Bro. J. S. will cease even to intimate that the North is chargable with all the horrors of the Southern rebellion, thus indirectly justifying the South in their attempt to pull down our glorious temple of liberty."

I have not even "intimated" that the North was chargable with all the horrors of our present unhappy and most unnecessary civil war. I have made no intimation the one way nor the other. I have been endeavoring to show some things wherein we of the North have erred in the unfortu-

---

(1) Rom xiii, 8.

nate qua*r*el, because I am writing for Northern readers, and addressing the Northern mind. In doing that, it is not necessary, nor even proper, to speak of the errors of those of the South. When I address the brethren of the South, (if I should ever have the opportunity of doing so,) then will be the proper time to show the errors into which they have fallen. In my opinion, grave errors have been committed, and are being committed, both North and South; and neither "is chargable with all the horrors" of the present distress. People like to have the faults and errors of others pointed out, but not their own. The Lord and the apostles, however, did not teach that way. And as my lot is cast in the North, my duty is to cast in my mite, to aid us in the North to come to the light on the subject. We ought not to shun coming to the light of God's truth, lest, perchance, our deeds should be reproved. "He that *doeth truth* cometh to the light, that his deeds may be made manifest that they are wrought *in God*."[1] And it is a weak excuse for not coming to the light, when it reproves our conduct, to say that it will indirectly justify the conduct of somebody else. It will not do so;[2] but even if it will, "let God be true, but every man a liar."[3] That is what inspiration says in the premises.

May the Lord enable us to come to the light, as He is in the light.   J. S.

---

(1) John iii, 20--21.

(2) As evidence that this proposition is true, I will cite what the great British statesman Edmund Burke said in the time of our revolution. Speaking of those who were opposed to the policy of the government, he said:

"They have been told that their dissent from violent measures is an encouragement to rebellion. Men of *great presumption* and *little knowledge* will hold a language which is contradicted by the whole course of history. General rebellions and revolts of a whole people never were *encouraged*, now or at any time. They are always *provoked*. But if this unheard of doctrine of the encouragement of rebellion were true; if it were true that the assurance of the friendship of numbers in this country toward the colonies could become an encouragement to them to break off all connection with it, what is the inference? Does any body seriously maintain that, charged with my share of the public councils, I am obliged not to resist projects which I think mischievous, lest men who suffer should be encouraged to resist? The very tendency of such projects to produce rebellion is one of the chief reasons against them. Shall that reason not be given? Is it then a rule that no man in this nation shall open his mouth in favor of the colonies; shall defend their rights, or complain of their sufferings? or when war finally breaks out, no man shall express his desire of peace? Has this been the law of our past, or is it to be the terms of our future connection? Even looking no further than ourselves, can it be true loyalty to any Government, or true patriotism toward any country, to degrade their solemn councils into servile drawing-rooms, to flatter their pride and passions, rather than to enlighten their reason, and prevent them from being cautioned against violence, lest others should be encouraged to resistance? By such acquiescence great kings and mighty nations have been undone, and if any are at this day in a perilous situation from rejecting truth and listening to flattery, it would rather become them to *reform* the errors under which they suffer, than to reproach those who *forewarn* them of their danger."—*Burk's letter to the sheriffs of Bristol, published in April*, 1777.

(3) Rom. iii, 3–4.

REMARKS.

As Bro. J. S. has paid his respects, in a very kind and respectful manner to the *Record*, duty and the rules of reciprocity demand a few remarks from me. Bro. J. S. supposes that it was the railings, evil speaking and evil surmizings of others, that led me to say—" Whether the bodies and souls of men for whom Jesus died, may be chattelized and sold on the auction block, in common with horses and mules, without incurring the displeasure of the great Father of all, is a question of no small moment. Still, as thousands of our fellow citizens and even christians, have, been taught from infancy to believe this all right, in the eyes of God and the light of the Bible, the subject demands serious, scriptural investigation."

In this my Bro. is mistaken. Evil surmizing and evil speaking does not thus effect me. My remarks were prompted by facts. But Bro. J. S. says—" no body has been so taught, as he (I) states." What! Nobody taught that slaves may be sold on the auction-block in common with other property, without incurring the displeasure of God!! Bro. J. S., "I speak that I know, and testify that I have seen." I know that many good and pious men in the slaveholding States mourn over this state of things, and shed tears at the sight of such sales; but still it is true, that thousands, and tens of thousands are taught and therefore believe that the sale of slave-man is just as righteous as the sale of a horse or mule. Our good brother thinks I should have said " Slaves,' and not " the souls and bodies for whom Jesus died." Did not Jesus die for the slave as well as for the master? If so, my phraseology is correct. Even the term *servant*, would sound a little more softly on many ears than the word *slave*. But this is no reason why the naked truth should not be spoken; or, that things should not be called by their proper names. I have found a few persons who denied that Christ died for Africans, or the negro race; but surely this is not what Bro. J. S. means. Yet he says, to express the term *slaves*, by " the souls and bodies of men for whom Jesus died," is " a false paraphrase " !

But Bro. J. S., admits that slaves are sold on the auction block under three classes of circumstances. That admission is enough to place the whole institution under the ban of condemnation.[1] Bro. J. S. says, slaves can not be sold at auction by a sheriff, or admidistrator where the christian law, to "owe no man anything," is kept by the master. But such sales often become necessary to make equal divisions of estates. And then that law is not always kept according to the strict letter, even by christians; and thousands of slaveholders do not profess to be governed by the law of Christ. Good men often become involved so that their property falls into the sheriff's hands. Hence, I conclude that any law that places human beings on a level with brute property, and subjects them to be thus exposed by the imprudent trading of their master, is an unrighteous law.

Bro. J. S. denies that he has ever "intimated that the North is chargeable with 'all' the horrors of our present unhappy and most unnecessary civil war." It was in view of the following paragraph that I made the remark to which he refers, as found in the 18th number of our weekly:

"But it has been harped so long [that slavery is a sin] that thousands of excellent people have got to believe that it is true, THAT IT IS A SIN; and hence, as they desire to eradicate all sin from the earth, they have entered into crusades against it, increasing in intensity and vigor, till our present woful condition exists."

My conclusion from this was, that Bro. J. S. blamed this awful war, with all its horrors, upon the slavery agitation in the North, and, indirectly, justified the South in their rebellion. I am glad, however, that I have given him the occasion to explain; and that he now tells us that he did not mean to be so understood. That great national evils have been committed both North and South, I admit; but I am far from admitting that the course pursued by a few fanatics in the North who had but little influence either North or South, has caused this horrible rebellion. But this is no time to inquire who caused the rebellion. Let the storm be passed, and the nation become sober, before we agitate that question.

---

(1) What a strange notion! What passage of scripture proves this assertion of brother Goodwin?

[From the Christian Record of June 17th, 1862.]
FANATICISM OF ERROR.

Bro. Goodwin:—I regret to be under the necessity to occupy more space in the *Record*, and more of the time and attention of its readers, in a discussion with J. S. without the prospect of soon reaching the real subject of discussion. If J. S. and myself are to give our views upon the subject of slavery, it were time that we began the argument. If that is not the purpose, we need not trouble ourselves, or the readers of the *Record*, with so lengthy a logomachy. I suppose, however, that I must still follow J. S. so far as to notice briefly some of the contents of his last article.

J. S. still regards me as having fallen into the "fanaticism of error," while I regard him as its willing captive. Which of us is the best illustration of that species of fanaticism, is a question upon which, as a matter of course, we should differ, and upon which the reader will form his own opinion without reference to ours.

J. S. complains that I have done him injustice, in my remarks upon his paralleling the institutions of marriage and slavery. Some injustice may have been done by those remarks, to his unexpressed sentiments and convictions, but I still think I gave a fair construction of the language he used. He spoke of both marriage and slavery as simple institutions of civil government, and neither assigned to the one a higher, or the other a lower rank. I accept his disclaimer of any intention to represent them as equal, but still he has not assigned to them, or to either of them, any other rank. In the event of his prosecuting this discussion, if he does not yet attempt to exalt slavery to the rank of a divine institution, I shall be agreeably disappointed.

In reference to a court of conscience in the Lord's kingdom, and the propriety of an agreed or hypothetical case for the trial of slavery there, I have nothing to retract from what I have said upon that subject. To my conception, there is a quality, faculty, or power of the mind, which investigates and decides upon the moral character of acts done or contemplated. It is its province to hear and determine the case presented, and hence, by no unauthorized figure of speech, it may be called a court. That quality. faculty, or power of the mind, I call conscience, and it is so called by the common consent of mankind. It tries and determines the moral character of acts contemplated, as well as of acts done. To do this, the act contemplated is in mental contemplation regarded as done, and thus an agreed or hypothetical case is made out and submitted to the decision of conscience. This J. S. calls fiction, and gravely talks of my "proneness to deal in fiction," and keeps repeating, for my benefit, the apostolical injunction, "think of whatsoever things are true." I claim that I have not violated truth in this matter, and that J. S. has sufficient intellect to appreciate that fact. It is unworthy of him, and of the subject, to resort to a species of pettifogging, for the purpose of prejudicing the minds of the readers against me, and against such arguments as I may use in opposition to chattel slavery.

But I ought, perhaps, to excuse J. S. for although he has long been a citizen of the Lord's kingdom, he has not yet learned that there is in that kingdom a court of conscience, and doubtingly requests me to "cite to the passage of the New Testament establishing it." It would draw me from my present purpose to attempt that now; but perhaps when the matter in hand is disposed of, I may find leisure to attend to his request. But for the present, to use another figure of speech in reference to the conscience, or another fiction, if J. S. will so regard it, let me say, that to my contemplation, the conscience is the Lord's garden in the human heart. It has cost him much of labor, much of suffering, to make it good, to cleanse, purify, and enlighten it, and to render it a fit and proper place of his resort, for the purpose of holding communion with the human soul. And when, in the cool of life's summer day, he shall come to walk in this his garden, happy is the man who, with humble boldness, can meet and commune with him there. But it is to be feared that, upon such occasions, many other than Father Adam will be found holding themselves from his presence, not, perhaps, in the shadow of the trees of the ancient paradise, but beneath the deeper shadows of those specimens of political growth called civil institutions.

I can not attempt to follow J. S. in all he says upon the subject of slavery. His track is too intricate, or at least diverges too far from my line of thought to induce an effort on my part to do so. I will, however, notice some of the items.

J. S. understands me to have admitted, "that the institution of slavery is not a sin—that it is not sin to hold the relation of master to a slave—in other words, that it is not sin to own a slave." I have made no such admission, not even in reference to the *institution* of slavery, contemplated in the total exclusion of its incidents and qualities—its effects and consequences. If he will revise my remarks, he will find, that by fair construction, my language has directly the opposite meaning. I said, however, that the discussion of the moral character of the institution—the simple theory of slavery so contemplated—would be unprofitable. I did not refer to the relation of a master to a slave, or to the claim by one man to own another as slave property. These are some of the incidents and qualities of slavery—the effects and consequences of the institution. The moral character of the relation and of the claim, I have not yet declined to discuss with J. S. The subject is fully embraced in the proposition I have submitted. I hold, that the legalized relation of the master to the slave is sinful, and that the legalized claim of one human being to another as his slave, his chattel property, is sin.

The agitation of the subject of slavery has deeply "vexed the righteous soul" of J. S. With or without reason or appropriateness, and both in season and out of season, he makes hostile demonstrations against those whom he calls agitators. Hence, he cites freely, and at random, from portions of the Holy Scriptures, designating various crimes and offences, italicising such of these crimes and offences as he regards as applicable to these agitators. The italics are intended to give them point, and indicate the purpose for which the quotations are made. They have no appreciable reference to the subject of which he is treating. But if I mistake not, these missiles will much more frequently light upon his own head than reach the mark at which he aims them. He had better reserve his fire, and not waste his ammunition, by firing at long range, under circumstances that leave his presumed antagonists ever in doubt, whether he is aiming at them. Should he reach the field of conflict, he will need all his ammunition then, and still may find himself under the necessity of retiring for the want of more. At any rate, he should exercise more judgment and discretion in the selection and use of his missiles, lest he should inflict upon himself the wounds he intends for others.

J. S. has said, that the institution of slavery is a question of political economy—an institution of civil government—a civil institution—a State institution—and as such is not sinful, and yet he declines to discuss the question of the moral character of American slavery, and talks gravely about the impropriety of designating slavery as American. He thinks it would sound strange, if one who proposed to inquire into the sinfulness of adultery, or drunkenness, should insist upon confining the discussion to American adultery or drunkenness. If adultery and drunkenness were institutions established, legalized and protected by State laws—if they were institutions of civil government, such limitation of discussion in reference to them would seem to me appropriate. There is, we are told, in the territory of Utah, an institution of adultery, legalized and protected by the Utah laws, and there it would be most pertinent and most appropriate to discuss the moral character of Utah adultery.

The agitation of which J. S. complains so bitterly, is and has been wholly in reference to *American* slavery, and the claims and conduct of the master to the slaves, as legalized and protected by American laws. Of this J. S. is well aware, and if disposed to meet the real question at issue, he will consent to discuss my proposition, or some other one, involving about what is intended to be expressed by it. He has submitted no proposition himself, nor has he suggested any one in tangible form. I therefore conclude that he does not intend to discuss the question, but simply seeks an opportunity to discharge a few arrows, Parthian like, at the advancing antagonists of chattel slavery. Unless his next article, should he think proper to furnish another, shall be at least some approximation to the point, my impression now is, that I shall not attempt to follow him further. However, as I have submitted a proposition, and as yet have offered no argument to sustain it, I may be disposed, with the consent of the editor of the *Record*, to make some effort, in an article or two, to prove that American slavery is sin. But I leave that matter open for further consideration. O. B.

FANATICISM OF ERROR.

REPLY OF J. S. TO E. G.

A few remarks are proper in reply to Bro. Goodwin.
If any man "consent not to wholesome words, he is proud, * * * but doting about questions and strife of words, whereof cometh envy, strife, railings, evil surmisings, perverse disputings, (gallings one of another, *marginal reading*,) of men of corrupt minds (wholly corrupted in mind, *New Translation*,) and destitute of the truth."[1] We are enjoined not only to hold fast "sound words," but even "the form" of them.[2] Well might we be so enjoined and commanded, and how great heed should we take to observe the injunction when we speak of matters pertaining to the Lord, his laws and kingdom, may be seen, when we consider that the Lord himself gave to his disciples, and through them to us, "the *words* which thou [the Father] gavest me."[3]

Bro. Goodwin said: "Whether the bodies and souls of men for whom Jesus died, may be chattelized and sold on the auction block, in common with horses and mules, without incurring the displeasure of the Great Father of all, is a question of no small moment."

Let us calmly, and in the fear of God, look at this a few moments.

The *bodies* of slaves are not "chattelized," but they belong to the slaves during their lives, and at their death they are returned to the earth, the mother of us all. The *souls* of the slaves are not "chattelized," but they belong to the slaves, and to the God and Father of all our spirits. What is it, then, about slaves that are "chattelized?" It is their *services and labor*. That is what is chattelized; that is what is bought and sold on the auction block and otherwise; and it is not either the bodies or the souls of men for whom Jesus died that are either chattelized or sold, owned or possessed. If the bodies were used for meat, or the skins for leather, then it might be said that the bodies were chattelized. Chattelized, however, is an improper term, because it produces ["whereof cometh,"] "strife, railings, evil sur-

---

(1) 1 Tim. vi, 3–5.   (2) 2 Tim. i, 13.   (3) John xvii, 8.

misings, gallings one of another." But neither the bodies of the slaves, nor any portion of them, are ever used as property by the masters, but they are delivered up to the earth.

Hence, I said, that "the bodies and souls of men for whom Jesus died," was a false periphrasis for the word *slaves*. It is false. For "the services and labor of men," is the true periphrasis for the word. And the clause "for whom Jesus died," is an unnecessary appendage, and, it seems to me, is added only to make improper impressions upon pious and kind-hearted brethren and sisters, and is a random use of words and phrases that christian teachers should not indulge in. Bro. Goodwin's labor and services, and mine, and all the christian brethren and sisters' labors and services, belong to, and are owned by the Lord—so did Paul's; and by looking at 2 Cor. xi. 23–33, we will see what great and hard labors and services were exacted of him by the Lord. Having done this, let us reflect a moment, and see what we think of using such language as, the body and soul of a man for whom Jesus died, five times whipped with thirty-nine lashes each time; thrice beaten with rods; once stoned; thrice shipwrecked; a night and a day in the deep; in traveling, often in the perils of the water, of robbers, of Jews, of the heathen, in the city, in the wilderness, in the sea, and among false brethren; in weariness and painfulness, and watchings, often in hunger and thirst, and fastings, in cold and nakedness; and besides all these things of outward bodily sufferings, the daily mental labor and anxiety of the care of all the churches placed on him; and he finally put to a violent death by a wicked heathen; *all this exacted by his master*. Can this be done? Can such an institution exist "without incurring the displeasure of the Great Father of all"?

It does look somewhat like both Paul's body and soul were "chattelized;" but they were not. His services, labor and sufferings were all of Paul, that the Lord reduced to property, when he "captured" him, and "reduced" him to his service. But slave-owners only have property in the labors and services of their slaves—not in their sufferings, nor lives, as the Lord had in Paul, and has in all christians.

Bro. Goodwin thinks that the admission that slaves (he there uses the term) are sold on the auction-block, is enough

to place the whole institution under the ban of condemnation; and he concludes that any law allowing it, is an unrighteous law. Here we see that it is *the law* that he objects to, and not to slavery. Well, as neither the Savior nor the apostles ever gave an opinion of the goodness or badness of any of the laws, or of any of the kingdoms of this world, I shall refrain from discussing that question in a religious discussion, in a religious paper. In a political forum, I am, and always have been, ready to do it, but not here. J. S.
June 11, 1862.

REMARKS ON THE ABOVE.

Upon the foregoing from our esteemed Bro. J. S., a few remarks may be necessary. I have no disposition to enter into a general discussion of the subject of American slavery with J. S. or any other person, especially the political phase of the subject. Particularly would this be improper on my part, while the preliminaries of a discussion of that subject, between Bro J. S. and another brother, are in course of adjustment. I know, too, that this is a very exciting subject, and one that is difficult to either oppose or defend, without becoming extravagant in the use of terms.

Bro. J. S. seems to think that I have become guilty of this extravagance, because I used the terms, "souls and bodies of men for whom Jesus died," to express slaves, and he gravely informs us, "that the bodies of slaves are not chattelized, but they belong to the slaves during their natural lives, and at death they are returned to the earth, the mother of us all. The souls of the slaves are not chattelized, but they belong to the slaves, and to the God and Father of all our spirits."

I am inclined to think this is a new definition of slavery, formed to suit the occasion. The body and soul of the slave belongs to the slave, and the slave's service belongs to the master! Where, then, is the slave? The slave owns the body and soul—who is that slave? If the slave owns the slave's body, he has a right to use that body as he may think proper. Suppose a certain slave should conclude to move his body, which belongs to him, from Kentucky to Canada, what would the master do or say? I am inclined to think he would pursue the slave, and, if caught in the United States, would compel him to bring that body back by the force of the fugitive slave law. In vain might the slave claim that the body was his own; the master would claim the man, and all that goes to constitute the man.

But what is the fact in the case? Look over the tax-list of a slave State, and you will see horses, mules and slaves, put down as property, without any distinction being made between the slave man and his service. When a man is put up at auction, the cryer does not call for bids on the services of the man, but on the man himself. 'Tis true, the purchaser expects to get service out of the slave, but he buys the man in the hope of the service. Just so when he buys a horse or mule. He buys the animal for the sake of the service he can get out of him. Thus the man and the mules are sold in common. Let us hear what Mr. Cobb, the great expounder of slave law and defender of American slavery, says. He says:

"Of the other great absolute right of a freeman, viz: the right of private property, the slave is entirely deprived. His person and his time being entirely the property of his master, whatever he may accumulate by his labor, or is otherwise acquired by him, becomes immediately the property of the master."

There is the plain truth in the case, stated by one of the ablest defenders of the institution, of the present age. Bro. J. S. admits virtually, that Christ died for the souls and bodies of slaves; and that it would be wrong, therefore, to chattelize them, and sell them in common with horses and mules. Such a thing is too revolting for his moral feelings. Hence, he is not willing to admit that any body does it. Still he must admit that the master has supreme control over the body of the slave. Thus my statement of the case is correct, as shown above. Bro. J. S. thinks the phrase, "for whom Jesus died," is "an unnecessary appendage." I think not. It shows the worth of the person sold. Should I say my neighbor killed my horse, the offence would appear great; but if I should say, my horse for which I paid five hundred dollars, the crime would appear still greater. So, to sell a man seems hard, but when we add the man for whom Jesus died, it gives us a more just conception of the magnitude of the offence. That the person is sold and becomes the property of the purchaser, we have proved; and as it takes both soul and body to make the person, then the souls and bodies for whom Jesus died, is chattelized and sold. We did not use the phrase to make improper impressions upon the minds of the brethren and sisters, as our brother seems to suppose. Our object was to place the practice in its true color before our readers. I know we may conceal the enormity of a crime by giving it a pretty name; but, that we may see things as they are, we should call them by their proper names. Bro. J. S. don't like the name; then let him not defend the thing.

What does Bro. J. S. mean by the example of Paul which he here introduces? The Lord claimed the services of Paul, and the master claims the services of his slave; all the difference that he makes between the claims of the Lord upon Paul, and the claims of the master upon his slave, is, that the Lord claimed Paul's life and sufferings, while the master only claims the slave's services. But Paul's master rewarded him for his toils—do slaveholders reward their slaves according to their works?

If Bro. J. S. is unwilling to defend the traffic in human flesh, let him say no more in favor of the institution.

[From the Christian Record of July 17, 1862.]

FANATICISM OF ERROR.

Absence from home prevented an earlier notice of the articles of brethren O. B. and the Editor, which appeared in the *Record* of the 17th of June.

Our heavenly Father has been so kind to our fallen and sinful race, as not only to provide a way for redeeming, regenerating and elevating us from our fallen and ruined condition, to a position higher in the scale of existence than Adam held before he sinned, but he has, by and through the Lord, instructed us, and revealed to us his will in the premises, and what he requires of us. He has not only revealed in his good word, what he requires of us, but, to prevent any mistake or misapprehension, he has, in his word, defined most of the *things* that it is important for us to *know* to understand his commands to us, and our duty as members of the Lord's kingdom in this world. And we are commanded to hold fast to sound words—wholesome words—in speaking of the Lord, his laws, and the matters pertaining and relating to his kingdom; and we are explicitly told that those who will not consent to wholesome words, the words of our Lord Jesus Christ, are proud, knowing nothing, &c. Hence, my objections to words and phrases used by brother O. B. and the Editor, are not because they are "revolting to my moral feelings," nor because I "don't like them," but because they are untrue, unsound, and unwholesome. Neither our "moral feelings," or "sensibilities," nor our "consciences," are tests of truth in ascertaining the Lord's will; but the Scriptures given by inspiration are the tests; and they "thoroughly furnish the man of God to every good work," and give him "instruction in righteousness," that he "may be perfect."[1]

In the good word of the Lord, *sin* is defined; *righteousness* is defined; and *slavery* is defined.

Sin is doing what is forbidden, or failing to do what is commanded.

Righteousness, is doing what is commanded.

Slavery, like many other things, is neither sinful nor righteous; hence, brother O. B. need not be alarmed lest I should "attempt to exalt slavery to the rank of a Divine institution." I here simply state these things without adducing the proofs. I will do it when proper.

Slavery, is *obedience* to some person or thing.

In proof of this, I adduce the following passages of Scripture, quoting each as in the common version, in Wesley's Translation, and in the New Translation, published by Bro. Campbell.

1. To whom you yield yourselves servants (slaves) to obey, his servants (slaves) ye are to whom ye obey.[2]—*Common Version.*

Wesley's is the same, except that *to* before *whom* is omitted in the last clause.

To whom ye present yourselves servants, (slaves) *by obe-*

---

(1) 2 Tim. iii, 16, 17.   (2) Rom. vi, 16.

dience, his servants (slaves) you are whom you thus obey.—*New Translation*.

2. For of whom a man is overcome, of the same is he brought into bondage.[1]—*Com. Vers*.

For by whom a man is overcome, by him is he also brought into slavery.—*Wesley*.

For every one is enslaved by that which overcomes him.—*New Trans*.

3. Whosoever committeth sin is the servant (slave) of sin.[2]—*Com. Vers*.

He that committeth sin is the slave of sin.—*Wesley*.

Whosoever commits sin is the slave of sin.—*New Trans*.

The Lord, while here, was a slave and a master, and his slaves were his brethren.

He took upon himself the form of a servant, (slave) and being found in that form, he became a slave by humbling himself and becoming *obedient*. He became obedient to his Father unto death, even the ignnominious and painful death of the Cross.[3] "Ye call me Master and Lord: and ye say well; for so I am."[4] "One is your Master, even Christ."[5] "Whosover shall do the will of my Father, is *my brother*."[6] "Inasmuch as you have done it to one of the least of these, my brethren," &c.[7]

The Lord, then, while here, was a slave; he was also then, and now is, a Master, and a master too over his brethren. He occupied both positions in the relation of master and slave. Yet he was without sin.[8] He neither sinned by being a slave, nor by being a master.

I state this that Bro. Goodwin may see what I mean by this example; inasmuch as he inquires what I meant by the example of Paul, in my last. The Lord was a Master to Paul, and Paul was his slave; and I showed what great labor, services and sufferings the Lord exacted of Paul, much worse than selling his services and labor upon the "auction block," to a cotton or sugar planter, would have been; and that this was done by the Lord, "without incurring the displeasure of the great Father of all."

Yet brother Goodwin insists that the definition I gave of slavery in my last is a new definition, though as old as the

---

(1) 2 Pet. ii, 19. (4) John xiii, 13. (7) Matt. xxv, 40.
(2) John viii, 34. (5) Matt. xxiii, 8, 10. (8) Heb. iv, 15; 1 John iii, 5.
(3) Phil. ii, 7, 8. (6) Matt. xii, 50.

apostolic writings; and he quotes Mr. Cobb. I respectfully insist that the good word of the Lord is more reliable than the word of Mr. Cobb, though he may be a "great expounder of slave law." "A greater than Solomon" is the authority that I respectfully beg leave to submit to, myself. Others, of course, will decide and act for themselves, as to which authority they will accept, as we each have to account separately for himself, and not for another. *Obedience* is *slavery*, and *overcoming* is *mastery*, according to that authority which is greater than Solomon.

Brother Goodwin says:

"If Bro. J. S. is unwilling to defend the traffic in human flesh, let him say no more in favor of the institution" of slavery.

Here "traffic in human flesh," and "the institution of slavery," are used as convertible phrases, meaning exactly the same thing. And I suppose that he thinks that this is a correct definition, and that he is using "sound words, wholesome words, even the words of our Lord Jesus Christ."

Is not traffic in hog flesh, cattle flesh and sheep flesh, respectively, traffic in pork, beef and mutton, slaughtered and ready for market? It certainly is. Is the institution of slavery traffic in the flesh of slaves, slaughtered and ready for market in the butcher's stall? What a monstrous use of words! what an abuse of words! and in a religious discussion in a religious paper!!

Thus miscalling things, and misrepresenting the institution of slavery, has been, and is, a principal means used to mislead the public mind of the brotherhood upon the subject. And the principal thing to do, to disabuse the public mind, and let in the light of divine truth, by which we can look at things and see them as they are, is to correct this reckless and improper mode of expression.

"Persons held to service or labor," are to be given up and returned back, says the Constitution of the United States.[1] The Constitution gives the same definition of slavery that the inspired writers do. Held to service and labor is the language; that is, held to serve and labor for the master—not held that the master may traffic in their flesh in the butcher's stall. In the meantime, the bodies

---

(1) Const. art. iv, § 2.

and souls of the slaves are as much theirs, as those of the masters are theirs. And the fact that the bodies of the slaves are the slave's bodies, while their services and labor belong to their masters, no more entitles the slave "to use that body as he may think proper" in going to Canada or otherwheres, so as to deprive the master of the labor and services of the slave, than brother Goodwin is entitled to use his body as he may think proper, by becoming a thief, a robber, or keeping a doggery, or a brothel, and so deprive the Lord and the christian brotherhood of his labor and services as a christian preacher and editor. And will brother Goodwin say, that, as this is so, his body and soul do not belong to him? I apprehend not; and yet it can be as truly said of him as of any Kentucky slave. Would he say that he was chattelized; that his flesh was trafficked in? I apprehend not. Would he, instead of saying as the ancient and inspired slaves of the Lord did—Paul or Peter, a slave of Jesus Christ, &c.—say, the body and soul of one Elijah Goodwin, for whom Jesus died, chattelized by Christ, &c. I am certain that brother Goodwin would not use such language. He says that he did not use the phrase "for whom Jesus died," to make an improper impression. If not, and he only wanted to use a proper phrase descriptive of the person, why did he not use the phrase, "who die in Adam?"[1] That is equally true with the other, and would have placed "the practice in its true colors before our readers," as much as the other did—yea, and more; for there is a mawkish, morbid condition of the public mind at present on the subject, created by long "harping," that makes such a use of the phrase produce an improper impression at the present time. The "thing" brother Goodwin speaks of, I do not "defend." I object to the name he gives it, not because I dislike it, but because it is untrue, and contrary to the directions given us in the good word of the Lord as to the use of *words*, and the contemplation of *things*. But, with him I say, "that we may see things as they are, we should call them by their proper names." And this is what I am trying to get him to do.

Brother Goodwin says, "Paul's Master rewarded him for his toils—do slaveholders reward their slaves according to their works?"

---

(1) 1 Cor. xv, 22.

If they do not, their sin is in failing to discharge their duty as masters to their slaves, as laid down in the christian Scriptures, and not in owning the slaves. Masters, as well as fathers, have great responsibilities resting upon them. I am opposed to the institution of slavery as a question of political economy; and, were that out of the way, and I lived where the institution existed, I should not assume the relation of master. I have a wife and eight living children, which gives me full as much responsibility, as a husband and father, as I want to have to bear, without adding to it the responsibility, as a master, of one or more slaves. But because Paul and all the christians have a good Master in the Lord, while some masters of slaves are "forward," and sin greatly in their conduct toward their slaves, that's being so, neither proves the one slavery righteous, nor the other slavery sinful. It only proves the one master "perfect," and the other a great scamp (if I may use the term.) The Lord was made perfect through the suffering he endured while a slave, and as a slave.[1] Does brother Goodwin know how much nearer perfect the slaves of the United States are than the same race is in Africa, whence they came?[2] Does he know why the Israelites were enslaved in Egypt, though they were the elect people of God? Does he know why the Lord humbled himself and became obedient (that is, a slave) unto death, even the death of the Cross, to make him perfect through sufferings? If he does not—if these are "deep things of God,"[3] that he can't fathom any more than I can, (and I confess I can't) let him not, on that account, berate his and my brethren who live in the slave States, and their institutions and domestic relations, and call them hard names unwarranted, and even condemned by the

---

(1) Heb. ii, 10; and v, 8, 9.

(2) That the reader may see the condition of the negro race in Africa, and compare it with the condition of the negro race in the slave States of this Union, I append the following:

SEVEN THOUSAND NEGROES BUTCHERED.—The *West African Herald* publishes statements of the horrible massacres recently committed by his ebony Highness, the King of Dahomey. Several persons agree in stating that the number of negroes slain on the occasion was estimated at 2,000, but another correspondent gives the number at 7,000. He says he was present by compulsion, and that the blood swept past him like a flood into a large reservoir. Another gentleman, referring to these inhuman butcheries, says: "I assure you, it made me quite sick, and at the same time I felt stunned. The poor wretches met death with perfect indifference."

(3) 1 Cor. ii, 10; and Rom. xi, 33. Because God's judgments or determinations as to the negroes, are unsearchable, and his ways past finding out, the abolitionists essay to take the matter into their own hands, and undertake to manage it for him.

Scriptures, and thereby stir up wrath, envy, strife, railing, evil surmising, and gallings one of another.

Whatever brother O. B.'s "conception" may be as to the quality, faculty or power of the mind, and his system of philosophy as to conscience, and his "figures" about gardens, and his philosophy thereon, I respectfully beg to be excused from considering them. For the Lord has warned me to "beware lest any man spoil you through philosophy and vain deceit, after the traditions [teachings] of men," and not after the teachings of Christ;[1] and as he declines to cite me the passage of Scripture establishing the court of conscience in the Lord's kingdom, I decline to have anything to do with his philosophy, in a religious inquiry after the truth.

He still insists that legalizing slavery and adultery makes them sinful, and that the "legalized claim of one human being to another is sin." Does the legalizing of either of these, by human governments, make it a sin, when, if it were not legalized, it would not be a sin? Slavery is not legalized in Indiana, but it is in Kentucky. Are we to understand him, that to hold a slave in Kentucky, by the laws thereof, is sin; but not so if a slave is held in Indiana, for it is not legalized here? If this is not what he means, why does he talk so much about legalized slavery? It is apparent that he wants to discuss, *not slavery*, but *the laws* of the slave States. That is, he wants to enter into a *christian* (?) discussion of the *things* of the kingdoms of this world—a thing that neither the Lord nor the apostles did, and a thing that they forbid christians to do! He says, as adultery is legalized and protected in Utah, there it would be most pertinent and most appropriate to discuss the moral character of Utah adultery. *Query:* Did legalizing it make it either more or less sinful? and is Utah adultery more or less sinful than Indiana adultery? Will he answer? *Query 2:* As slavery is not legalized in Indiana, is it "most pertinent and appropriate to discuss the moral character of" Kentucky slavery here? and if we do, do we not become busy-bodies in other men's matters?

Brother O. B. says I have submitted no proposition, nor suggested any one in a tangible form. The reader, by

---

(1) Col. ii, 8.

looking back, can see what weight this is entitled to. I have stated repeatedly the proposition, and in a postscript to my article in the *Record* of May 27th,[1] I stated that, if O. B. or A. R. B., or any of that school of opinion, would take the affirmative of it, I would discuss it. To stop all cavil, I will state it in form. Slavery is sinful. Slavery is sin. Is slavery sinful? Is slavery sin. It is stated here four ways. I take the negative of each of them. Will O. B. affirm any of them? If he will, let him say so. If he will not, let him quit denouncing it as a sin. And let him quit denouncing it in words, when, what he supposes to be its effects, and, the laws of the slave States, is what he means by the denunciation. Let him not say one thing and mean another. Political questions (and questions in relation to the laws of the slave States, are political questions) should not be discussed in the christian congregation, nor in a christian paper. The political forum is the place to discuss them. And it is, in that forum, "most pertinent and appropriate" for us of Indiana to discuss Indiana laws, and leave the citizens of Kentucky and other slave States to discuss the laws of their States respectively.

J. S.

June 23d, 1862.

REMARKS ON BRO. J. S.'S ARTICLE.

In another colum will be seen an article from Bro. J. S. most of which is intended to be a reply to my response to his former article. I will not enter into any lengthy reply to this response, as the subject referred to is in the hands of Bro. O. B., who will reply in his own way.

What unexpected turns matters will sometimes take! When Bro. A. R. B.'s article on "The Fanaticism of Error" was published in the *Record*, neither he nor I had any idea that it was going to lead to a discussion of the question of American slavery. Nor did I suppose that my friendly hint to Bro. O. B. and J. S., in reference to the manner in which the discussion should be conducted, was going to involve me in the discussion.

I can not see the propriety of illustrating American

---

(1) Ante, p. 66.

slavery by the obedience of Christ to his heavenly Father, nor by the subjection of Paul, Peter, and other christians, to the will of Christ. The claims of Christ upon the service of his people, and the claims of masters upon their slaves rest on very different principles, which Bro. J. S. will see by consulting an editorial in the weekly *Record* for June the 17th, on "The Claims of Christ." The claims of Christ rest upon the following considerations:
1. "All things were made by him and for him."
2. He "upholdeth all things by the word of his power."
3. He died for all, that they who live should not live unto themselves, but unto him who died for them and rose again.

Now, if the slaveholder can establish his claims to his slave on such a basis as this—if he made them and upholds them by the word of his power, and if he has redeemed them by his own blood, then I have no more to say against the institution of American slavery; if he can not, then Bro. J. S.'s comparison has no bearing on the subject, but, in my humble opinion, approaches very near to the profane. But I forbear.

[From the Christian Record of July 15th, 1862.]

REPLY TO J. S.

If an apology were necessary for my not having sooner noticed the article of J. S., published in the *Record* of the 1st inst., I could find one in the fact that my time has been too much occupied to attend to this matter. It may, however, be thought more necessary for me to apologize for noticing the article at all, than for not having done so sooner. I feel that a discussion without a proposition, and apparently without a purpose, desultory and rambling as ours is, can hardly be regarded as profitable by the readers of the *Record*. And yet, I am disposed to believe, that the articles of J. S. are better calculated, than anything I can say, to defeat the cause which he is attempting to sustain, and I am therefore content to lead him on still further in the discussion.

J. S. has undertaken the defense of slavery, and the pressing necessities of the argument have driven him to the irreverent, and, to my apprehension, the blasphemous assertion that the Lord Jesus was himself a slave. J. S. is a bold man, and does not hesitate to accept and avow the ultimate of his own vicious reasonings.

He has given us an entirely new and strange definition of the term slavery—a definition at war with the common use and common understanding of the meaning of the term, and not to be found either in the lexicons, or in the laws and judicial decisions upon the subject of slavery. As defined by J. S., "obedience is slavery," and to prove the correctness of this definition, he cites sundry passages from Holy Writ, into which he takes the fearful responsibility of interpolating very freely and frequently his favorite word. Without such interpolations, the passages will not answer his purpose, or show that they have any connection with the subject. If we allow his interpolations, and admit the correctness of his definition—if obedience is slavery—the the passages he has cited proves that obedience is sometimes sinful, and sometimes righteous; that its moral character depends upon the question whether it be rendered to God or to Satan—to the Lord or to the Adversary. And in so far as it is proved sinful, the proposition that slavery is sinful, is proved by J. S. himself.

But this is far from the question at issue between J. S. and myself. We are not discussing, or at least I am not disposed to discuss the question of the moral character of obedience or service in the abstract, and I shall have no controversy with J. S. upon the question in that shape.

The words slave and slavery are of very common use, especially in American society, and they have admitted and well established meanings in common parlance. They are defined in the lexicons, and also in the laws and judicial decisions of the slave States. J. S. has denounced, in the bitterest terms, those whom he calls abolitionists and agitators of the subject of slavery, and he knows full well, that there never has been any agitation of the subject of slavery in the sense in which he now professes to use the term. The whole controversy has been, and is, in reference to slavery, as that word is used and understood in popular language, and as it exists in American society, under the sanction and protection of the laws of the slave States. The effort to remove the question entirely from the admitted field of controversy, by giving a forced and hitherto unheard of definition to a word having so clear and definite a meaning, is, as it seems to me, a backing out of the controversy which he has himself challenged and provoked. If he will not defend American slavery, it would be much for his credit to say frankly and honestly, that he regards it as indefensible, and not resort to the subterfuge and evasion of new and unrecognized definitions to cover his withdrawal from the field. But if he wishes to defend slavery, as that word is used and understood in popular language, and as it exists in American society, under the sanction and protection of the laws of the slave States, I would give him the opportunity to do so. If, however, it is something else, which he may term slavery, which he purposes to defend, and especially if that something else is construed to embrace the willing service, and obedience of man to his Maker, and of the christian to his Lord, I can certainly have no controversy with him upon that subject.

Defining slavery as above, I affirm the proposition that "Slavery is sinful." This is the form suggested by J. S., and of course he will not object to it. What I may have to say upon the proposition will be directed to the consideration of the moral character of American slavery, referring, if at all, to servitude of other character, simply for the purpose of argument or illustration. J. S., of course, will choose his own manner of argument, and may occupy a field as extensive or as limited as he pleases. I shall not feel bound to follow him any farther than I may think it necessary to do so to establish the proposition, so far as it relates to American slavery. The proposition that "slavery is sinful," embraces the proposition that "slavery, as it exists in American society, under and by virtue of the laws of the slaveholding States, is sinful," and if I choose to make my own remarks, specially applicable to the latter form of the proposition, J. S. can not complain, as I am willing to allow him the full latitude of the other form.

It is not true that I have insisted, " that legalizing slavery and adultery makes them sinful." J. S. must have been aware of his perversion of my language, when he made that statement. The idea which I intended to present, and which, I think, is clearly apparent to every honest and intelligent reader, is, that the legalizing of either slavery or adultety does not change its moral character, or purge it of its native sinfulness. Although legalized and protected by the laws and usages of civil communities, slavery and adultery are yet sins against God and against humanity. This is certainly comprehensible to every one to whom the Great Father has furnished an ordinary share of brains, and I do not suspect J. S. of deficiency in this particular.

There are other matters in the article of J. S. which it may be proper to notice in their proper place. They will probably again be presented should this discussion proceed, and may then require some attention. I therefore pass them now.

To escape this perpetual moving in a circle, or, perhaps, I should rather say, this rambling and purposeless discussion with J. S., I will introduce here one argument to prove the proposition, that "slavery is sinful." If J. S. chooses to reply, I hope that he will attempt the refutation of this argument.

"For if our heart condemn us, God is greater than our heart and knoweth all things." 1 Jonn iii, 20.

Above and before all logical reasonings, the intuitions of man's moral nature assert the sinfulness of slavery. To these, to the enlightened christian conscience, to the moral convictions of the human heart in communion with God our heavenly Father, and in fellowship, and sympathy with Jesus the Lord, I appeal, as my first and best evidence upon this issue. Whatever else I may say, however elaborate may be the further argument, upon this intuitive perception of the right, and conviction of the wrong, in the heart, enlightened by God's word, and humanized by his love, I rely most confidently to sustain the proposition.

Let me briefly state this argument. The love of liberty, the desire for personal freedom, is the strongest feeling in the human breast. It is the universal, all pervading sentiment of humanity. Probably no individual of the human family can be found who does not desire liberty above all other earthly good. Each one feels that he has a right to himself—to the control of his own actions, and to the enjoyment of the fruits of his own labor, against the claim of any and all other human beings. The fiercest soldiers of the most unprincipled despotism are led to the battle-field by the war-cry of liberty, and in the fond delusion that they are fighting for this right to personal freedom. So highly is this boon prized by all men, that the very words, which are used to express it in human language, are chosen by inspiration to represent the highest joys of the christian state, on earth and in heaven. Hence the following and innumerable other similar expressions in the word of God: "The glorious *liberty* of the children of God;" "The truth shall make you *free;*" "If the son shall make you *free*, you shall be *free indeed;*" "But Jerusalem which is above is *free;*" "Stand fast, therefore, in the *liberty* wherewith Christ has made us *free.*" It is possible that those terms are here used in a more literal sense than many are willing to admit, but if we regard them as figuratively used, for the purpose of presenting to the mind the fullest and most correct ideas of the joys of the christian state here and hereafter, which can be communicated in human language, such use of them proves that liberty—personal freedom—is regarded as the greatest and highest blessing among men. I may venture to affirm, that of all the human family, there probably can not be found one individual, whatever may be his condition and circumstances in life, who is willing to be enslaved—to be made the property and subject to the absolute control of any other human being. We all desire that others should yield to us the right, and leave us in the enjoyment of personal freedom.

The Master has commanded that "all things whatsoever you would that men should do to you, do you even so to them." Hence, desiring liberty ourselves, and wishing above all else, that our personal freedom may not be taken away from us, we are forbidden, by this express command of the Lord Jesus, to enslave, or attempt to enslave others. In the light of this divine command, no man may, without sin, become a master, or owner of another, who would not himself be willing to become the slave and property of his fellow man. This argument appeals to the conscience of every christian, and clearly and conclusively fixes the guilt of sin upon American slavery. Hence, I say, that the intuitions of man's moral nature, in the light of the divine law, and under the promptings of an enlightened christian conscience, assert with deep earnestness the truth of the proposition, that "slavery is sin."

O. B.

[From the Christian Record of July 29th, 1862.]

DISCUSSION OF SLAVERY.

Brother O. B. has at last agreed to affirm that *Slavery is sinful*, and to undertake to prove it.

As I have agreed to discuss it with him on equal terms, if he would take the affirmative of it, it may now be understood as settled, that there is to be a discussion of that proposition.

It is true that he puts a "defining slavery" with his agreeing to affirm the proposition; but does not make that defining a part of the proposition; hence, I am not to be understood as accepting his "defining slavery" as the proper definition of it. Should he insist upon his definition, in the discussion, and so place himself on the record therein, I will then attend to it.

In order to arrange the equal terms upon which the discussion is to proceed, I propose for his consideration the following:

DISCUSSION OF SLAVERY.

Proposition—Slavery is sinful.
O. B. affirms; J. S. denies.

RULES OF THE DISCUSSION.

1. Each party is to have equal space, say two columns, of the *Christian Record*, to each number; any excess or deficiency of space in one or more numbers shall be allowed for in subsequent ones, so as to make the whole space occupied by the parties equal.

2. Each party shall have ten numbers, O. B. opening and J. S. replying, and so on, until the numbers shall be completed on each side.

3. When the discussion shall be completed, it shall be published in book form, inserting these preceding articles as an introduction, at the joint expense of the parties, each having an equal voice in the publication, if the parties shall then be willing to so publish it; but if either shall decline to so publish it, the other shall have the right to do so at his own expense.

These terms being equal and fair, I suppose he will accept them. If so, he may proceed at once to open the discussion with number one of his articles. If he wants any modification of the rules, let him state it for my consideration. I will agree to any terms that are equal and fair.

Having disposed of this preliminary business matter, I will now notice what he says in his last article.

He says: "J. S. has undertaken the defence of slavery," &c. O. B. affirms that slavery is sinful; I deny it. Instead of saying that I deny that slavery is sinful, he says that I have undertaken the defence of slavery! Let us look at this manner of speaking, using it in relation to another subject about which our reasons and intellects are not beclouded. O. B. says Napoleon was a base hypocrite. I deny it. Then O. B. says: "J. S. has undertaken the defence of Napoleon! his Russian campaign, his overturning the free government of France and all," when I had only denied his charge that Napoleon was a hypocrite.

In searching after truth, we should speak of things truly.

He says: "J. S. has denounced, in the bitterest terms, those whom he calls abolitionists and agitators of the subject of slavery." I do not use bitter terms. The reader will please look back and see whether he can find them.

O. B. introduces "one argument to prove the proposition that slavery is sinful," and it is this: "The intuitions of man's moral nature assert the sinfulness of slavery;" and he says that this is his "first and best evidence upon this issue."

Well, this is his first, and, with him, I think it is his best; and it is no argument nor evidence at all. For the intuitions of man's moral nature are not tests of sin and righteousness—tests of truth. It is the spirit of truth that guides us into truth;[1] and it is not our intuitions, nor any-

---

(1) John xvi, 13.

thing that pertains to us, that we are to take or follow as a guide to the truth. And this spirit of truth guides us to the truth, by taking the things of the Lord and showing them to us,[1] in and by the word of inspiration, which is the word of God; and his word is truth.[2] Hence, what the spirit of truth shows to us of the things of the Lord, is properly called by inspiration "the knowledge of the Lord," and is the only source of knowledge that we have. All else is "imagination," in which men become "vain," and get their "foolish hearts" "darkenened." "Professing themselves to be wise they become fools."[3] They walk "in the vanity of their mind," as Gentiles walk, and not as christians walk, "having their *understanding* darkened, being alienated from *the life of God* through the ignorance that is in them."[4] But christians do not "war after the flesh;" that is, in this Gentile and human manner of warring for the truth; they war "casting down *imaginations* (reasonings, *marginal reading*,) and everything that exalteth itself *against the knowledge of God*, [the knowledge God has revealed to us,] and bringing into captivity *every thought* to the obedience of Christ," to the word of God— the truth of God.[5]

In briefly stating that first and best argument, he says: "The love of liberty, the desire of personal freedom, is the strongest feeling in the human breast." This is contradicted by the whole history of the human race, as well as by inspiration, both of which prove that lust—the love of pleasure and enjoyment—is the strongest feeling in the human breast.

He quotes as a text for this first best argument, 1 John iii, 20: "For if our heart condemn us, God is greater than our heart, and knoweth all things." This is a divinely inspired assurance to us, that, if we are conscious ourselves, that we have disobeyed, or are disobeying God, by doing what he has forbidden us to do, or by failing to do what he has commanded us to do, that God is greater than our hearts, our own perception and consciousness of the fact, and knows all things, and hence, knows that we have disobeyed, or are disobeying. This being what that passage says, brother O. B., by quoting it to prove slavery sinful, says:

---

(1) John xvi, 15. (3) Rom. i, 21, 22. (5) 2 Cor. x, 3–5.
(2) John xvii, 17. (4) Eph. iv, 17, 18.

"Because, when we are conscious ourselves of disobedience, we may be assured that God knows it; *therefore*, slavery is sinful!" What logic! If his sense of the passage be the true sense, the next verse must be taken in the same sense. It reads: "Beloved, if our heart condemn us not, then have we confidence toward God." And as the slaveholders' hearts condemn them not for holding slaves, they properly have confidence toward God, and it is all right with them. And as all idolaters' and anti-christians' hearts condemn them not, they may have confidence toward God that all is right. But the truth of God is, that sin and righteousness, right and wrong, are not thus tested, measured and ascertained. The word of the Lord is the test and measure. "The word that I have spoken, the same shall judge him in the last day,"[1] and not his heart, nor his conscience, nor his intuition, nor his anything else, shall judge him, either O. B., myself, or the slaveholder. Sin and righteousness are not only thus tested and measured by the word of the Lord, and we judged by it at the last day, but in this life, if we live according to the will of God, we live, not by our intuitions, our hearts, our consciences, our moral feelings, nor our sensibilities, "but by every word that proceeds out of the mouth of God."[2]

Brother O. B. hoped I would attempt a refutation of this his first best argument. The reader will see that I have attempted it, and will determine for himself whether I have succeeded in the attempt.

He quotes the "golden rule." This does not prove slavery sinful; but it is so much relied upon by those who agree with Bro. O. B., I will defer its consideration until it takes its regular place in the discussion, only saying now, for his and their benefit and consideration, that the phrase, "in like circumstances," which was interpolated into it in the catechisms and school-books I used to see when a boy, has to be interpolated into it to give it the sense, bearing and application he and they give it.

J. S.

July 21*st*, 1862.

---

(1) John xii, 48.   (2) Matt. iv, 4; Deut. viii, 3.

[Editorial in the Christian Record of July 29th, 1862.]

THE DISCUSSION.

Our readers will learn from the article of Bro. J. S. in this issue, that the discussion of the moral character of slavery is about to proceed. With this some are very much delighted, while others are fearful it will result in evil. To all such we would say, be not uneasy; these brethren are among our old, well tried and experienced brethren; they have passed the age of fiery youth; they both belong to the legal profession, and of course know how to conduct a discussion. This may not be the most favorable time for such a discussion, still, I am inclined to the opinion, that, if properly conducted, it will result in good. We have just received a private communication from Bro. J. S. from which we take the following:

"BRO. GOODWIN:—May we all be able to come to the knowledge of the truth; I know I want nothing else; and if I am in error, I hope to be shown it, and for which I will be thankful. Being of the opinion that the error is on the other side, and that much mischief has been done, and is being done, by that error, is the reason why I feel it my imperative duty to cast in my humble mite to enable us all to come to the knowledge of the truth. I honestly believe we all want to find the truth, and pursue it. I know it to be the duty of all to do that; and as some of us are wrong, it is the duty of all of us to try to find where that wrong is, that those of us who are in error may amend our ways."

This breathes the right spirit, and expresses a good reason for the discussion. While brethren discuss points of difference for the sake of learning the truth, and not merely for the sake of the mastery in argument, good will result from the effort. That this may be the result of this investigation, is my prayer.

There is one rule proposed by Bro. J. S. to which, as the proprietor of the paper, I have a right to object, namely, that when one of the parties fail to fill two columns with an article, he shall make up the deficit in a subsequent number. This might lead to an occasional article of too great length. The other rules proposed by Br. J. S. may be disposed of as the parties may agree.

DISCUSSION OF SLAVERY.

PROPOSITION—*Slavery is Sinful.*

O. B. AFFIRMS; J. S. DENIES.

[From the Christian Record of August 5th, 1862.]

O. B.'s FIRST AFFIRMATIVE.

The editor of the *Record*, in noticing the proposed discussion between J. S. and myself, (which he seems to regard as a fixed fact,) says of J. S. and myself: "These brethren are among our old, well-tried and experienced brethren. They have passed the age of fiery youth; they both belong to the legal profession." The readers of the *Record* will, of course, accept this statement of the editor as an assurance that the discussion, if it proceeds, will be conducted in the true christian spirit, and upon fair and honorable principles. But to J. S. and myself it is an admonition, and an intimation of what will be expected of us. I so accept it. J. S., in a private note to the editor, professes a desire to come to a knowledge of the truth, and if in error, hopes to be shown that error, &c. I am not sure that a public discussion, either for or against any given proposition, is the right way to conviction of error on the part of either disputant, and I have never been vain enough to suppose even for a moment, that my powers of argument were sufficient to convince J. S. of the sinfulness of slavery after he should have committed himself publicly to disprove the proposition. The days of miraculous conversions are supposed to be past. For J. S. then, I have no hope of t conversion. Others, who are not so committed, may be reasoned with to more advantage. I partake largely in the doubt expressed by the editor, that "this may not be the most favorable time for such a discussion." The argument has been assumed by a Logician, stronger and more in earnest than any human reasoner. His arguments are facts, fearful, terrible facts—deducing conclusions, and forcing convictions upon reluctant masses of men, which were hopeless of attainment by human reason. Awed and abashed by the developments of this stern logic, the friend of the oppressed is disposed to "stand still and see the salvation of God," and, in the presence of the "burning bush" of the Great Deliverer of Horeb, to feel rather than hear the admonition, "Draw not nigh hither, put off thy shoes from off thy feet, for the place whereon thou standest is holy ground." But it may be, that, notwithstanding past derilictions, the professedly christian church is not yet wholly rejected as an agency in the accomplishment of God's purposes—there may still be work for it in the moral field of his controversy. The Great Deliverer may yet accept the tardily proffered services of his people in the consummation of his purpose for the deliverance of the oppressed. The hope and trust that this is so—the anxiety, not for the abolition of slavery, for that I regard as God's work, and sure of being accomplished, either with or without the aid and co-operation of either church or State; but that the church and people of God may be his willing agents in this work, I am induced to make an effort to prosecute this discussion so far as my time will permit, and as I may think it profitable to do so.

But to the article of J. S. He says that I have "at last agreed to affirm that slavery is sinful, and to undertake to prove it." He may take to himself his own admonition, 'In searching after truth, we should speak of things truthfully." If I understand myself, I have from the *first* affirmed that "slavery is sinful," and my venturing to suggest that it was "a collossal crime," stirred him up to challenge this debate. But first and last I have declined to discuss any other form of slavery than that which is legalized in American society. With the distinct avowal that I should so limit myself, I have consented to the form of the proposition suggested by J. S. As I have the affirmative of the question, it will be both my privilege and my duty to lead in the discussion. It would be a work of supererogation for J. S. to defend where I make no attack, and it may, perhaps, be as much as he can accomplish to meet and refute successfully the arguments against American slavery. Should he make an effort to lead me farther, he will pardon me if I should not choose to follow. While American slavery is bringing upon us the rage, and the tempest of fiercest war, wrapping our towns and cities in flames, drenching our land in blood, and covering our fields with our slaughtered friends and relatives, I have no heart to turn aside from this one great question to discuss with J. S. the moral character of West India Cooleyism, Mexican peonage, Russian serfdom, former English villianage, ancient Jewish servitude, or even Roman slavery. So far as any or all of these may be legitimately drawn into the discussion of American slavery, I may give them the attention which I may deem necessary, but beyond that, I leave to J. S. the undisputed possession of those fields.

J. S. does not like to be regarded as having undertaken to defend slavery. His restiveness under the imputation is a favorable indication. I hope that restiveness may increase, until he shall be induced to make a much stronger disclaimer. The hypothetical case he puts does not, as I perceive, help him out of the difficulty.

With the foregoing explanation of my own position and purpose, I am willing that the proposition should stand as stated by J. S. As to the rules of discussion which he proposes, they seem to me to contemplate a discussion more formal than I anticipated. I from the first declined a formal discussion, for the reasons that my health was too poor, and my time too much occupied, to enable me to promise so much. These reasons, especially the last one, exist now in still greater force than formerly. I am willing, however, to make an effort to sustain the proposition by some arguments to be presented from time to time, as may be convenient for me, to which J. S. can reply as he thinks best. So far as it depends upon me, I am willing that it be understood, that each of us have the privilege of using an equal space in the *Record* for the presentation of our arguments, and in the order named by J. S., and that the limit or extent of the privilege be determined by the editor of the

Record, either in advance or otherwise, as he may think best. I would further stipulate for J. S. that in the absence of argument to fill up his portion of the space, he have the privilege of selecting at random, and incorporating in his argument, without reference to their pertinency or applicability to the question at issue, such portions of Holy Writ as he may desire thus to reproduce; for the Scripture "is profitable for doctrine, for reproof, for correction, for instruction in righteousness." The want of argument can not probably be better supplied; for however inapplicable to the subject, the quotations will be profitable, for some purpose, to the devout reader.

I had not contemplated writing a book. My impression is, that it would be an unprofitable investment, either pecuniarily or otherwise. I suppose, however, that either party would have the right to publish the discussion at his own expense, as no copy-right is contemplated by either. As J. S. has intimated his desire for such publication, I wish it understood, that neither party will make the publication without the co-operation of the other, unless the other first decline to co-operate on equal terms.

Having disposed of these preliminary matters, I come now to the proposition itself. I affirm that "slavery is sinful." I have not room in this article to introduce any new argument, but will re-state my former one, and notice the reply of J. S. to it.

It is unfortunate either for me, or for J. S., that he does not seem to understand that argument. It shows a want of capacity, either in me to state an argument clearly, or in him to comprehend it when so stated. Let me try again, and perhaps I may be better understood. The argument is capable of being presented in the form of a syllogism, and I will endeavor, by reversing the order in which it was stated, to so present it now.

The first and major proposition in the syllogism may be stated as follows:

The Lord Jesus commanded that "all things whatsoever ye would that men should do to you, do ye even so to them."

The second and minor proposition may be stated thus:

The love of liberty is an intuition—an instinct of humanity. Above and before all logical reasonings, each one desires for himself personal freedom, and rejects and repels, as most abhorrent to his nature, the idea of being made a slave, and held in bondage, subject to be used, controlled, and disposed of, as property, by any other human being.

These two propositions are the premises of the argument.

The conclusion to be deduced from these premises is: That to deprive a human being of liberty, to reduce him to slavery, and hold him as property, subject to be used, controlled, and disposed of, as other property, is a transgression of the law of the Lord, embraced in the first proposition, and consequently sin. This conclusion is the inevitable sequence of the premises; and if there be no error, no defect in either of the propositions, the argument proves beyond doubt or controversy, that "slavery is sinful."

Is there error or defect in either proposition? The first is the command of the Divine Master, and in the very words of the Holy Writ. It is addressed to man, under all circumstances, and in every condition in life, and covers the whole field of man's relation to man. It "is a discerner of the thoughts and intents of the heart," and appeals to man's intuitions, prompted by his self love, and claiming sympathy, consideration, assistance and justice from others, deducing from these intuitions, these promptings of a man's selfish desires, an infallible and unerring rule of conduct for him, in his actions towards others.

J. S. will hardly venture to deny this proposition, whatever else he may say of it, to avoid its force in this argument. He does not, however, seem to know that it is a part of the argument as heretofore stated by me. I regard it as the basis of the argument, yet he passes it by with scarcely a notice, except to say that he "will defer its consideration until it takes its regular place in the discussion." As I have the affirmative, the onus of the proof of the proposition lies upon me, and it is both my privilege and my duty to lead in the discussion. J. S. has the negative, and it is therefore incumbent on him to dispose of my arguments as I introduce them. When he shall have accomplished that successfully, his work will be done. I have introduced this divine command as the major proposition, in what I have termed my "first and best evidence" in support of the main proposition. I so term it, for the reason that it covers the whole field, and pervades, with the light of a divine command, the whole subject of controversy. I expect that J. S. will give it proper attention.

The second or minor proposition of the syllogism, as above stated, needs little to support it more than I have already said of it in my former articles, to which I refer the reader. The intuitions of man's nature, the very instincts of our being, are the proof which I adduce to sustain it. My proof is in the heart and consciousness of each reader. To the reader I appeal: "Would you willingly surrender your liberty—your personal freedom? Do you desire to be made a slave, and held in bondage, subject to be used, controlled, and disposed of, as property, by any other human being?" For a reply you would not pause to reason, and to canvass the advantages and disadvantages of such a position, but above and before all reasoning, and precluding all deliberation, out of the intuitions of your own hearts would come the prompt and indignant answer: "No! Death rather than slavery." Were I to put the same question to J. S., I doubt not he would give them the same prompt and indignant reply. He could not so far forget his own manhood, and belie the instincts and intuitions of his own nature, as to hesitate or pause even to reason upon such a subject. This proposition of the syllogism I regard then as established beyond controversy, and have no fears that J. S will be able to refute it.

The premises being established, the conclusion follows as a natural and inevitable sequence. That conclusion is, that to enslave a human being, and hold him as property, subject to be used, controlled and disposed of as other property, is a transgression of the divine law, in refusing to do to others as we would that they should do to us—and is therefore sin.

Hence, I have said, and now repeat, that the intuitions of man's moral nature, in the light of the divine law, and under the promptings of an enlightened conscience, assert, with deep earnestness, the truth of the proposition that "slavery is sinful."

In conclusion, I again quote from Holy Writ, and the quotation may perhaps be regarded as pertinent here: "For if our heart condemn us, God is greater than our heart, and knoweth all things. Beloved, if our hearts condemn us not, then have we confidence towards God."[1]   O. B.

---

(1) 1 John iii, 20, 21.

[From the Christian Record of August 12th, 1862.]
FIRST REPLY OF J. S.

I confess that I am surprised at the course of my brother O. B. Instead of accepting the rules proposed by me for the discussion, or proposing them in a modified form•for my consideration, he has gone on in a rambling way, and settled nothing definitely.

Logical discussion, to elicit truth, should be carried on under explicit rules, equal and fair. And the erratic course of those who denounce slavery as sinful, makes it the more necessary in a discussion with any of them, to have explicit, definite rules of discussion. They are rambling and erratic in their course, "wandering stars,"[1] and should be tied down to pursue a rational course, when a grave examination, by "the word of truth," of their hallucinations, is undertaken. But it seems that this can not be had. They must first be restored to reason—to their "right mind"[2]—before they can be induced to act rationally; and I suppose I ought to have known that this is so.

The first two paragraphs of O. B.'s last article present another strong evidence of "fanaticism of error." The "wild notions" contained in them could as properly have been expressed by the Saracens of the year 650, and by the Crusaders of the year 1098, as by my brother O. B. Whether such "wild notions" will be adhered to now as they were on those occasions, till as much mischief is done as was then done, the Lord only knows. May he yet avert such awful calamities, is my devout prayer.

"American slavery bringing upon us the rage and the tempest of the fiercest war"!! &c., says O. B. in his last. If slavery brought on the war, why did it not bring on war during the first fifty years or this government? as it existed then more in proportion to the whole people, than now. All, however, was peace, till fanaticism sprang up. As well might the Crusaders have said, that the tomb of the Savior brought upon them the rage and tempest of war; and have added, as is now added, that it must be exterminated, to take away the cause of the war, and give us lasting peace!

(1) Jude 13.   (2) Mark v, 15.

It is strange what hallucinations can seize and lead captive the human intellect. Alas! that it is so. But inspiration informs us, that because we receive not the love of the truth, God sends upon us such strong delusions.[1] To cast in my humble mite, to bring us back to the love of the truth, and free us from such delusions that are working such great calamities among us, I shall, with the blessing and permission of God, proceed with this discussion in the rambling, erratic course that my brother O. B. seems disposed to take. If this is not "the most favorable time," it is certainly the time when it is most needful to find the truth and pursue it.

I will say to the editor of the *Record*, that I did not contemplate, in making up for deficiency of space, to have any articles of so great length as to discommode him. The fair construction of the rule I laid down, is, that the articles should all be, as nearly as may be, of two columns length; but not necessarily of that length; and excesses or deficiencies afterwards allowed for in other articles—not in one. Brother O. B.'s last article fills a little over two and a quarter columns.

His argument, as reversed and re-stated, is entirely a different syllogism from that previously stated. I will examine it as last stated.

"Therefore, all things whatsoever ye would that men should do to you, do ye even so to them: for this is the law and the prophets."[2]

1. If this part of the word of the Lord did forbid slavery, and make it sinful, and if holding slaves was a violation of this Golden Rule of the Lord, that includes both the law and the prophets in it, the inspired apostles would certainly have so informed slaveholding masters, when converted to christianity, and would have required them to free their slaves. But they did not do so. They, by divine inspiration, prescribed rules by which the masters and slaves should govern themselves in their respective states and conditions to each other, as master and slave, and did not inform them that that relation was sinful—was a violation of the Golden Rule of the Lord—and that they must dissolve it. Paul substantially quoted this rule in two of his epistles, and yet in one

---

(1) 2 Thes. ii. 10, 11.   (2) Matt. vii, 12.

of these very epistles, he enjoined upon masters and slaves their duty to each other, without saying that the relation they held to each other was a violation of the rule, and hence sinful; but instead of doing that, he ordained, *in all the churches*, that, in whatever state or condition in life each one was called into the christian kingdom, that he should remain in that state or condition, whether bond or free, circumcised or uncircumcised; that if any were called, being a slave, to care not for it; but if he could be made free, to use it rather, that is, prefer it.[1] He sent the slave, Onesimus back to his master, Philemon, with an apostolic letter, in which he *did not* say that holding Onesimus as a slave was a violation of the Golden Rule. How different this teaching and action from that of those who run underground railroads, their aiders and abettors!

Much more apostolic precept and action could be cited to show, that they did not construe the Golden Rule as forbidding slavery; and their construction of that rule is conclusive to all who are willing to take God at his word and live, or square their conduct by it.

2. But the Lord expressly says that this rule is both the law and the prophets. It includes both. What is the law, then? See Ex. xxi, 1–21; Lev. xxv, 39–55; Deut. xv, 12–18; which establish slavery, and prescribe rules and regulations for its government. And the Lord said that the Golden Rule was this law, instead of saying that it counteracted, contradicted, or repealed, or superseded it, as brother O. B. argues. It is better to regard what the Lord says, than what O. B. says. And the prophets, what are they on this subject? See Jer. xxxiv, 8–22, where sore punishments are denounced for disobedience of this law of slavery. Other passages might be quoted to the same effect from the prophets. And this is the Golden Rule as expounded by the Lord.

3. These interpretations of the Golden Rule, by the inspired apostles, and by the Lord himself, settle its meaning and construction authoritatively and conclusively. But there is no harm in us poor, weak, uninspired mortals, looking at it ourselves, and seeing the apositeness and correctness of the divine interpretation of it.

---

(1) 1 Cor. vii, 17–21.

Does a master want others to free him? No: because he is not in bondage. The Golden Rule, then, does not require him to free his slaves, because he does not want them to free him. Hence the necessity, to give the rule O. B.'s meaning, of interpolating into it the phrase, "in like circumstances," so as to make the rule read to the master thus: If I were a slave, I would want my master to free me; therefore, I must free my slaves; because, if I were in their circumstances, I would want to be freed. And, as whatsoever I would that men should do to me, *were I in their circumstances*, I must do so to them—I must free my slaves. But brother O. B., and those who think and act with him, do not stop at freeing his or their own slaves; they set to work, with a will, to free everybody else's slaves. And this comes from a construction of the Golden Rule obtained only by interpolating it! But we must take the word of the Lord as it is, and must neither add to nor take from it.

Does brother O. B. want others to free him? No, he does not. Then the Golden Rule, *as laid down by the Lord*, does not require him to free, nor attempt to free any one. Does brother O. B. want others not to interfere with his domestic arrangements in his family, including his wife and children, and servants, hired and bound? If he does, the Golden Rule *requires* him not to interfere with the domestic affairs of others. Does brother O. B. desire that others should not intermeddle with, nor become busy-bodies in his affairs? If he does, the Golden Rule, as well as another law of the Lord *requires* that he should not be a busy-body in other men's matters. Does brother O. B. want others to live in peace, harmony and concord with him? If he does, the Golden Rule *requires* him to so live with others. Does brother O. B. want others not to denounce, decry, and speak evil of him and his domestic affairs and arrangements, including his servants, hired and bound? If he does, the rule requires that he do not denounce, decry, and speak evil of others and their domestic affairs, including their servants, hired and bond. Does brother O. B. desire that others should not stir up emulation, wrath, strife and sedition around and about him? If so, the Golden Rule *requires* him not to stir up such things round and about others. Does brother O. B. desire others to make war upon him and his neighbors, to break up, destroy and upturn his and their families, and domestic arrangements and order of society? If he does not, the Golden Rule does *not* require him to make war upon others for such purposes; but *enjoins him* not to do it. These and a great many other things, the Golden Rule teaches and enjoins upon Bro. O. B. and me, as well as upon all others; but it does not authorize any of us to be picking at the motes in our brethren's eyes, instead of pulling the huge beams out of our own; nor to get up crusades against them, if they do not square their conduct according to *our notions* of right and wrong. That was the spirit that actuated the Crusaders, Saracens, anti-christians of every grade, and *all tyrants;* and is, itself, at war with the spirit of Christ.

His major proposition, as he has arranged his syllogism in his last, failing to answer the purpose he quotes it for, logic does not require me to examine his argument further. He narrows his minor (major, as he stated before,) down to desire of personal freedom, and the abhorrent "idea of being made a slave;" and he draws his conclusion, wild and rambling, "that to deprive a human being of liberty, to reduce him to slavery, and hold him as property," is a violation of this Golden Rule; and slavery is sinful.

Now, he has protested, all the time, that American slavery is the only slavery that he will discuss; and it does not include *depriving* human beings of liberty, and *reducing* them to slavery; for that was all done while the British government held this country as colonies, and during the first twenty years of the existence of this government, and has been no part of American slavery for fifty-four years. Holding of slaves, as property, in his language, or, truly, holding them to serve and labor, is the only one of his three that is included in American slavery. And I have clearly shown that the Golden Rule does not require the master to change the relation that he and his slaves did not make, but find themselves in. All American slaves were born so, and have not been *deprived* of liberty and *reduced* to slavery by any one; they have only been and are held to serve and labor for their master. Slavery, itself, is obedience or rendering service. So O. B.'s conclusion to his syllogism covers two things not existing in American slavery, nor in slavery itself. Man-stealing is a sin, and always was.[1] Joseph's brethren committed a great sin in stealing him, depriving him of his liberty, and reducing him to slavery; but Potiphar committed no sin in buying him, and holding him a slave. The law (which the Golden Rule is) allowed persons to sell *themselves* into slavery, (see chapter above quoted) to *deprive* themselves of liberty, and to *reduce* themselves to slavery. Why must brother O. B., in undertaking to prove slavery sinful, talk about two other things—depriving men of liberty and reducing them to slavery—instead of confining himself to slavery itself? It comes from that reckless, loose; careless, rambling manner of speaking, that has been so long used by anti-slavery agitators, that it has become a second nature with them, and it seems as impossible to cure them of the fault, as it is to rid a people of provincialisms in dialect.

I sufficiently showed in my last, that 1 John iii, 20, did not relate to slavery at all. But as he has quoted it again, without any attempt to avoid the objections I raised in my last to the use he was trying to make of it, I will quote it, with its context, here, which is sufficient to show the reader the utter absurdity of quoting it to prove slavery sinful. I quote from the New Translation—the reader can look at it in the common version. "We *know* that we have passed away from death to life, because we *love* the brethren. He who *loves* not his brother, abides in death. Every one who hates his brother is a man-slayer; and you *know* that no man-slayer has eternal life abiding in him. By this we *have known* the love of Christ, because he laid down his life for us; therefore, we ought to lay down our lives for the brethren. Whoever, therefore, has goods of this world, and sees his brother in need, and yet shuts up his compassion from him, how abides the *love* of God in him? My little children, let us not *love* in word nor tongue; but in *deed* and in truth. For, *by this we know* that we are of the truth, and *shall assure* our *hearts* before him. But if our heart condemn us, certainly God is greater than our heart, and knows all things. Beloved, if our heart do not condemn us, we have confidence with God. And, whatever we ask, we receive of him, because *we keep his commandments*, and *do the things* which are pleasing in his sight:" and, therefore, are assured

---

(1) Ex. xxi, 16.

in our hearts. Whereas, when we do not keep his commandments, and do the things that please him, our hearts condemn us for the derilection; and God being greater, knows it as well as we.

J. S.

August 6th, 1862.

[From the Christian Record, of August 19th, 1862.]

O. B.'S SECOND AFFIRMATIVE.

"And the Lord commanded the man saying, of every tree of the garden thou mayest freely eat. But of the tree of knowledge of good and evil, thou shalt not eat."[1]

I pass for the present without notice the reply of J. S. to my former argument. I hope, however, that the readers of the *Record* will preserve it for future reference, as I propose hereafter to give it some attention. I desire here to introduce another argument upon the proposition under discussion, and will not have room for more in this article.

American slavery, both in law and in fact, is based upon the assumption of the right of one man to enslave another, and to buy and sell, hold and possess, use, control and enjoy him as property. In the language of the law, and of judicial decisions, a slave is a chattel, and as such is subject, as all other property is, to be used, controlled and disposed of by the master at his own will, and for his own profit or pleasure, irrespective of the will or consent of the slave. This assumed right of property in man is the basis of the whole slave system, the *sine qua non* of slavery, both in American thought and in American law. It is the trunk of the deadly Upas tree, which has sent its roots deep into the southern soil, and has spread its branches wide over the fairest portions of the republic.

Within the assumed boundaries of the Union, about four millions of human beings, claiming with us a common pa-

---

(1) Gen. ii, 16, 17.

ternity, and a common brotherhood, are chattelized—held as property, like cattle, hogs and horses, subject to be used, controlled and disposed of, as may suit the pleasure, caprice or necessities of their masters. The aggregate market value of this species of property has been estimated at some two thousand millions of dollars. The legality of the claim—the validity of the title in heaven's high chancery to all this property—are involved in the proposition under discussion. J. S. appears for the claimants. He could not ask a more important case, or one involving a heavier property interest. My purpose is to prove that the claim is false, defective, and vicious—that it can find no support in the divine law, but on the contrary is a violation of that law.

The love of dominion over external things—the desire to possess, enjoy and control property, is universal in the human breast. It was planted there by the Creator of man, for good and wise purposes, and might almost be regarded as that characteristic which distinguishes man from the brute. When rightly and properly directed and employed, it is perhaps the principal agency in the civilization of man The right to acquire, possess and enjoy property, is by some writers even classed among the inalienable rights.

The laws of *meum et tuem*—of mine and thine—fill much the largest space on the pages of the statute books of States and nations, and engross much the most of the attention of judicial tribunals. These facts show that the civil government claims, and to it is conceded, the proprietorship of, and the dominion over, all those things which are regarded as the subjects of property, and the right and duty of controlling their distribution among the members of the community—of determining to whom shall pertain the exclusive use and enjoyment of the several portions thereof, and of protecting each in such use and enjoyment. So far as property rights are concerned, these are the peculiar, perhaps the only province of civil government.

But this is admissible only in reference to those things which may rightfully be regarded as property, and in and over which human governments may legitimately claim the ownership and proprietorship. The purpose of my present argument is to show that man—that any human being is not rightfully the subject of such a claim of ownership, either on the part of a civil commuunity, or of any member thereof. I present the argument in a series of propositions, which, if true, lead to the conclusion above stated.

1. God the heavenly Father, is the Creator, Preserver, and Proprietor of man, and of all things. His they were and are. His right and title are supreme, and above and before any and all others.

Does this proposition need proof? Listen, then, to the voice of inspiration: "So God created man in his own image; in the image of God created he him; male and female created he them."[1] "Thou, even thou art Lord alone; thou hast made the heaven, the heaven of heavens, with all their host, the earth, and all things that are therein, the seas and all that is therein, and thou preservest them all; and the host of heaven worshippeth thee."[2] "Behold the heaven, and the heaven of heavens is the Lord's thy God, the earth also, and all that therein is."[3] "The earth is the Lord's, and the fullness thereof; the world, and they that dwell therein."[4] "Lord, thou art God, which has made heaven, and earth, and the sea, and all that in them is."[5]

2. Any and all right or title, which any man, or any civil community, can rightfully have or claim to property in either men or things, must be derived from God the Great Proprietor, and held by and under a grant from him.

The christian has no need of proof for this proposition. His own moral intuitions—the spirit of God dwelling in him—teach him that all that he has, and all that he is, are the gift of God; that " every good, and every perfect gift," is from God, who "giveth to all life and breath, and all things."

3. The gifts and grants of God to man are either special or general, and all of them, in which we of the present day can have any interest, or under which we can claim any right, are recorded in the Record of His Will, as revealed to us in the Holy Scriptures.

4. A special grant is a gift or grant to a designated person, or to a specified class or number of persons, or to a particular family or civil community, of rights, privileges, immunities, or property, to the extent and for the purposes specified in the grant. The grantees alone—those who are what the law terms parties or privies to the grant—are en-

---

(1) Gen. i, 27. (3) Deut. x, 14. (5) Acts iv, 24.
(2) Neh. ix, 6. (4) Ps. xxiv, 1.

titled to claim anything under it. All others are strangers to the grant, and can claim no right or property under it, or derive any benefit from its provisions.

I call special attention to this proposition, as I may have further use for it, in the consideration of the subject under discussion. The Scriptures afford many cases of such grants. I notice but one now. God gave to the children of Israel the land of Canaan for a possession upon certain terms and conditions specified in the grant. Among other things, he commanded them to exterminate the Canaanites then dwelling in the land, and he made their obedience to his commands, the condition of their possession. It will not be contended that the American Republic, or any State of the Union, can rightfully claim either the land of Canaan, or any other portion of God's earth, under that grant, or that the command of God to Israel to exterminate the Canaanites is or can be a justification to us to exterminate any people, and take possession of their land. God, the sole owner and proprietor of all things, "doeth according to his will, in the army of heaven, and among the inhabitants of the earth; and none can stay his hand, or say unto him, what doest thou."[1] There is not in the divine record any special grant, under which we can claim property in man, or the right to hold, use, control, and dispose of as property any human being.

5. A general grant is a grant to the family of man, without distinction or discrimination of particular individuals, families, nations, or communities, of rights, privileges, immunities, or property, to the extent and for the purposes specified in the grant. In such grant, aggregated and universal humanity is the grantee, and each member of the human family may claim under it an equal right and title to partake of the benefits conferred by it.

There are upon the divine record two such general grants. It may be well to refer to them, and consider them, and consider them carefully, to ascertain whether they, either in their letter or spirit, confer upon any one or more of the human family, the right to hold others as property. The first of these grants was made soon after the creation, to our first parents, as the head and representative of all their

---

(1) Dan. iv, 35.

posterity. It is in these words: "And God blessed them, and God said unto them, Be fruitful, and multiply, and replenish the earth, and subdue it: and have dominion over the fish of the sea, and over the fowl of the air, and over every living thing that moveth upon the earth. And God said, behold I have given you every herb bearing seed, which is upon the face of all the earth, and every tree, in the which is the fruit of a tree yielding seed; to you it shall be for meat. And to every beast of the earth, and to every fowl of the air, and to everything that creepeth upon the earth, wherein there is life, I have given every green herb for meat."[1]

The other of these general grants was made to Noah and his sons, as they descended from Mount Ararat. They were then the head and representatives of a new race of men. Before and around them lay a new and a purified world awaiting their possession. The grant was a renewal, somewhat changed and enlarged, of God's former grant of dominion, and property to humanity. It is in these words: "And God blessed Noah and his sons, and said unto them, be fruitful, multiply and replenish the earth. And the fear of you, and the dread of you, shall be upon every beast of the earth, and upon every fowl of the air, and upon all that moveth upon the earth, and upon all the fishes of the sea; into your hands are they delivered. Every moving thing that liveth shall be meat for you; even as the green herb have I given you all things. But flesh with the life thereof, which is the blood thereof, shall ye not eat. And surely your blood of your lives will I require; at the hand of every beast will I require it, and at the hand of man; at the hand of every man's brother, will I require the life of man. Whoso sheddeth man's blood, by man shall his blood be shed: for in the image of God made he man."[2]

If there be any other general grant of property to man, it is probably included in what is called the primeval curse, in which God said to Adam, "In the sweat of thy face, shalt thou eat bread." Whatever else is involved in this curse, it may fairly be construed as granting to man the products of his own labor, and to have for that purpose a comprehensiveness of meaning, embracing the whole field of man's legitimate labors.

---

(1) Gen. i, 28–30.   (2) Gen. ix, 1–6.

These several general grants are very extensive in their application. They embrace all—everything that man may rightfully claim as property. It is not my purpose here to show what is granted by them, or to point out the means and manner of the individual possession and enjoyment of the things granted. To do so, even to the most limited extent, would require more space in the *Record* than I can now ask. One thing is not embraced in either of these grants, and it is the one thing which is the subject of the present discussion, not in either of these grants, not in any common or general grant from God to humanity, is the right of property in man conferred upon or vested in man, or in any part or portion of the family of man. On the contrary, the latter portion of the grant to Noah and his sons contains what the law terms the exclusion of such a conclusion upon this subject. The idea of property in man is excluded by the terms of the grant. This is simply a property grant; and what relevancy or pertinency can the concluding sentences have, unless they are significant of such exclusion. Man is set apart, sanctified, shrouded in the image of God, and to him is given the protecting ægis of God's word. "Whoso sheddeth man's blood, by man shall his blood be shed, for in the image of God made he man."

The argument may be briefly re-stated thus: God, the Creator, is the original and absolute owner and proprietor of man, and of all things.

No person or community can rightfully claim any dominion over, or property in, either man or things, except under and in virtue of some gift or grant from God.

No general grant from God to humanity has conferred upon man, or upon any portion of the human family, the right of property in man.

No special grant from God to us, as individuals, as States or as a nation, or in any other way, has conferred upon us the right of property in persons of the African race, or indeed any right of property in man.

The conclusion from these premises has been well and forcibly expressed by one of our distinguished writers. It is, "No one but God can own a man." To assert and exercise the right of property in man, is on the part of any human being or civil community, an usurpation of God's right and prerogative, a sacrilegious invasion and appropriation of that which he has reserved to himself, and upon which he has stamped his own "image and superscription." Such act is disloyalty to God, and treason against heaven. Slavery involves all these; and hence, the mildest form of reprobation which can properly be applied to it, is in the language of the proposition—"slavery is sinful."

O. B.

[From the Christian Record of September 2, 1862.]

SECOND REPLY OF J. S.

Brother O. B. calls his last article a reply to me; and yet it does not reply to anything I have said. It entirely abandons his "first and best argument," and strikes out into a new field.

Sin and righteousness are not ascertained and determined by inference. The papacy was built up and is sustained by inferential determination of what is sinful and what is righteous. So all the discord and jarring that exists among Protestants is brought about and kept up by inferential measures of right and wrong, of sin and righteousness. I have already shown that christians are commanded by the good word of the Lord to beware, least any man spoil them through such philosophy and vain deceit, after the traditions or teachings of men, after the rudiments (elements or principles of reasoning and action,) of the world, and not after the law and teaching of Christ.[1] And that such vain imaginations of the rudiments or elements of the world, darkened the hearts and made fools of those who yielded themselves to their guidance.[2] And that those who thus walk in the vanity of their minds have their understanding darkened, and become alienated from the life of God through the ignorance that is in them, because of the blindness of their heart, in following such philosophy and vain deceit of their own imagination and reasoning powers, instead of fol-

---

(1) Col. ii, 8.   (2) Rom. i, 21, 22.

lowing the plain word and command of the Lord.[1] And hence the ambassador of the Lord, the inspired Paul, cast down such reasonings, and every high thing that exalteth itself against the knowledge communicated of God, and brought into captivity every thought of his mind to the obedience of Christ, in giving to his disciples, and through them to us, the words which the Father gave him, instead of giving them philosophy, imaginations, reasonings according to the elements or rudiments of the world.[2] If he did so, how much more necessary is it for us uninspired people to do so too. And, as christians are commanded to come out of Babylon, and as we of the reformation profess to be coming out of her, we must abandon and eschew her practices of determining right and wrong, sin and righteousness, by inference, philosophy, imaginations or reasonings, or any otherwise, howsoever, than by the word of truth.

"Sin is the transgression of the law."[3] It is not the transgression of an inference, or of a conclusion from a course of reasoning, either long or short. Sin is not determined by a course of argumentation, but by finding the law that it is a transgression of. Hence, brother O. B.'s two and a half columns of reasoning and deduction contained in his last article, if it was all true and logical, would not prove slavery sinful. But it is neither true nor logical; and, although what I have already said, is a sufficient answer to it, yet I will notice some of its parts.

He says there were two general grants from God to man, and quotes those given to Adam, and to Noah and his sons.[4] And he says: "If there be any other general grant of property to man, it is probably included in what is called the primeval curse, in which God said to Adam, 'In the sweat of thy face shalt thou eat bread.'" But there is another general grant included in another curse which he does not notice, and which stands in the same chapter with the grant to Noah and his sons, and by which Ham's posterity was cursed. "Cursed be Canaan; a slave of slaves shall he be unto his brethren. * * Blessed be the Lord God of Shem; and Canaan shall be his slave. God shall enlarge (or persuade) Japhet, and he shall dwell in the tents of Shem; and Canaan shall be his slave."[5]

---

(1) Eph. iv, 17, 18. (3) 1 John iii, 4. (5) Gen. ix, 25-27.
(2) 2 Cor. x, 5; John xvii, 8. (4) Gen. i, 28-30; ix, 1-6.

Servant is the word used in the common version: but slave expresses the true idea.

The curse upon Adam and the curse upon Canaan are both equally the fiat of God; and the history of the human race, from the times of their denunciation respectively to the present, shows that they have existed all the time, and still exist, as much so as that the fiats that the serpent should go upon his belly, that enmity (hostility) should exist between him and the human race, and that the fear of man and the dread of man should be upon the animal creation, have existed all the time, and still exist. Was not this a curse upon the posterity of Ham, through Canaan, and a grant to the posterity of Shem and Japheth? It was more so than the curse upon Adam was a grant to each of his posterity of the fruits of his labor.

But in addition to the general grants to Shem and Japheth of the posterity of Ham, God gave to Israel the heathen round about them for slaves of inheritance,[1] with power to take the life of the slave, *because he was his money.*[2] So brother O. B.'s assumption that there is no grant by God of property in man, is contradicted by the divine record. But he may say that this grant was to Israel. Well, so it was. But inspiration (not our reasoning) informs us who Israel is. They are not all Israel which are of Israel; neither because they are of the seed of Abraham; but the children of promise are counted for the seed;[3] and christians are the children of promise.[4] Hence, christians now constitute the true Israel of God, and have ever since the christian kingdom was set up. Has this grant to the true Israel of God, when it was planted in Canaan by Joshua, ever been revoked or resumed by the Lord, and taken from his true Israel? If it has, I hope brother O. B. will do me the favor to cite me to the passage of the divine volume wherein the grant is revoked, and the thing granted resumed by the Lord. The christian law, as laid down in the apostolic writings, changes the *duties* respectively of the master and slave to each other, from those laid down in the laws of Moses; but does not change the *relation*, nor *revoke* the grant given to Israel through Moses. Brother O. B. being a christian is one of the grantees of this grant.

---

(1) Lev. xxv, 44, 46.   (2) Ex. xxi, 21.   (3) Rom. ix, 6–8.
(4) Gal. iv, 28. See also Rom. ii, 28, 29; John viii, 39; Matt. viii, 11, 12.

The Lord dwelt among the children of Israel in Canaan.[1] He was both their Lord and their God. He was their master, and they were his slaves,[2] because he redeemed them from bondage in Egypt.[3] He sold them six different times into slavery, to the petty kings and nations round about them, for their sins against, and disobedience of, him, and redeemed them back to himself upon their repentance and reformation. Some of the servitudes he sold them into were very grievous—as bad as, if not worse than, being sold South is, or ever was, which is the punishment that has been inflicted by American slaveholders, for the sins and disobedience for their slaves. These six servitudes amounted in all to one hundred and eleven years before Samuel judged Israel. So the Lord himself not only granted the heathen to his people Israel, but he sold Israel itself six different times to the heathen, before Samuel's day, and redeemed or bought them back again. Yet what christian will reproachfully say that he "trafficked in human flesh"?

So there is a divine grant of property in man to all the posterity of Shem and Japheth, in the curse of Canaan; and a grant to all Israel, in the law given by Moses, *both of which are unrevoked.*

But O. B. says that there is no grant from God to us as individuals, as States, as nations, of property in man; and that "to assert and exercise the right of property in man, is, on the part of any human being, or civil community, an usurpation of God's right and prerogative, a sacrilegous invasion and appropriation of that which he has reserved to himself," &c.

Does he not know that our government (a civil community) is now asserting and exercising the right of property in all of us free American citizens between the ages of 18 and 45 years, and drafting us into her service and labor; and not only that, but claiming our lives, if need be? Does he not know that there are now, and have been ever since he was born and before, States of this Union that assert and exercise the right of property in the services and labor of persons of African descent? Does he not know that these powers exist, and have existed all his life? Certainly he does. Well, inspiration says, and christian inspiration

---

(1) Num. xxxv, 34.   (2) Lev. xxv, 55.   (3) Deut. xv, 15.

at that, that there is no power but of God; that the powers that be, or exist, including both our National and State governments, are ordained of God; that whoever resists the power, resists *the ordinance of God;* and that they that resist, shall receive to themselves damnation.[1] And the law of the Lord enjoins upon christians to submit themselves *to every ordinance of man* for the Lord's sake.[2] These things being so, will brother O. B. insist that our government has no right of property in its citizens, and is usurping God's right, and guilty of a sacrilegous invasion of his reserved rights, and hence resist the draft? or will he, as a good christian should, submit himself to that ordinance of man for the Lord's sake. And the same interrogatories can properly be asked him in reference to the claim and exercise of the right to the service and labor of the negroes that is claimed and exercised by the slave States. The National and State governments are ordinances of God. The calling out the draft, and the establishment and keeping up the institution of slavery, are ordinances of man. There is this difference, however, in brother O. B.'s case: he, if of the proper age, is operated upon, and affected by the draft; but as he and I live in a free State, and are not slaves, we are not affected personally, and have nothing whatever to do with the slave question of the slave States. Though the governments of those States are powers that be, yet they do not affect us. But if they did, (as O. B. and those who think and act with him, have got it into their heads that they do) then, as good christians, they should submit *themselves (?)—no, their notions*—to these ordinances of man, of States and communities where they do not live, FOR THE LORD'S SAKE, and not disturb every body and the peace of society, by their constant clamor about them.

Governments exercise power over the property, services and lives of their subjects. They are ordained of God, (as a necessary evil, if I may use that expression in speaking of the ordinances of God) and obedience to them is enjoined upon christians. And there is no distinction made in the good word of the Lord between those governments that establish and sustain the institution of slavery, and those that do not. The power of both is put down as the

---

(1) Rom. xiii, 1, 2.   (2) 1 Pet. ii, 13.

ordinance of God. If slavery is sinful, government itself is sinful; and so O. B.'s sees it. For he denies to civil society, to-wit: government, property in man, equally as much as he denies it as to individuals.

Hence, O. B.'s last long argument is untrue, and hence illogical.

He is very anxious to put me into the affirmative, by making a supposititious case that does not exist, and saying that I "appear for the claimants." The reader will remember, however, that I deny what he affirms of slavery, and do not appear for any one.

J. S.

August 25th, 1862.

[From the Christian Record of September 9th, 1862.]

O. B.'S THIRD AFFIRMATIVE.

"And the serpent said unto the woman, ye shall not surely die, for God doth know that in the day ye eat thereof, then your eyes shall be opened, and ye shall be as God, knowing good and evil."[1]

In my last, published in the *Record* of August 19th, which the editor inappropriately headed, "Second Reply to J. S.," I made no response to the reply of J. S. to my first argument. I stated that I had not room in that article to do so, but desired thereafter to notice it. Subsequently J. S. has replied to my second argument. Both of these replies are unanswered by me, and a proper response will require more than I can crowd into this article. I will first attend to the first of them, and will endeavor to limit myself strictly to those matters which are in reply to my argument. Other matters are introduced incidentally, and for effect into each of the replies, some of which I would like to notice, but must forego that pleasure, at least for the present.

---

(1) Gen. iii, 4, 5.

It will be recollected that the major proposition in my first argument was the well known command of the Lord, commonly called "the Golden Rule." In the construction of the language of this command, J. S. has attempted to give it an exposition, directly, and positively at variance with its spirit—its true intent and meaning. I am almost ashamed to reproduce his construction, as emanating from a professed disciple of our Lord Jesus. But we must hear J. S. He says: "Does a master want others to free him? No; because he is not in bondage. The Golden Rule, then, does not require him to free his slaves, because he does not want them to free him." And again, "Does brother O. B. want others to free him? No—he does not. Then the Golden Rule, *as laid down by the Lord*, does not require him to free, or attempt to free any one." These quotations show the construction which J. S. gives to this divine law. It were better and more in character, as it would seem to me, in the mouth of the arch deceiver, than of a disciple of the Lord. According to this construction, the person who has an abundance of this world's goods—who knows no personal want—who could have no desire that others should give him in charity either food, clothing or shelter—and who indeed would not receive such charities from others, is not bound, nor indeed is he permitted to bestow such charities upon others, whatever may be their condition and necessities. The widow and the orphan may weep on, for there is no help—no sympathy for them. The sorrowing, the sick, the afflicted, and the oppressed may suffer and endure, in hopelessness and despair, for there is no relief, no "balm in Gilead" for them. No one may offer help or consolation, but those who are in like need, and they of course have not the power to bestow either. The door is thus effectually closed against the efforts of any and every philanthrophy, of any and every charitable and benevolent enterprize, and man wrapped in the mantle of selfishness—a selfishness baptised in this divine command—is permitted, nay, more, enjoined, if he have "goods of this world, and sees his brother in need," to "shut up his compassion from him." Incongruous and inharmonious with this construction, is the lengthy and most welcome quotation by J. S., from the writings of the loving and beloved disciple. The construction in such an atmosphere of love, seems the serpent disporting itself in the very fountains of the waters of life. The spirit of the command—the intent and meaning of the language of the Lord—are sufficiently obvious, without any effort on my part to refute the construction which J. S. has put upon them.

In reference to the concluding words of this command, to-wit: "for this is the law and the prophets," J. S., for the purpose of obtaining the Lord's sanction to the Hebrew law of servitude, insists upon the ultraism of a literal construction. He says "that the Lord expressly says that this rule is both the law and the prophets. It includes both." To adopt to the full extent the construction for which J. S. seems to contend, we must be firm believers in the extremest doctrine of transubstantiation, and suppose, that by some miraculous process, this rule of the Lord is transmuted into, not only the very precepts of the law, but also the very bodies and blood of the ancient prophets. This would be too literal even for J. S. It is better to adopt the plain and obvious intent and meaning of the language. To illustrate that meaning, let us suppose that J. S., upon being consulted on some matters involving legal and constitutional questions, should, in giving his opinion, say of it, "this is the constitution and the law." This form of expression would be fully justified by common usage, and there would be no danger of a misapprehension of its meaning. How ridiculous it would be for me to say in reference to it, that J. S. claimed that his opinion included the whole body of both the constitution and laws.

The term *the law*, when used by the Jews in that definite form and singular number, referred specially to the Decalogue, the commands of the two tables. In reference to the law of these tables, the Lord upon another occasion said: "Thou shalt love the Lord thy God with all thy heart, and with all thy soul, and with all thy mind. This is the first and great commandment. And the second is like unto it, Thou shalt love thy neighbor as thyself. On these two commandments hang all the law and the prophets." It does not appear that these commands, in this form and language, were upon the tables; but the first is the embodiment, in their spirit and meaning, of all the commands of the first table, and the second a like embodiment of all the commands of the second table. They were so adopted and held by the Jews before this utterance of them by the Lord.

The Golden Rule, which we are considering, has reference to man's duty to man. It covers the whole field of the commands of the second table, and of the teachings of the prophets in reference thereto—no more and no less. It is an authoritative exponent of, and substitution for, that law and those teachings. It gives the law in another form, and in other language, the better to correct the too limited, too technical, and too literal construction of that law, by the Jewish doctors and lawyers. Some Judge Somebody, among the Jewish lawyers, had probably suggested that the term neighbor in the law was a term specific and limited in its meaning, and that in its utmost extent it embraced none others than the members of the Jewish family, and that all others were strangers, dogs and enemies. This was the general, perhaps uniform construction of the law of the second table among the Jews, and hence the maxim, "Thou shalt love thy neighbor and hate thine enemies," to which the Lord refers. The term love in the law was also liable to a like misconstruction. Love is literally an emotion, and not an act; and hence it may have been said that the law had no reference to man's *conduct* to his neighbor, but simply and only required *kindly affection* and *friendly feelings* toward him. The Lord, in the Golden Rule, which he substitutes for this law, corrects both these errors of construction. For *loving* he substituted *doing*, and made our own selfish desires the measure of our charity, and the rule of our conduct to others. For *neighbor* he substituted *men*—all men—thus enlarging the boundaries of neighborhood to embrace the whole human family. This, too, is in accordance with all his other teachings, and especially in the parable of the good Samaritan. The apostles also taught the same lesson in all their teachings and writings "Go ye into all the world and preach the gospel to every creature," is the great commission. "God is no respecter of persons, but in every nation he that feareth God and worketh righteousness, is accepted with him."[1] "As we have therefore opportunity, let us do good unto all men."[2] "Love worketh no ill to his neighbor, therefore love is the fulfilling of the

---

(1) Acts x, 34, 35.   (2) Gal. vi, 10.

law."[1] "For all the law is fulfilled in one word, even this, thou shalt love thy neighbor as thyself."[2] "God is love, and he that dwelleth in love, dwelleth in God, and God in him. If a man say I love God, and hateth his brother, he is a liar. For he that loveth not his brother, whom he hath seen, how can he love God whom he hath not seen?"[3] If humanity would bathe in that fountain, and breathe of that atmosphere of love, which God has prepared for us, and to the free enjoyment of which he invites us, there would be no more slavery—no more sin in the world.

I have, as I think, shown the futility and absurdity of the effort to wrest from the Golden Rule of the Lord his approval of the Jewish municipal law of servitude, as of universal and perpetual obligation. Hence, the consideration of that law is not demanded in this discussion. However, when the matters which I regard as more relevant to, and more pertinent in this discussion, shall have been disposed of, I may make an effort to show that that law is misunderstood and misinterpreted by those who would deduce from it an argument in favor of American slavery.

The teachings of the apostles, and the practices of the first christians, are referred to by J. S. to prove a construction of the Golden Rule different from the one I give it, and more in harmony with the views of J. S. But the reference is too general and indefinite to demand a specific response. I claim that those teachings and practices are in harmony with my construction of the rule. If J. S. will specify the parts of the writings of the New Testament upon which he relies, I may be able to give him a more specific response, and to prove from his own witnesses the truth of the proposition under discussion.

J. S. has made an important admission. He says "man stealing is a sin, and always was.[4] Joseph's brethren committed a great sin in stealing him—depriving him of his liberty, and reducing him to slavery." This, together with the context, fully authorizes me in claiming, that J. S. admits, that to enslave a person—to deprive him of liberty, and reduce him to slavery—is sin. This is one position yielded; and if no more is gained, the truth of the proposition that "slavery is sinful," is established by his own ad-

---

(1) Rom. xiii, 10.   (2) Gal. v, 14.   (3) 1 John iv, 16-20.   (4) Ex. xxi, 16.

mission. Slavery originates in the enslavement of persons, and if it originate in sin, it must of necessity be sinful. I claim to hold the position thus yielded in all the future of this discussion.

To suppose, as J. S. does, that the transfer of the enslaved, by sale or otherwise, from one person to another, would purify and perfect a title, vicious in its origin, founded in wrong and sin, is bad civil, and worse moral law. By the civil law, the purchaser acquires no better title than the seller possessed; hence the maxim, "Buyer, beware of whom you purchase." Hence, too, the statute for the equal punishment of the thief, and the receiver of stolen goods. But J. S., anticipating the difficulty of the position, says: "All American slaves were born so, and have not been *deprived* of liberty, and *reduced* to slavery by any one." Is this so? God is the Creator of all men. He has made no person a slave. "All men are created free." "God is no respecter of persons."[1] He has put no difference between them.[2] "And he has made of one blood all nations of men, for to dwell on all the face of the earth."[3] Freedom is the noamal and normal condition of man. It is necessary to his rationality. It is essential to his accountability. God made man, and to manhood, freedom is an indispensable requisite. Hence God made him free. Slavery is a condition created by human laws, and other human agencies. It is superinduced upon humanity. It avails not to say, that it attaches to the person at the moment of his birth. Freedom was the first—the normal condition. Slavery the superinduced—the unnatural condition. In logical sequence, if not in the order of time being, the personal existence precedes slavery. That personal existence is a prerequisite to the enslavement of the person. Hence, every person who is held in slavery has been and is deprived of liberty, and reduced to slavery. That the whole life, instead of a portion of it, has been and is thus offered a living sacrifice upon the altar of this modern moloch, is certainly no extenuation, but rather an aggravation of the crime.

If this argument be sound, and I can see no defect in it, except in the imperfect manner of its statement, the admission of J. S. yielded the whole field covered by the proposition, at least as far as American slavery is concerned.

---

(1) Acts x, 34.   (2) Acts xv, 9.   (3) Acts xvii, 26.

This article has been so far limited to the consideration of the reply of J. S. to my first argument. In his reply to my second argument are some matters which should receive attention. He there introduces two arguments for slavery; the one founded upon the curse of Canaan, the other upon the supposed grant, of the right of property in man, to Israel, which he construes to mean the spiritual Israel. Whatever I may think of the strength or soundness of these arguments, they embody perhaps the whole scriptural argument in favor of slavery, and will therefore require more attention, and a fuller consideration, than I can give them in this article. I will endeavor hereafter to notice them, and show that they afford neither support of, or argument for American slavery.

O. B.

[From the Christian Record of September 16th, 1862.]

THIRD REPLY OF J. S.

My brother O. B. has retrogaded in his last article, and I must follow him, erratic as he is.

I shall not repeat what I have already said in my first reply. The reader will please look back over it. It is itself nearly a full answer to what O. B. says upon the Golden Rule in his last article. I shall only say now, here, what may be necessary in addition to what I have said, to meet what my brother has said in his last.

Charity, alms-giving, furnishing food and raiment to the needy, visiting the sick and afflicted, and administering to their wants, &c., do not rest on the Golden Rule as the basis that makes them christian duties and obligations, but upon other Scriptures. They are ascertained and determined to be acts of righteousness, by other parts of the divine volume than the Golden Rule; and it is not necessary nor proper to wrest the Golden Rule from what *it says*, and interpolate it, to make it a precept for those virtues; and it can not be made a precept for those virtues without an interpolation. Brother O. B.'s construction of it will not obtain, without an interpolation, express or implied. But we must take the Lord's word as he uttered it, without interpolation; and must not make one precept a precept for a thing or things that it is not a precept for, to justify such interpolation. Having seen the mischief done by such a course having been pursued by the apostacy, we should take warning and not follow in its footsteps.

"For this is the law and the prophets," said the Lord, of the Golden Rule. *For* is here used in the sense of *because;* the injunction, therefore, is, whatsoever ye would that men should do to you, do ye even so to them; *because* this is the law and the prophets. But brother O. B.'s position and argument says that "this" is not the law and the prophets, but is inconsistent with, supercedes and repeals that portion of the law and the prophets that relates to slavery. The Lord, however, said otherwise; and we must determine, each for himself, whether we will heed the Lord or brother O. B. This Golden Rule stands near the conclusion of the sermon on the Mount, in which the Lord had frequently said, you know it was said of old, so and so, but *I say* to you so and so; sometimes contradicting and changing what was said of old; sometimes modifying, and sometimes only explaining and applying what had been said of old; in none of which was the law of slavery mentioned, contradicted, changed, modified or explained; and after all of which comes this Golden Rule with a *therefore* prefixed, which is equivalent to saying, *for these reasons,* "all things whatsoever ye would that men should do to you, do ye even so to them; *because* this is the law and the prophets;" which is equivalent to saying it is consistent with them, it is the law and the prophets in a nut-shell; and hence is entirely consistent with what had been said of old in relation to slavery.

What O. B. says about love as a christian duty, would all be well enough if he would apply it rightly to the subject under consideration. He applies it to the slave only, and not to the master and slave both; while the christian injunction to love, and the christian duty to love, applies equally to both. Bro. O. B. expends all his love upon the slave, while it is to be feared that his hate only is given to the master. Let him extend his love equally to the master and the slave, and then, as he is neither a master nor a slave, and is equally the "neighbor" to both, let him look to the Golden Rule, *as it reads*, to see how he should conduct himself *to both*, and conduct himself acordingly, and he will then be in the letter, and, I apprehend, will begin to feel the spirit of the law of the Lord on the subject under consideration.

The apostles, in all their teachings and writings, nowhere said that slavery was a violation of the Golden Rule, and hence sinful. I can not make this reference to their action and teaching any less "general," and I rely upon all that they said and wrote. If brother O. B. can find where they did, let him point it out, and thus make the reference particular. My reference must necessarily be general. And I will now add, that the Lord never said that slavery was a violation of the Golden Rule, nor that it was sinful, though it existed all around him where he taught.

Brother O. B. is very much elated at "an important admission" that he says I have made; and he "claims to hold the position thus yielded in all the future of this discussion." I am glad to see him pleased, and am entirely willing that he "hold" the position I have admitted. But in this grave discussion, it is my duty not to let him *deceive himself* into elation, even for a short time.

Quoting Ex. xxi, 16, I said, "man-stealing is a sin, and always was. Joseph's brethren committed a great sin in stealing him, depriving him of his liberty, and reducing him to slavery; but Potiphar committed no sin in buying him, and holding him a slave." This is the "important admission" I made. I am willing to be held to it "in all the future of this discussion."

O. B. says that by this I admit "that to enslave a person, to deprive him of liberty, and reduce him to slavery, is sin"! How crotchety a man's intellect becomes when he becomes an abolitionist! Or, it may be that the truth of the case is properly stated thus: How crotchety a man's intellect must become, before he can become an abolitionist! Is stealing a man, and depriving him of his liberty, and reducing him to slavery, the same with simply depriving him of his liberty, and enslaving him? Certainly not. Yet O. B. puts them down as identical! In the same twenty-first chapter of Exodus, which makes man-stealing a capital offence, it is provided that if a six-year Hebrew servant "plainly say, I love my master, my *wife* and my *children*, I will not go free;" then he might be deprived of his liberty, and reduced to slavery forever, verses 5, 6; and that if a Hebrew man *sell his daughter* to be a maid servant, she shall not go out at the end of six years as the men servants do, verse 7. Hence, in the mind of the divine law-giver, there was quite a broad distinction between man-stealing and reducing people to slavery. And I hope my brother O. B. will be blessed with ability to see it.

The larceny of Joseph and the selling of him was the sin of Joseph's brethren.[1] Potiphar did not sin in buying him, and holding him; first, because the divine record does not say he did; and second, because God blessed Potiphar on account of Joseph.[2] It is not necessary to talk about the stolen title he bought: The question is, did he sin by holding Joseph by it? It is a question of fact, not of casuistry and speculation. The testimony of God is, that he did not; because he does not bless people for sinning, nor in sinning. He cursed the Philistines for sinning in keeping the ark; while he blessed Obed-edom for the righteousness of keeping it in his house.[3]

The receiver of stolen goods does not sin against the civil law of the land, unless he receives them *knowing them to be stolen*. What title to real or personal property exists among us that has not been tinctured with force or fraud at some stage of it? and if that is to affect it in our hands, who of us has a good title for anything? But I forbear to pursue this thought. We are to determine this question by the law of the Lord, and not by the law of civil society. And title is not the question; but it is, Is the holding the title, and exercising the rights of ownership of the title, a sin?

To prove that all men are created of God free, and are born free, in the face of the fact patent and existing all his life, and also in all ages of the world, that the slaves of the United States have all been born slaves, and that the subjects of the despots of Europe and Asia are, and have been in all ages, born subjects, and not freemen, O. B. says:

---

(1) Deut. xxiv, 7.　　(2) Gen. xxxix, 5.　　(3) 1 Sam. v; 2 Sam. vi, 11, 12.

"God is the Creator of men. He has made no person a slave." "All men are created free." God is no respecter of persons.[1] He has put no difference between them.[2] "And has made of one blood all nations of men for to dwell on all the face of the earth"[3]—to which he should have added Dow's text, "top-knot come down."[4]

When the secret that had been hid in God from the beginning of the world,[5] hid from ages and from generations,[6] which secret was, "that the Gentiles should be fellow-heirs and of the same body, and partakers of his promise in Christ by the Gospel;"[7] when this secret was first made known, and revealed to Peter, and the astounding fact burst upon him, he exclaimed, "Of a truth I perceive that God is no respecter of persons; but in every nation, he that feareth him and worketh righteousness is accepted of him."[8] And Peter, in telling of this transaction afterwards, said, that in the admission of the Gentiles into the kingdom, God put no difference between the Jews and the Gentiles, purifying their hearts by faith, as the Jews' hearts were purified by faith.[9] And O. B. quotes these occurrences to prove that those born slaves are actually born free! when what the passages prove is, that God has no respect of persons as to receiving them into his kingdom from one nation or people more than another; and puts no difference between them as to the manner of purifying their hearts, purifying the hearts of all of them alike by faith. And when Paul stood upon Mars Hill in Athens, and told the idolatrous Athenians that God had made of one blood all nations of men *for to dwell on all the face of the earth,* * * * that they *should seek the Lord,* if haply they might feel after him and find him, O. B. quotes this to prove that all the human family are born free! It would come near proving that all are born christians; but I suppose no one will be so silly as to quote it to prove that. In all seriousness, O. B. should properly have closed these quotations with Dow's text, "top-knot come down,"[10] to prove that slaveholders should manumit their slaves, as Dow used it to prove that the ladies should take the top-knots off their bonnets.

---

(1) Acts x, 34.
(2) Acts xv, 9.
(3) Acts xvii, 26.
(4) Matt. xxiv, 17.
(5) Rom. xvi, 25; Eph. iii. 9.
(6) Col. i, 26.
(7) Eph. iii, 6.
(8) Acts x, 34.
(9) Acts xv, 7-9.
(10) Matt. xxiv, 17.

We should all be careful not to handle the Word of God deceitfully.[1]

As I am engaged in a religious discussion, and not a political one, I shall not notice the political quotation he makes—"all men are created free"—but will say, that, in a proper forum, I can, as I have frequently heretofore done, show that it is equally misapplied and perverted with the above passages from the divine volume.

All his philosophy and vain imaginings about the *noamal* and normal conditions of man, I pass by as unworthy of notice, for the reason already twice given, why it is proper to thus treat philosophy and vain deceit, contradictory to facts patent to all, and unsupported by inspiration, which is the true source of knowledge. The slaves of America have not been *deprived* of liberty, for they never had it; and they have never been *reduced* to slavery, for they were always there; and the hair-splitting idea that being precedes slavery, is as sophistical and unsupported by fact, as that being precedes heirship. Being, existence, heirship, all actually take place at the same time, whether the infant heir be heir to thousands, to penury, or to slavery.[2]

My dear brother O. B. has undertaken to prove that slavery is a sin. Sin is the transgression of the law. It is time that he had cited us to the law that slavery is a transgression of. He has issued his third number, and next will come his fourth. I respectfully request that if he can cite us to any law of the Lord of which slavery is a transgression, he will do it in his next. He has not done it hitherto. And I want him to bear in mind, that to be a sin, it must be the transgression of *a law*, and not the transgression of some inference that he or some one else may draw, nor of a conclusion from a course of argument. No thing can be established to be a sin by argument or inference. No one was ever held accountable as a sinner, and for a sin, that was deduced by argument, or rested on an inference; and no one ever will be. From the day God said to Adam, of a certain tree in the garden, "thou shalt not eat," down to

---

(1) 2 Cor. iv, 2; ii, 17.
(2) The chief captain bought the franchise of being a free Roman citizen with a great sum; but Paul was born a free Roman citizen. Acts xxii, 28. Inspiration here recognizes the fact which the whole history of the human race proves to be true, that some are born free and others not free; and yet abolitionists reject all this light, clear as the noon-day sun, to build up their wild false theory, upon the false assumption that *being precedes slavery*.

the close of the Apocalypse, God has laid down the law, plain and unmistakable, in every case where he has held man accountable as a sinner for the breach of it; and so, too, of works of righteousness. And theorizing, and reasoning, and inference, and conclusion from arguments, as to both sin and righteousness, have always led, and still will lead, to apostacy from God. So let my dear brother drop his reasonings and his conclusions, and his philosophy, (falsely so-called,) and look up the law of the Lord of which slavery is a transgression, and thus show it to be a sin in the only way in which it can be done, if done at all. And let him bear in mind, that calling slavery hard names, as "modern Moloch," in his last, or saying spiteful things of it, does not prove his proposition, and is out of place in a grave, christian discussion. And, as Jude informs us, that the archangel Michael, when contending with the Devil even, about the body of Moses, durst not bring a railing accusation against him;[1] and as it may seem to some of our readers that what he says in his last about "arch-deceiver," and "the *serpent* disporting itself in the very fountain waters of life," are railing accusations brought against me. To prevent such unjust and untrue impressions getting into the minds of any readers, perhaps he had better not use such mode of expression any more.

May the Lord aid us all in coming to the *knowledge* of the *truth*, is my devout prayer.

J. S.

September 10*th*, 1862.

[From the Christian Record of September 23, 1862.]

O. B.'S FOURTH AFFIRMATIVE.

"And when the woman saw that the tree was good for food, and that it was pleasant to the eyes, and a tree to be desired to make one wise, she took of the fruit thereof, and did eat; and gave also unto her husband, and he did eat."[2]

---

(1) Jude 9.   (2) Gen. iii, 6.

In looking over the last article of J. S., I can perceive little in it which would seem to require much attention. It is mostly a re-statement of his former argument, somewhat extended, but not, as I perceive, strengthened. There is in it an abundance of assertions; but no proof, no logical argument. I might desire to notice some portions of it, but as J. S. is moving somewhat in a circle, he will probably give me an opportunity to do so at a more appropriate place in this discussion. I must not suffer myself to be drawn away from my own course of argument, to pick up the fragments of his, especially when I regard those fragments as of little value. I propose now to respond, more especially to some matters in his article of the first of September, to which I hope the reader will refer.

Slavery is based upon the idea of the right of one man, or class or race of men, to property in other men. It means the holding and trafficing in the persons—the bodies and souls of men as chattel property. Disguise it as we may, modify and qualify it as we will, this is its true significance in American thought, and in American law. In a former number, I endeavored to show that there is no such right—that God, the Creator, is the original, absolute owner and proprietor of man, and of all things—that man has no right of property except such as he derives from the grant of God—that by no grant from the Creator is man, or any class or race of men, invested with the right of property in man; but that, on the contrary, God has reserved man, and all property in man to himself, for his own special use and service. As a clear and unmistakable indication of such purpose of reservation, he has stamped his own image upon man, "for in the image of God made he man." And from this I drew the conclusion, which seems to me necessary and inevitable from the premises, that American slavery— the enslavement of the African race in American society, and under American law—is sinful.

To this J. S. has pleaded the Noachian utterance of the curse of Canaan, and the accompanying blessings of Shem and Japheth, claiming this as God's curse upon the posterity of Ham, and his grant of them as property to the posterity of Shem and Japheth.

He has also pleaded the Hebrew law permitting the children of Israel to buy bondmen and bondmaids of the heathen round about them, claiming this as a grant to all christians—the true Israel—of the right of property in the heathen.

If these can be regarded as grants, they are inconsistent, and in conflict with each other. The grantees in the first are all the posterity of Shem and Japheth, and in the second all the members of the true Israel. The subjects of the first grant—the persons claimed to be granted by it—are all the posterity of Ham, and of the second all the heathens. To reconcile and harmonize these, we must adopt a new and hitherto unknown system of theology—a gospel of salvation not found in the Scriptures. We must conclude that the descendants of Shem and Japheth are the elected, foreordained members of the true Israel, and as such unconditionally entitled, not only to the ownership of the children of Ham, but to all the blessings of the new covenant, and that all the descendants of Ham are in like manner the elected, foreordained reprobates of earth and heaven, doomed not only to perpetual slavery here, but to perdition hereafter. J. S. will perceive the necessity either of correcting his faith, or withdrawing at least one of his pleas. To enable him to act advisedly in the premises, I suggest that the heathens round about the children of Israel were mostly of the descendants of Shem, and many of them justly claimed the paternity of the patriarch Abraham. The text of this second pretended grant will probably come under consideration again, should I attempt an exposition of the Jewish law of servitude. For the present, I leave it with the suggestions already made in reference to it.

The first pretended grant—the Noachian utterance—will require a more lengthy consideration, not as I think on account of any intrinsic merit, or strength in it, either as argument or evidence to support the claim set up under it, nor indeed wholly or principally for the reason that J. S. has adduced it, and relies upon it, but because it is made the basis of every Scriptural argument to sustain slavery. Every advocate of the system vauntingly and dogmatically quotes it, in mere wantonness and total disregard for the accuracy of his quotations, as heaven's sanction of the iniquity of American slavery.

The following is the text of this utterance of Noah, as

recorded in the sacred history, and to it I ask the careful and close attention of the reader:

"And Noah awoke from his wine, and knew what his younger son had done unto him: and he said, cursed be Canaan; a servant of servants shall he be unto his brethren. And he said, blessed be the Lord God of Shem, and Canaan shall be his servant. God shall enlarge Japheth, and he shall dwell in the tents of Shem, and Canaan shall be his servant."[1]

This utterance can justly claim no higher character than the prophetic. It can not reasonably be regarded as more than an inspired prophecy of events then future; and even for this, there is no other evidence than historic facts, showing the fulfillment of its predictions. It claims to be no more than the simple utterance of Noah, under a feeling of just indignation against Ham, for his irreverent and impious conduct toward his father. In the light of subsequent history, it may, however, be accepted as a prophecy. As the fiat and decree of God, it can not be sustained. The sacred record neither claims or intimates that it possesses that character. No other similar utterance, either of any of the patriarchs, or any other human being, referred to in the Scriptures, is regarded as possessing the character of a divine decree. God's decrees, his blessings and his curses, are recorded either as pronounced by himself, or as the word of the Lord by the mouth of his prophet, and never as the simple language of any man without reference to God's authority for the utterance.

Regarded as a simple prediction of events then future— the developments of human wickedness and depravity, dependent upon merely human agencies—the utterance possesses none of the characteristics of a grant, and can neither be pleaded as such, or in extenuation of, or excuse for the events predicted.

For the purpose, however, of examining the subject further, I am willing, for the present, to treat this utterance of Noah as the decree, the fiat of God, which J. S. claims that it is. Noah had three sons, Shem, Ham and Japheth, of whom Ham was the youngest, as we infer from this text. Ham had four sons, Cush, Mizraim, Phut and Canaan, of

---

[1] Gen. ix, 24-27.

whom it is supposed that Canaan was the youngest. Noah had partaken too freely of the fruit of the first vintage, and had become drunken and helpless. In his exposed condition, Ham had been guilty of a gross act of irreverence, and impiety to him; and when he awoke from his wine he uttered this curse. It is not necessary here to inquire whether the conduct of Ham was the cause of, or simply the occasion for this utterance. Let the casuist settle that question for himself in such a manner as may be consistent with his own ideas of divine justice. We have to do now only with the utterance itself, and not with either the cause of, or the occasion for it.

The utterance is in clear, precise and strong language. The curse involved rested upon the head of Canaan; and if it be God's curse, *God himself selected the victim*. J. S. says that it is the curse of Ham through Canaan. The curse was a bitter one, at the best—a terribly bitter one, if it have the import which J. S. contends that it has. And yet it is too limited in its terms to suit the idea of justice, which J. S. entertains. He thinks the curse should have fallen upon the head of Ham, that *all* his children might have been involved in it; and he really attempts, at this late day, to correct this omission of the Just One, and involve Ham and all his posterity in the curse of Canaan. The intent and meaning of the utterance can not, at least in this particular, be mistaken by any one not predetermined to pervert it. For greater certainty, the name of the doomed one is thrice repeated in the utterance. The curse rested solely upon Canaan. From him it might flow in the descending line to, and over all his posterity. By no law or usage, divine or human, could it flow back in the ascending line to Ham, or outward into collateral channels to Cush, Mizraim and Phut. The silence of the record in reference to Ham, and these, his three sons, the total want of any reference to them in the deed, is conclusive evidence that neither its blessing or its curse was intended for them. This, together with the grief which Ham must have felt, that his younger, and perhaps his favorite son, was so cursed and so doomed, might perhaps have been regarded as a sufficient punishment to him for his wicked act. The African race of the present day are admitted to be the descendants of Cush. No one claims that they are the descendants of

Canaan; and hence whatever may be the import of the curse of Canaan, it can not affect the African race. They are not under it, or involved in it, and American slavery can receive no support from it.

Here I might rest this argument so far as this Noachian utterance is concerned. But I desire to push it further, and examine some, at least one other, of the terms used in the text.

It is quite strange that one professing so much reverence for God's word as J. S. professes, should take the liberty to tamper with it as he does. He quotes often from the Scriptures, and yet rarely makes a quotation without introducing his own interpretations and amendations. In the text which we are considering, he has gone still farther. He has stricken out some words and substituted others in their place. The term *servant*, wherever it occurs in the text, is stricken out by him, and the term *slave* substituted for it. For this he gives no reason, and offers no apology, but simply his own assertion that that is what it means. If J. S. were a thorough Hebrew scholar, his opinion might be entitled to some consideration. But to both J. S. and myself the Hebrew " is all Greek." We neither of us know a letter of the alphabet, or can pronounce a word of the language. I will not be guilty of the folly, nor the pedantry, of discussing with J. S. the meaning of Hebrew words and phrases. And yet there is a process of reasoning open to us, and to all who have an ordinary knowledge of the English language, by which our confidence in the correctness of the common English version of the Scriptures may be either strengthened or weakened. Let us, then, inquire what are the probabilities of error in the common version, in the use of the word servant, either in this text or elsewhere in the Scriptures.

The words *servant* and *slave* are not synonymous terms. Each has its own peculiar meaning, and one can never be made the equivalent of the other. *Servant* is a generic term, and designates any and every person rendering service to or for another, whatever may be the character or quality of the service, though usually, in popular language, applied to persons engaged in the lower classes of voluntary service. *Slave* is a specific term, and designates a species of property—a person held as property, for use, consumption, or traffic, as other property. A slave may be, and usually is, a servant also, but not necessarily so. A slave-dealer may own a thousand slaves, and not have a servant among them all. A servant may be a slave also, but is not necesssarily or usually so. The word servant involves the idea of service—no more and no less. The word slave involves the idea of property as clearly and distinctly as does the word horse or ox. In common language—in American thought, and in American law—these are the significance of the two words. These terms and their meaning and import were fixed and established in the English language, and in common use in English society, long before the common version, or King James' translation was made. And, indeed, at the time of that translation, owing to the condition of society in England, and the prevalence and activity of the slave-trade, the distinctive meaning of these terms was even more definitely and clearly marked, in the English use of them, than it is now in American society and in American use.

The purpose of the translation was to express the true idea and meaning of the original in equivalent English words and phrases. The use of any word or phrase not so equivalent, would have been a false translation. We have seen that the words servant and slave are not synonymous, and do not represent equivalent ideas. The presumption is, that the translators have selected the right words to express the meaning of the original, and this presumption amounts to almost a certainty, so far as these words are concerned, when we consider the circumstances under which the translation was made, the prejudices and opinions of the translators, and the influences which were operating upon them. Whatever may be thought of English opinion, either now or at any time since the translation, it was then decidedly favorable to slavery. The slave-trade was then in active and vigorous operation, stimulated by the countenance and favor of the Crown. The English King was a partner in the nefarious traffic. England's nobility favored it, and her merchants invested largely in the profitable business. There was no popular sentiment against it, and even the moral sense of the church was quiescent or approving. The translation was made under the auspices of the English Crown, and under the pressure and within the circle of all these influences favorable to slavery. It would be more than folly—it would be some evidence of insanity—to doubt that the translators, thus situated, would have used the word slave, or some equivalent English word, in the translation, whenever and wherever they could, as scholars, have felt justified, or even have found a plausible excuse for so doing. Whenever they used the word servant, we may feel the utmost confidence that the word slave would have been an improper one, and a false translation. The word slave occurs but twice in the whole English Scriptures, and in one of these instances,[1] it is in italics, showing that it is not in the original, but was introduced by the translators to supply an elipsis. The context shows that the word there should have been servant, and not slave, and its introduction shows the disposition of the translators to use the word slave whenever they could find an excuse for doing so.

If this argument be a sound one, as I am fully convinced that it is, the word slave, substituted by J. S. in the text under consideration, must be rejected, and the word servant, as found in the common version, restored to its proper place. The argument goes further, and applies to every case of the use of the word servant in the common version. I shall, therefore, have further use for it, in considering other portions of the sacred record.

I have thus shown, and I think clearly, that slavery was not involved in the curse of Canaan. But, it may be asked, what then does it involve, and to what does it doom the posterity of Canaan? We need not here follow the fortunes of the other sons of Noah, for it is only with Canaan and his posterity that this argument has to do. When Abraham first emigrated to the land of Canaan, he found the descendants of Canaan in possession of it. Even then they had become extremely wicked, and God punished their wickedness by the destruction of Sodom and Gomorrah. God promised that land to Abraham, as a possession for his posterity, but told him that the iniquity of its inhabitants was not then full; that his own posterity would be made to serve in another country for generations, before they could come in possession of the land. This service was accom-

---

(1) Jer. ii, 14.

plished in Egypt, when God commanded the children of Israel to go up and possess the promised land, advising them that the iniquity of the Canaanites was full, and commanded them to exterminate all the inhabitants of the land.

The decrees and the commands of God must of necessity be consistent and in harmony with each other. We can not suppose that God would command the extermination of the Canaanites, if obedience to such command would conflict with his before expressed purpose and decree. And hence, if we regard the curse of Canaan as the fiat of God, we must look for the full execution and accomplishment of that curse before, or at the time the children of Israel came into full possession of the land of Canaan. Whatever remnant was left of Canaan after that event, was not sufficient to have been regarded, either in God's purpose or prophecy, or in subsequent history, as the people represented and symbolized by Canaan in the text. We must look, then, to the history of the Canaanites antecedently to the settlement of the Israelites in the promised land for the fulfillment of the curse. While the Israelites were servants in Egypt, the Canaanites were spread over the land of Canaan, engaged in replenishing and subduing the earth; in enclosing and cultivating fields; in planting vineyards; and in building houses and cities. No doubt they thought that they were laboring for themselves, and that these things—the results and products of their own labor—were to be theirs for a perpetual possession. Yet history shows, that, in all this service and labor and toil, they were the servants of the Israelites—the *servants of the then servants of the Egyptian.* If Israel served the Egyptian, God had appointed the Canaanite to serve the Israelite at the same time, and Israel, in due time, entered into their labors. Thus, the curse was fulfilled, accomplished, and exhausted, when Israel found himself quietly settled in the land of Canaan, occupying houses and cities which others had builded for him—cultivating the fields which others had subdued and enclosed—and eating of the fruit of the vineyards which others had planted and prepared for him.

Perish, then, that *"philosophy and vain deceit, after the traditions of men, after the rudiments of the world, and not after Christ,"*[1] which would build upon this text a hideous

---
(1) Col. ii, 8.

system of chattel slavery, as cruel and inexorable as death, and as enduring as time. Let ours be that better philosophy, *which is after Christ*—founded in God's love to humanity, as manifested in sending his Son " to preach the gospel to the poor—to heal the broken-hearted—to preach deliverance to the captives, and recovering of sight to the blind—to set at liberty them that are bruised—to preach the acceptable year of the Lord."[1]

O. B.

[From the Christian Record of September 30th, 1862.]

FOURTH REPLY OF J. S.

My brother O. B.'s articles increase in quantity, if not in quality. The last contains three and a half columns of matter. He has commenced each of the last three with a quotation from the beginning of Genesis, of no pertinency whatever to the subject under consideration. It may be that he has commenced at the beginning of the Bible, intending to quote it all through, to see if he can not find a passage constituting a law, of which slavery is a transgression. If this is his object, I fear our readers' patience can not stand the infliction.

He asserted that God never granted property in man. I produced the grant to the posterity of Shem and Japheth, of property in the posterity of Ham, in or following the curse pronounced on Canaan, and also the grant to the children of Israel of property in the heathen round about. I also showed that civil governments had, and exercised, property in man; and that the power of the civil government was the ordinance of God. I said that these grants to Shem, Japheth and Israel, had not been revoked nor resumed by the Lord; and called upon O. B. to cite us to the passage of the Bible revoking them, if they had been revoked.

(1) Luke iv, 18, 19.

How does he meet these things in his last? He says that the curse pronounced by Noah did not apply to Ham, but to Canaan only, who is named in the curse; that while Israel was serving the Egyptians, the Canaanites were serving them, and thus were "the servants of the servants of the Egyptians;" and that "thus the curse was fulfilled, accomplished and exhausted." He takes no notice of the grant to civil governments, of property in man, and very little of that to Israel.

The question was, Had God ever granted property in man? I showed that he had in Noah's day, in Moses' day, and in the Apostolic day; three different times and ways. He meets it by the above special plea, or, as lawyers would call it, quibble, taking three and a half columns of the *Record* to state it in. The question was grant or no grant. He meets it by stating that one of the grants was not as large as I stated it to be—that it was confined to Canaan, and to his service to Israel, and was fulfilled, accomplished, exhausted, in Palestine before Israel got there!

But Canaan was to be Japheth's servant as well as Shem's; and Israel was not Japheth; therefore O. B.'s fulfillment was not a fulfillment, accomplishment, exhaustion, of what Noah said. When Israel was in bondage in Egypt, and also during the forty years that Israel was in the wilderness, the Canaanites were not serving Israel, but themselves. And the curse was, that Canaan was to be a servant of servants *to his brethren*, of course of the family of Ham, and not of the families of Shem and Japheth; for the three are distinctly stated, his brethren, Shem and Japheth. The *curse* made him a servant of servants to his brethren, and was followed by *a grant* of him, as a servant, to Shem and Japheth. And as Israel was not his brethren, but a part of Shem, serving Israel would not be serving his brethren. And hence O. B.'s fulfillment could not be a fulfillment, if it was true in fact that Canaan served Israel as he says he did. But he did not. Canaan has always been understood to stand for, and represent the posterity of Ham; but as to the question of grant or no grant of property in man, it is immaterial whether he represent the posterity of Ham, or his own.

He takes the reason given why murder should be expiated by the blood of the murderer—" for in the image of God made he man" as proof, "a clear and unmistakable indication," according to his reasoning and conclusion from the passage, "that by no grant from the Creator, is man, or any class or race of men invested with the right of property in man; but that, on the contrary, God has reserved man, and all property in man, to himself;" when, in fact, his reasonings and conclusions are directly contradicted by the knowledge communicated of God in the above three specified grants of property in man. This is, in him, exalting his own "imaginations" "against the knowledge of God"—a thing that we are forbidden to do.

Why did not O. B. cite the passages of Scripture revoking these grants to Shem, Japheth and Israel? and why was he entirely silent as to the grants to the civil governments, State and National, exhibited by me from the writings of the apostles?

He has a column upon the terms *servant* and *slave*. Though I have, in a preliminary article, given the Scripture definition of slavery, yet, as clear ideas and a correct understanding of the terms used, are necessary in ascertaining truth, I will now investigate that matter fully.

The merciful Lord has not only clearly told us what to do, and what not to do, but he has clearly defined most of the *things* necessary for us to understand, in order to understand what he has told us to do, or not to do. Among the things thus defined are *slaves* and *slavery*.

"Know ye not, that to whom you yield yourselves *servants* to obey, his *servants* ye are to whom ye obey; whether of sin unto death, or of obedience unto righteousness? But God be thanked, that ye were the *servants* of sin, but ye have obeyed from the heart that form of doctrine which was delivered to you. Being then made *free* from sin, ye became the *servants* of righteousness."[1]

"They answered him, we be Abraham's seed, and were never *in bondage* to any man; how sayest thou ye shall be made *free*? Jesus answered them, verily, verily I say unto you, whosoever committeth sin, is the *servant* of sin."[2]—*Common Version.*

They answered him, "we are Abraham's offspring, and were never *enslaved* to any man; how sayest thou, ye shall

---

(1) Rom. vi, 16–18. (2) John viii, 33, 34.

be made *free?* Jesus answered them, verily, verily I say unto you, he that committeth sin, is the *slave* of sin."—*Wesley's Translation.*

Some made answer, "We are Abraham's offspring, and were never *enslaved* to any man; how say you, you shall be made *free?* Jesus replied, most assuredly, I say to you, whosoever commits sin, is the *slave* of sin."—*New Translation.*

"While they promise them *liberty*, they themselves are the *servants* of corruption; for of whom a man is overcome, of the same is he *brought into bondage.*"[1]—*Common Version.*

"While they promise them *liberty*, themselves are the *slaves* of corruption; for by whom a man is overcome, by him he is also brought into *slavery.*"—*Wesley.*

"They promise them *liberty*, whilst they themselves are *slaves* of corruption; for every one is *enslaved* by that which overcomes him."—*New Translation.*

These contain clear Scriptural definitions of *slaves* and *slavery*, without determining whether Hebrew is all Greek to brother O. B. and me, or not.

In Romans 6th, the word *servant* is used in all the three translations quoted. Whether the word used in the original there, is the same used in the other passages quoted, it is not necessary to know, to ascertain the truth in the case. Being *free* is put in contrast with being a *servant;* and *freedom* is the contrast of *bondage.* Sin is said to have "dominion" over them, (verse 14) and to "reign" if "obeyed," (verse 12). Read the whole chapter.

But the Lord settles it in the passage in John viii. The Jews said they were never in bondage or slavery; for bondage in the Jewish law was slavery.[2] The Lord said that whosoever commits (or serves) sin, is the *slave* of sin; for *bondage* is what they said they were not in, and he said that by serving sin or sinning, they were in bondage, that is, in slavery. Then the service of sin, as mentioned by Paul in Rom. 6th, placed those who served or committed sin, in bondage to sin, as explained and defined by the Lord himself. The *thing* spoken of by Paul in Romans, was defined by the Lord to be *bondage*, translated by Wesley, and in the new translation *slavery.* And abolitionists say, and

---

(1) 2 Pet. ii, 19.   (2) Lev. xxv, 42.

have long said, that Wesley said that slavery " was the sum of all villianies;" and hence he would not be favorable to the word *slave* over *servant* in translating. And so of the translation of the passage in 2d Peter.

Hence, it is clear, that the Scripture definition of *slavery*, is *obedience* or *servitude;* and of *slave* is, *one who obeys or serves.*

The definition of *a slave* in the Constitution of the United States, is *a person held to service or labor.*[1] This is in accordance with the Scripture definition.

The definition given by Scripture, and by the Constitution, which is the highest law of the land, is conclusive in a religious discussion of slavery, and as to American slavery.

But I will also show what lexicographers say.

And first, Walker:

SLAVE—One mancipated to a master, not a freeman, a dependent.

SLAVERY—Servitude, the condition of a slave, the offices of a slave.

SERVANT—One who attends another, *and acts at his command;* one in a state of subjection; a word of civilty used to superiors or equals.

☞ This is one of the few words which has acquired by time, a softer signification than its original, *Knave*, which originally signified only a servant, but is now degenerated into a *Cheat;* while *servant*, which signified originally a person preserved from death by the conqueror, *and reserved for slavery*, signifies only an obedient attendant.

Secondly, Webster unabridged:

SLAVE—1. A person who is wholly subject to the will of another; one who has no freedom of action, but whose *person* and *services* are wholly under the *control of another.* 2. One who has lost the power of resistance, or who *surrenders himself to any power whatever*, as a slave to passion, to lust, to ambition. 3. A mean person; one in the lowest state of life. 4. A drudge; one who labors like a slave.

SLAVERY—Bondage; the entire state of subjection of one person to the will of another.

Slavery is the obligation to labor for the benefit of the master without the contract or consent of the servant.— *Paley.*

---

(1) Const. art. iv, § 2.

Slavery may proceed from crime, from captivity, or from debt. Slavery is also "voluntary" or "involuntary;" "voluntary" when a person *sells* or *yields* his own person to the absolute command of another; "involuntary," when he is placed under the absolute power of another without his own consent.

SERVANT—1. (After two definitions under this head, comes this, the last sentence in this paragraph.) Every slave is a servant, but every servant is not a slave. (Bro. O. B. contradicts this in his last article.)

2. One in *a state of subjection*.

3. In *Scripture*, a slave a bondman; one purchased for money, and who was compelled to serve till the year of jubilee; also, one purchased for a term of years. (Exod. xxi.)

SERVANT OF SERVANTS—One debased to the lowest condition of servitude. (Gen. ix.)

Hence, lexicographers agree with the Scripture definition, and with the definition of the Constitution of the United States; and I modestly claim that I have spoken in accordance with them, throughout this discussion. And hence, I have not taken "the liberty to tamper" with "God's word," in saying that *slave* expresses the true idea of the word *servant* in the curse of Canaan. For Webster says, that in Scripture *servant* means: first, a slave; second, a bondman; and that *servant of servants* means the lowest condition of servitude; and *servant of servants* is the expression used in that curse. Canaan was first cursed to the lowest condition of servitude or slavery to his brethren, and then given over, as a slave, to Shem and Japheth. Walker says that *servant* is one of the few words that has acquired a softer signification by time; that originally it meant a person preserved from death by the conqueror, and reserved for slavery. Hence, the translators of the common version, who acted over two hundred years ago, used the word *servant* in the harder sense, instead of being inclined to use the word *slave* if the original would justify it, as is charged by O. B. And Webster sustains this position of Walker, by giving the definition of *servant*, as used in the Scriptures, to be a slave, a bondman.

And it is clear also, that the word *slave* does not "involve the idea of property" "as does the words *horse* and *ox:*"

for *slave* involves the idea of property in the services and labor only of the slave; while *horse* and *ox* involve the idea not only of property in their services and labor, but also in their bodies, meat, hides, tallow, horns, &c. And hence, also, it is clear, that *slavery* does not mean "holding and trafficking in the persons—the bodies and souls of men— as chattel property." That is only an abolition exaggeration, that they have made use of so long and so often, that they believe it; and "because they receive not the love of truth," they have been, by the Good Being, allowed to believe it.[1]

Brother O. B. closes his last article with the quotation of Luke iv, 18, 19, a passage often quoted by abolitionists, and I propose to examine it now, as I have space enough.

This was the commencement of the Lord's public ministry, after his immersion and temptation, and was the first time after these events, that he had been in the synagogue on the Sabbath day, at Nazareth, where he had been raised. He went, as his custom was, and stood up to read. He found the place in Isaiah, chapter sixty-one, and read the first verse and part of the second, and closed the book and sat down and said: "This day is this Scripture fulfilled in your ears." The fulfillment was, that the spirit of the Lord God was then upon him, (having come upon him at Jordan,) because he had annointed him to preach and do these things. He went on and preached, and did these things for three years and a half; was crucified, arose, and ascended to the right hand of God, sent power to his apostles, who, by his command, preached throughout all the world, and finished the work.

The Lord and the apostles, then, "preached deliverance to the captives," and "set at liberty them that are bruised," in the true sense of the prophecy by Isaiah. And though there were then 30,000,000 of slaves in the Roman Empire, in which they were, and in which they preached, yet they did not say that they must be, or ought to be emancipated; nor give them "deliverance," nor "liberty," in the abolition sense in which they quote this passage. If they did, let brother O. B. show it; for, after the thing he was to do has been done, the proper way to show what he was to do, is to

---

(1) 2 Thes. ii, 10, 11.

show what he did. He did not preach abolitionism. If he did, show it. On the contrary, he and the apostles gave directions to both the masters and the slaves how to conduct themselves to each other, as masters and slaves, without telling them that the relation they held to each other was sinful, was a violation of the Golden Rule, and hence should be dissolved.

J. S.

September 25th, 1862.

[From the Christian Record of October 14th, 1862.]

O. B.'S FIFTH AFFIRMATIVE.

"Ye shall make the trumpet sound throughout all your land. And ye shall hallow the fiftieth year, and proclaim liberty, throughout all the land to all the inhabitants thereof, it shall be a jubilee unto you."[1]

In the opening of this discussion, I expressed the opinion that the question of slavery was no longer a debatable one— that the argument of words had been exhausted—that those who still persisted in maintaining the right of property in man, were past conviction by human argument, and that God himself, by the logic of the fearful and terrible events transpiring, was working out the solution of the dark problem.

Events, the most fearful in human history, fraught with the fortunes of the present, and the destinies of the future, have passed, and are now passing, with the velocity of thought. In their contemplation, the mind becomes dizzy and bewildered, and in their presence the human intellect "reels to and fro, and staggers like a drunken man." Clouds and darkness, storms and tempests, involve the whole area of this, the "conflict of ages." And yet, the just and the merciful One "rides upon the tempest and directs the storm." God is in all history. How fearfully, how terribly is he manifesting himself in this. It is the trumpet of the

(1) Lev. xxv, 9, 10.

Lord's jubilee, proclaiming "liberty throughout all the land, unto all the inhabitants thereof." Hope has waited long for a responsive note from our National authorities to this proclamation of the just and holy One, conscious that our national life depended upon the character of such response. It has come at last. The response is made in the recent proclamation of the President of the United States, proclaiming liberty to all the slaves, in all portions of the national domain, which shall be in rebellion on the first day of January next. Who shall doubt that this national act is in harmony with God's purpose, and believing this, we may not despair of the salvation of the nation, and the preservation of the Union. "If God be for us, who shall be against us." "And I heard as it were the voice of a great multitude, and as the voice of many waters, and as the voice of mighty thunderings, saying Allelulia, for the Lord God omnipotent reigneth. Let us be glad, and rejoice, and give honor to him."[1]

The great question of American slavery is solved, not by man's argument, or reasonings, but by the inexorable logic of events, guided and controlled by the hand of the Omnipotent One. The conflict, the storm, and the tempest, are still raging, and for a time may be even more fierce, bitter, and intense, than heretofore, but the christian will not doubt that there is a glorious day approaching—a day of peace, prosperity and happiness to the church, the nation and the people.

More deeply than heretofore, do I feel that the question is no longer a debatable one, and have therefore the less inclination to pursue the discussion. I shall, therefore, endeavor to be as brief as possible, in following the line of argument which I had proposed to myself. J. S. must excuse me, if I do not give to his fragmentary arguments the notice to which he may think them entitled.

I have, as I think, satisfactorily disposed of his argument drawn from the curse of Canaan, and have shown that American slavery can find no support from that curse.

I propose now to notice the Hebrew law of servitude, which J. S. claims sanctions chattel slavery among christians, and has been neither repealed or annulled. It is a

---

(1) Rev. xix, 6, 7.

most singular position, for one professing to be a christian, to take that the Hebrew law is in force in the kingdom of the Lord Jesus. I might cite many passages from the christian Scriptures to prove that the Lord himself fulfilled the law, and annulled it, nailing it to his cross, and himself gave a full and perfect law to his disciples, and that the Hebrew law never has been, and never can be, the law of the christian kingdom. But to do so, would seem to indicate a doubt of the intelligence of the reader, for such is the whole tenor of the christian Scriptures. So fully and so strongly is this taught, that Paul said to those Jewish scribes, who, like J. S., still insisted upon the law of Moses, "Christ has become of no effect unto you, whosoever of you are justified by the law, ye are fallen from grace."[1] I need not say more to the christian reader upon this subject, than to ask him to re-read the Gallatin letter. Whatever the Hebrew law of servitude may have been, the christian can not avail himself of its provisions, to sustain his claim of property in man. But the Hebrew law is not liable to the reproach of sanctioning chattel slavery, even among the ancient Israelites. On the contrary, its provisions were humane and benevolent, and wholly antagonistic to such claim.

Good and wise laws are necessarily adapted to the circumstances and condition of those for whom they are made. When those laws were given to Israel, the Israelites had just escaped from a bondage of ages, to a people who at the present time would at the best be regarded but as semi-civilized. Under their long oppression, the Israelites had became even more debased and degraded, and less self-reliant, than the negroes of the South at the present day. The people in and around the land of Canaan were not sufficiently advanced in social life, in civil organizations, and in the arts and sciences to be entitled to be characterized as semi-civilized. We have, perhaps, at the present day, no better representatives of these, than the inhabitants of the interior of Africa. Thickly settled over all the land of Canaan, and the surrounding countries, the necessities of civil government, for the protection of persons and property, were keenly felt by them; but there was no appreciation of what

---

(1) Gal. v, 4.

DISCUSSION OF SLAVERY. 161

was or should be the nature, character, or purposes of such government. Might ruled, and everywhere, in social life and civil organizations, the power of the strongest prevailed over the right. The people were separated, and formed into almost innumerable petty communities, called kingdoms, which were constantly preying upon each other, and were sunken in idolatry, and steeped in crime. God proposed to use the degraded fugitives from Egypt, to exterminate that portion of these people then inhabiting the land of Canaan, and to establish there a wider, stronger, and more enduring nationality—a civil government founded upon the idea, then new and strange to humanity, of the rule of law instead of might. In a country not larger than an ordinary State of our Union, thirty-two kingdom's were overthrown, and the inhabitants exterminated to make room for Israelites. The Hebrew laws were made for the Israelites in their inhabitancy of this country, in the condition and under the circumstances above named. God's purpose was not solely the establishment of a larger and more enduring nationality; but also, and perhaps principally, the elevation and civilization of the Hebrew race, and their preservation as a separate, distinct and peculiar people, as the depositors of his Holy Oracles, until the promised Messiah should come. It was inevitable that the Israelites would have intercourse with the surrounding heathens. Those heathens would seek the security and protection of their stronger nationality. Humanity required that such intercourse be permitted, so far as might be, without endangering the religious faith of the Israelites, or their distinctive and peculiar national character. The Hebrew laws, and especially the laws of servitude, were apparently framed for that purpose.

It will not, I presume, be contended by any one, that the law, so far as it related to Hebrew servants, involved the idea of chattel slavery, or property in man. That law may be found, Ex. xxi, 2–11; Lev. xxv, 39–43, and 47–55; Deut. xv, 12–18. There are also in other portions of Ex. xxi, some provision in reference to stealing, killing and smiting a servant, which seem to apply specially to Hebrew servants, as none other are named in the connection.

A Hebrew might be sold for theft, or for debt, or he might sell himself, or perhaps his children. These two last, although called sales, would be simply contracts for his own service, or the service of his children. However sold, the law made no distinction in the condition of the Hebrew servants. The service could not continue for more than six years, unless at the end of that time the servant voluntarily, and in solemn form, contracted to serve until the year of jubilee next thereafter. He could not bind himself for a longer time. The law specifically and positively provided for his kind treatment, and for the protection and preservation of his manhood, his individuality, and his rights, as an Israelite. Certainly no idea of chattel slavery could apply to his condition.

Another class of servants is named in the Hebrew law, and these are called bondmen. These in their condition approximate nearer to the condition of slaves than any other known to Hebrew law. The law in reference to them is as follows: "Both the bondmen and the bondmaids, which thou shalt have, shall be of the heathen that are round about you; of these shall ye buy bondmen and bondmaids. Moreover, of the children of the strangers that do sojourn among you, of these shall ye buy, and of their families that are with you, which they begat in your land, and they shall be your possession, and ye shall take them as an inheritance for your children after you, to inherit them for a possession, they shall be your bondmen forever."[1]

This is the whole of the Hebrew law for the establishment or sanction of bondage in Israel; and perhaps, were there no other provisions to modify or explain what is here intended, we might infer that something like chattel slavery was contemplated by it. This, however, would be an inference not fully warranted by the terms of the law. The heathen or the stranger might sell himself, or the stranger might sell his children to the Israelites, provided these children were natives of the land. Such sale was a contract for service between the master and the bondman, or the parent of the bondman, if a child. Although the claim for the service of the bondmen descended to the heir of the master, yet the obligation to serve did not descend to the children of the bondmen.

The year of jubilee discharged and enfranchised the bondman, for the law provides as follows: "And ye shall

---

(1) Lev. xxv, 44–46.

hallow the fiftieth year, and proclaim liberty throughout all the land to all the inhabitants thereof, it shall be a jubilee unto you."[1] Hence every bondman must be freed at the jubilee next after his service began, be that time longer or shorter. In these particulars, Jewish servitude differed from American slavery in some of the most revolting features of the modern institution. Nor were these the only differences.

From the bench of our highest national judicial tribunal, it has been declared, that "the African has no rights which a white man is bound to respect." Harsh and unfeeling as this seems, it is nevertheless legally true in reference to slaves, wherever chattel slavery exists. It is the necessity, the inevitable sequence of the claim of the right of property in man. Was that true of the Hebrew bondmen? Had they no rights under the Hebrew law, which the Hebrews were bound to respect. The heathen, whether inhabiting other lands, or sojourning among the Israelites, were called strangers by them, and are so spoken of in their law. That law says in reference to strangers, "and if a stranger sojourn with thee, in your land, ye shall not vex him. But the stranger that dwelleth with you, shall be unto you as one born among you, and thou shalt love him as thyself, for ye were strangers in the land of Egypt. I am the Lord thy God."[2] "If thy brother be waxen poor, and fallen into decay with thee, then thou shalt relieve him, yea, though he be a stranger or sojourner, that he may live with thee."[3] "One law and one manner shall be for you, and the stranger that sojourneth with you."[4] "Hear the causes between your brethren, and judge righteously between every man and his brother, and the stranger that is with him."[5] "Love ye, therefore, the stranger, for ye were strangers in the land of Egypt."[6]

These passages, and many more which might be cited, indicate the spirit of the Hebrew law, in reference to the heathen, the type of the African of our day, and are in direct conflict with the spirit of our laws, as indicated by the decision above named. I blush for the civilization and christianity of the age, in which such barbarism could find utterance in the court of a professedly civilized and chris-

---
(1) Lev. xxv, 10. (3) Lev. xxv, 35. (5) Deut. i, 16.
(2) Lev xix, 33, 34. (4) Numb. xv, 16. (6) Deut. x, 19.

tian people. And yet the sentiment is essential to the existence of chattel slavery. The fact that the Hebrew law was wholly antagonistic to such a sentiment, is conclusive proof that chattel slavery was not only not contemplated, but was forbidden by that law. The servitude of the bondmen was not slavery. It was instituted for the mutual benefit and convenience of the parties. It commenced in their voluntary contract, and its continuance depended upon their option. Especially might the bondman terminate it at any time, by leaving his master. The Lord forbade his being returned. "Thou shalt not deliver unto his master the servant which is escaped from his master unto thee. He shall dwell with thee, even among you, in that place which he shall choose, in one of thy gates, where it liketh him best. Thou shalt not oppress him."[1]

The relation between master and bondman was one of mutual choice, and of mutual benefit and convenience. When we consider the civil and social condition of the heathen, in and about the land of Canaan, their weakness and their wants, their insecurity in person and property, under the prevailing rule of might and tyrannical force on the one hand, and the civil and social condition of the Israelites, possessing a strong nationality, and living under the rule of laws, just and equal, alike to the Israelites and the stranger, offering to the stranger protection, and the enjoyment of civil and social rights on the other hand, it would not surprise us to know that the condition of bondmen to the Israelites was frequently sought by the weak, the defenceless, and the unprotected, among the heathen. Especially might they desire this, as a means of becoming naturalized and adopted into the Hebrew nation.

It was not the policy of the Hebrew laws to favor the incorporation of the stranger element with the Israelites, for the reason that too large an accession of that element might endanger the religious faith and the peculiar national character of the Israelites. Yet so far as such danger could be avoided, such accession was permitted. Hence, the law says, "Thou shalt not abhor an Edomite, for he is thy brother. Thou shalt not abhor an Egyptian, because thou wast a stranger in his land. The children that are begotten

---

(1) Deut. xxiii, 15, 16.

of them shall enter into the congregation of the Lord in their third generation."[1] Hence, if the children of the heathen became bondmen to the Israelites, their children were entitled to citizenship in the Hebrew commonwealth. This seems to have been the general rule. There are, however, some exceptions to it named in the law. The Moabites and the Ammonites were not entitled to citizenship for ten generations. But it seems that the rule did not refer to the heathen females married to Israelites, for Ruth, the great grandmother af David, was a Moabitess.

I may admit here, that by a sort of common law of nations—an international law, founded upon the wicked and barbarous customs of that age—captives taken in war were held and regarded as slaves—the property of the captors—and were held for ransom, or for service, or traffic as property. Their persons—their bodies and their souls—were regarded as articles of merchandize, and were in later times inventoried as articles of traffic in the hands of the merchants of Tyre. In Ezekiel xxvii, 13, they are thus spoken of. But the policy of the Hebrew law was wholly adverse to such a system, and its provisions rendered the enslavement of captives impracticable. The captives of the Hebrews were sometimes released upon condition of paying tribute. Otherwise they were slain and destroyed in obedience to the requirements of their law. Under certain circumstances, the female captives might be spared and retained, not, however, as slaves, or even as servants, but for wives for the Israelites, to satisfy the demand of their institution of polygamy. The precepts and examples, in reference to the treatment of captives, are numerous in the Hebrew law, and in Jewish history. It is unnecessary to cite them here.

The law was given to Israel in an age of great barbarism and crime—an age in which the practices and usages of slavery obtained almost universally among men. Yet the Hebrew law is not liable to the reproach of having sanctioned that iniquity by any of its provisions.

There are some other matters which I would like to notice in this connection, but I omit them now, as this article is already too long.

O. B.

---

(1) Deut. xxiii, 7, 8.

[From the Christian Record of October 28th, 1862.]

FIFTH REPLY OF J. S.

My dear brother O. B. has undertaken before the public to prove that slavery is sinful. Sin is the transgression of the law.[1] It is not the transgression of an argument, nor of a conclusion from an argument, nor of an inference. The LAW of the Lord, by which we mortals are to determine and ascertain whether anything is sinful or not, is found only in the Scriptures, given by inspiration of God. There only it is we learn what is sinful or wrong, and become thereby reproved and corrected; and there only it is we are instructed in righteousness, or told what is right; and by them the man of God—the man who obeys and follows God's directions—is *thoroughly furnished* unto all good works, and of course to the avoidance of all evil works.[2] This man of God who thus does, being thus thoroughly furnished, does not need any argument, or inference, or philosophical disquisition, to show him what is sin or what is righteousness. He only has to look into this law of the Lord contained in the Scripture given by inspiration; it is "the perfect law,"[3] and is the only perfect law that was ever made. Being perfect, it has left nothing to "doubtful disputation," or argument, or inference, so far as sin and righteousness are concerned.

As brother O. B. had not, in his first three numbers, cited any law of the Lord of which slavery is a transgression, and thereby shown that it was sinful, in my third reply I respectfully requested him, in his next number, to cite us to *the law* of which slavery is a transgression, if there was such a law. He has hitherto failed to do it, and has taken no notice of my respectful request; and in his last number thinks that the question is not debatable. As he has given no proof to sustain his proposition, it does seem that there is no room for debate. And it is a very easy way, and perhaps the only way, for a disputant who can offer no proof to sustain his propositions, to say it is indisputable, and stop there.

But he goes off into a paroxysm, and speaks of the

---

(1) 1 John iii, 4.   (2) 2 Tim. iii, 16, 17.   (3) James i, 25.

"logic of the fearful and terrible events transpiring," as being proof; gets "dizzy and bewildered;" seems to think that the President's abolition proclamation settles the question, and asks "who shall doubt" that it is an emanation from God; shrieks like a maniac in "the conflict, the storm, and the tempest" now unhappily existing in our beloved country; and says that it is God's work.

"It was the Puritan meddling with the moral *status* of slavery that inflicted this fearful contest upon us," and not the good Lord. And when called upon to sustain the Puritan assertions as to the moral *status* of slavery by the good word of the Lord, such hallucinations are given us in a grave discussion of the question!

"Fanaticism is the bane of harmony. It has disturbed many States, and overturned many governments. It is one of the most difficult social evils to deal with. It is a growth of prosperity, and yet gains strength under persecution. It often appeals to the most generous prejudices of humanity; it often wears the garb of religion and morality; it has wonderful powers of proselytism; it has great capacity to make wrong look like right, and to deck errors in the robes of truth. IT IS A TERRIBLE APOSTLE OF EVIL. Discord follows its lead, and revolution, too often, is the end of its career."

O. B. asserted that God had never granted property in man. I produced three instances from the divine volume where he had granted property in man—to Shem and Japheth, to Israel, and to the civil governments. He tried to avoid the first by asserting that the Canaanites served Israel, while the Israelites were serving the Egyptians, and thus fulfilled and exhausted that grant. I replied that Israel was not Japheth, and was only a part of Shem; and that the curse of Canaan, to be a servant of servants to his brethren, meant being servants to the posterity of Ham, and not to Shem and Japheth, or any portion of either, as Israel was. To meet this, he says he has "satisfactorily disposed of his [my] argument drawn from the curse of Canaan!" Well, if this statement is true of my brother O. B. and those who agree with him, abolition intellects are easily satisfied. But it is consonant with the assertion that the question is not debatable—his proposition is to be taken as indisputably true without proof.

But he says that I claim that the Hebrew law of servitude sanctions chattel slavery among the christians! I have claimed no such thing. I quoted the Hebrew law of servitude *as proof* that God *had granted property in man*—granted it to Israel—and showed who Israel was since the Lord's kingdom was set up. I quoted it as proof of a grant of property in man, which he asserted God had never made; and he thus tries to dodge it by changing the issue. But I shall not let him do it. I know how slippery those who take his position are; and it is my duty, in this grave discussion before the brotherhood and the world, to not let him dodge out of the issue in that way, without exposing the dodge. Whenever those who are constantly asserting slavery to be sinful, are impaled upon the sword of the Spirit, which is the word of God, they always attempt to dodge away from it, by raising another and different issue. Brother O. B. is attempting it now, and it is my duty to show it to our readers.

He asserted that God had not granted property in man. I showed that he had through Noah. He tried to dodge it as above stated; which really was an admission that there had been a grant made; but the dodge was, that it was not a very large grant, and it had been fulfilled and exhausted. I showed that God had granted the heathen to Israel. He tries in his last, to dodge that, by raising a new issue, and insisting that the laws of God gave to govern the slave property created by that grant, were different from the laws of the slave States of this Union. What a weak attempt at a dodge! He admits the grant of property—the very thing in issue—but tries to get round the admission, and do away its effect, by raising in the mind of the reader a new issue, as to whether the laws given by God to govern the Hebrew enjoyment of slave property were the same or different from the laws governing the enjoyment of slave property in the United States. That question is not material in determining whether God has granted property in man or not, and in determining whether it is a sin to hold such property, and exercise the rights of such ownership.

I said that the grants of property in man given through Moses had not been revoked by the Lord, and the things granted resumed by him; and I desired my brother O. B. to cite us to the passage of the divine volume revoking those grants, if there was one. He, in his last, cites us to Gal. v, 4, which reads thus: "Christ is become of no effect unto you, whosoever of you are justified by the law; ye are fallen from grace." *Justified* is here used in the sense of *saved* or *pardoned;* and hence, what Paul here asserts is, that those who seek to obtain pardon of their sins, in the manner and by the means prescribed in the law, are fallen from grace or favor, which is the means of pardon set out in the Gospel. And this O. B. quotes as a revocation of the grant of property in man, when it only shows that there had been a change in the system of pardon or justification in the christian dispensation of grace or favor, from the system prescribed in the law of Moses for pardon. He requests us to read the whole of the letter to the Galatians. Well, I have done it, and I hope our readers will do the same, and they will see, as I see, that which inspiration teaches plainly, that it was the "*handwriting of ordinances*," that the Lord "blotted out" "and took out of the way, nailing them to his cross,"[1] and "abolished in his flesh the enmity *even the law of commandments concerning ordinances*,"[2] and not grants of property given through Noah or Moses. Those grants are not hand-writings of ordinances. And there are many other grants besides those under consideration, as the grants of the earth and the animal creation to man, and of the land of Canaan to Israel, &c. None of these were blotted out or taken out of the way by the Lord, because they were not hand-writings of ordinances, nor commandments concerning ordinances. But recurring back to things under consideration, the laws governing the enjoyment of the slaves granted to Israel, of the heathen, were hand-writings of ordinances, and were blotted out and taken out of the way, and the laws prescribed in the apostolic writings for the government of masters and slaves, and the enjoyment and use of slave property, were substituted for, and took the place of, the laws given through Moses for the government of the relation of master and slave, and the use of slave property; and the grant of property in slaves still stood untouched. Whether my brother O. B. has not acquired this "knowledge of God," that is, knowledge communicated of God, or,

---

(1) Col. ii, 14.   (2) Eph. ii, 15.

if he has, whether he wants to prevent the brotherhood from "coming to" this "knowledge," it is not material to this discussion to have answered; but it is my duty to see that the brotherhood are not kept from this "knowledge," under any pretense whatever. It was the hand-writing of ordinances that was taken away by the Lord and nailed to his cross, and not any grant of property or privilege, or prescription of morals set out in the Decalogue, that was taken away by the Lord. Peter, in his speech in the college of apostles recorded Acts xv, when the question was, whether the Gentiles should be circumcised, and keep the law of Moses, the hand-writing of ordinances, said, that that yoke should not be put upon the disciples, but that through the favor of the Lord Jesus Christ—the means of pardon prescribed by him—all *should be saved*, and not by being circumcised and keeping the law of Moses.

Whether the slave laws prescribed through Moses were better or worse than the slave laws that were prescribed through the apostles, and which took the place of those prescribed through Moses, is wholly immaterial to the inquiries, Did God grant property in man? Is holding and enjoying that property sin? Neither is it material whether the slave laws of the slave States of the Union are better or worse than those of Moses, or of the apostles, in determining whether the relation of master and slave is sinful. The laws governing the marriage relation in a State may be bad, but that does not prove the relation sinful. So the laws of a slave State, governing the relation of master and slave, may be bad, but that does not prove the relation sinful.

I am thus particular in stating these matters, that the reader may not be misled by the two columns of disquisition on the Mosaic slave laws given by O. B. in his last, and to fully explain the effort he is making to change the issue. In a good portion of his disquisition he is in error; but it is entirely immaterial to the question in issue in this discussion to show it; and I intend not to be drawn off from the issue. But there is one thing that he says that I shall notice, because of the gross manner in which the public mind has been abused by it. He says:

"From the bench of our highest national judicial tribunal, it has been declared, that 'the African has no rights which the white man is bound to respect,'" and then goes on to argue as if the court had so held.

In the Dred Scott case, the Supreme Court of the United States, speaking of public opinion in relation to the negroes, that "prevailed in the civilized and enlightened portions of the world at the time of the Declaration of Independence, and when the Constitution was formed and adopted," stated, as a historical fact, that,

"They had for more than a century before been regarded as beings of an inferior order, and altogether unfit to associate with the white race, either in social or political relations; and so far inferior that they had no rights which a white man was bound to respect."

The court did not say whether that regarding was correct or incorrect; but merely stated it as a historical fact that they had been so regarded for more than a century before the Declaration of Independence. And yet brother O. B., from that, and that alone, affirms what is above stated. It has been affirmed thousands of times. *A cause that resorts to such perversions and falsifications, it seems to me, must be sinful.* O. B. lets off nearly a column upon this false assumption, as to what the Supreme Court adjudicated. He is too good a lawyer not to know that the authority does not sustain what he assumes that it does. His premises being false, of course his argument is at fault, and his conclusions erroneous. And more than that, they are immaterial to the question at issue, whether true or false.

The assertion that God had not granted property in man, is a main foundation pillar in the abolition theory. O. B. set out with it, and still asserts it, notwithstanding I have shown to the contrary three instances of the grant. I will now add these others: that the husband has property in the wife, and the wife in the husband; parents have property in their children, and children in their parents; all granted by God, and enjoined by him in every dispensation. This assumption that God has not granted property in man, like every other assumption of the abolition theory, is untrue.

I again respectfully request and insist that brother O. B. cite us to the law of the Lord of which slavery is a transgression. The debate is half out now, and it is time that he would furnish us some proof of his proposition.

I also respectfully request him to inform our readers, if

slavery is a sin, and slaveholders sinners, why are they not so specifically denominated in the christian Scriptures? Murder, adultery, lying, covetousness, idolatry, evil-speaking, evil-surmising, emulation, wrath, strife, sedition, heresy, or making sects, &c., are all specifically denounced as sins; and murderers, adulterers, liars, covetous, idolators, backbiters, false accusers, &c., are all specifically denounced as sinners. If slavery was a sin, and slaveholders sinners, why did not the apostles say so in enumerating sins and sinners? There were then, when they wrote, as much slavery as there was adultery, and as many slaveholders as there were adulterers; why was one specified and the other not, if they were equally sins and sinners? And so of the others.

And I will say, in all kindness, that those who honestly desire to "come to the knowledge of the truth" of God upon this, and upon all moral questions, must look to, examine, and study his word, his revealed will, and not run off, nor allow others to lead them off, into such wild rhapsdies as are contained in the first four paragraphs of O. B.'s last article. He, and those who agree with him, have erroneously worked themselves into the belief that slavery is sin. His having failed so far in this discussion, to show the law that slavery is a transgression of, and therefore a sin, shows that he and they are in error. But upon that error, for years, "they have sown the winds," and alas! our unhappy country and people are now "reaping the whirlwind."[1] And whilst the storm is raging so fiercely and fearfully, to refer to the fact of its existence as proof that they and he are right, is the wildest fanaticism, and wholly out of place in a grave religious inquiry after the truth of God upon the subject.

J. S.

October 20th, 1862.

P. S.—Professional duty requiring me to attend the court of an adjoining county last week, I was thereby prevented from getting this number ready in time for to-morrow's *Record*.   J. S.

---

(1) Hosea viii, 7.

EPISODE.

Abolition tactics, and "the moral character," not of slavery, but of the abolition conduct that carried out and executed those tactics, make it my imperative duty to put on record here, and lay before the public certain facts and transactions that never should have occurred; but, having occurred, had the law of Christ been followed and acted upon, they would have been buried in the tomb of the Capulets, and consigned to perpetual oblition.

I am sometimes inclined to think that this necessity has been imposed upon me in the providence of God, that the deformities of abolitionism may be the more fully exposed, by having this phase of it exhibited to the public. But whether this is so or not, future events must determine.

As stated in the postscript to my last article, professional duty required my attendance at the Circuit Court of the adjoining county of Jay, on the 15th of October, 1862. Gross personal outrages were perpetrated upon me there by certain sons of Belial, set on and incited by certain political demagogues, that drove me from court, and prevented me from attending to my business there According to the old, homely, but true proverb, "If I do you a wrong, you can forgive me; but if you do me a wrong, you can never forgive me," the men who instigated the perpetration of this great wrong upon me, could not forgive me for the wrong they had done me, but followed it up with a still greater wrong. They caused to be published in the *Winchester Journal*, an abolition hebdomadel paper printed in the town where I reside, a grossly scurrilous article concerning me and that transaction. It appeared in that paper of the date of Friday, the 24th of October. On that day, two of the demagogues went to Indianapolis, and on Monday morning, October 27th, the scurrilous article appeared in the *Indianapolis Journal*, the abolition sess-pool of all the political filth and falsehood of Indiana.

It was too gross to have a place in any decent print, and, of course, can not be inserted here. In addition to the fact that all its statements of the facts of the transaction were false, it falsely charged me with "being drunk, and swearing worse than an Algerine pirate;" with "swearing terribly, and using the most abusive language;" with saying that Shanks and "all his supporters were G—d d—d niggerites;" with "ringing the changes of the most profane vocabulary, denouncing the soldiers also as a set of G—d d—d tories, and secessionists and traitors;" and that I "now swore more terribly, denouncing Shanks as a traitor, and calling the soldiers 'd—d traitors and secessionists,' and swore that had (I) been at Mumfordsville when our soldiers were taken prisoners, and had the authority, (I) would have hung every G—d d—d one of them, as they were all d—d traitors.

I am sorry to have to soil my pages with such filthy falsehoods; but thus much is necessary that the reader may understand what follows.

Upon my demand, the conductors of the *Winchester Journal*, though somewhat reluctantly, published my defence in their next succeeding paper, of the date of the 31st of October, 1862.

Without any communication whatever with me, either orally, by letter, or through third persons, my brother GOODWIN published in the *Record* of the 4th of November, 1862, the following:

DISCUSSION OF SLAVERY.

Our readers have noticed a discussion of the moral character of slavery by O. B. and J. S., which has been publishing for some weeks in the *Christian Record*. The discussion has been read so far with a good degree of interest by many; but just as it was assuming a greater degree of interest, by approaching the New Testament argument, we have seen certain reports in the public prints, touching the recent conduct of J. S., which compels us to close our columns against the further prosecution of the discussion until he sets himself right before the religious public. If Bro.

EPISODE. 175

O. B. wishes to give his views of the New Testament Scriptures in reference to the duties of masters and servants, without referring in any way to the discussion, he may do so through our columns.

Thus the reader will see, that, notwithstanding I was in his editorial house, mansion, or church, and in there as a christian, and a christian disputant or debater, and with his assent and permission as such christian disputant and debater, without taking one step, or doing one act required by the law of Christ in such cases, as well as by common courtesy between man and man, even of those who never recognized the relation of brethren in Christ as existing between them, my *quondam* brother GOODWIN so far endorsed these foul charges as to publicly in his paper, before the whole brotherhood, so far as his paper circulated among them, excommunicate, or rather thrust me out of his religious paper, house, mansion or church, and tell my *quondam* opponent to proceed, but to get on into the New Testament, and give his (the abolition) views of what that says about the question under discussion. He, GOODWIN, was not only *a bishop* and *an elder* in that religious journal, but he was sole bishop, elder, and autocrat of it.

Immediately on the reception of his paper of the 4th of November, I sent the following communication to him:

ELDER E. GOODWIN, *Editor Christian Record:*—As I presume from what you say in the *Record* of the 4th inst., that it would be offensive to you for me to call you brother, I do not so address you; for the Lord commands me to " give none offence, neither to the Jews, nor to the Gentiles, nor to the church of God;"[1] and my desire at all times is to avoid sinning by transgressing his commands, though alas! I daily more or less transgress, and thereby sin. And were it not that the good Lord has opened up a way and given me access to the Father, and is there an Advocate for me, whereby I may obtain the forgiveness of my sins thus daily committed, I would be ruined and lost, entirely and hopelessly.

You say: " We have seen certain reports in the public

---

(1) 1 Cor. x, 32.

prints touching the recent conduct of J. S., which compels us to close our columns against the further prosecution of the discussion, until he sets himself right before the religious public."

Did you know that those "certain reports" were written out and circulated in "the public prints," by two political demagogues, who are infidels in religion? Did you know that "the public prints" that circulated those reports were political partizan prints, and hence nought but sess-pools of filth and falsehood? Did you pursue the course laid down by yourself, under the head of Discipline, in the Address on the Government and Discipline of the church, published in the *Record* of October 28th, as proper to be pursued?[1] Did you follow the rules you there laid down, that "in dealing with members charged with crime, the *first* object should be *to secure to all* their rights, and do *justice* to all; and the final object should be *to save* the offender, if possible; and *if this be not possible*, to save the church from

---

(1) That the reader may see the difference between brother Goodwin's statements of the law, and his action in this case, I append the following extracts from that address:

"On this subject I remark, first, that we may contemplate all the offences claiming the attention of the overseers of the church into two classes: first, such as arise from disagreements between brethren, or where one brother does a wrong to another; and, secondly, breaches of the law which affect the whole brotherhood alike, such as profane swearing, drunkenness, and such like. Now, in dealing with members charged with crime, the first object should be *to secure to all their rights*, and to do justice to all; and the final object should be *to save the offender, if possible;* and if this be not possible, to save the church from scandal."

* * * * * *

"In cases of the first class named above, the elders should see the parties as soon as possible, and endeavor to reconcile them to each other. This should be done without making special charges against either. If the matter is not generally known, and the reconciliation is effected, nothing more is necessary in the case; but if it has been noised abroad, and the members of the congregation generally, or any considerable number of them know that any such difficulty has existed, then the elder presiding at the first meeting of the church subsequent to the reconciliation, should announce to the congregation that the difficulty had been adjusted, and that the parties are now reconciled to each other."

* * * * * *

"A similar course should be pursued in reference to the second class of offences. If a member of the church should be guilty of profane swearing, or drunkenness, or any other violation of the law of Christ, the elders, or some one of them, who would be likely to have the most influence with him, *should visit him in kindness, and tell in love the crime that he is said to be guilty of, and try to restore him.* If he should deny the charge, and the report is so generally known and *believed** as to bring a reproach upon the good cause, let him be requested to meet the elders in their official meeting; let those knowing the facts appear as witnesses, and let the accused brother make his defence. If found guilty, *an effort should be made to bring him to repentance.* If this point is gained, he should come before the church, and, either in person, or through one of the elders, make confession of his fault, and state his determination to do so no more, *upon which he should be forgiven.* But if he remain stubborn, and refuse to make satisfaction for his wrong doing, it should be announced to the church that he has forfeited the fellowship of the brotherhood, and can be no longer regarded as a member." And then, and not till then, may the offender be publicly kicked out of a religious paper, if he refuses to go out without being thus publicly expelled.

---

* This foul charge in my case was not believed even partially, much less generally, by those who knew me.

scandal"? Or, did you from "certain reports," written by infidels, and circulated by them in filthy partizan prints, without taking any of the steps laid down by yourself in that address, as being those to be taken to comply with the divine injunction, "Let all things be done decently and in order," that is to say, without visiting, without trial, without conviction, without effort to bring to repentance, and without any knowledge on my part of what you were about to do, excommunicate me, whom you have heretofore professed to regard as a member with you of the body of the blessed Lord, and publish that excommunication, not only to the church of the brotherhood, but to the world?

The answer to these questions already exist for eternity. I do not ask them to accuse or criminate you, (for God forbids that I should be an "accuser of the brethren,") but because the word of the Lord says: "Brethren, if any of you do err from the truth, and one convert him, let him know that he who converteth a sinner from the error of his way, shall save a soul from death, and shall hide a multitude of sins."[1]

After having thus adjudged, and convicted, and excommunicated me, you tell me I may set myself right before the religious public. Well, this is a privilege for which I am very thankful. It is true that your course, like that of the administration for a year past, first to condemn, seize, and incarcerate, and then to let the culprit, if he can in his dungeon, prove that he is not guilty of anything, is similar to the civil and religious liberty enjoyed when the Inquisition in religious, and despots in civil governments, had universal control of Christendom, and looks to me like retrogression to the dark ages, instead of being a still brighter effulgence of the Gospel light, and of the liberty wherewith Christ has made his people free, and an advance of civil liberty in the freest form of government, and hitherto the freest government ever constructed or existing for man, in these United States of America, in the afternoon of the nineteenth century. But still as I am not blessed with transcendental notions of "free speech, free press, free soil, free men, and Fremont," I suppose that I must, out of courtesy to those who are so endowed, accept it as progression in light and liberty, civil and religious.

---

(1) James v, 19, 20.

I will therefore proceed to state the efforts I have made to set myself right before the world, including the religious public, since the gross and false libel of me was published in the *Winchester Journal* of the 24th of October, and copied into the *Indianapolis Journal* of the 27th.

I prepared an article, which, though the conductors of the *Winchester Journal* winced considerably at having to publish it in their paper, they thought proper not to refuse to do so. On the day of its publication, I wrote a letter to the Indianapolis Journal Company, directed to J. M. Tilford as its President, of which the following is a copy:

WINCHESTER, Oct. 31st, 1862.

To the Indianapolis Journal Company:—As the article libelous of me was copied from the *Winchester Journal* of the 24th instant into your paper of the 27th instant, I claim, as an act of justice, that my article contained in the *Winchester Journal* of to-day be forthwith copied into your paper; and I hope you will not refuse to comply with this request. Respectfully, &c.,
JER. SMITH.
J. M. Tilford, Pres. Ind. Journal Co.

Accompanying which, I sent a private note to Tilford, of which the following is a copy:

BRO. TILFORD :—I send the enclosed to you as the President of the Journal Company, and all that I have to say now, is, that divine writ informs us that the "serpent cast out of his mouth water [lies, vituperation and slander] as a flood after the woman, that he might cause her to be carried away by the flood," and I, as one of the least among "the remnant of her seed,"[1] have to receive my portion of that flood of calumny, it seems.

May the good Lord, out of his abundant mercy, pardon all who have been concerned in doing me this great wrong, and thereby sinning, is my prayer.
Affectionately, &c.,
JER. SMITH.

---

(1) Rev. xii, 15-17.

My article not having appeared in the *Journal*, on the 5th of November I sent the following:

WINCHESTER, Nov. 5th, 1862.

J. M. TILFORD, *Pres. Indianapolis Journal Co.—Sir:—*
On the 31st ult. I sent a request to the Journal Company, directed to you as its President, that my reply to the gross and false libel of me, published in the *Winchester Journal* of the 24th of October, and copied into your paper of the 27th of October, be copied into your paper as an act of justice to me. It has not yet been done. I write this to again urge that it be done; for I am anxious to avoid the necessity of having to bring a suit for libel against the Journal Company. Whether all sense of truth and justice has left the earth, and law is dethroned, and only fraud, force, and anarchy exist in our unhappy country, I am not able to say; but I really fear that it is so.

Respectfully, &c.,

JER. SMITH.

My article has not yet appeared in the *Journal*, nor have I received any communication from them; which fully shows the fairness, uprightness, and christian *spirit* and *conduct* of the conductors of that sheet; and demonstrates the facilities they have afforded me to set myself right before the world and the religious public; and the extreme anxiety they have to make amends, and undo the wrong they have done me. Tilford is a bishop of the church at Indianapolis; the foreman and the clerk in the *Journal* office are deacons of that church; and I suppose they have seen the divine injunctions, " to speak evil of no man,"[1] and " to do justly, and love mercy."[2] Paul had "perils amongst false brethren."[3] Is it possible that I am entitled to the honor of suffering as he did?

As your paper is printed by that company, and your office is in their building, I think it probable that you had knowledge of these things as they transpired.

As you have brought the matter to the notice of your readers, by publishing your condemnation and excommunication of me upon the false libel, without notice, or hearing,

---

(1) Tit. iii, 2.   (2) Micah vi, 8.   (3) 2 Cor. xi, 26.

or trial, or attempt to reclaim me, I herewith enclose a copy of my published defence, and request you to lay it, with this communication, before your readers. And I hope you will comply with this request. If you do not, I shall have to find some other means of getting them before the public. For, if the Lord spares me, I intend to have all these things laid before the public in some form; for all is known to the Lord, and will be known to all at the great day, and had as well be made known to the public now, though it may be some time yet before they get there. If so, I must exercise, as I am commanded to do, the christian virtue, PATIENCE. I confess, however, here, that in this case it is hard to exercise it. But I am commanded to, and will, "let patience have her perfect work."[1] "Some men's sins do go before, and others they follow after."

It may be, and I have no doubt is, very convenient to O. B. and those who agree with him, to have the discussion choked down now; for he was getting into a very tight place. But truth is mighty, and will finally prevail, though she travels in a slow coach, while falsehood, slander, and detraction, run on the wings of the wind.

It is proper to say here, in conclusion, that the charge of drunkenness made against me in the libel, was not noticed in my published defence herewith enclosed, for good and sufficient reasons, which I have given, and will hereafter give, when proper. All that is necessary or proper here and now to say, is, that the charge is false.

Repeating the prayer, "May the God and Father of all, out of his abundant mercy, forgive all who have been concerned in doing me this great wrong, and thereby sinning," I am, Very respectfully, &c.,

JER. SMITH.

November 10th, 1862.

[From the Winchester Journal.—Enclosed in the foregoing.]

TO THE PUBLIC.

An article in the *Winchester Journal* of last week, abusive of me, an humble citizen in the private walks of life, quietly attending to my own business without molesting or disturbing any one in attending to his, is so utterly false, that I

---

(1) James i, 4.

deem it proper to notice it, lest my silence should be taken as an admission of the truth of the statements contained in it.

That I swore worse than an Algerene pirate, or swore at all, or used profane language, is false. That I said that Shanks and all (or any) of his supporters were traitors and niggerites, is false; but I said that all the niggerites had voted for him, which all know is true. I did not speak about soldiers, nor use the word soldier in either of the conversations hereinafter mentioned; and, of course, did not call them tories, traitors, or secessionists; and I did not say a word about Mumfordsville, nor hanging soldiers, nor hanging any body else. All this was manufactured out of the whole cloth at the time, by those whose object it was to raise a mob.

I went to Portland on the 15th day of October, the day after the election, to attend to some professional business in court. When I arrived there, knowing that Mr. Black, the landlord, was a Democrat, and, of course, an anti-Shank man, I jocularly remarked as I drove up, as I have heard remarked perhaps a hundred times in my life, "Is this a Shank tavern? If it is, I guess I'll go farther." Mr. Black, coming up to my buggy, remarked, "I guess it's all right, Judge; get out." I again jocularly remarked that I did not want to patronize an abolition house.

Some of the persons around (none of whom I knew) angrily began to denounce me as a secessionist, &c., and I denounced abolitionists back again, and within a minute of the time I stopped my buggy, Mr. Underwood came up to my buggy, and said that he was Marshal of the county, and warned me how I talked. This fired me up, and I said excitedly, "Well, you had better arrest me and take me to Fort Lafayette; I dare you to do it." He mildly replied, that we dare to do things that we do not want to do; and to get out and put up. His manner and language at once calmed my excitement, and I remarking, " Let these scoundrels not bother me then," or " keep away from me," or "let me alone;" I do not remember which way I said it; got out of my buggy, and went into the sitting-room of the hotel.

Having sat there some twenty minutes, I went to the court-house, and remained till the court adjourned. Mr.

Hawkins, the clerk, came and saluted me, and I chatted with him till all had left the court-house, when I returned to the hotel.

After supper, in the dusk of the evening, I started out to the stable to see my horse, as it is my custom. Mr. Joseph Maddox met me on the way, and commenced talking with me about politics, he urging Republican views, and I sustaining Democratic views. The conversation was mild and respectful by both of us, and continued some five or ten minutes, perhaps longer. In the meantime, a considerable crowd gathered around us, when a young man at my left hand said, "Old man, you must hush up." Another immediately, at my right hand, said with an oath, "You must leave." Maddox immediately crouched down and slid away from between them. I was surprised, but was immediately convinced that there was concert among them to do me personal violence. The two men who thus first spoke I did not know, and they were dressed in soldier's clothing. About a half dozen voices immediately spoke up. I stepped a few paces to the fence, and placed my back against it. I was wholly unarmed. The cries were, "you must leave in twenty minutes;" "where's a watch;" "hang him;" "ride him on a rail;" where's a rail," &c. I said I had come to court to attend to my business in court, and I had a right to stay and attend to it. "You shan't;" "let it go undone;" "you called us secessionists," &c., were halloaed back in the crowd. I continued, and said that I had started to the stable to see to my horse, and came across Mr. Maddox, and stopped and talked with him; and I have said nothing disrespectful of any of you—which was true. All this transpired within two minutes of time. A kind of lull then occurred. I saw a little opening in the crowd to my left hand, towards the house. I started to the house; the second or third step I was tripped and fell. A friend, whose voice I knew, stooped over me and told me to get up, and come with him into the house. I did so, and at the instance of friends, I was conducted to a place of concealment, where I remained an hour or more, I should guess. A friend then came and told me that my buggy was ready, and it was agreed that I should get into it and go to Mr. Jonas Votaw's. I went with him to my buggy, surrounded by a crowd, got into it, and drove off. Soon after I crossed the creek, Mr. Votaw came riding on behind me. We went on to his house, put up our horses, and I stayed all night.

Next morning, after breakfast, while the mail was being opened by Mr. Votaw and lady, the soldiers' wagons came along, and stopped in the road opposite the house. One of them came in whom I knew to be the second one who had spoken on the night previous at my right hand, but did not know his name. He stayed in some five or ten minutes, eyeing me sitting in the public room, and then went out; and after a while they started off. Had he or any of them then offered violence to me, I should have killed them. My friends had furnished me arms, and I then had them. Had I had them on the previous night, I should have killed two men. I am glad that I did not have them; for God knows that I do not want to shed the blood of a fellow creature.

Brave men do not, fifteen or twenty of them together, attack a single unarmed man, whether they wear soldier-clothes, shoulder-straps, or have held a seat in Congress. Cowards only are cruel to the weak and defenceless.

I remained publicly at Mr. Votaw's till after dinner. By the advice of friends, whose counsel it was my duty to respect, I did not go back to Portland, but came home in the evening, arriving there before dark.

As to the contemptible lies about John Bowden, in the article:

I sold him a farm in Jay county three years ago last March. He has paid but about $80 on it, and has had the use of it for four crops, worth $400; and has sold off and destroyed the timber. He promised me a year ago, when I took judgment for $1,086 92 of the purchase money then due and unpaid, that he would pay $400 by Christmas, and I agreed to wait a year for the balance without security, if he made the payment; and it was so entered in the record of the judgment. He did not make the payment, and I sued out execution, and it was returned no property found. In May last he promised me to pay $500 by harvest, or surrender the title-bond without costs or trouble. He did not do it, and I wrote twice to him afterwards, and could get no answer from him, nor the bond. About the first of September, I had an offer for the land at a loss to me of only about $200, and the offer was to stand open till Christmas. I again wrote to Bowden, reminding him of what he had promised, and requesting him to surrender the bond, or I should take steps at the fall court to sell out his equity. He failed to answer, and about that time volunteered. I brought the suit; went out to take my decree and sell out his equity, and get *my* property into my possession, which I had a clear, legal, and equitable right to have. He, with the assistance of two others, got up the mob, resulting as above stated, notwithstanding the court and all its officers were present. The law was powerless in protecting me in my legal rights, and afforded me no protection. Bowden got the decree rendered, giving him to July next before a sale of his equity can be made, *without his giving any security whatever for the purchase-money, all being due.* He will not pay it, nor a cent of it, and is utterly insolvent and worthless, and will get nearly another year's use of the farm, making $500 in all. I lose a sale, and by that time, the farm will probably not sell for more than half what is due me, including the costs which he has compelled me to make. Thus he affected the object he had in raising the mob. Had I dreamed it possible he could have so succeeded, I should have gone back to court, though I should have been thereby put under the necessity of killing three or four persons, and perhaps of losing my own life. And now, in addition to all this, to try to cover up these gross outrages perpetrated upon me, this torrent of abusive falsehood is published to overwhelm me if possible.

I had no *personal* hostility to Mr. Shanks. I had *political* hostility to him for two reasons: 1st. He is wholly unqualified to fill a seat in Congress. 2d. He sustained measures in Congress utterly subversive and destructive of the Constitution and the Union, both of which I am very anxious to preserve for my posterity as I have enjoyed them. And when my country's all is at stake, as it now is, in a choice between its interests and personal friendships, I hesitate not a moment to take my stand for my country.

Gross and groundless as these outrages are to me personally, I sorrow less for them on that account, than because they add another to the many evidences we have of the rapid speed with which the Constitution and the laws are being overturned and destroyed, and anarchy, internecine strife and the reign of terror are being inaugurated in our beloved but unhappy country. The result of the recent elections give me a gleam of hope that daylight is coming. Had abolitionism succeeded again in the elections this fall, our beloved Union, and the Constitution that forms it, and the Government, would have been hopelessly gone. The abolitionists and the secessionists are but the two blades of the same pair of shears, that have been, and are, shearing this Union and Government to shreds. Either without the other would be powerless and harmless. But together, how potent for mischief they are, and have been! This I have said, and warned my countrymen of, for years. And now it is shown by what an intelligent rebel officer, taken prisoner at the battle of Antietam, recently said, as reported in the *Boston Courier*, an old line Whig paper. He said:

"I tell you there is not one thing old Jeff. prays for so much as to have Wadsworth put in Governor of New York. I was in Richmond when the papers with the nomination came, and they all said there could not have been a more lucky nomination. * * * * The abolitionists have got control of the North just as we have of the South, and they don't want us any more than we do them; and what persons on both sides don't want, they won't have. If Wadsworth should be beaten, and Andrew should be beaten, and the rest of them, it would just show that a majority of the North want us back in the old Union, and there are so many now in the South who want the same thing, we should have to come back. But I tell you, the abolitionists will have it all their own way, and your Northern old line Unionists and their relatives down South, will have to cave in."

Thank God! the abolitionists have not had it all their own way so far, and every patriot and true Union man prays God that they may not have it all their own way in the elections to come off next week, so that old line Unionists, of whom I am proud to know that I am one, and always have been, will not have to cave in either North or South, and our glorious Union, and the Constitution, formed by the fathers of the Revolution, and sealed with their blood, and the Government created by that Constitution, will be saved from their present extreme peril, and handed down to our posterity as we received them from our fathers. And I rejoice, that I, even I, in my humble and obscure private position, "am counted worthy to suffer shame" for being an old line Unionist, and trying to bring about a consummation so devoutly to be wished.

JER. SMITH.

October 27th, 1862.

[*See Appendix.*]

By letter of the date of November 17th, 1862, Elder GOODWIN declined publishing the foregoing articles, on the ground that they were "too political in their character" for his columns; when in truth, at that time, and before, and since, at least two columns of every issue of his paper, were exclusively political, while much of the professedly religious matter of his paper was terribly mixed with politics. The charge itself was political, made by politicians, in political papers, for political purposes. This political matter was made the ground of excommunicating me from the *Record*, and forsooth, the *Record* can not publish my side of the affair, because it is political!

Paul was frequently mobbed by incitement of hypocrites, existing then as well as now, on charges of "disloyalty," and of being "a traitor," saying there was "another king, one Jesus," &c.; but the christians of that day protected him and sent him away,[1] instead of thrusting him out, and requiring him to set himself right before the community. Those christians, however, were not "philanthropists" and "humanitarians," such as modern abolitionists are.

In the *Christian Record* of the date of November 18th, 1862, the following article appeared:

DISCUSSION OF SLAVERY.

PROPOSITION—*Slavery is Sinful.*

O. B.'S SIXTH AFFIRMATIVE.

"If the son, therefore, shall make you free, ye shall be free indeed."[2]

I regret that there should have been any occasion for breaking off the discussion between J. S. and myself. Under the circumstances I feel much embarrassed in attempting to proceed further in the consideration of the subject.

---

(1) Acts xvii, 6–10, and 13–15; xix, 24–41; xx, 1.   (2) John viii, 36.

But as the argument would be incomplete without some reference to the christian Scriptures, and to those teachings of the apostles, which are frequently cited to prove the righteousness of slavery, I conclude to avail myself to some extent of the privilege which the editor of the *Record* offers me. I can not, however, avoid an occasional reference to the preceding discussion, as my arguments in it are parts and portions of the main argument, to prove the sinfulness of American slavery, and are regarded by me as preliminary to the consideration of the teachings of the christian Scriptures upon that subject. As the matter now stands, I shall make no effort to elaborate the different points of the argument, but simply indicate them, and leave them to the reflection of the reader. There are some things in the articles of J. S. which I had purposed noticing in the progress of the debate, but as the debate is closed, it is but right and proper that I pass them without notice.

I think I have shown, that God in no grant of property to man, has granted the right of property in man, but that, on the contrary, he has clearly reserved that right to himself. The only cases in the Old Testament Scriptures, under which such a grant has been claimed, are the Noachian curse of Canaan, and the Hebrew law of servitude. These I have examined separately, and have, as I think, satisfactorily shown that the idea of chattel slavery is not involved in either of them. I have shown further, that in the Hebrew law that condition is clearly excluded. A further argument to sustain this position might be drawn from the social condition and anti-slavery sentiments of the Jews in the times of Christ and of his apostles. The permanent laws and institutions of any people have a controlling influence in forming their social condition and moral sentiments. This is peculiarly true of the Jews. In speaking of them, of the time of the apostles, our Bro. Campbell, in some of his writings upon the subject of slavery, has said that they were a nation of abolitionists. Any one who studies their social condition, in the light of the New Testament history, and of the parables of our Lord, will be satisfied that chattel slavery had no existence in Jewish society, and that the moral sentiment was adverse to it. This, by clear inference, is one lesson taught by the parable of the prodigal son. The purpose of the parable required, that the prodigal, as the result of his folly and crime, should be reduced from a high social position—a condition of ease and affluence—to the lowest, most dependent, and most degraded condition known in Jewish society; and that in such condition, the repentant prodigal should be so humbled as to desire, and be willing to accept the lowest and most humble position in society, which, in the regard of the Master, was consistent with personal manhood, and the right and proper discharge of the duties of man to himself, to humanity, and to God. These that purpose required, and if these points are not reached in the representation of the life of the prodigal, the parable itself is a failure, for want of point and force. But the parable is not a failure. It was uttered by the infallible One; and while involving a moral lesson of the deepest import to humanity, delineates faithfully and truly the then conditions of Jewish society. The prodigal, who foolishly and wickedly took from his father an advancement of his whole portion of the paternal estates, " and gathered all together, and took his journey into a far country, and there wasted his substance with riotous living," was reduced to the lowest, most dependent and degraded condition of humanity known in Jewish society, which is thus described: " And he went and joined himself to a citizen of that country, and he sent him into his fields to feed swine. And he would fain have filled his belly with the husks that the swine did eat, and no man gave unto him."[1] Here is described the lowest condition of humanity known in Jewish society. It was truly low enough. It involves, to some extent, the sacrifice of personal manhood and the ability to discharge his proper duties to himself, to humanity, and to God. It was below the condition of a hired servant, for he labored, not for wages, but merely to sustain existence. It was not, however, the condition of a slave. No man held property in him. He could still dispose of his own person, and control his own actions, as his subsequent determination and action clearly show. That condition, however, was neither proper nor right for man, in the regard of the Master. It must have been regarded as sinful, for the prodigal, in his deepest repentance and humility, is represented as desiring to escape it, and to have the position of a hired servant. A hired servant, then, occupies the lowest condition of hu-

---

(1) Luke xv.

manity, approved by the Master. Humility can descend no lower. Whatever is beneath that, is personal debasement. Since the primeval curse, labor has been, and still is, the basis of all human society. Compensated labor is the basis of all good and virtuous society, and is so recognized by the Master in the parable of the prodigal. Society built upon the basis of enforced and uncompensated labor, is necessarily vicious and corrupt.

I have had occasion in a former number to speak of the meaning of the word servant, as used in common version of the Scriptures. I trust that the reader will recollect that argument. It applies perhaps as well to the use of the term in the New as in the Old Testament. Besides this, the New Testament Scriptures incidentally furnish some indication of the import of the term in New Testament use, which show very clearly that chattel slavery is not meant by it, or included in it. A slave, in legal contemplation, is like other property, held by a perpetual tenure, and is, in legal phrase, vested in the owner, his heirs and assigns forever. Of the servant the Lord said: "And the servant abideth not in the house forever; but the son abideth ever."[1] Perpetuity of tenure is an essential quality of slave property, and this saying of the Lord shows clearly that a servant had not this essential characteristic of the condition of a slave.

Not only in this particular, but also in the social condition of the servant, and in the character and qualities of his service, the Scriptures show that there is a clear and wide distinction between him and a slave. The slave is an abject, holding no position in human society, regarded as a thing, a species of property, an article of traffic, a menial and a servile, without independent volition, without manhood, put to the lowest uses of humanity. This is not the condition of a servant, or the character or quality of his service, in the view of the apostle Paul, as shown by the following language: "Now I say that the heir, as long as he is a child, *diffeleth nothing from a servant*, though he be Lord of all, but is under tutors and governors until the time appointed of the Father."[2] This shows that in his social condition of personal manhood, and in the character and quality of his service, the servant did not differ from the son;

---

(1) John viii, 35.   (2) Gal. iv, 1, 2.

hence he could not have been a slave—could not have been held and regarded as property.

Without attempting to define, these two passages illustrate the meaning of the word servant as used in the New Testament Scriptures. That meaning is wholly inconsistent with the idea of chattel slavery, and such an idea could not have been involved in the use of the term. This fact is well worthy of being remembered in the consideration of this subject.

In some translations later than the common version, the word slave is used in some places in which the word servant occurs in the common version. It is not necessary for me to question the correctness of these later translations. Possessing no knowledge of the original language, I am not qualified to decide upon their merit; but if correct, they afford additional evidence of the truth of the proposition under discussion. In the progress of society, there have been enlargements of the fields of thought, and a closer and more critical analysis of things and of ideas, requiring improvement in living languages, as well by the addition of new words as by using the old ones in a variety of secondary and figurative meanings. The English language, more than any other, has been thus improved.

While the word slave retains its precise, primary and literal meaning, it has, since the time of James II, obtained use in a secondary and figurative sense. Hence, we say of a person under the controlling influence of wicked, degrading and overmastering habits, that he is the slave of such habits. Of this character are the expressions, the slave of sin, the slave of lust, the slave of passion, &c. Of this character, too, are all the cases in which the word is so used in the later translations. Whenever and wherever this word is used in the secondary and figurative sense, it expresses the wickedness and degradation of the condition it represents. In this sense slavery is sinful. The fact that the word is so figuratively used, proves clearly that in its literal sense and primary meaning, it involves the idea of sin, that the slavery under discussion is sinful, for the word is never used to characterize the influence of correct and righteous habits and feelings. The propriety and correctness of the use of the term in the figurative sense rests wholly upon the admitted sinfulness of slavery in the literal and primary meaning of the word. This argument is conclusive, and singly and unsupported by other argument, would establish the truth of the proposition.

I purpose to attempt the examination and consideration of those teachings of the christian Scriptures, which are relied upon to sustain slavery, but can not do it now, as it would give this article too great a length. I therefore reserve that matter for a future number.

O. B.

Upon the reception of the paper containing the foregoing article, I wrote and sent to brother BUTLER the following letter:

WINCHESTER, Nov. 19th, 1862.

OVID BUTLER, *Elder of the Christian Church at Indianapolis, and President of Board of Directors of the N. W. C. University—Dear Brother:*—The plan to get rid of me as a disputant and respondent, in the discussion of slavery, and to neutralize the divine truths brought to bear upon the question by me, and to stop the ears of the brotherhood and public against them, is fully understood, and shall, if the Lord will, be thoroughly exposed.

The blessed Lord said: "The disciple is not above his master, nor the servant above his lord. It is *enough* for the disciple to be as his *master*, and the *servant* as his *lord*. If they have called the Master of the house Beelzebub, how much more shall they call them of his household? Fear them not, therefore; for there is nothing *covered* that shall not be *revealed;* and *hid* that shall not be *known*."[1] "For there is nothing *hid* which shall not be *manifested;* neither was any thing kept *secret*, but that it *should come abroad*"[2] "Beware ye [the disciples] of the leaven of the Pharisees, *which is hypocrisy*. For there is nothing covered that shall not be revealed; neither *hid*, that shall not *be known*. Therefore, whatsoever ye *have spoken in darkness*, shall be *heard* in the light; and that which ye have spoken *in the ear in the closets*, shall be proclaimed upon the housetops."[3]

It is better for you who aspire to be the leader among the brotherhood of the Northwest, and who really are the leader of the faction of the brotherhood of the Northwest,

---

(1) Matt x, 24-26. (2) Mark iv, 22; Luke viii, 17. (3) Luke xii, 1-3.

who are abolitionized; it is better for the faction of whom you are thus the leader; it is better for the entire brotherhood, and the American people; it is better for the cause of the blessed Lord and Master of us all; and it is better for the truth of God, that you open the columns of the *Record*, and proceed with the discussion to its conclusion. But I have no expectation that it will be done.

I received last night the *Record* of yesterday, in which I find your number six, in which you say "the debate is closed." If so, why do you continue it? Your continuance of it, after your respondent is silenced, is an admission by you, that you had failed to sustain your proposition in his presence. And now, after he is silenced, you wish to try to make the readers of the *Record* believe that your proposition is true.

As you say the debate is closed, I write this letter to know whether or not you will join in the publication of the debate in book form, according to the preliminary stipulations? An early answer is requested.

Very respectfully, &c.,
JER. SMITH.

To which I received the following reply:

FOREST HOME, Nov. 28th, 1862.

BRO. JER. SMITH :—I duly received yours of the 19th inst., but have not been able to reply sooner. I am but little disposed to notice the groundless charges and insinuations against me which yours contains. I am aware that any person who could make them with no better evidence to sustain them than you have, would not be apt to credit their simple denial. I will say, however, that I am not responsible for the closing of the debate between us. That responsibility rests with brother GOODWIN, who, as you well know, controls his own paper; and you know, too, if you will recollect the past, that he is not liable to the charge of being influenced by me. I spoke of the debate being closed as a fact previously announced by the editor of the *Record*, and without any reference to my own wishes upon the subject. I may, however, say in all frankness, that I think brother GOODWIN did right in thus closing the debate until you should vindicate yourself against the charges made against you in the public papers. Those charges are serious ones to be made against a man professing to be a disciple of Jesus. Unanswered by you, they would very naturally, though perhaps unjustly, affect any argument you might use in the debate. If indeed you are as you suppose, advocating divine truth, it is important to a proper and fair consideration of your arguments, that you first dispose of these charges. Whether it be a truth or error, righteousness or sin, that you advocate, I do not desire the advantage in the argument which the existence of those charges unanswered, or not satisfactorily answered, would give me. It would seem to me, therefore, that you have no reason to complain that the debate is closed, or suspended, until you can resume it with nothing extrinsic of the debate to prejudice your arguments. Nor can you complain that I have interposed an article which will give you the right to resume the argument whenever you shall place yourself right in reference to those charges. I do not doubt that brother GOODWIN is not only willing, but anxious, that you should vindicate yourself, and, that done, would open the columns of the *Record* to you. I trust that you can, and hope that you will, do this in time to resume the discussion before the readers of the *Record* shall have forgotten all about it. I propose waiting awhile for such resumption by you; but should you fail to accomplish it, I shall probably desire, in some form, to close my argment.

It is somewhat remarkable, that a person so strongly opposed to fiction as you profess to be, should deal so largely in it. What you say of my leadership or aspirations for the leadership among the Northwestern brethren, or any portion of them, is most decidedly of this character, so palpably so, that it needs no notice from me.

I need not reply to your proposition about the publication of the debate, until advised that you will make no effort to resume it. Whether you resume it or not, rests with you and Bro. GOODWIN. I can have no control over the decision of that question.

I may say now, as I said at first, that I have not contemplated the publication of the debate; but it is possible that, at the proper time for deciding, I may come to a different conclusion. Yours, &c.,

OVID BUTLER.

I then sent him the following:

WINCHESTER, Dec. 1st, 1862.

BRO. OVID BUTLER:—Your letter of the 28th ult. is just received, in which you say: "I say now, as I said at first, that I have not contemplated the publication of the debate; but it is possible that, at the proper time for deciding, I may come to a different conclusion."

Now is the proper time; and I want a categorical answer, yea or nay.   Fraternally, &c.,
                                    JER. SMITH.

P. S —I write this, presuming that you know what has passed between brother GOODWIN and me, and the Journal Company and me; which presumption I have no doubt is correct.   J. S.

And received the following:

FOREST HOME, near Indianapolis, Dec. 6th, 1862.

BRO. JER. SMITH:—I have yours of the 1st, asking a *categorical* answer to your proposition about publishing the debate, &c. You do not say how much you desire to publish—whether you would include the preliminary articles, or whether you would wish to add other and extrinsic matter. Were I disposed to unite in the publication, these would be necessary inquiries.

I see no good that can result either to you or me, by the publication of the debate in its present form; and it would seem that you have abandoned the idea of the discussion being again resumed.

You are mistaken in the presumption that I knew what has passed between you and brother GOODWIN, or between you and the Journal Company, in reference to the charges against you. I have read what has been published. Beyond that, I have been told that you had written some lengthy articles both for the *Record* and for the *Journal*, which the editors had not published for the reason, as I understand in each case, that they were too lengthy, and the matter regarded as irrelevant to anything which had appeared against you in the respective papers. I may be mistaken in this; but it is the impression I got at the time.

Your communications were not submitted to me. My advice was not sought, nor was it given, as to their publication. And so you will perceive that your presumption is not sustained by the facts.

I would much prefer that you would put yourself right before the public, and resume the discussion; but if you decide not to attempt that, you can let me know just how much and how little you desire to publish, and I will answer as directly to your proposition as it is in my nature to do.

Yours fraternally,
OVID BUTLER.

To which I sent the following response:

WINCHESTER, Dec. 10th, 1862.

BRO. OVID BUTLER:—Yours of the 6th instant is just received.

Of course, in the published debate, I "would include the preliminary articles;" and if you will go on in manuscript, we will finish out the whole ten numbers to each side, and include them.

Instead of my abandoning the idea of going on to the conclusion of the discussion, I was publicly thrust out of the forum, the door slammed in my face, and you told to go on, which you commenced doing. And you "say in all frankness, that I (you) think Bro. GOODWIN did right in thus closing the debate." I shall not again ask admittance into that forum, and, perhaps, ought not to occupy it if tendered, unless proper amends be made to me; though, in obedience to the law of the Lord, I forgive all trespasses committed against me, in the manner therein enjoined on me to forgive them.

You say that you prefer that I put myself "right before the public and resume the discussion;" and yet say that you do not know what has passed between brother GOODWIN and me, and the Journal Company and me. Not boasting of my rectitude, (for God knows I sin too often) I, however, beg leave to state, that I am nearer right before the All-seeing Eye, before the public, and *in curia*, as we lawyers say, than are those who have trespassed against me in getting up and *circulating* this slander. But that is a subject that I will not, neither now nor here, discuss nor expatiate upon. To my own Master I stand or fall, and not to those who judge another man's servant;[1] and, with his help, I will try and meet his approbation.

But do not understand that I "decide not to attempt" to "put myself right before the public." I have attempted it, but hitherto, however, with only partial success. But if the Lord spares me and permits, I purpose that it shall all come to the light, as I informed you in my letter of the 19th ultimo.

But all this has nothing to do with the business of this correspondence. Hence to it.

I desire to publish an introduction giving the reasons why it is important *now* to inquire and *ascertain* whether or not slavery is sinful; in which will be included the preliminary articles. Then the discussion as far as it has gone. If you will immediately proceed with the discussion, in manuscript, to its conclusion, the other five numbers on each side will of course go in. If you do not, it will be a refusal on your part to finish and publish the discussion jointly, and I shall publish it as far as it has gone, with such concluding arguments and matter as I deem proper to go to the public with it.

I again desire an early categorical answer, yea or nay; and if yea, send me your number six immediately, or say whether I shall take that already published in the *Record*, as number six, and reply to it.

Fraternally yours,

JER. SMITH.

To which I received the following long response:

FOREST HOME, near Indianapolis, Dec. 16th, 1862.

BRO. JER. SMITH:—I have yours of the 10th. Your answer to my inquiries as to what you desire to include in the proposed publication, is not as definite as I could have wished. I could perceive no motive which you could have for the simple publication of the debate in its present unfinished state, and could therefore but suspect that you proposed uniting with it, in the publication, your defence against the charges made against you in the political papers of the

---

(1) Rom. xiv, 4.

day. I could not perceive the connection of the debate, either with those charges, or with your vindication against them. For the purpose of ascertaining "how much you desire to publish, whether you would include the preliminary articles, or whether you would wish to add other and extrinsic matter," I asked you to "let me know how much and how little you desire to publish?" To this you reply that "you desire to publish an introduction, giving the reasons why it is important *now* to inquire and *ascertain* whether or not slavery is sinful, in which will be included the preliminary articles. Then the discussion as far as it has gone." You do not say that this is all, nor have you removed my suspicion that you wish to add to it other and extrinsic matter. You do not say how much or how little you desire to publish. If your purpose is simply the publication of the debate, I see no necessity of an introductory argument, "giving the reasons why it is important *now* to inquire and *ascertain* whether or not slavery is sinful." It would be asking me to co-operate in the publication of whatever you might *now* choose to write on that subject. To this I could not consent. Nor could I consent, under cover of publishing the debate, to co-operate with you in a publication, the real purpose of which would be to vindicate yourself against charges which have no connection with the debate, or with any matters named in it. I am not your accuser, and have no acquaintance with those who are. You do not need my help or co-operation in your vindication. You can manage that better without connecting me or the debate with it.

I have a right to object, and do object, to *your* publishing the debate in connection with your purposed vindication. You could have neither motive nor excuse for doing so, but by charging me with being your accuser, or with colluding with those who have accused you. Such a charge would be false, and would be an attempt to place me in a false position. Such a charge would be calculated to injure rather than benefit you, in your vindication. Your character and former habits, so far as known to me, afforded a fair presumption that the charges against you were false. I so stated when I first heard them, and you have no right to place me in a position of antagonism to you upon those charges.

I suppose I need not hardly say whether I will now consent or decline to unite with you in the sole and simple publication of the debate as it stands, with the preliminary articles as they stand, as I apprehend you do not contemplate making a proposition of that kind. Yet if so made, I should probably decline to unite in such a publication, as I am of opinion that the book would neither find sale, nor be read by the brethren, especially in the incomplete and imperfect state of the debate on both sides.

I am not inclined to proceed with the discussion in manuscript, as you suggest; for to do so, we would be simply writing for the benefit of each other, unless I should conclude, in advance, to unite in the publication when completed. If the debate should proceed, I am willing to abide by the terms of my own proposition in reference to the publication, and in reference to the number and length of the articles,[1] to which you agreed, but which you seem to forget, and strive to crowd me back on to your first propositions, which were not accepted by me.

I have had some talk with brother GOODWIN. He said he was willing that you should resume the debate upon terms to which he thought you would not object; and that he would write you upon the subject. I suppose he has done so. If he proposes anything satisfactory to you, please let me know. Yours fraternally,

OVID BUTLER.

About the time that I got the last preceding letter, I received the following from brother GOODWIN:

INDIANAPOLIS, Dec. 13th, 1862.

BRO. SMITH:—I supposed you would see the propriety of the plan suggested by me, in a former letter, for clearing yourself of those unfavorable charges which appeared against you in some of the public papers, and that you would adopt that plan. I hoped that ere this, I should have received a favorable decision from the proposed committee, by publishing which, you would be placed favorably before the christian public. I have felt much afflicted in mind, to

---

(1) Where is this proposition? If the reader can find it, he can do more than I can; and he has, in the preceding pages, all that brother Butler wrote, or that I agreed to on the subject.

think that one who stood so high in my esteem, should be made the subject of such serious charges, under any circumstances; and therefore I feel very anxious that you should clear yourself of them, if you are innocent, as you aver.

But you seem to have paid no attention to my friendly suggestions. For your sake, and for the sake of the cause of Christ, I do not feel willing for the matter to remain as it is. I therefore suggest, in all kindness, that you write and send me something like the enclosed article, and I will publish it. Then the charges will stand denied; and if any brethren should feel dissatisfied, it will remain for them to renew the charges, and ask an investigation. If no one should do this, your denial would stand approved.

I hope you will not regard it as presumptious in me to make these suggestions, and that you will let me hear from you on the subject at your earliest convenience.

Yours in hope,
ELIJAH GOODWIN.

"*The enclosed article.*"

BRO. GOODWIN:—You advised me, in a private note, to call a committee to investigate those slanderous reports that were published in some of the public prints against me, for the purpose of proving myself clear of those charges. I choose, however, simply to deny those charges; and let those who believe them, and think the cause of Christ is suffering thereby, bring them up in due form, before a competent tribunal, and I will be ready to answer for myself.

That I had an unpleasant difficulty with certain men that I believed to be soldiers, at the time referred to in those papers, by their attacking me without any provocation on my part, is true. That I may have done and said things, in the excitement, that the law of Christ would not justify, I admit; but that I was drunk, and swore profanely, or that I swore at all, on that occasion, I most positively deny.

Yours, &c.

I sent to brother GOODWIN the following answer:

WINCHESTER, Dec. 18th, 1862.

BRO. GOODWIN:—Your kind letter of the 13th inst., with its enclosure, came while I was absent from home.

Since my acquaintance with you, I have regarded you as possessed of a kind heart, and of uprightness of intention; and this letter is an evidence, that in so regarding you, I did you no more than justice.

But, my dear brother, permit me, in all kindness, in this private correspondence between us, to suggest to you, that you, in common with myself, and all other poor mortals of Adam's race, are liable to, and do, fall into errors of judgment, leading to, and resulting in, errors of action.

How much better it would have been, in my humble judgment, and how much more consonant with the divine law relating to such matters it would have been, had you written this, or a similar letter, to me, before, and instead of, *publicly* thrusting me out of the *Record* as a disputant in the middle of a discussion, stating that you were compelled to do so by certain reports in the public prints touching my recent conduct, thus giving the christian brotherhood, publicly, in your paper, a *quasi* endorsement of those reports. Having first done thus publicly, then privately, though in a kind spirit, and with an upright intention, to call on me *to clear myself*, reverses all rules, divine and human, governing such cases.

I am not certain that the manner you suggest *of clearing myself*, is the *best* way, or even a *proper* way, *taking all the facts that have transpired into consideration*, of vindicating me against the foul and false libels; and hence I can not at present accept your suggestions. If, when you learn this, you still "do not feel willing for the matter to rest as it is," you will, of course, do what, before the Master, is proper for his cause, for you, and for me.

It is proper, however, and my duty, now and here, to give you the reasons why I did not, in my address to the public, on the subject, notice the charge of drunkenness. They were two. In that address, I was in a political forum.

1. Had I been as drunk as charged, I should not, for that reason, have been mobbed. If I should, almost all the persons engaged in the mob should have been mobbed also. And men *who conduct leading Republican papers* should be also mobbed at least twice a week.

2. Temperance society men hold that if one partakes of spirits at all, he becomes intoxicated; while confirmed inebriates hold that one is not intoxicated so long as he re-

tains his consciousness and powers of locomotion; and all stages between these two extremes are held by some one or other in society as being the point at which intoxication commences. Hence, intoxicated or not intoxicated, is too vague an issue to make before the public, with political demagogues.

The truth is this: I saw some friends and drank some spirits on the way as I went to Portland, and felt the influence of the spirits I had drunk, somewhat, when I got to Portland, and, of course, the spirits could be smelt on my breath; *but I was not drunk in any fair sense of the term.* The demagogues seized upon the fact as it was, to make the charge—hence I committed a sin; for I was commanded to abstain from all appearance of evil.[1] And though I actually committed no evil in partaking of the spirits, yet the use the devil made of it at Portland, and through the press, gave it the appearance of evil—hence I sinned; and for that sin I have sorrowfully and bitterly repented, and have the word of God that I am pardoned for it.

I did not say or do things at Portland "that the law of Christ would not justify;" and hence, I can not say that I did, either publicly in your paper, or in this private correspondence with you. To my own Master, I stand or fall; and not to those who judge another man's servant;[2] and with his help, I hope to be able to meet his approbation.

May the good Lord enable us all to walk worthy of the vocation wherewith we are called,[3] and to be not high-minded but fear,[4] is my devout prayer. The God of peace be with you. Farewell.

JER. SMITH.

It is seen that brother GOODWIN, in his last letter above inserted, says that a public denial by me of the foul charges "would stand approved," unless brethren who believed them, and thought the cause of Christ was suffering thereby, "should bring them up *in due form* before *a competent tribunal,*" and "renew the charges, and ask an investigation." He was right in this. And, if this was correct and true on the 13th of December, 1862, when he wrote that letter, it was equally true and correct on the 10th and 17th of No-

---

(1) 1 Thes. v, 22. (2) Rom. xiv, 4. (3) Eph. iv, 1. (4) Rom. xi, 20.

vember, preceding. And the reader, by looking to my communication to him of the date of November 10th, which I asked him to publish, will see that in that communication I denied the charges, each and all of them. That denial "stood approved," unless brethren renewed the charges, brought them up in due form, and asked an investigation before a competent tribunal. But brother GOODWIN, on the 17th of November, refused to publish that denial; and said, in his letter refusing, that I had "adopted the wrong course" to set myself right before the world. In less than a month afterwards, however, to-wit: on the 13th of December, he said it was right, and recommended me then to take it—things still standing as they then were, before the brotherhood and the public.

The reader, by looking back, will see that I said in reply to that, that I was not certain that the manner then suggested by him was the *best*, or even *a proper* way of proceeding, taking all the facts that had transpired into consideration; and that hence, I could not *then* accept his suggestions. He had said that he did not feel willing to let the matter rest as it was, from which I had necessarily to understand that he intended to have it straightened out; and he wanted me to take the initiative. I thought, and still think, taking all the facts that had transpired into consideration, that it was his place to take the initiative, and not mine. If he believed the charges, he should have renewed them, and asked an investigation, *in due form*, before a competent tribunal. If he did not believe them, he should, in his paper, publicly, have taken back and undone the mischief he had done me by his publication in the *Record*, of the 4th of November. Had he done so, then the way would have been open for me to make such a publication as recommended by him on the 13th of December. I could not then accept that suggestion, because his publication of the 4th of November stood, and all that had passed between him and me, and the Journal Company and me, had been, and then was, suppressed and kept from the public. Things standing thus before the public, in publishing a denial of the charges, it was absolutely necessary that, with it, I should set out the facts and circumstances showing the *animus*, the spirit, object and purpose of those who had got up, and of those who had circulated the charges. These things my communication of November 10th did, and that recommended by brother GOODWIN on December 13th, did not do. He refused to publish mine of the 10th, I think, because it exposed the faults of the Journal Company and himself, rather than because it was too political, as he alleged. Hence, before I could properly appear in his paper, otherwise than as set out in my communication of the 10th of November, or move in the matter, he had to take the initiative: either to renew the charges and proceed *in due form*, or to remove the *quasi* endorsement he had given them by his publication of November 4th, and place me before the christian brotherhood and the public, as if that publication had never been made. Hence, I gave him the facts as to the charge of drunkenness, that he might have them to consider, with the others, in determining which course he would take. Yet he took neither, and "let the matter rest as it was."

He said I "adopted the wrong course" in the article I sent him for publication on the 10th of November. Well, I said, and I think I have shown in the preceding pages, partly from his own pen, that he adopted the wrong course in making that publication, when he did, and as he did. In my public denial of the charges to which he gave a *quasi* endorsement by that publication, sent to him for publication, I showed, as it was my duty to show, the impropriety of the course he, as well as the Journal Company, had pursued towards me, but included in it my prayer for their forgiveness for the trespasses they had committed against me, having set out and shown what they were. Is he to determine what is the proper course for him and me both? Is it not as proper that I should determine for both? And yet I do not claim the right, and would not exercise it, if I have privilege of determining for both. I judge him not; and "unto God would I commit my cause;"[1] "I would order my cause before him."[2]

Brother BUTLER said that a certain thing said as to him, was so palpably a fiction, "that it needs no notice from me."[3] These charges were so, as to me, with persons who had known my conduct for forty years in this community, where I live. They were so palpably false that they did not need a denial from me, with all who had so known me,

---

(1) Job v, 8.   (2) Job xxiii, 4.   (3) Ante, p. 193.

and who did not wish to believe evil of me—who did not wish the charges true; and those who did, I regard as beneath my attention, and unworthy of any notice from me. Such charges against brethren GOODWIN and BUTLER, even in a religious paper, much more in dirty, filthy, political, partizan sheets, would need no denial from them, with me; nor would I circulate such reports against them, emanating from such sources. Brother BUTLER says that he stated, when he first heard the charge, that my character and former habits afforded a fair presumption that they were false.[1]

What put it into brother BUTLER'S head, that in publishing the debate, I would unite with it my defence against the conduct of my accusers? And what put it into his head, that he would be charged with being my accuser, or with colluding with those who have accused me? I had said neither. The reader will please look back and see if I had. Did his "heart" condemn him? Or, did his "intuition" "before and above all reasoning," bring these things up in his mind?

Let us first state and look at the facts as they are. Brother BUTLER is a stockholder, and, I am told, a large one, in in the Indianapolis Journal Company. He is an influential member of that corporation or firm, whichever it may be. Tilford is the President of that Company, and of course a stockholder. They are the co-bishops of the Christian Church at Indianapolis, are both rabid abolitionists, and, of course, are in intimate social relations.

Brother BUTLER knows the Latin legal maxim, as well as that it is true, *Qui facit per alium, facit per se*—"What a man does by another, he does by himself;" and, that as to firms and corporations, the act of the firm or corporation is the act of each member; and that each member is presumed to know, that is, that it is taken as a fact that he does know, all the acts of the firm or corporation in the course of its business. Hence brother BUTLER knew and assented to the copying of the libel from the *Winchester Journal* into the *Indianapolis Journal*, and knew and assented to the refusal of the *Indianapolis Journal* to publish my defence, notwithstanding the presumption, in his opinion, was, that the charges were false. If he did not actually

---

(1) Ante, p. 197.

know of these things at the time they were done, as he says he did not, when they came to his knowledge, what was his duty, he believing them to be false, and in contemplation of law, the Journal Company's act being his act? It was to tell the Company to publicly, in their paper, withdraw the charges, or publish my defence. But instead of that, he says " my advice was not sought, nor was it given." Thus not only in contemplation of law, but in fact, he assented to, and assumed the acts of the Journal Company. Had he then forgotten what he so eloquently said in his third article of the debate about love, as exhibited in action—in doing?[1] Had he forgotten the Scriptures he then partly quoted? "As we have therefore opportunity, let us do good unto all men, *especially unto them who are of the household of faith.*"[2] "Love worketh no ill to his neighbor."[3] "If any man say I love God, and hateth his brother, he is a liar: for he that loveth not his brother whom he hath seen, how can he love God whom he hath not seen?"[4] And had he forgotten the divine commands that he did not there quote? "Above all things, have fervent charity (love) among yourselves: for charity (love) shall cover a multitude of sins."[5] "Charity (love) suffereth long, and is kind; * * * thinketh no evil; rejoiceth not in iniquity, but rejoiceth *in the truth.*"[6] But this "fountain" of love brother BUTLER could not "bathe in," and could not "breathe of that atmosphere of love" in my case, because (as I can only suppose) I was not of the proper race and color to be the recipient of the ebulition of abolition love. Yet he says the Lord took this law of love from "neighbor," and applied it to "men"—" all men."

And he approved brother GOODWIN's publication of the 4th of November, closing the debate until I should "vindicate" myself against the slander he had, through the *Indianapolis Journal,* sent all over the State, and had refused to send my "vindication" in the same sheet. The *Winchester Journal* was limited in its circulation to 300 or 400 copies, and they in the region of country where I have been known,

---

(1) Ante, pp. 131-2-3-4, which the reader will please turn to and read.
(2) Gal. vi, 10.   (3) Rom. xiii, 10.   (4) 1 John iv, 20.
(5) 1 Pet. iv, 8. Wesley, in his note on this passage, says: "He that *loves* another, *covereth his faults,* how many soever they be. He turns away his own eyes from them; and, as far as possible, *hides them from others,*" instead of publishing them broadcast in his paper.
(6) 1 Cor. xiii, 4-6.

and have lived for forty-odd years. Its circulation and dissemination of the slander, was measurably futile and harmless; but brethren TILFORD and BUTLER, by their journal, sent it upon the wings of the wind, all over the State, and even out of the State, to thousands, to whom neither I, nor my conduct, are known.

Brother BUTLER was greatly alarmed lest, if the debate should be published, my defence would be published with it. Why should he be? He says he "could not perceive the connection of the debate, either with those charges, or with your (my) vindication against them." No connection between the debate and the charges? Well, I thought so too. But what are the facts? Brother GOODWIN with brother BUTLER'S approbation, stopped the debate because of the charges; and did this publicly, not privately, as he should have done, if he did it at all. How, then, does it become necessary to notice the charges in this book? Let the facts answer. I invited brother BUTLER to go on and close the debate in manuscript, and told him that if he did, it would all go to the public in the book, having informed him that it would be published in book form—with him if he went into the publication, and by me if he refused; and that if he refused to finish the debate, I should "publish it as far as it had gone, with such concluding arguments and matter as I should deem proper to go to the public with it." Yet he said that I did not say whether or not I would not stop the book at the end of the discussion as far as it had gone! and that he would not proceed and close the discussion in manuscript, because it would "be simply writing for the benefit of each other"!! Had he gone on and finished the debate, it would have appeared in this book unbroken, and there would have been no need of saying anything about the charges, or of the suspension of the publication of the debate in the *Record;* and nothing would have been said *in this book* about either, unless he had in his subsequent articles alluded to the charges, or to the excommunication of me from the *Record,* in which case it would have been done. But as he refused to finish the discussion, the debate necessarily appears in this book abruptly broken off in the middle. This makes it absolutely necessary that the reason why it is so abruptly broken off, be given to the reader. Hence this Episode. The *facts* as to that breaking off, constitute a full "vindication" of me. And the reader will see, that this book disproves the charge he makes, that "the real purpose" of my publishing it, is to "vindicate" myself. When I undertook the labor of this debate, I did it with the intention of giving it to the public in book form. I would not have undertaken the labor for a mere newspaper debate. The real purpose of this book, is to combat abolitionism through its chief dogma that slavery is sinful.

At the outset, brother BUTLER professed to be anxious to have the discussion resumed, and said if it was not, he would desire, "in some form, to close" his argument. But when invited to resume the discussion and finish it, and informed that it would go to the public in book form, he declined on the ground that we would only be writing for ourselves! The rational inference from these facts is, that at first he supposed he had me permanently shut down upon and hushed up, and he wanted to close his argument without my replies, because he had found them to be too damaging. For when I offered to close the discussion with him, he refused. He did not place his refusal on the ground of the charges. He stated twice in that letter, that the debate had no connection with the charges. Still he refused to close the debate to go to the public in a book, in which he might be joint publisher if he would. This shows that he wanted to suppress the debate, equally as badly as he wanted to suppress me.

His broad assertion that God had never granted property in man, I had totally demolished; and in my last article, I exposed and laid bare the dodge he was trying to make, to shift the issue on that question, to other and collateral matters. These, in my humble opinion, were the true reasons why he did not want to conclude the debate with me, to go to the public in a book, or otherwise; and these were the reasons why he wanted to close his argument in some form, (but without my replies) scuttle-fish like, to cover up his defeat. The language of the article in the *Record* of November 4th, satisfies my mind that it was framed in consultation with him, if not by him. He said he approved it. The *Winchester Journal's* article was a God-send to the Indianaoplis abolition clique. It came very opportunely, when I had them, through their champion, in a very tight place upon their darling dogma. It was seized upon by them with avidity, and sent *by them* broadcast over the world, so far as their political organ, the *Indianapolis Journal*, could send it. In their religious organ, the *Christian Record*, on the pretext of the libel they had disseminated against me, they shut me out of the debate, telling me to set myself right before the public against their fulmination, refusing me space in the columns of both their organs to do it! Instead of proceeding in proper form, to establish the charges *they had given to the public against me*, they called upon me to prove myself clear of them. Their brother Boggs said "the accused party is not under obligation to prove himself *not* guilty. But on the contrary, the *onus probandi* rests entirely upon the accuser."[1] But they reversed the rule when *they* accused *me*.

On the 28th of November, 1862, the following editorial article appeared in the *Winchester Journal:*

ONCE MORE AND FINALLY.

An inadvertence of workmen in the office compels allusion again to the Judge Smith Portland affair. Until within a very short time, the present editor had not assumed entire control of that department; and from what had been the custom, he was not surprised to see, in proof, a short article from the *Independent* in reference to the above matter. So soon as his eye fell upon it, he made the request, that it by all means be thrown out, as he wished to have done with that matter. This was readily agreed to by the other partner; and he could have almost sworn, when his attention was called to it on the morning of publication, that it was not in his paper. It came about thus:

It was not read in proof at all, but taken back into the compositor's department and set aside, but not distributed. In this way it was found by a hand who happened to make up the forms for the outside of that paper, but knew nothing of the circumstances, and placed in a space it was adapted to fill. In this way the whole edition was worked off with the obnoxious article in its columns. No one, perhaps, regrets it more than the editor. He would not have had it appear knowingly on any account.

A final word about this whole matter. We published the original article, because we thought it gave a true statement

---

(1) Ante, p. 29.

of the "affair." The Judge replied *in extenso*. As the "town was full of people," it was expected that something further would be said by witnesses on one side or the other. Everybody else keeping silence, we intended to do the same.

Towards our neighbor and fellow townsman, Judge Smith, we never have had an ill-feeling. Take him out of politics, and we have few neighbors with whom we have got on more agreeably; and we have had considerable intercourse and dealings with each other.

To our way of regarding things, his political principles are highly obnoxious to the growth of true liberty in this country, and to the preservation and integrity of the Government. It was as a politician, as an intelligent, influential and determined exponent and defender of the devil-daring, pro-slavery, secession-sympathizing 8th of January Democracy, that he was spoken of in this paper, in reference to the rather notorious affair—"more in sorrow than in anger." It was the politician that went to Jay county on that memorable "October day." The politician had seen in the results of the election "a gleam of hope." The politician felt elated. The politician doubtless had taken an extra glass of wine when he drove into Portland; and further this deponent sayeth not.

This pretty much takes back all the charges of the libel. It apologizes for the appearance, in the previous week's paper, of a filthy article from Beecher's *Independent* about it. Says that it supposed the statements of the libel true when he published it; that I had denied it, and it had not been sustained by witnesses, though the town was full of people. Speaks of me personally "out of politics." Says it was as a politician, using a hard epithet, that I was spoken of in the libel. That I was elated about the result of the election; had doubtless taken an extra glass of wine; but further as to the charges of the libel, it said not—in other words, would not re-affirm them.

A single remark. The political press can properly discuss only public measures, and the acts of public men as to public measures. Private character, and the acts of men in private life, are not proper subjects for comment and criticism of the public political press. Whenever the political press does inveigh against men in private life, it is an improper act, and is never done only for base party purposes; and the very fact that it is done, is proof that what is so said, should be wholly disregarded. And all good citizens so treat it. I was a private citizen, in private life, was not a candidate, and had not been ; and hence was not a proper subject of comment in the political press. All this Tilford, Butler and Goodwin knew, as well as it was known at Winchester.

Notwithstanding the keen-sightedness of the Indianapolis Journal Company in seeing the libel in the *Winchester Journal*, and their promptness in copying it into their paper, they could not see and copy this article from the *Winchester Journal* of the 28th of November. And notwithstanding brother Goodwin had seen the charges, and publicly expelled me from the *Record* for them, he could not see this article, and say in his paper, that the *Winchester Journal*, whence the charges against J. S. emanated, having virtually withdrawn those charges, we announce the fact, and invite him to renew in our columns the discussion of slavery ; leaving out any expression of sorrow, if he did not feel any, for having rudely, publicly expelled me on baseless charges.

I have set out before the reader, in this Episode, this phase of abolitionism, which I would have been much rejoiced if necessity had not been laid upon me to do. It is, however, in its main feature, consonant with the general character and conduct of abolitionism, which is, to malign, libel and falsify every person and thing opposed to it. Such has been its course for years, till even excellent men, such as brother Goodwin (and he is an excellent man,) are led to make such gross assertions as "the bodies and souls of men for whom Jesus died are chattelized," and "the institution of slavery is traffic in human flesh;" he not being conscious that abolition evil-speaking and evil-surmising, for years, had led him into such erroneous conduct.

My discussion of their pet dogma was becoming so damaging, that they resorted to their common practice of libel and vilification, to get rid of me and of the discussion, as set out in this Episode. They have not succeeded. Their efforts to blast my reputation have been measurably harmless. I have taken other means than their organs, of getting the discussion, including the balance of what I had to say, before the public. What they will do when this book goes before the public, I do not know; but judging from the uniform conduct of abolitionism for years, I suppose that the libel is but as a drop in the bucket, in comparison to the torrents of vituperation and slang that will be poured upon my devoted head. I expect to show before I close this book, and prove, not by inference, but by the law of the Lord, *the sinfulness of abolitionism.* And I confess in advance, that I sin more or less daily; and were it not that the Lord has made propitiation for my sins, and is an Advocate for me with the Father, whereby I have the word of God that I may obtain pardon for my sins, I should have no hope. A difference between my *quondam* abolition brethren and me, is, that I frankly confess that I sin; while they will not admit their sins, but Pharisee-like, thank God that they are not like other men—like us poor anti-abolitionists, for instance. " If we say that we have no sin, we deceive ourselves, and the truth is not in us."[1]

The Lord has given me warning and notice, that as they called him Beelzebub, how much more will they call me, humble and frail as I am; but he has told me to fear them not; for their machinations shall all be developed, exposed, and made known.[2] With humble confidence in, and reliance upon his promise, I cast away fear, and say, let their vituperation come, and to God I commit my cause.

---

(1) 1 John i, 8. (2) Matt. x, 25–27.

DISCUSSION OF SLAVERY.

DEBATE WITH ELDER THOMAS WILEY.

I desire to lay before the reader all that has been said to me by our brethren in favor of the proposition, *Slavery is sinful*, before I proceed to my *ex parte* discussion of the question. Hence, I have concluded to insert a partial discussion of the question, that took place between me and brother THOMAS WILEY, pastor of the Christian Church at Union City, Indiana, in the winter and spring of 1861. I do this, as well because I want all that those who assert the proposition, have said, to go to the reader, as that brother WILEY presented some views and reasons why slavery is sinful, that I should not have thought of being urged for such a purpose; and yet I have no doubt that thousands of honest well-meaning people, accept them as sufficient proof. In answering brother WILEY I answer them.

Brother WILEY had originally but a limited education; but he was a man of strong mind, and by application, he made considerable progress in the acquisition of knowledge. He earnestly loved the truth, and followed it when he became satisfied where it led, though to do so required the abandonment of previous opinions. This I knew him to do on three or four occasions, during our acquaintance of more than twenty years.

In January, 1861, in a friendly conversation with him, I stated to him for the first time, that I did not admit that slavery was sinful; that I had investigated the subject, and was satisfied that it was not sinful. This seemed to astonish him, and he seemed to think that there could be no doubt but that it was sinful. I suggested that he had before found some previous notions he had entertained to be erroneous, and it might be, that if he would investigate this, he might find it to be so too. The result of the conversation was, that we agreed to enter into a friendly investigation of the matter in writing, and I drew up four propositions, substantially like those I sent to brother Boggs shortly afterwards, sent him a copy of them, and retained one myself. The following is the correspondence that ensued between us. I make some slight changes in brother WILEY's articles, merely, however, as to style, such as using *I* where he used *we*, &c.

ELDER WILEY'S NUMBER ONE.

JER. SMITH—*Dear Brother:*—I received your propositions, and am entirely willing to *affirm* that *Slavery is a sinful institution,* and do the very best I can to prove it.

Your first proposition says that *slavery is an institution of civil society;* and you suppose that we will both agree to this. Now, all I have to say on this proposition, at this time, is this: I believe that slavery originated in paganism, and that its tendency is back to paganism again. But I pass to notice your second proposition, as it involves the real issue between us. The proposition reads: The institution of slavery is sinful.

Now, as I understand you to mean American slavery, I will attempt to defend the truth of the proposition by the christian Scriptures. In order for us to discuss this proposition understandingly, we must know what *sin* is. We must know what constitutes an institution *sinful.* What is it? Let the apostle answer. He says, "Sin is the transgression of the law." Again, "All unrighteousness is sin."[1] Here we have the question clearly defined. Every institution that is *contrary* to God's law, is sinful; all unrighteous-

---

(1) 1 John iii, 4; v, 17.

ness, every act which is *opposed* to the law of God, is *sinful*. I am now prepared for an effort to sustain the truth of my affirmative proposition.

1. My first argument is based on the following language of the apostle, when speaking of the God that made the world, he said, "hath made of one blood all nations of men for to dwell on all the face of the earth."[1] Here we learn that *all* nations of men are made of one blood, and therefore have one common Father. This confirms the truth of what has long since been said, that "none but God can own a man." Now, as God has never given to man authority to reduce his brother or fellow-man to the level of a brute beast, as does the institution of slavery; and as human laws are essential to the existence of slavery, and as slavery does reduce human beings to that of chattel property, the only legitimate conclusion which can be drawn from the premises, is, that the institution of slavery is a *sinful institution*. A word more at this point. If it can be shown that a class of persons of a certain cast or color, can be *sinlessly* enslaved, then it can be shown that *all*, in their turn, of every cast, color, or nation, may be enslaved, and *no sin committed*. Now, let it be remembered, that he who labors to show the righteousness of the institution of slavery, is laboring to show that he may be *righteously enslaved himself*. FOR ALL ARE MADE OF ONE BLOOD.

2. The Savior, in speaking of the institution of marriage, says: "For this cause shall a man leave his father and mother, and shall cleave to his wife: and they twain shall be one flesh. Wherefore they are no more twain but one flesh. What therefore God hath joined together, let not man put asunder."[2] This passage shows that marriage is a *divine institution*. The institution of "American slavery" is of human origin; it is supported and carried on by human authority. It separates husband and wife, parents and children; and regardless of God's authority, it sunders all the holy and endearing ties of the family relation. This American slavery *does do*. Now, as sin is the transgression of the law of God, and as the *institution* of slavery is rebellion against God's government, by sundering every tie of natural affection, it is therefore a *sinful institution*. Now, brother

---

(1) Acts xvii, 26.   (2) Matt. xix, 5, 6.

Smith, we *must* have this difficulty removed before we can believe that the institution is not sinful. And remember, too, that in *this* case the institution of slavery is directly opposed to the "words," "even the wholesome words of our Lord Jesus Christ, and the doctrine which is according to godliness."

3. My third argument is based upon the following words of the Savior: "The spirit of the Lord is upon me, because he hath anointed me to preach the Gospel to the poor; he hath sent me to heal the broken-hearted, to preach deliverance to the captives, and recovering of sight to the blind, to set at liberty them that are bruised, to preach the acceptable year of the Lord."[1] These are also the words, "the *wholesome* words of our Lord Jesus Christ, the doctrine which is according to godliness." This is the doctrine of the reign of favor, "the acceptable year of the Lord." But alas! the institution of slavery stands directly opposed to the doctrine. The subjects of the peculiar institution are the poor, blinded, bruised, broken-hearted captives, and they are not permitted to receive the Lord's Gospel—the blessings of the "acceptable year of the Lord." Now, as the institution of slavery is, in this case, clearly seen to stand opposed to the Gospel of Christ, and as sin is the transgression of the law, it follows as clear as a sun-beam, that the institution of slavery is a sinful institution. Now, dear brother, these contradictions between slavery and christianity *must* be removed, or we never can believe that the institution of slavery is right.

4. My fourth argument is founded on the following words of the Savior: "Therefore all things whatsoever ye would that men should do to you, do ye even so to them; for this is the law and the prophets."[2] Here the Savior concentrates the law and the prophets, and makes out a case to be taken home to the hearts of every individual person. This is indeed the "golden rule." It is not merely one or two things, but it is *all things whatsoever ye would that men should do to you, do ye even so to them.* This rule tries men's souls. When this rule is properly regarded, it is no mere seeing visions, and dreaming dreams; it is communing with realities. And he who is not willing to be reduced to the degrading institution of slavery, as are the slaves of the

---

(1) Luke iv, 18, 19.   (2) Matt. vii, 12.

South, can not favor the peculiar institution without violating this precept of our Lord Jesus Christ; without violating the "words, even the wholesome words of the Lord, and the doctrine which is according to godliness." In this case, the institution of slavery is directly opposed to the doctrine of the Lord Jesus Christ, and is therefore seen to be a sinful institution.

5. My fifth argument is founded upon the following language of the apostle: "But if ye have respect to persons, ye commit sin, and are convinced of the law as transgressors."[1]

This case really needs no comment. I think no one in this enlightened age will pretend to say that there is no difference between slavery and freedom—between the slave and his master. Surely no one will take the position, that the same respect is shown to the slave that is shown to the slave owner. This being true, and I think it can not be denied, then it follows that the institution is a sinful institution.

6. This, my sixth argument, shall be based upon the Lord's final decision. The case reads as follows: "Then shall the king say to them on his right hand, come ye blessed of my Father, inherit the kingdom prepared for you from the foundation of the world: for I was a hungered and ye gave me meat: I was thirsty and ye gave me drink: I was a stranger and ye took me in: naked, and ye clothed me: I was sick and ye visited me: I was in prison, and ye came unto me. Then shall the righteous answer him, saying, Lord when saw we thee a hungered and fed thee? or thirsty and gave thee drink? When saw we thee a stranger, and took thee in? or naked and clothed thee? Or when saw we thee sick, or in prison and came unto thee? And the king shall answer and say unto them, verily I say unto you, inasmuch as ye have done it unto one of the least of these my brethren, ye have done it unto me. Then shall the king say also unto them on the left hand, depart from me, ye cursed, into everlasting fire prepared for the devil and his angels: for I was a hungered and ye gave me no meat: I was thirsty, and ye gave me no drink: I was a stranger, and ye took me not in: naked, and ye clothed me not: sick

---

(1) James ii, 9.

and in prison, and ye visited me not. Then shall they also answer him, saying, Lord when saw we thee a hungered, or athirst, or a stranger, or naked, or sick, or in prison, and did not minister to thee? Then shall he answer them, saying, verily I say unto you, inasmuch as ye did it not to one of the least of these, ye did it not to me. And these shall go away into everlasting punishment; but the righteous into life eternal."[1] The particular in this connection, upon which my argument is based, is this: It is here clearly shown, that, as we treat the Lord's disciple, so we treat the Lord himself. Now, as the institution of American slavery does whip, abuse, starve, imprison, and even sell the disciples of Christ, it most assuredly does these things to the Lord himself. And when Judas sold his Lord for silver, it was certainly a sinful act. And now, as the institution of American slavery *does* sell Christ's disciples, and takes the money for them, it is most assuredly a sinful institution.

7. This argument is based upon the following language: "Let this mind be in you, which was also in Christ Jesus."[2] A few words here, and I close for this time. *The mind of Christ.* Ah! what was the mind of Christ? or what is the mind of Christ? He was "holy, harmless, undefiled, separate from sinners," and made higher than the heavens. He could say, "Father, not my will but thine be done." Was he minded to have slavery? Where, where, we ask, did he ever show a mind like that of slaveholding? The divine Savior suffered death—yea, he was willing—he had a *mind* to suffer death for the redemption of poor, blinded, bruised, broken-hearted captives, such as slavery's bonds are fettering to-day. Now, as slavery binds, and the Lord's Gospel frees, it follows that the institution of slavery is a sinful institution.

THOS. WILEY.

Now, Bro. SMITH, the foregoing are some of the reasons why I believe that the institution of slavery is sinful. I have more; but I expect to hear from you soon. Please write a plain hand. Send my first back when you send your first. T. W.

---

(1) Matt. xxv. 34–46.   (2) Phil. ii, 5.

JER. SMITH'S REPLY NUMBER ONE.

My Dear Brother Wiley:—Your number one, though left for me some time ago, only reached me yesterday.

Slavery is an institution existing in fact. It must be an institution of civil society or civil government; or it is an institution of the christian kingdom; for there are but the two—the kingdoms of this world, and the kingdom of our Lord and Savior Jesus Christ. I aver that it is an institution of civil society or civil government; you do not deny it, but say that it originated in paganism, and that its tendency is back to paganism. If this is true, it is not an institution of the Lord's kingdom, but of civil society, or the kingdoms of this world. I understood you in our conversation, in which this friendly discussion was agreed upon, to agree with me that it was an institution of civil society. You do not, in your number one, deny it, but do not, in words, admit it, but pass on to the second proposition, " as it involves the real issue between us," in your opinion. I notice this first proposition, as it is well for us to understand each other as we go along, and " not strive about words to no profit, but to the subverting of the hearers,"[1] and set it down that we agree that slavery is an institution of civil society.

" Whosoever committeth sin transgresseth also the law; for sin is the transgression of the law."[2] " All unrighteousness is sin."[3] These divine rules and definitions you quote in part. Of course they are right, because they are divine. But that we may fully understand it, I will quote some further: " Whosoever *abideth in him*, sinneth not."[4] " He that keepeth his commandments, *dwelleth in him*, and he in him."[5] " If ye *keep my commandments*, ye shall abide in my love; even as I have kept my Father's commandments, and abide in his love."[6] " He that doeth righteousness, is righteous, even as he (Christ) is righteous."[7]

From these divine oracles we learn that sin is a transgression of the law of God; that if we abide in the Lord, we will not sin; that if we keep his commandments, we

---

(1) 2 Tim. ii, 14.   (3) 1 John v, 17.   (5) 1 John iii, 24.   (7) 1 John iii, 7.
(2) 1 John, iii, 4.   (4) 1 John iii, 6.   (6) John xv, 10.

shall dwell or abide in him, and in his love, as he abided in his Father's love by keeping his Father's commandments; that if we do righteousness, that is, keep the Lord's commandments, we shall be righteous as the Lord was righteous, who was not left alone by the Father, because he did "always those things that pleased" the Father,[1] that is, the things that the Father had commanded him to do.

Having premised these things, I will proceed to notice your arguments, *serialim*.

1. Your first argument, thrown into the form of a syllogism, is: The whole human family have one common origin, to-wit, God and Adam; therefore the institution of slavery is sinful!! The conclusion does not follow from the premises. It has no logical relation to the premises. As well might the conclusion be: therefore the relation of monarch and subject, in all monarchical governments, is sinful; or, therefore is the relation of President and subordinate officers, and the relation between them and citizens, in this government, sinful relations! This argument is a fallacy, brother WILEY.

You quote, in this argument, a scrap of home-made Scripture, that I think proper to notice, to-wit: "None but God can own a man." This is not only home-made, but it is contradictory of divine Scripture; as will appear before we get through this discussion. Let us stick to the "Scriptures given by inspiration," in our investigation; for they alone are "profitable for doctrine," and "for instruction in righteousness,"[2] to-wit, for instruction in keeping the commandments of God; for, keeping the commandments of God, is righteousness.

Some other matters thrown in by you under this head, I will notice, though irrelevant to the investigation before us. You *assume* that the institution of slavery reduces man "to the level of a brute beast," to "chattel property," &c. This is untrue, brother WILEY; the *institution* does no such thing; and it is a great pity that so many good men and women are misled by this, and similar mis statements that have been made for years, and are still being made, as to what the institution does. In almost every particular, is the relation of master and the slave, different from that between the owner and the animal of brute creation. *Some*

---

(1) John viii, 29. (2) 2 Tim. iii, 16.

bad masters may treat *some of their slaves* like brute beasts; but it is the *man*, and not the institution, that does that. The institution itself regards both master and slave as human beings, and not as brute beasts; but either or both may, by their conduct, become like brute beasts, and each may treat the other as if he were a brute beast. But it is the man that does this—not the institution. Many husbands and wives treat their companions as brute beasts. Does that prove the institution of marriage sinful? Certainly not.

Another item under this head: In this investigation, it is not incumbent on any one to "labor to show the righteousness of the institution of slavery." It is incumbent on you to show that it is sinful, that is, a transgression of the law of God; it is not incumbent on me to show that it is commanded of God; for that is required to make it righteousness in one to become or remain a slaveholder or a slave. The *onus* or burden of proof is on you, not on me. You are to produce the law of God that the institution itself is a transgression of; I need not produce any law of God ordaining it.

2. The institution of slavery is not violative of the marriage rights, any more than is civil government itself. Civil goverment may, and often does, separate husband and wife, parent and child, brother and sister, when the public defence, the public welfare, or public justice requires it. In time of war, husbands and sons are drafted into the army; and when the public health, public duty, or public justice requires it, husband, wife, son, or daughter, is separated from the rest of the family, by the civil government. Because of these facts, will brother WILEY say that the institution of civil government is sinful? Of course not. Bad rulers or bad masters may commit sins by violating marital rights; but that is their sin, not the sin of the institution either of government or of slavery. The master may have bad regulations, or the State may have bad laws where slavery exists, as to the marriage rights and relations; but that is the sin of the master or of the legislature—it is not to be charged up as the sin of the institution.

The "wholesome words of Christ" will be attended to in due time; I am glad you have named them.

3. Your third authority is what Christ read from Isaiah

as recorded in Luke iv, 18, 19. This was done when he was entering his ministry, and was simply a reading of what the spirit had said 700 years before, through the prophet, that he should do when he came. Among the things that the prophet said he should do, was "to preach deliverance to the captives." As he has fulfilled that mission, and has ascended up on high, we must, to understand the prophecy, look to what *he did preach*, instead of looking to what it was said he would preach when he came. If your construction of the prophecy is right, we can find that he preached that slavery is sinful, and that masters should let their slaves go free. And that is the passage to cite me to. The passage you cite, is where he announces what he is to do; show us where he did it, in your sense of preaching deliverance to the captives, and that will be the law, the transgression of which will be sin. I apprehend, my brother, that you can not find where he preached deliverance to the captives in your sense of deliverance; if you can, please cite me to the place.

I must correct another erroneous statement you make under this head, that slaves "are not permitted to receive the Lord's Gospel." As great a proportion of the slave population is christian, as there is of the white population christian, either North or South. The whole race in Africa is heathen and pagan, while a large portion of the slaves in the United States are christians. The institution has brought them within the sound of the Gospel; while, if they had remained in Africa, they would not have heard, and, of course, would not have "received," the Gospel, and would have been pagans or heathens, as those that have remained there are. "God moves in a mysterious way." We can not comprehend fully why the chosen people of God were enslaved 430 years in Egypt; nor why the Africans have been enslaved in the United States 220 years, and still are enslaved. Let us "be not righteous overmuch; neither make ourselves overwise."[1] Let us not get wise above what is written. The spirit only, searcheth the deep things of God.[2] What he does not reveal to us in the Scriptures, we have no right to know, nor to try to know.

4. Your fourth proof that the institution of slavery is

---

(1) Eccl. vii, 16.   (2) 1 Cor. ii, 10, 11.

sinful, is the Golden Rule. Be careful, my beloved brother, that you do not get to "seeing visions and dreaming dreams." If the observance of this rule requires masters to sever the relation existing between them and their slaves, by freeing their slaves, how came it that the apostles, in writing to christian masters, and laying down the divine law to govern them, as masters, did not so state, and direct them to free their slaves? If your construction of this rule is correct, the apostles were greatly at fault—Paul particularly, when he wrote to Philemon. According to your construction of it, inasmuch as you and I are not willing to be reduced to the situation of subjects of the British, French, or Austrian empire, unless we endeavor to make those governments give proper political franchises to their subjects, we violate this precept; or, if we insist that our government should live in peace and amity with those empires, we violate the rule. I could, by many other instances, show the absurdity of your construction and application of this truly Golden Rule. But I forbear at present.

5. The fifth proof is what is said in James ii, 9. This is a law for christians in the assembly of saints, or house of God, as is evident from what is said from the beginning of the chapter up to the ninth verse. Saints in the house of God should have no respect of persons among themselves, on account of poverty or riches; and if they do, they sin. This law says nothing about what respect to persons christians should pay outside of the house of God, and in the civil government, and, as to the civil government, its officers and institutions, one of which institutions, in part of the States of this Union, is slavery. The law relating to this part of the conduct of christians, is found, Rom. xiii, 1–7; 1 Pet. ii, 13–18; 1 Tim. vi, 1–5, &c. This last passage is the one you quote from so often about "wholesome words." I shall notice it at full length hereafter, as this number is too long already. If your construction of James ii, 9, is correct, Paul and Peter were wrong in the passages above quoted. But Paul and Peter were right, and so was James; for he spoke of having respect to persons in a different relation than that of master and slave.

6. Your sixth proof also misses the case. As I have filled so much space already, I must condense now, and elaborate hereafter, if necessary. The master can feed his

hungry slave, give him drink when thirsty, clothe him when naked, and visit him when sick or in prison, as fully and as well as he could if the relation of master and slave did not exist between them. Your inference from the premises, "that as we treat the Lord's disciple, so we treat the Lord himself," and therefore, if we sell a christian slave, we sell the Lord, is not proved by the passage; but I will not now take the space to show it. Judas' crime was treason against the Lord of the universe—not the selling of him.

7. My dear brother, this is as far off lame a proof that slavery is sinful, as the old covenant argument is, as a proof of sprinkling. Do not take fright, and be scared to death, dear brother, when I say to you that the Lord is "minded to have slavery," and show you "where! where!!" In Matthew xxiii, 10, he avowed "to the multitude, and to his disciples," that Christ was *their Master*. In John xiii, 13, he told his disciples that they called him Master and Lord, and that they said well, or truly, "for so I am." Paul said to the church of God at Corinth, to them that were sanctified in Christ, and all that in every place call upon the name of Jesus Christ our Lord, both theirs and ours,[1] that they were *bought* with a price, by their said Master.[2] Paul also taught that all, including you and me, brother WILEY, are slaves either of sin or of this Lord and Master, that has bought us with so great a price,[3] the first verse of which teaching, *defines slavery*. And he taught masters of slaves, that they also had a Master in heaven,[4] who is the Lord.

In conclusion, I will say that you have given no law of the Lord of which slavery is a transgression. If slaveholding was in itself a sin, when the apostle was denouncing fornicators, idolaters, adulterers, thieves, covetuous, drunkards, *revilers*, extortioners, &c., and saying that none of them could inherit the kingdom of God, why did he not include slaveholders, if slaveholding is sinful? The law of God, as to human action, is explicit and plain. What God forbids, he forbids plainly and directly. What he does not so forbid, we have no right by reasoning (vain philosophy inspiration calls it) to declare forbidden, and incorporate our conclusions, from our reasoning, into the law of God. The law given to Adam was plain and explicit. So has

---

(1) 1 Cor. i, 2.   (2) 1 Cor. vi, 20.   (3) Rom. vi, 16-20.   (4) Eph. vi, 9; Col. iv, 1.

been every other law since given by God, as to the actions of men. If the institution of slavery is sinful, it is so because it is forbidden, and so forbidden as explicitly as drunkenness, adultery, &c., are. You have not found such a prohibition; and to make out your affirmative, you must find such a one.

JER. SMITH.

February 24th, 1861.

ELDER WILEY'S NUMBER TWO.

JER. SMITH—*Dear Brother:*—Your reply to my first article is now before me, and I feel called upon, before proceeding with my regular file of argument, to correct the errors into which you have fallen, and to show that my arguments still remain with all their force against the sin of slavery.

In regard to slavery being an institution of civil society, you say: "It must be an institution of civil society or civil government, or it is an institution of the christian kingdom."

Now, brother SMITH, upon a moment's reflection, you will certainly see that you are mistaken. You certainly will admit that paganism, civilization, and christianity, produce *three* kinds of society. Barbarism is the legitimate out-growth of paganism; civil institutions are the legitimate results of civilization; and christianity consists in strict conformity to the government of Christ's kingdom. From these *facts*, it is clearly seen, that slavery is not *necessarily* an institution either of civil society, or of the christian kingdom. It certainly can not properly belong to either. I am willing, however, to admit that slavery has been forced into civil society; but it is nevertheless a relic of paganism, and in *fact* forms no part of civil governments. Having now placed this item before you, in its proper light, I pass to notice your reply to my arguments, reviewing each item in proper order.

1. You labor to construe my first argument into what

you would call a "sophistical syllogism;" but still you fail to meet my argument. In view of the fact that God " made of one blood all nations of men to dwell on all the face of the earth,"[1] I claim that all men have one common origin. And as human laws are essential to the existence of the institution of slavery, and as God has never given to man authority to reduce his (brother) fellow-man to a level with the animal of brute creation, as does the institititution of American slavery, and as the institution, in this particular, does conflict with the law of God, therefore it is a sinful institution. This is the argument, and it remains with all its force against the sinful institution of slavery.

Again, after quoting my words, "that the institution of slavery reduces man to a level with the animal of the brute creation," you say: "This is not true, brother WILEY. The institution does no such thing."

Now, brother SMITH, I am willing to risk the whole controversy upon the truth of this declaration. If it can not be shown that the institution of slavery reduces human beings to a level with animals of the brute creation—if it can not be shown that it makes property of men, women, and children—then I am willing to give up the whole controversy. But if *this* can be shown, then you are bound to yield the whole question; for when you say " the institution does no such thing," you virtually admit that if it does, then it is a sinful institution.

Again you say: " In almost every particular is the relation between master and slave different from that between the owner and the animal of the brute creation." You have, however, *failed* to give one single instance in support of the truth of this declaration. You speak of the brutal conduct of master and slave, and of husband and wife, toward each other; but this comes not within a thousand miles of the issue between us. There is brutal conduct to be seen frequently between the owner and the horse or ox. The owner makes a brute of himself by becoming intoxicated, and abusing his property; and the animal of the brute creation becomes indignant, and retaliates with brute force upon the owner; but this does not prove that the owner and the brute sustain the same relation to each other that exists be-

---

(1) Acts xvii, 26.

tween the husband and the wife, which would be the case if your reasoning be true. You were talking about brutal conduct; I am talking of the sinful institution.

Again, you say that I quote a "scrap of home-made Scripture." I quoted nothing for Scripture without giving book, chapter, and verse. In harmony, however, with the great .truth, that "God made of one blood all nations of men," the following words were quoted: "*None but God can own a man.*" This was not quoted for Scripture; but it was spoken by one possessed of more wisdom than either of us; and is certainly true.

The following is rather a shrewd thought, and is not a little amusing. You say: "In this investigation, it is not incumbent upon any one to labor to show the righteousness of slavery." It was indeed thoughtful in you, brother SMITH, to make this suggestion; but it does not release you from the solemn responsibility of "laboring to show" that slavery *is a righteous institution.* Every affirmative has its negative, and *vice versa;* therefore, if the institution of slavery is not sinful, it must be righteous. It must be either right or wrong.

2. In regard to my argument based upon the institution of marriage, you say: "The institution of slavery is not violative of the marriage rights, any more than is civil government itself." Your proof of this assertion is, that civil government may, and often does, separate husband and wife, &c., "when the public defence, the public good, or public justice requires it." Now, dear brother, will you point to the law, even in our own State, that will separate husband and wife, in the *same sense* that slavery does this? No, you can not do it! Never! no, never!! You may point to the case of the criminal, taken from his companion for crime, and sent to prison or to death; but this is not a parallel case. The institution of American slavery—not for public good, not for public safety, not for public justice, *not for the commission of crime*—ruthlessly separates husband and wife, thus sundering God's institution of holy matrimony. If such an institution is not sinful, then it is in vain to labor to show that anything on earth is sinful.

3. In regard to my argument based upon Luke iv, 18, 19, you say: "Among the things that the prophet said he (Christ) should do, was 'to preach deliverance to the cap-

tives.'" This is right, brother Smith. And he was to "preach the Gospel to the poor;" to "heal the brokenhearted;" to preach the acceptable year of the Lord." The divine Savior has done all this, but did it through his inspired apostles. The prediction of the prophet, made some 700 years before the Savior's advent into the world, embraced more than the simple reading of the two verses. Preaching the Gospel to the poor, healing the brokenhearted, preaching deliverance to the captives, the recovering of sight to the blind, setting at liberty them that are bruised, preaching the acceptable year of the Lord, were all embraced in the work of the Lord's apostle, in preaching the Gospel to the world.[1] Jesus said in prayer to his Father, "As thou has sent me into the world, even so have I also sent them into the world."[2] Again the Savior says: "He that believeth on me, the works that I do shall he do also; and greater works than these shall he do; because I go unto my Father."[3] Now, brother Smith, from these *facts*, you are bound to admit that the minister that "preaches deliverance to the captives," preaches as did the Lord and his apostles; and that the institution that captivates and enslaves men, women, and children, is a sinful institution.

4. In regard to my argument based upon the Savior's words, "therefore all things whatsoever ye would that men should do to you, do ye even so to them; for this is the law and the prophets," you say: "Be careful, my beloved brother, that you do not get to 'seeing visions and dreaming dreams.'" This is as strong a point as you made against my fourth argument; and as I can't meet it, I will pass with this remark: that no man can practice the institution of slavery, as it is practiced in the South, without violating this rule given by the Savior.

5. Your reply to my fifth argument goes to establish the truth of my position. The argument is founded upon the following passage: "But if ye have respect to persons, ye commit sin, and are convicted of the law as transgressors."[4] And you say, "this is a law for christians in the assembly, or the house of God." Again you say: "This law says nothing about what respect to persons christians should pay

---

(1) See Acts xxvi, 16, 17, 18; Eph. iii, 8.
(2) John xvii, 18.
(3) John xiv, 12.
(4) James ii, 9.

outside the house of God," &c. Now, if you mean by "the assembly, or house of God," *the church of Christ*, then you admit the truth of my position. But if you mean nothing more than the association of christians assembled in a house, then you have two laws, one to govern christians in regard to the respect they have for each other when they are at meeting, and another law by which to regulate their conduct toward each other, when meeting is over.

Now I aver that the apostle James furnishes most conclusive evidence to show that the institution or law of slavery, is sinful. He puts in contrast most forcibly the law of *liberty*, and the law or institution of *slavery*. He says: "Whoso looketh into the perfect law of liberty, and continueth therein, he being not a forgetful hearer, but a doer of the work, this man shall be blessed in his deed."[1] Again he says: "So speak ye, and so do, as they that shall be judged by the law of liberty."[2] *The law of liberty* is here put in contrast with the *law of slavery*. "The perfect law of liberty" is the "Gospel law"—"the law of the spirit of life"—and it admits of no partiality or respect to one above another, as the law of slavery does. Thus the apostle shows clearly, that the institution of slavery conflicts with the Gospel of Christ, and is therefore a sinful institution.

6. In reply to this argument based, on Matt. xxv, 34–46, you say of me: "Your inference from the premises, 'that as we treat the Lord's disciples, so we treat the Lord,' is not proved by the passage; but I will not now undertake to show it." With an expectation that you will try to meet this argument at some future time, I pass for the present.

7. As you approach this argument you say: "Do not take a fright, and be scared to death, dear brother, when I say to you that the Lord is 'minded to have slavery,' and show you where!" You then cite Matt. xxiii, 10; John xiii, 13, to prove that Christ was a Master; for he said to the disciples that he was their Master, and they called him Master. You then quote 1 Cor. vi, 20, to prove that all christians are *slaves* This looks well. But in order to use this argument to advantage in this discussion, you should have pointed to the passage of the Savior's "slave code," where he *sold* his slaves—where he separated husband and wife, parents and children, brothers and sisters, &c.—and if this

---

(1) James i, 25.   (2) James ii, 12.

can not be found in the Lord's slave code, nor in his "mind," nor in his practice, then your labor is all lost. But this is not the worst of it. The Lord says to his disciples: "But be not ye called Rabbi (Master) for one is your Master even Christ, and all ye are brethren."[1] This puts an everlasting *veto* upon all human slave codes. Now, dear brother, you say "what the Lord commands must be done;" and so say I. There can be no christian masters without disregarding the Lord's word. But this is not all. The apostle says: "If the son therefore shall make you *free*, ye shall be *free indeed*." This shows that the christian is the Lord's freeman; and he "*shall* be free indeed." To become a servant of Jesus Christ then, destroys every relation that would make one man the property or slave of another; or that would allow one man to be called the master of another. This is what the Gospel does. You claim that "if the institution of slavery is sinful, it is so because it is forbidden; and so forbidden as explicitly as drunkenness, adultery, &c." Now, brother SMITH, you certainly know that getting drunk is not an *institution*, neither is committing adultery an institution; such actions are corrupt, wicked, brutal actions, and are the results of the sinful institution of slavery. American slavery is an institution, and it does tolerate the practice of adultery, and is therefore a sinful institution. And as certainly as adultery is sinful, the institution that tolerates it is sinful; and as certainly as adultery is forbidden, so certainly is the institution of slavery that admits it forbidden.

Having now examined your reply, and removed every thing out of the way, I will proceed with my regular file of arguments.

8. This argument is founded upon the following passage, embracing the law of love. It reads as follows: "Render therefore to all their dues; tribute to whom tribute is due; custom to whom custom; fear to whom fear; honor to whom honor. Owe no man any thing, but to love one another; for he that loveth another hath fulfilled the law. For this, thou shalt not commit adultery, thou shalt not kill, thou shalt not steal, thou shalt not bear false witness, thou shalt not covet; and if there be any other commandment, it is briefly comprehended in this saying, namely, thou shalt love

---

(1) Matt. xxiii, 8

thy neighbor as thyself. Love worketh no ill to his neighbor; therefore love is the fulfilling of the law."[1]

The point embraced in this passage is this: The Gospel law is a law of love; and as it requires its advocates to *love their neighbors as themselves*, and as *love* is the fulfilling of the law, it "therefore briefly comprehends" all the acts of benevolence necessary to adorn the christian character, and puts an everlasting end to the institution of slavery, which reduces human beings to a level with the animal of the brute creation.

Here I plant myself, and here I expect to stand, fearless of anything that can be said in favor of the righteousness of the institution of American slavery.

This law of love comprehends, in one general view, *all* the good contemplated in the Gospel of Christ; and condemns every species of wickedness—yea, everything that opposes the principles of the Gospel of Christ. Card-playing, horse-racing, and polygamy, are not once named in the New Testament; but the Gospel law, called by Paul " the law of the spirit of life ;" called by James "the perfect law of liberty," condemns all such wickedness.

9. This argument is based upon the following words of the apostle: " Behold, the hire of the laborers who have reaped down your fields, which is of you kept back by fraud, crieth ; and the cries of them which have reaped are entered into the ears of the Lord of Sabaoth."[2] The whole connection in the fifth chapter of James goes to show that this is a practical demonstration of slavery, and justly incurs the judgments of God. American slavery is no modification of the above case. If the *Bible* condemns any thing, it condemns oppression ; and if there is anything upon this broad green earth that can rightfully be called oppression, it is the institution of American slavery.

Now, brother SMITH, you must come right up to the work, and meet these arguments, or yield the cause, and admit that the institution of American slavery is a sinful institution.

THOMAS WILEY.

March 20th, 1861.

---

(1) Rom. xiii, 7-10.   (2) James v, 4.

JER. SMITH'S REPLY NUMBER TWO.

MY DEAR BROTHER WILEY:—Your number two is before me.

Clear ideas are essential to correct reasoning and just judgment. To have clear ideas, we must have correct definitions of the terms used; or, rather, we must understand the terms used in the sense in which they are used. Hence, I will try again, to explain the sense in which certain terms are used in this our friendly investigation.

In the proposition, *Slavery is an institution of civil society, or civil government*, let us settle what is meant by the terms *civil society* or *civil government*; for the two are used as synonymous.

Civil government is used in contra-distinction to *ecclesiastical* government. This nomenclature arose more than a thousand years ago, and really grew out of papistical notions and ideas. *Civil* and *ecclesiastical* were the terms used to designate the two orders of government; *secular* and *holy* the terms used to designate the officers of each respectively. The government of the Roman Emperors and their officers, were called *civil* and *secular;* while the government of the church (as it was called) and its officers were designated as *ecclesiastical* and *holy*. That nomenclature was carried into the common law when it arose in England; *civil government* was used to designate the government of the King and Parliament; and *ecclesiastical government* was applied to the church or religious government. We borrowed these terms, and the ideas conveyed by them, from the common law of England, which we inherited from her. So *civil government* or *civil society* means the government of the State, or secular government, whether it exists among a pagan people or a christian people, and whether the people were civilized or barbarous. Barbarism did not always exist among pagans; for the Greeks and Romans were pagans, and yet they were the most civilized and polished nations of antiquity. But christianity, lived up to truly, will, of course, produce a higher state of civilization, than the Greeks and Romans attained to. But I am wandering too far off.

Civil is the counterpart of *ecclesiastical*. We, of this

reformation, in our designation of things, using terms as we have for near forty years, would use the terms *human government* and *divine* government to designate them. The way they are designated in the christian Scriptures is this: Civil or secular governments, as designated by Catholics and the common law, and human governments, as we designate them, are, in the christian Scriptures, called "the kingdoms of this world;" while ecclesiastical and holy government, as designated by Catholics and the common law, stand, in their notions, in the place of what we call divine government, and in the place of what is designated in the christian Scriptures as "the kingdom of our Lord and Savior Jesus Christ." In the nomenclature of the christian Scriptures, there are but two governments—the kingdoms of this world, and the kingdom of the Lord Jesus Christ. The kingdoms of this world include all human governments, whether savage, barbarous, or civilized; and the kingdom of the Lord is the divine government during the christian dispensation. When that dispensation shall end, the Lord will surrender the kingdom to God.[1] But during its existence, it is, in the Scriptures, called the kingdom of the Lord Jesus Christ.

So the terms *civil government, civil society*, is used, and will be used by me throughout this discussion, in the sense of *human governments, kingdoms of this world;* while *divine government* and *divine law* will be used to designate the *government of the Lord Jesus Christ* and *his laws*. And, in that sense, I say that American slavery is an institution of civil government; and you agree to it in that sense; for in your last, you say "human laws are essential to the institution of slavery." So much for this; and I hope we will understand one another hereafter, and that you will attach the same idea to the words I use, that I do myself, when I use the phrases civil society, civil government, and divine government and divine law.

Another preliminary matter relating to definitions, and the having of clear ideas of things about which we talk.

You set out by quoting from John the definition of sin, that it is *a transgression of the law*. I accepted it, because it is of divine authority, and hence true. But I went on further, to give the Scripture definition of righteousness,

---
(1) 1 Cor. xv, 24–28.

that it was doing what God commanded. Sin then, is *the transgression of God's law;* and righteousness is *doing his commandments—keeping his law*. Let us keep these ideas clear in our minds, brother WILEY, when we go to examine to see whether anything is sinful or righteous. If it is a transgression of God's law, it is sin; if it is doing a command of God, it is righteous. Hence, doing a thing not forbidden of God, is not sin; and doing a thing not commanded of God, is not righteousness. Hence, to make slavery sinful, it must be forbidden: to make it righteous, it must be commanded. You have undertaken to prove it sinful; I have not undertaken to prove it righteous. But you seem to think that my denying that it is sinful, is an averment that it is righteous. Not so, my brother. But you say "it must be either right or wrong." That may be true, and still it may not be either sinful or righteous, in the Scripture sense of sin and righteousness. I will try and show you that this is so. To migrate, or travel from one place to another, may be right or wrong, that is, it may be proper or improper, expedient or inexpedient, for any particular person to do so at a particular time; but it is not righteousness to do it unless it is commanded of God, nor sinful to do it unless it is prohibited of God. Now, when Abram left Haran and went to Canaan, he did an act of righteousness, because God had commanded him to do so: and, if the apostles had gone by the way of the Gentiles, or into the cities of the Samaritans, when the Lord sent them, during his ministry, they would have sinned, because he commanded them not to do so. Any other person that went at the time Abram went, or at any other time, from Haran to Canaan, did not "do righteousness" by that act; nor did any other persons that went by the way of the Gentiles, or into the cities of the Samaritans, sin by so doing. A great many other instances could be given from Scripture to the same effect. Hence, we see the necessity, if we want to understand "the mind of Christ" and "grow in the knowledge of" him, to keep correct ideas of sin and righteousness before our minds when we presume to call anything sinful or righteous.

I will now proceed to review what you have said in your last, under the respective numerical heads.

1. As you seem to think I have "failed" to give a single

instance in support of the truth of the declaration that "in almost every particular, is the relation between master and slave different from that between the owner and the animal of the brute creation;" and reiterate the assertion that "the institution of slavery reduces human beings to a level with animals of the brute creation," I will elaborate these matters some further.

Does the institution of slavery deprive human beings of speech, of thought, of the reasoning powers, of the mental faculties generally, of the affections, of the erect attitude or upright position in which God formed man to go, of an immortal spirit, and of religious aspirations toward his Maker? It must do all this, and even more, before it can be *truly* said that it reduces human beings *to a level* with animals of the brute creation; for they lack all these things. I can not now call to mind but *one* particular in which the relation between master and slave, and the relation between the owner and the animal of the brute creation, is the same, and that particular is the relation of owner and owned. In everything else that I can now think of, the relation between them is different. The relation between the master and the slave is that of man and man, with all the concomitants of conversation, society, &c., &c., including the high and holy relation of brethren in the kingdom of Christ; while the relation between the owner and the animal of the brute creation, is simply that of man and brute, differing in almost every respect from that of man and man.

Now, though you are "willing to risk the whole controversy on the truth" of the declaration that "the institution does no such thing" as reduce human beings to the level of brutes, I shall not hold you to it, though I have shown that it "does no such thing." My object is to convince your judgment, not to obtain a mere polemic victory, in this friendly investigation. It is best, however, as I think you will see now, to come down to sober truth, and drop all such exaggerated assertions that have been asserted and re-asserted so long by excited, if not demented persons, that many good people have unfortunately fallen into the belief of them, without examination as to their truth.

I did not complain that you did not quote chapter and verse for your home-made Scripture, nor that you quoted it for Scripture. I only tried to induce you to rely upon

Scripture itself, and not upon home-made scraps of any kind. I do not know who is the author of the scrap, "none but God can own a man," and do not pretend to say but that he was "possessed of more wisdom than either of us;" but I have said that "it is contradictory of divine Scripture, as will appear before we get through this discussion," which I now reiterate, and add to it, that the scrap is untrue, notwithstanding the wisdom of its author, as any one may be convinced who will travel from Cincinnati south to the Gulf of Mexico, in which travel he will find that others than God not only can, but actually do, own many men.

According to your own opinion of your first argument, as you state the argument in your last number, *that slavery reduces man to the level of the brute creation*, is a necessary part; and as I have shown that proposition to be untrue, that argument fails. As I said in my first, this argument is a fallacy. Stripped of all verbiage, it is this: All men have a common origin, therefore slavery is sinful! Most illogical! And it is contradicted by a fact patent to every one. Parents and children are of the *same blood*, and yet parents have property in their children, and the children property in their parents, both by civil law and divine law.

But there is another thing that exists in this argument, that exists in nearly all the others, and I had as well notice it here, once for all. It is, that you come to the conclusion that a thing is sinful, through three or four deductions from some passage of Scripture, or from some principle taught in the Scriptures. Now, that method of proceeding is called in the Scriptures "philosophy and vain deceit, after the traditions of men, after the rudiments of the world, and not after (or according to) Christ;" and the command is, to "beware lest any man spoil"[1] us through it. To this I will at this time add, that from the day that God put Adam into the garden of Eden, and gave him the law of his conduct, down to the close of the book of Revelations, there is no recorded case of God's holding any one accountable for a sin, and as a sinner, for violating something that was arrived at only by some two, three or four deductions from something that God had said. And in all cases where God held any one accountable as a sinner, it was for the violation of something that God had directly said. Sin and

---

(1) Col. ii, 8.

righteousness, based upon inferences, built up the papacy, and, with other things, brought on the long night of moral darkness, which has now, thank God, nearly passed away. We should come out not only from Bablyon, but from her practices. If we follow her practices, we are so far a part of her. Coming out of the communion and ecclesiastical body of the Man of Sin, does not prevent us from being a part of the Man of Sin, if we follow his practices and do his work. We must not only come out of Babylon, but we must leave there everything Babylonish, even though it be "a goodly Babylonish garment,"[1] of reasoning men to act from their deductions from what God has said, instead of acting directly from what he has said, without the deduction or the inference. I say these things that you may reflect upon them, and examine the good word of God to see whether these things are so: and that you may cease to try to prove slavery sinful by inference, and begin to look up direct proof of its sinfulness.

2. The laws of Indiana divorce men and their wives, and take children from one or both of the parents, as the case may be, for all time to come; and slave laws do it for no longer a time. Indiana has never had occasion to do it— but she may; and other States of the Union have had occasion to draft husbands, fathers and brothers, from wives, children and sisters, and take them to battle where they were slain and never returned. And the European governments are now constantly doing this.

I must correct another incorrect assertion, brother WILEY. The institution does not "ruthlessly separate" husband and wife. Bad masters may, and perhaps sometimes do; but not a thousandth part of the instances that have been constantly represented throughout the North, during the last ten or fifteen years, ever existed in fact. When masters do so, it is their sin, and is so set down in the law of God governing in the premises; and not a word of condemnation, in that place, of the *institution* or relation existing between the master and the slave, is found.

3. I admit, brother WILEY, that what the apostles preached and taught, is the preaching and teaching of the Savior; for he sent them as he was sent. But please to cite me to the passage where either he or the apostles preached "de-

---

(1) Josh. vii, 21.

liverance to the captives," in your sense of deliverance, to-wit, freeing the slaves, (and all the country they all preached and taught in was full of slaves,) and that will show that it is right to preach abolitionism, and that your construction of the prophecy that the Savior read,[1] is right. The passages you cite me to, Acts xxvi, 16–18; Eph. iii, 8, say nothing about slavery, freeing the slaves, or even about captives. The first is a rehearsal, by Paul, of his conversion; and the second says he was to preach *the unsearchable riches of Christ*—not that the slaves should be freed, nor that slavery was sinful. Would it not be well for preachers to do that way now?

4. The Golden Rule. I warned you about visions and dreams, because you had, in your first number, mentioned visions and dreams. You wholly fail to answer my inquiry, why, if your construction of the Golden Rule is right, the apostles, in writing to christian masters and slaves, did not tell them so, and direct the masters to free the slaves. You, however, close with the broad assertion, " that no man can practice the institution of slavery, as it is practiced in the South, without violating this rule." What a pity that Paul made so great a mistake in Philemon's case, in sending Onesimus back to serve him, instead of telling Philemon that he could not retain Onesimus as a slave, without violating the Lord's Golden Rule; and that he must let Onesimus go; and that if he did not, he would sin. But it needed the light of modern wisdom, without revelation, to so learn Paul his duty in that case, and the other cases where he wrote to masters as to how they should demean themselves to their slaves.

Let us examine this Golden Rule a little, and see whether you understand it. In creeds and larger and shorter chatechisms, and in spelling books, when I was a boy, it was put down thus: *Whatsoever ye would that men should do to you*, in like circumstances, *do ye even so to them*. But that is not the rule; yet your interpretation makes that the rule. But the rule is: *Whatsoever you would that men should do to you, do ye even so to them.* Let us apply this to the master and slave directly. Does the master want the slave to free him? No: because the master is free. Hence, he need not free the slave, as he does not want the slave to

---

(1) Luke iv, 18, 19.

free him. Does the slave want the master to free him? Though it might be, and is otherwise with most of the slaves, let the answer be, yes. But the slave can not do to the master what he wants the master to do to him, because the master is already free. So that in the case in discussion, to-wit, that between the master and the slave, where the slave wants to be liberated, the Golden Rule does not direct the master to liberate the slave, and the master's failing to do it, is not a violation of the Golden Rule, *unless the phrase*, in like circumstances, *be interpolated into the rule.* All your argument from this rule requires that interpolation into it. Brother WILEY, we do not want the Scriptures interpolated; and it seems now, from the examination, that Paul and Peter were right, in not telling christian masters, in their epistles, that slaveholding was a violation of the Lord's Golden Rule.

5. The Lord has two sets of laws for his disciples; one to govern them and their conduct in his house and kingdom, and with and towards their brethren in Christ, and one to govern them in their conduct " towards them that are without,"[1] and as being members or subjects of the kingdoms of this world. But to "rightfully divide the word of truth,"[2] on this subject, will come up hereafter, and will take too much space here. The "law of liberty" mentioned by James is not a law to free slaves who are slaves by the laws of the kingdoms of this world; but I forbear to elaborate and show that at present.

6. I can now only briefly say, that worshipping the Lord's disciple, is not worshipping him; hence the passage, Matt. xxv, 34-46, does not prove that as we treat the Lord's disciples, we treat him. But more of this hereafter.

7. The Savior is a good Master, and keeps his Father's commandments; and hence does not violate any of the divine laws relating to masters. And as to selling, separating husband and wife, &c., which is uppermost so much in heated imaginations, I have not space to elaborate now. I will only at this time briefly say, that he chose Paul, saying at the time he "captivated" him, that he would "show him how great things he had to suffer" for him;[3] which things Paul did suffer, even to the giving up of his life. Stephen, James, Peter, Paul, and, it is said, all the apostles except

---

(1) Col. iv, 5; 1 Cor. v, 12, 13.   (2) 2 Tim. ii, 15.   (3) Acts ix, 16.

John, were "sold" even unto death, in the service of the Lord, as well as into prison, to stripes, &c. So much is not exacted of slaves in any State of this Union! The Lord took upon him the form of a slave, and was *obedient* unto death, *even* the death of the Cross, which, by the Roman law, was inflicted only on slaves and malefactors. Such obedience is not exacted of any slave in the United States. This was the "mind" that was in Christ, that we are directed to have in us.[1] Look at the passage carefully, and you will see that for his so demeaning himself, he was highly exalted, and given a name above every other name. We, by being like-minded, and conducting ourselves as he did, will be exalted also. With an abolition imagination, *and manner of speaking of things*, but actually sticking to the facts, and not exaggerating or adding to the facts recorded of these slaves of the Lord, and the Lord himself, quite a raw-head and bloody-bones account could be framed. But I will not do it. Such exaggerated pictures, it is not proper for christians to draw, even of matters pertaining to the laws and administration of the civil government, much less of those appertaining to the kingdom of the Lord. Christians' speech should "be seasoned with salt,"[2] and they should think on "whatsoever things are true,"[3] and not contemplate exaggerated fictions. When I have space, I shall dwell somewhat at length upon this branch of the inquiry. I will now only say, that in the kingdom of God, we have but one Pope, that is, Father, who is God; one Lord, that is, Master, who is Christ; and all of us are brethren;[4] while in the kingdoms of this world, there are gods many and lords many.[5] And the divine law gives rules to govern christians in their conduct in both kingdoms. And becoming a member of the Lord's kingdom, does not free us from the kingdoms of this world, and from our duties in them, while we live on earth.

8. I can notice this but very briefly now. "Render therefore to all their dues." What dues, brother WILEY? Why, dues under the civil government, its laws, institutions and regulations. Slaves, in our Constitution, are defined to be persons held to service by the laws of a State. The services of the slave, therefore, in our kingdoms of this

---

(1) Phil. ii, 5–9. (3) Phil. iv, 8. (5) 1 Cor. viii, 5.
(2) Col. iv, 6. (4) Matt. xxiii, 8–10.

world, are "dues" to the master. This divine law, to render to all their dues, is an injunction to the christian slave to render to his master the service "due" the master by the laws of the State; to the christian subject of a monarchy, to render the taxes military and other services "due" the monarch, by the laws of the kingdom; to the christian citizen of this republic, to render to the other States, and to the citizens of the other States, their "dues" under the Constitution and laws, that is, to let them have peace and quiet, and to give them kindness and courtesy in our conduct towards them personally, and protection to them and their institutions, *including the slaves held to service to them, by the laws of their States,* &c. These are their "dues" under our Constitution, and the Union formed thereby. More on this subject hereafter.

Card-playing and horse-racing are modern sins, manufactured by the same methods that manufactured the Man of Sin. They may, and generally do, lead to sin; but are not sinful by the law of the Lord. Polygamy is forbidden in the christian Scriptures.

9. Because those who *hire* laborers to reap down their fields, and then keep back the *hire* of the laborers *by fraud*, commit sin thereby that entereth into the ears of the Lord of Sabaoth; therefore, slavery is sinful! This is the argument. This must be a curious passage of Scripture; for it seems that anything can be proved by it. An excellent brother, who had insisted rather unsuccessfully that I should pay him for certain of his missionary labor that he said he had been doing, finally thundered this passage at me. In reply, I simply informed him that I had not *hired* him to reap any field for me. So a christian master can reply to you, that he has not *hired* his slaves; and in addition to that, he can say, that he regularly "renders" to his slaves their "dues." Brother WILEY, this passage fits neither my missionary brother's case, nor yours.

I have tried to "come right up to the work, and meet" your arguments, brother WILEY; and I apprehend that you will do me the justice to admit that I have "come right up" at least: I think I have met them.

Yours in christian bonds,
JER. SMITH.

March 26*th*, 1861.

ELDER WILEY'S NUMBER THREE.

Dear Brother Smith :—Your reply number two is now before me, and I am truly glad that our labors have been characterized thus far by a kind christian spirit.

In your last article, you labor extensively to show the meaning of certain words and phrases; and to prove that, according to *your* use of them, American slavery is an institution of "civil society."

You define "civil society or civil government" to mean *all human governments*, whether savage, barbarous, or civilized. And, in "that sense," you say: "American slavery is an institution of civil society or civil government." And you further say, " that is the sense in which you have used, and intend to use these terms." In your definitions you have given the *legal* or technical meaning of those terms; and your solution of the question stands thus: Civil society or civil government *means all human governments*, savage and barbarous, as well as civilized. Now, brother Smith, I cheerfully accept your definitions; for you have fully sustained the truth of my position on this point.

My position in the very commencement of this discussion was, that slavery originated in paganism, and that its tendencies are back to paganism again. I did not claim that slavery *is* paganism, but that it originated *in* paganism, and that its tendencies are back to where it originated.

In my second article, it was shown that barbarism is the legitimate outgrowth of paganism; and that barbarism, paganism, and civilization, form *three* kinds of society: and this you admit. And as the *barbarous* institution of slavery, a relic of paganism, has been *forced* into civil society, it therefore forms no part of civil society in *fact;* it belongs to civil society, *only* in your qualified sense, which is, that civil society *means savage*, and *barbarous* society. This was my position at the commencement of this discussion, and this is the truth of the case. Slavery is indeed a savage, barbarous, sinful institution, turn it which way you will. The proposition, that "slavery is an institution of civil society," is not the question we proposed to discuss; but still I am much pleased with what you have said upon it. Your definitions have fully established the truth of my position; and it will hereafter be clearly understood, that slavery belongs to savage, barbarous society, technically called "civil society." And it will be remembered also, that every effort you make, brother SMITH, to show that American slavery is not sinful, you are laboring to show that savage barbarity is not sinful. And if it can be shown that savage barbarity *is* sinful, *then is American slavery sinful*. And if you admit that savage barbarity is sinful, (and this you must do) then you admit, upon purely logical principles, that slavery is a sinful institution. From these conclusions there is no way of escape.

The next item to be noticed is the *criterion* by which the proposition in debate must be settled. It will be remembered, that at the commencement of this our friendly investigation, it was shown that *sin* is the transgression of God's law; and to this you agree. It was also shown that "all unrighteousness is sin." Now, according to these definitions of sin, given in the precise words of the Scripture, it will be seen, that whatever an individual does that is not righteousness, must be sinful. And hence I repeat it, that slavery must be either right or wrong.

But you labor to show that sin and righteousness depend entirely upon positive express commands. That to *do* a positive express cammand, is righteousness; and to *do* what is positively and expressly forbidden, is sinful. And, upon the principle of positive and express requisitions, you suspend the *whole* of the righteousness or sinfulness of the acts of the human family. And, in order to establish the truth of this position, you illustrate by two given cases: the case of Abram and the Lord's apostles. You say: "When Abram went from Haran to Canaan, he did an act of righteousness, because God commanded him to do so;" and "if the apostles had gone by the way of the Gentiles, or into the cities of the Samaritans, when the Lord sent them during his ministry, they would have sinned, because he commanded them not to do so." Then you add: "Any other person that went at the time Abram went, or at any other time, from Haran to Canaan, did not do righteousness by that act; nor did any other person that went by the way of the Gentiles, or into the cities of the Samaritans, sin by so doing."

Here is your argument, brother SMITH, to establish the

truth of your proposition, that the sinfulness and righteousness of man *wholly* depends upon disobedience or obedience of the *positive, express* commands of God. You have committed a fatal error at this point, as I will now proceed to show.

While there is no man who believes more in positive divine institutions than myself, and while no one believes more fully than I do, that God has given to man, in his written word, a *full* and *complete* plan of salvation, still there are *moral* obligations and *moral* duties, as clearly set forth in the Gospel, as there are positive express commandments. There are *positive, moral,* and *relative* obligations or duties to be performed. And as no one but Abram was commanded to go to Canaan, in the same sense that he was, therefore it was a special case, and comes within the purview of *moral* obligations of the Gospel of Christ. As well might an individual bring up the case of the thief on the Cross, to prove the *general* rule or plan of salvation, revealed in the christian Scriptures, as to bring up Abram's case to establish the truth of your position. Sending out the apostles was another *special* case, a parallel case with the one just examined; and no more establishes the truth of your position, than the case of the palsied man being miraculously cured, establishes the *plan* of salvation.

In order to show more forcibly the total failure of your position, and to exhibit the *moral* obligations set forth in the Golden Rule—the law of love—I will instance a few cases. There is, or has been, systems, legalized systems of gambling, called lotteries, in our country; and still there is not one *express* command in the Scriptures about them. Are we, therefore, left in the dark on this subject? Or could we all engage in such business and not commit sin? Again, men assemble together at the card-table, stake their money, and play cards, win or lose; and still there is no *positive, express* command on the subject. Can individuals, therefore, practice gambling of this kind and not commit sin? Or does the *moral* government of the Lord Jesus Christ—" the Golden Rule "—condemn all such things? It most assuredly does. Once more: Were a company of persons, in a clandestine manner, to place some obstruction in the pathway between your mansion-house and your office, and cause you to get some of your limbs broken, could they do so, and not commit sin? There is no such thing positively or expressly forbidden. But the law of love—the moral principle of the gospel—clearly forbids and condemns all such things.

Many more cases might be offered; but one more will suffice for the present. Were a company of persons to fasten the iron grasp upon you and me, brother SMITH, and force us and our families from our comfortable dwellings, and place us entirely in the same condition that the institution of American slavery places human beings, could such an act be done and no sin committed by it? Let this be answered according to the Golden Rule—according to the law of love, and the whole question will be forever settled.

The next item is in reference to the institution of slavery *reducing* human beings to a level with the animal of the brute creation.

On this point you say: " Does the institution of slavery deprive human beings of speech, of thought, of the reasoning powers, of the mental faculties generally, of the affections," &c.

Now, brother SMITH, I did not say that slavery *makes* of human beings animals of the brute creation, as you would have me to say, or as your reply indicates; for that would be a contradiction of terms; but I did say, that the institution of slavery *reduces* human beings to a level with the animal of the brute creation. That is what I said; and in the true sense of this subject, that position can be maintained.

You ask, " Does the institution of slavery deprive human beings of speech?" I answer, yes! It does not always deprive them of the *power* of speech, but it does indeed deprive them of the *liberty* of speech,[1] and that is the *true* sense in which I am discussing this subject; and in that sense it does *reduce* human beings to a level with the animal of the brute creation.

In the true sense of the institution of slavery, and in reference to the *fact* of it *reducing* human beings to a level with the animal of the brute creation, I will offer the following: As the animal of the brute creation is an article of

---

(1) Were brother WILEY alive now, what would he say of Burnside and his order " No. 38," and Hascall and his order " No. 9 " and of the banishment of Vallandigham? Would he not say that those Generals and the administration were reducing free American citizens to the level of the animal of the brute creation, and hence sinful institutions?

merchandize, so is the slave. As the animal of the brute creation is taught to know the meaning of words expressive of the will of the owner, so is the slave. As the animal of the brute creation is compelled by *force* to obey the will of the owner, so is the slave. As the animal of the brute creation is deprived of owning anything, so is the slave. As the animal of the brute creation may be deprived of nurturing and enjoying the association of its offspring, so may the slave. As the owner of the animal of the brute creation can sell the animal at pleasure, even so can the slave be sold. As the owner of the animal of the brute creation disregards the affections (for the animal of the brute creation, brother SMITH, has both mind and affections) of the animal by separating it from its mate, and its offspring, even so does the institution of slavery disregard the affections of the slave, by separating him from his companion and offspring, and thus *reducing* him to a level with the animal of the brute creation.

In all these cases, and in many more, does the institution of slavery reduce, or bring down, human beings to a level with the animal of the brute creation. And I am still willing to risk the whole controversy upon the truth of this one item. "Sober truth" is enough for me.

"None but God can own a man." You inform me that if I will take a tour to the South, I will certainly see that the above quotation is not true. Well, I am willing to admit that, by the authority of the *sinful* institution of slavery, one man is permitted to own another, as an article of merchandise; but *none but God can own a man*, in the true sense of ownership. No man can own his fellow-man, only by authority of the sinful institution of oppression, made by man, in direct opposition to the law of the divine lawgiver.

Next in order comes the item of separating families. On this item you say: "The laws of Indiana divorce men and their wives, and take children from one or both of their parents, as the case may be, for all time to come; and the slave laws do it for no longer time." Now, brother SMITH, these remarks of yours fail to reach the point I made. My argument went to show, that husbands and wives, being separated by divorce, or parents and children, being separated by being called into the service of their country, does not separate families in the same sense that slavery separates them. This must be done, brother SMITH, otherwise the argument fails to reach the case. But you claim that I have fallen into an error by saying that the institution of slavery *ruthlessly* separates husband and wife. This is not an error; it is strictly true. Take for example the following: Deacon A., quite a respectable man, by the authority of the peculiar institution, owns a number of slave families, men, women, and children; he is kind to them, even better than the law requires; but he is suddenly called by death away, and they are left to the tender mercies of the institution : what now is done with them? What will the peculiar institution do for them? They are *forced* to the auction block, where the institution, with all its tender mercies, *ruthlessly* separates husband and wife, parents and children, to realize all the horrors of perpetual bondage. This, dear brother, is what the institution of slavery does do; and if such an institution is not *sinful*, then it is no use to talk about anything being sinful.

The next item is your reply to my argument on Luke iv, 18, 19. But you so signally failed to remove, or to even weaken the force of my argument, that it is unnecessary to make any further defence of it now.

But again: In regard to the Golden Rule you say: " What a pity Paul made so great a mistake in Philemon's case, in sending Onesimus back to serve him, instead of telling Philemon that he could not retain Onesimus as a slave, without violating the Lord's Golden Rule; and he must let Onesimus go free; and if he did not he would sin." I am glad that you brought up this case; for I am prepared, by it, to show two facts: first, that Philemon and Onesimus were brothers according to the flesh; and second, after Onesimus was converted to christianity, he was no longer bound to service. If this can be done, then one of two things must be true. He was not a servant in the sense of American slavery; or the Gospel, when it converts a man, destroys the relation of master and slave. If the truth or the above statements is questioned, I pledge myself to sustain them; but for the present, I will pass to notice some other remarks made in regard to the Golden Rule. You say: " The slave can not do to his master what he wants the master to do to him, because the master is already free."

The Golden Rule says, "All things whatsoever ye would that men should do to you, do ye even so to them." But you say this can not be done! "The slave can not do to his master what he wants the master to do to him." Thus you have shown, that the institution of slavery makes it impossible for the Golden Rule to be obeyed. The Lord has given this rule, and its moral obligations rest upon every human being; but you have shown that it is morally, yea, utterly impossible for the slave, while he remains in slavery, to obey it. Now, brother SMITH, you certainly can see, that, according to your own showing, it is the sinful institution of slavery that places individuals in such a condition that they can not obey God. The slaveholder won't obey the Golden Rule and free his slaves, as he would that others should do to him; and therefore the slave can not obey it, according to your own showing. If an institution, that makes it impossible to obey the moral obligations plainly set forth in the word of the Lord, is not sinful, then it is in vain to try to show that anything is sinful. But if masters would obey the moral obligations contained in the Golden Rule, and free their slaves, then the slave could also obey the moral obligations of this rule.

Again you say: "The Lord has two sets of laws for his disciples; one to govern them in their conduct in his house and kingdom, and with and towards brethren in Christ, and one to govern them in their conduct towards them that are without, and as being members or subjects of the kingdoms of this world." But you passed from this item without defining yourself; and I think that you have placed yourself in a dilemma, turn which way you will. But I wait to hear from you again.

In your next item you say: "The Savior is a good Master;" but you fail to show his *slave code*, or to show that he *sold* his slaves for money. I can not see what you introduce this item for, unless it was to prove that American slavery is a righteous institution. If this is your object, then you must show *where* the Lord made merchandise of his disciples, and bought and sold them for money. If this is not your object, then your pleadings on this point has no bearing on the subject in dispute.

In reply to my argument, based upon the passage, "Render therefore to all their dues," you ask, "What dues, brother WILEY?" Then you answer: "Why, dues under the civil government, its laws, institutions, and regulations." Again, you say: "Slaves, in our Constitution, are defined to be persons held to service by the laws of a State. The service of the slave is, therefore, in our kingdom of this world, due to the master." Thus it is seen, that your reply is *wholly* based upon the assumption that the institution of slavery is a righteous institution. You are compelled first to go to the law authorizing slavery; and then *assume* that it has the *divine sanction* upon it; and then you *assert* that the apostle, when he said, "render to all their dues," *meant* the service of the slave to his master. But as you promise more on this point, I will wait to see if you have anything better.

Your last item in reply number two, is an *attempt* to meet my 9th argument; but for some cause, either for the want of time, or space, or ideas, you failed to reach the argument. You related an anecdote about some good missionary brother, and closed your argument, and left my argument standing, with all its force against the institution of slavery.

I will now proceed with my regular file of arguments.

10. This, my tenth argument, is founded upon the following words of the apostle: "Where there is neither Greek nor Jew, circumcision nor uncircumcision, Barbarian, Scythian, bond nor free: but Christ is all in all."[1] This passage shows that the Gospel of Christ sets aside Judaism, Barbarism, or slavery, and makes all one in Christ; and that "Christ is all in all." Thus it is shown that the barbarous institution of slavery is sinful.

11. This argument is drawn from the following passage: "And whatsoever ye do in word or deed, do all in the name of the Lord Jesus, giving thanks to God and the Father by him."[2]

To do anything *in the name of the Lord*, is to do it by the *authority* of the Lord. And this passage says, "whatsoever ye do in word or deed, do all in the name of the Lord Jesus." No man, or set of men, can enact a slave code, and bring human beings into perpetual bondage, as the institution of American slavery does, without committing sin, unless the Lord Jesus has authorized it; and, as he has

---

(1) Col. iii, 11. (2) Col. iii, 17.

never authorized any such thing, therefore the institution of American slavery is a sinful institution.

Now, brother SMITH, you must meet these arguments with plain sober truth, or fail in your undertaking.

Yours in christian love,
THOS. WILEY.
April 9th, 1861.

JER. SMITH'S REPLY NUMBER THREE.

MY DEAR BROTHER WILEY:—Your number three, dated April 9th, is before me.

It seems that I must pay some more attention to the meaning of words and phrases, that we may, if possible, arrive at clear and distinct ideas. We must do that if we desire to reason correctly, and "come to the knowledge of the truth;" and if we do not, we will "never be able to come to the knowledge of the truth;" but as Jannes and Jambres withstood Moses, so we will also "resist the truth," and become of the sort who creep into houses, and lead captive silly women.[1] And, without arriving at clear, and distinct, and *correct* definitions and ideas of the words and phrases used in the good word of the Lord, we will "strive about words to no profit,"[2] which we are commanded not to do; and if we do, we sin.

I said in my last, that "*civil government* or *civil society* means the government of the State, or the secular government, whether it exists among a pagan people or christian people, and whether the people were civilized or barbarous;" and that "the terms *civil government, civil society*, are used, and will be used by me throughout this discussion, in the sense of *human governments—kingdoms of this world.*" You, in your last, state this thus: "Civil society or civil government means all human governments; savage and barbarous as well as civilized;" and you cheerfully accept that. Now look and see how you have mis-stated what I said. I spoke of civilized and barbarous *people*, while you convert

---
(1) 2 Tim. iii, 6–8.   (2) 2 Tim. ii, 14.

it into savage, barbarous, and civilized *governments*—a very different thing. But in the next step, you get still further off, and say: "It (slavery) belongs to civil society, *only* in your (my) qualified sense, which is, that civil society *means savage* and *barbarous* society"!! and afterwards, getting still further off, you go on to say, "it will hereafter be clearly understood that slavery belongs to savage, barbarous society"!!! and then you assume that I must show that "savage barbarity" is not sinful, and that you are to show that it is sinful, instead of showing that slavery is!!!

Why do you take *savage* and *barbarous*, and leave out *civilized*, when you talk of my definition of society and government, when, according to what you "accept" as what I said, it included *civilized* "as well as" *savage* and *barbarous*? Why did you not say, as you might properly have said, that "it will hereafter be clearly understood that slavery belongs to *civilized society*"? Brother WILEY, this method of proceeding is not the proper one by which to come to the knowledge of the truth.

"Sin is the transgression of the law;" "all unrighteousness is sin." Righteousness is doing the things commanded of God. These are Scripture definitions; the last, though not in the exact words of the Scripture, is scripturally accurate.

In your last you say, "whatever an individual does that is not righteous, must be sinful." Here, in a nut-shell, is the difference between us. Let us go to work, right here, and ascertain which is in error; and, having done that, we can see clearly our way further on.

Righteousness is doing God's commands. What, then, must be *unrighteousness*? Clearly *not* doing God's commands; for *un*, placed before a word, is *not*, or the negative of what is expressed by the word. Hence, the *unrighteousness* that is sin, is *the not doing of what God commands*. Consequently it is not true, that "whatever an individual does that is not righteous, must be sinful."

I desire you, brother WILEY, to examine this with that calm, candid scrutiny, that I know you have the disposition to exercise, and I am confident that you will see that it is as above stated. The above statement itself, clearly shows its truth. If, however, further elucidation of it should be necessary, 1 shall furnish it hereafter.

To call the cases of Abram's going from Haran, and the apostles' going by the way of the Gentiles, or into the cities of the Samaritans, special cases, does not aid you; for they were *laws of God* to those persons. The case of the thief on the Cross was not a law, but *a blessing bestowed*. The Savior did not command him to do anything; but because the thief believed on him, and turned and applied for aid, he pardoned him and promised him paradise. So of the palsied man, though in addition to the blessing bestowed upon him, he had a command given to him, which he obeyed.[1] But to Abram and to the apostles, commands were given, which makes those cases entirely different from the thief's case.

But I will now show that the same rule obtains in God's law to all mankind, that did in the laws cited as to Abram and the apostles.

"The wrath of God is revealed from heaven against all ungodliness and unrighteousness of men, who hold the truth in unrighteousness; *because* that which may be known of God is manifest in them; *for God hath shown it unto them*."[2]

The *wrath* of God (which is the penalty of God's law) is revealed against *not* godliness and *not* righteousness of men, who hold the truth in *unrighteousness;* that is, in disobedience of the truth, or law of God, made known of (or by) God, and manifested to them, and shown to them by God. This is shown to be so, if any more showing is necessary, in the fifth chapter of Ephesians, where it is shown that the wrath of God comes upon the *children of disobedience* Disobedience is there used to mean the same thing that *unrighteousness* is used to mean in Romans.

And upon examination you will find it to be true throughout the Scripture record, that the wrath of God came always upon disobedience or unrighteousness, both meaning the same thing. I will name some of the instances. Saul disobeyed and saved some of the spoils of Amalek. For this the wrath of God rejected him from being king, and cut off his house and posterity. The Jewish nation disobeyed the law of God given by Moses. For that the wrath of God *sold* them into *captivity* to the Babylonians, and took away their place and nation. The same nation afterwards dis-

---

(1) Matt. ix, 1-7; Mark ii, 3-12; Luke v, 18-25.   (2) Rom. i, 18-19.

obeyed God in disobeying and rejecting the Lord. For this, together with the transgression of the law they committed in murdering the Lord, the wrath of God visited the sorest vengeance and punishment upon them, which is still being inflicted, as they imprecated his blood on them and their children.[1]

You did not attempt in your last, my brother, to show any recorded case in the Bible, where God held any one to be a sinner, in any other case than for the violation of something that God had directly said—where he ever accounted any one a sinner for constructive sins, or such as were made sins by inference only from what God had said. Until you do so, it is entirely unnecessary to think about or examine what you say about gambling, lotteries, card-tables, &c. Winning money, or articles of value, is dishonesty—not providing things honest in the sight of all men, and is denounced as sinful in the christian Scripture, a half dozen times. The case of some one placing an obstruction where I was to walk, by which I would get a limb broken, is a violation of the express command to put away from us all malice, recorded three different times in the divine law.[2] But enough.

You may call slavery a "sinful institution," a "barbarous institution," &c., in every paragraph or page you write, but you do not thereby show it to be sinful; nor will you, until you show it to be in violation of something that God has directly said as a command or direction to man; and your effort to do so by inferences—two, three, or four, and sometimes five or six inferences—from a command or direction of God, is labor lost; and it looks to me like it is useless for you to further do so, until you have produced *at least one instance* where God has ever accounted any one a sinner by inference.

This is the point to which you must come, brother WILEY. But I will still go on to show that the Scriptures quoted by you do not prove slavery sinful. Many of them are so wholly irrelevant to the proposition to be proved, that it looks to me unnecessary to notice them; but, as we are laboring for our mutual instruction, I must examine them as far as space will permit.

---

[1]) Matt. xxvii, 25.   (2) Eph. iv, 30; Col. iii, 8; 1 Pet. ii, 1.

To reduce human beings *to a level* with animals of the brute creation, is to reduce them to the same position in the order of creation and existence that is occupied and filled by brutes. They must have just such powers, faculties, and qualities as brutes have, and no more. Human beings that are not brought down to that place in the scale of existence, are not reduced *to a level* with them. Slavery does not so reduce human beings.

You say it does not deprive them of the *power* of speech, but it does of the *liberty* of speech. That is another error; for they are allowed all *lawful* speech, proper for persons in their state and condition in life. Unlawful speech, which is *licentiousness of speech*, they are deprived of. Christians are deprived of the same thing, by the law of the Lord; and does that reduce christians *to a level* with animals of the brute creation? Certainly not. Here is the law of the Lord doing that: "There are many unruly and vain talkers and deceivers, specially they of the circumcision, *whose mouths must be stopped;* who subvert whole houses, teaching things which they ought not."[1] We have as many such talkers now as they had in Paul's time; who subvert not only whole houses, but whole communities; and they make great clamor about liberty of speech, when licentiousness of speech is what they mean by it.

"None but God can own a man," you now admit to be untrue in this country. I have said that it will appear before we get through this discussion, that it is contradictory of divine Scripture. I think it is now time for this to begin to appear.

"And the anger of the Lord was hot against Israel, and he delivered them into the hands of spoilers that spoiled them, and he *sold* them into the hands of their enemies round about, so that they could not any longer stand before their enemies."[2] "And the anger of the Lord was hot against Israel, and he *sold* them into the hand of Chusan-rishathaim, king of Mesopotamia."[3] "And the Lord *sold* them into the hand of Jabin, king of Canaan, that reigned in Hazor."[4] "And the anger of the Lord was hot against Israel, and he *sold* them into the hands of the Philistines, and into the hands of the children of Ammon."[5] These

---

(1) Tit. i, 10, 11. See, also, James i, 26; iii, 2–6.
(2) Judg. ii, 14.
(3) Judg. iii, 8.
(4) Judg. iv, 2.
(5) Judg. x, 7.

children of Israel were the people of God, his chosen people and possession; and we see that the Lord *sold* them these different times; and when he sold them, others than God *owned them*. It is immaterial how long, or how short the time between the sales, and the delivery or redemption of Israel by God again. After sold and before redeemed, Israel *was owned* by those to whom Israel had been sold. If it be said this was because of Israel's sin, the reply is, how do we know but that the Africans' being sold into slavery here, in the United States, is because they have sinned? We have no revelation on the subject. The providence of God, exhibited in the fact that they are enslaved here, is all that we have. Whether it is because they have sinned, or to reclaim them from the "barbarism" in which they were and still are, in Africa, and christianize them, and finally make them the means and instrument of renovating and elevating their race in Africa, we are not informed by revelation; and our reasoning and philosophical guesses at the purpose and object of God in their enslavement, are useless, if not wicked. The Spirit alone searches the deep things of God; and if they are necessary and proper for us to know, God reveals them to us by his Spirit.[1] If they are not, his judgments and determinations in the premises, are unsearchable, and his ways (Providences) are past finding out.[2]

I might as well say here, what is a reply to what you say under another head, that this is one of the ways that the Lord "sold his slaves," and "made merchandise of his people, and bought and sold them;" for it was the Lord that made these sales, and redeemed or delivered them again.

Separating families. As you have said so much about what the institution of slavery does on this subject, and about the ruthlessness of it, I will elucidate some further. "I am come to set a man at variance against [separate him from] his father, and the daughter against her mother, and the daughter-in-law against her mother-in-law. * * He that loveth father or mother more than me is not worthy of me: and he that loveth son or daughter more than me is not worthy of me. And he that taketh not his cross [of the severance of these family ties,] and followeth after me, [though these ties are thereby severed,] is not worthy of

---
(1) 1 Cor. ii, 10. (2) Rom. xi, 33.

me."[1] "If any man come to me, and hate not his father, and mother, and wife, and children, and brethren, and sisters, yea, and his own life also, *he can not be my disciple.*"[2] Is this "ruthless" and "barbarous," brother WILEY? Are those words—*ruthless* and *barbarous*—"sound words," "wholesome words," to use in speaking of it? It is a part of the Lord's system of slavery. Is christianity, therefore, sinful? Your deacon case, if it was true of the institution of slavery in our "kingdom of this world," is not as near ruthless as this in the Lord's kingdom is. But it is the laws for the levying of debts by the execution and sale of property, that makes your deacon's case, and not the institution of slavery, nor the law creating it. By them, upon deacon A.'s death, *his slaves descended to his heirs.* If he died in debt beyond the means of payment left by him, so as to require the sale of his slaves to pay his debts, and the separation of families was caused thereby, that was brother deacon A's sin, not for owning the slaves, but for transgressing that *express* law of the Lord, which commanded him to "owe no man anything, but to love one another;"[3] and it was not the sin of the institution. And if he did not die so in debt, and his heirs, in partitioning among themselves the slaves inherited by them from him, separated families, that was their sin, (if it was a sin) and not the institution's. So this ruthless matter you are so alarmed about, brother WILEY, is not the institution's at all; and, if it was, it is not any more ruthless, if as ruthless, as the system in the Lord's kingdom.

Your third argument, to-wit, Luke iv, 18, 19, is fully answered until you cite me to the passage where the Savior or the apostles, in preaching deliverance to the captives, preached that the slaves should be emancipated, or that it was sinful to hold them. I am waiting for you to cite the passage.

The Golden Rule. The rule does not require or direct the master to free the slave; because the master being free, does not want the slave or any one else to free him. And, though the slave wants the master to free him, that does not make it the duty of the master to do it under the rule; and the slave can not free the master, not because "the institution of slavery makes it impossible for the Golden

---

(1) Matt. x, 35-38.   (2) Luke xiv, 26.   (3) Rom. xiii, 8.

Rule to be obeyed," but because the master being already free, can not be freed; and that being the case, the Golden Rule does not require the slave to free the master, and hence it is not disobeyed by the slave. So the "moral obligation" of the rule (and that is nothing more than what the rule imposes by its language) does not require the master to free the slave, nor the slave to free the master; and "the institution of slavery" does not "place" any one, either master or slave, or any one else, "in such a condition that they can not obey God."

I will hear and consider what you have to say about Onesimus.

The time has not yet come, in this friendly investigation, to "rightly divide the word of truth,"[1] in relation to our duties and obligations as "members of the body of Christ," and with and towards our fellow members, and with and towards "those that are without." We will reach it in due time, if it should, by that time, be necessary to go into the investigation of that matter. The passages quoted by you from James, under your fifth argument, to be understood in the sense of inspiration, must be considered under that division.

Under your eighth argument, in reply to what I said in my last, you say I am "compelled first to go to the law authorizing slavery, and then *assume* that it has the *divine sanction* upon it." I do not *assume* it, brother WILEY, but the law of the Lord says it. For, in our "kingdom of this world," as I showed in my last, the services of the slaves are "due" the masters; and the law of the Lord says that "there is no power [in civil governments] but of God; the powers that be are ordained of God. Whosoever, therefore, resisteth the power [that ordains that the services of the slaves are "due" the masters, as well as other matters established by the civil governments], resisteth the *ordinance of God:* and they that resist shall receive to themselves damnation. For rulers are not a terror to good works, but to the evil. For he [this power of the civil government] *is the minister of God* to thee [christian] for good. * * * * Wherefore ye [christians] must needs be subject, not only for [or on account of] wrath [punishment inflicted by this civil government] but also for conscience sake. For,

---
(1) 2 Tim. ii, 15.

for this cause [that they may keep up the regulations of their civil government] pay ye [christians] tribute also : for *they are God's ministers*, attending continually upon this very thing. [You christians must] render therefore to all their dues," under the laws and regulations of these civil governments or kingdoms of this world.[1] "Submit yourselves to every *ordinance of man for the Lord's sake*," even to the ordinance of man that establishes the institution of slavery; for so is the will of God."[2]

Your ninth argument or proof, was fully met by showing that masters did not "hire" their slaves, and, of course, did not keep back their *hire by fraud*.

Your tenth argument or proof text, does not show " that the Gospel of Christ sets aside * * slavery," and prove that the "institution of slavery is sinful." It does not have any relation whatever to slavery.

11. "Whatsoever ye do in word or deed, do all in the name of the Lord;" therefore, when you "submit yourselves" to the "ordinance of man," establishing slavery, you do it in the name, or by the *express* authority of the Lord, as above shown; but when you "resist," "in word or deed," you do not do it in the name of the Lord, or by his authority, but directly against it; and they that resist, &c.

Affectionately yours,
JER. SMITH.

April 15th, 1861.

This last letter was never answered by brother WILEY, and the discussion ended here. Whether it was because he began to doubt the correctness of his abolition opinions, and that he might examine more fully and carefully the good word of the Lord upon the subject, before he proceeded further with the discussion, I do not know; but I am inclined to believe that that was the reason. He was a very honest, candid man with himself, as well as with all others. And when he had reason to fear that he was wrong in anything, he went to work, faithfully and honestly, to ascertain the truth of the matter; and if he found himself in error, to correct it. That trait in his character was a principal reason why I entered into the friendly investigation with him.

He lived more than a year after the close of the forego-

---

(1) Rom. xviii, 1–7. (2) 1 Pet. ii, 13 and 15. See, also, Matt. xxii, 21.

ing correspondence, and died in August, I believe, of 1862. He was an excellent man, and I have no doubt has gone to be with the Lord. He went to prepare a place for his disciples, that where he is, there they may be also.[1] I have no doubt but brother WILEY has gone there. O! that I may so conduct myself as to meet him in those happy mansions, is my prayer.

As all who undertook to sustain the proposition, *Slavery is sinful*, desisted before the discussion was concluded—in brother Boggs' case before it was begun—I shall now proceed to close the discussion, *ex parte*. I would much prefer having an able, candid opponent, that all that can be urged in favor of the proposition might be considered. Proceeding alone, I may overlook some things that many honest people think go to sustain the truth of the proposition.

I shall, as I proceed, so far as it falls in my way, show the sinfulness of abolitionism.

June 20th, 1863.

---

(1) John xiv, 2, 3.

CONCLUSION

OF THE

DISCUSSION OF SLAVERY.

FOR SIN IS THE TRANSGRESSION OF THE LAW.[1]
FOR WHERE NO LAW IS, THERE IS NO TRANSGRESSION.[2]
SIN IS NOT IMPUTED WHERE THERE IS NO LAW.[3]
FOR BY THE LAW IS THE KNOWLEDGE OF SIN.[4]
I HAD NOT KNOWN SIN BUT BY THE LAW: FOR I HAD NOT KNOWN LUST, EXCEPT THE LAW HAD SAID, THOU SHALT NOT COVET.[5]

These are all divine oracles. They are plain and easy to be understood. They clearly teach that sin is the transgression of the law; that where there is no law, there is not, and, of course, can not be transgression of law, which constitutes sin; and hence, that sin is not imputed when there is no law. They also clearly teach that we acquire the knowledge of sin by the law; that we know what is sin only by the law; because we would not have known inordinate desire, or lust, if the law had not said, Thou shalt not covet, or desire inordinately. See *New Translation*.

Yet brother BUTLER labored through many of the preceding pages, as the reader will see, to bring me and our readers to the knowledge that slavery is sin, by argument, reasonings, philosophical deductions, " the inexorable logic of events, guided and controlled by the hand of the Omnipotent One,"[6] notwithstanding these divine oracles, emanating

---

(1) 1 John iii. 4.
(2) Rom. iv, 15.
(3) Rom. v, 13.
(4) Rom. iii, 20.
(5) Rom. vii, 7.
(6) Ante, p. 159.

from the Omnipotent One, show that he does not bring us to the knowledge of sin by logic, exorable or inexorable, nor by events, but by his law. And brother WILEY also thought that I "committed a fatal errror" in insisting upon what these divine oracles assert.[1]

As these men who had been a long time in the reformation, still had such ideas and notions when they wrote what precedes, and could not be convinced of the error they were in, by what I have already said on the subject, hundreds and thousands of others, who are honest and good people, who have, in word and theory, come out of Babylon and eschewed everything Babylonish, of course, still adhere to this course of ascertaining sin and righteousness; which method of determining and ascertaining what is sinful and what is righteous, was, and is, the very cause and sustenance of the great apostacy, and which created, built up, and sustained the Man of Sin and the Mother of Harlots, with all her harlotrous brood; hence, I deem it proper to dwell some longer upon this subject, before I proceed to the further direct discussion of the proposition, *Slavery is sinful.* Because, if we of this reformation follow this practice of the old Harlot, we will only add another one to her already numerous brood.

By the law is the *knowledge* of sin. I had not *known* sin but by the law. KNOWLEDGE, then, is an important *thing* to be understood; hence, I must briefly examine what it is, and how and whence we acquire it.

Knowledge is defined by lexicographers to be certain perception; learning, illumination of the mind.

Knowledge, as possessed by the various, perhaps myriads, of orders of intelligences, ascending from man up to God, we can have no conception of; much more, of that possessed by God himself. Our intellects are wholly incapable of having perception, much more *certain* perception of the knowledge of which superior intellects are possessed, and capable of being possessed. Take an instance, which will give us the idea. God has revealed to us the fact that we are to have a future existence after death. We are told that our bodies shall be raised spiritual bodies. The Lord was raised, and was exhibited openly after his resurrection, during forty days. We know these to be truths because

---
(1) Ante, p. 244.

they come from God. Yet we can not have "certain perception" about our future bodies, and our existence in the future state. The beloved disciple John could not; for to him, it did " not yet appear what we shall be: but we know that, when he shall appear, we shall be like him; for we shall see him as he is."[1] John saw the Lord after his resurrection, and when he ascended, but he could not say how he would appear when he came again. All that he could comprehend and communicate by revelation to us, was, that we shall be like him when he does come. Hence, *knowledge* beyond our sphere, and the things of our sphere, we can not have. While in this state of existence, things beyond our sphere rest with us, in *faith* and *hope*.

KNOWLEDGE, then, with us, relates to man, to his origin, his habitation, his mission, his history, and his destiny. Of these things we can acquire knowledge; and whatever we know of, or relating to these things, WE DERIVE FROM GOD.

God communicates knowledge to us, through his word, by his Spirit. "In the beginning [of creation] was the word; and the word was with God; and the word was God. This was in the beginning with God. All things were made by it; and without it, not a single creature was made. In it was life, and the life was the light [illumination] of men."[2] "And the word became incarnate, and sojourned among us * * * full of *favor* and *truth*."[3] He is the true light that enlightens or illuminates the human family.[4] He is the light or luminary of the world of mankind.[5] He walked with Adam in the garden of Eden; he talked with Abraham; he dwelt with the children of Israel;[6] his delights were with the sons of men;[7] his testimony is the spirit of prophecy;[8] in him are laid up *all the treasures* of wisdom and knowledge;[9] and he is both the POWER of God, and the WISDOM of God,[10] "who of God is made unto us wisdom, and righteousness, and sanctification, and redemption."[11] The knowledge that he communicates to the human family, is "the knowledge of the Lord," which is finally to cover the earth as the waters do the sea.[12]

Much of the knowledge communicated to the human family God revealed through the prophets and apostles,

---

(1) 1 John iii, 2.
(2) John i, 1-4, *N. T.*
(3) John i, 14, *N. T.*
(4) John i, 9.
(5) John viii, 12.
(6) Num. xxxv, 34.
(7) Prov. viii, 31.
(8) Rev. xix, 10.
(9) Col. ii, 3, *new translation*.
(10) 1 Cor. i, 24.
(11) 1 Cor. i, 30.
(12) Hab. ii, 14; Is. xi, 9.

"by his Spirit; for the Spirit searcheth all things, yea, the deep things of God. For what man knoweth the things of a man, save the spirit of man which is in him? even so the things of God *knoweth no man*, but the spirit of God."[1] Hence, they received "the Spirit which is of God; that they might know the *things* [proper or necessary for us to know] that were freely given to them of God,"[2] to communicate to us. "Which things also" they spoke, "not in words taught by human wisdom, [philosophy or reasoning] but in words taught by the Spirit, explaining spiritual *things* in spiritual *words*,"[3] or words taught by the Spirit. See what pains were taken to express the *things* that God by his Spirit revealed to us, by words selected by the Spirit, that we might fully understand them. And we are commanded to "let no one deceive himself. If any one among you thinks to be wise in this age, [the christian age] let him become a fool [throw away all his human wisdom, and philosophy and reasoning in matters pertaining to God, and his government and control of us as a part of his creation,] that he may be wise. For the wisdom of this world is foolishness with God; for it is written, 'he entangles the wise in their own craftiness.' And again, 'the Lord knows the *reasonings* of the wise, that they are vain.'"[4] Mr. Wesley, on the above clause, *he entangles the wise in their own craftiness*, says: "Not only while they think they are acting wisely, but by their very wisdom, which *itself* is their snare and the occasion of their destruction." Hence, we should cast down or destroy "reasoning, and every high thing which exalteth itself against the knowledge of God."[5] "Knowing this first, that no prophecy of Scripture is of private impulse: for never, at any time, was prophecy brought by the will of man; but the holy men of God spoke, being moved by the holy Spirit."[6]

The human family *knows* absolutely nothing of its origin, whence or how it came; of its habitation—this globe, whence and how it came, and what is its destiny; of its mission—what it was made for, and what it has to do; of its history—from its origin; and of its destiny—what is to become of it; except what God, through the Lord, by his Spirit, has taught it.

---

(1) 1 Cor. ii, 10, 11. (3) 1 Cor. ii, 13, *N. T.* and *Wesley*. (5) 2 Cor x, 5, *Wesley*.
(2) 1 Cor. ii, 12. (4) 1 Cor. iii, 18-20, *N. T.* and *Wesley*. (6) 2-Pet. i, 20, 12, *N. T.*

Who, without revelation, can tell the origin of our race? Look at the vague and crude notions of the ancients before the christian era, for an answer.

Who, without revelation, knows anything of this globe; of its origin, how long it has existed, what it was made for, and what is to become of it? Geologists tell us something of the changes it has undergone; but revelation alone tells us that in the beginning of creation, God created it, without telling us how long ago the beginning of creation was, for that it was, and is not material or necessary for us to know; that it was without form and void, and darkness was upon the face of the deep, but how long it was in that condition, is not material for us to know, and is not revealed. Then when revelation begins to inform us of the geological changes effected upon it to prepare it for the abode of man, its future lord, and for whom it was made, it becomes more definite and particular. By the word of God, we also learn that the heavens were of old, and the earth standing in the water and out of the water; whereby the world that then was, being overflowed with water, perished by a flood; but the heavens and the earth which are now, by the same word (of God) are kept in store, reserved for fire against the day of judgment and perdition of ungodly men: wherein the heavens shall pass away, being on fire shall be dissolved, and the elements shall melt with fervent heat, the earth also, and the works that are therein, shall be burned up. Nevertheless, after this general conflagration of the earth, and the works that are therein of sin and crime, which have been accumulating for now nearly six thousand years, we know by the same word of God that there will be new heavens and a new earth, (perhaps formed of the matter of the present one purified by fire) wherein will dwell righteousness, sin contaminating it no more.[1]

Without revelation, who can tell what the mission of the human family is, what it was made for, and what it has to do? Let the history of the heathen and pagan worlds answer. The best and ablest of the whole heathen world, Socrates, feeling after the knowledge of the Lord, if haply he might find him,[2] during a long and useful life, died directing a sacrifice to be made to a false deity.[3] The

---

(1) 2 Pet. iii, 5–7 and 10–13.   (2) Acts xvii, 27.   (3) Rol. Anc. Hist. B. ix, ch. 4, § 7.

world by wisdom knew not God,[1] and never could thus know him. No man knoweth the Father save the Son, and they to whom the Son will reveal him.[2] We can know God only by revelation, and, of course, we can not know what our mission and duty is, until we know our Maker. And this knowledge of God that we acquire by revelation of him to us by the Lord, is a rational knowledge of him and of his relation to us, and not a monkish moody knowledge, such as has been taught as being the proper one, for fifteen centuries. The knowledge of God was communicated by the Lord to Adam and to Noah, the progenitors of the antediluvian and post-diluvian worlds of mankind, and by each of them communicated to their posterity. But as the human family apostatized from God, it lost the knowledge of God, and inspiration accurately describes the effects and consequences of the apostacy, which effects and consequences were and are the same then as now, and now as then. "Because that when they knew God, they glorified him not as God, neither were thankful; but became vain in their imaginations, [*reasonings*, Wesley and N. Trans.] and their foolish heart was darkened. Professing themselves to be wise, they became fools, and changed the glory of the incorruptible God into an image made like to corruptible man, and to birds, and four-footed beasts, and creeping things. Wherefore God also *gave them up* to uncleanness through the lusts of their own hearts, to dishonor their own bodies between themselves. Who changed *the truth of God* into *a lie*, and worshipped and served the creature more [or rather] than the Creator, who is blessed forever. Amen. For this cause God gave them up unto vile affections: for even their women did change the natural use into that which is contrary to nature: and likewise also the men, leaving the natural use of the women, burned in their lust one toward another; men with men working that which is unseemly, and receiving in themselves that recompense of their error which was meet. And even as they did not like to retain God in their knowledge, God gave them over to a reprobate mind, [*a mind void of judgment*, marginal reading] to do those things which are not convenient; being filled with all unrighteousness, fornication, wickedness, covetousness, maliciousness; full of envy, murder, debate,

---

(1) 1 Cor i, 21.   (2) Matt. xi, 27; Luke x, 22.

deceit, malignity; whisperers, back-biters, haters of God, despiteful, proud, boasters, inventors of evil things, disobedient to parents, without understanding, covenant breakers, without natural affection, implacable, unmerciful."[1] This is man when left to himself, to rely upon his own *knowledge*, wisdom, and virtue.

The history of the human race for the first three thousand years would now be wholly lost, were it not for revelation. God, by his providence, caused Moses to be raised up at the court of Pharaoh, and "learned in all the wisdom of the Egyptians,"[2] then perhaps the most learned nation in the world. Some two thousand five hundred years after the creation of the human race, God caused Moses to bring Israel out of Egypt, sustained Israel by a constant miracle in the wilderness for forty years, during which time, Moses, by inspiration of God, who was sustaining him and the whole camp of Israel every day by a miracle, wrote a history of the race of man from its origin to Moses' death. The inspired apostles, and the Lord himself, frequently referred to this history and the facts therein recorded as authentic; and no rational man, who examines the proofs, can doubt their inspiration. And as the Spirit, through them, endorsed the record Moses made of the origin, and of the first two thousand five hundred and fifty years of the history of the race, it is the testimony of God himslef, that the record of Moses is true.

Not as knowledge communicated of God, but as my opinion after pretty extensive examination, reasoning from facts and truths communicated of God and by profane history, I state as my conclusion, that letters were not invented by man, but are a revelation of God. That the first written language "was the writing of God,"[3] "written with the finger of God,"[4] by the Lord,[5] upon the first two tables of stone, which Moses broke when he came down from the Mount. That the second written language was the second set of tables written by Moses in the Mount, during the second forty days that he was there,[6] under the tuition, instruction, and direction of the Lord, who taught him the letters and their use, and how to write. In eighty days tuition, Moses, then eighty years old, learned the alphabet,

---

(1) Rom. i, 21–31.　(3) Ex. xxxii, 16.　(5) Luke, xi, 20.
(2) Acts vii, 22.　(4) Ex. xxxi, 18.　(6) Ex. xxxiv, 28; see marginal reading.

its use, and how to write alphabetical writing. In his youth, he had been brought up in all the learning of the Egyptians, which included hieroglyphical writing, which was the only writing used by the Egyptians long after Moses' day. Among the Greeks, Cadmus was called the inventor of letters. But he took them to Greece from Phoenicia, (Philistia) or Syria, two years before Moses' death. And as the original Hebrew alphabet consisted of nineteen letters, all of which are in the Decalogue, written by the finger of God; and as Cadmus took sixteen letters to Greece, and the characters were the same as the Hebraic characters: and Cecrops, the founder of Athens, the seat of learning among the Greeks, went from Egypt and founded Athens the year before Cadmus went from Phoenicia (Philistia) and founded Thebes, called by him Cadmea, if letters had existed in Egypt, Cecrops would have taken them to Greece the year before Cadmus did, and would have been called by the Greeks the inventor of letters, and not Cadmus. But he knew only the Egyptian hieroglyphical method of writing; and as Cadmus' alphabetical method superseded it in Greece, and as alphabetical writing was then first known in Greece, the Greeks called Cadmus the inventor of letters; and, inasmuch as it was then called an invention, it was not known before. The presumption in my mind is, that Cadmus, who was a Philistine or Canaanite by birth, visited the Hebrew camp, stayed with Moses till he learned the then newly revealed alphabet and alphabetical method of writing, and saw enough of the wonderful works of God exhibited in the camp of Israel to convince him that his people—the Canaanites—were doomed to destruction; so two years before Joshua crossed the Jordan, and after Balak and Balaam had tried in vain to drive away Israel by exorcism, he fled the country with his people, went to Greece, took the Hebrew letters and learning with him, and founded the city of Thebes, and got the name among the Greeks of being the inventor of letters, when they were actually a revelation from God to Moses.[1]

But the destiny of the race of man: Who would know it without revelation? Socrates and Plato, the wisest men of the heathen world, taught the immortality of the soul; and Cicero almost argued himself into the belief of it; but none

---
(1) 1 Roll. Amc. Hist. B. i, part 2; B. v, art. 4.

of them ever dreamed of the redemption of the body from the grave. Life and immortality were brought to light through the Gospel, and through that alone.[1] Christ was the first fruits of them that slept,[2] and thus brought life and immortality to light, and showed light to the people and to the Gentiles.[3]

I have passed very briefly over these matters to show that all our knowledge is derived from God; and that those who want to acquire knowledge, should study the word of God. Daniel, though inspired, understood by the books of the word of the Lord, that he would accomplish seventy years in the desolations of Jerusalem.[4] If he went to the inspired record to acquire knowledge, how much more should uninspired men. The knowledge and wisdom with which his mind was thus stored by the study of the inspired books, made him chief minister both in Nebuchadnezzar's and in Darius' governments, notwithstanding both of them were heathens. And even the prophets inquired and searched diligently, searching what the Spirit of Christ that was in them, did signify.[5] So should we inquire and search diligently what God has communicated to us by his Spirit. If the inspired prophets searched and inquired to ascertain what the oracles of God uttered by them taught, how much more should we appeal to them to acquire the knowledge of God.

In thus studying and diligently acquiring the knowledge of God in relation to the mission of man—of what man has to do—we must look to *the righteousness of God.* This righteousness of God is not the good acts of God, or the beneficent things that God does; but it is the things that he has prescribed for us to do. The righteousness of God, now in force for all the human family, is revealed in the Gospel.[6] When we do that—obey the righteousness revealed in the Gospel—we are righteous even as Christ is righteous.[7] When we do not do that, either from ignorance or wilfulness, and set up and act upon our own notions of right and wrong, derived from our reason, from argument, from our "moral sensibilities," our hearts, our consciences, or from any other source than from the righteousness of

---

(1) 2 Tim. i, 10.
( ) 1 Cor. xv, 20-23.
(3) Acts xxvi, 23.
(4) Dan. ix, 2.
(5) 1 Pet. i, 10, 11.
(6) Rom. i, 16, 17.
(7) 1 John iii, 7.

God revealed in the Gospel to us, we go about to establish our own righteousness, and do not submit ourselves to the righteousness of God;[1] in which case, though our zeal for God may be ever so fervent, yet it is not according to KNOWLEDGE: and not being according to knowledge, it is fanatical, and the more zealous we are, the more fanatical we are.

In the revelations of God, relating to man's origin and his destiny, there are things difficult to comprehend and understand; but in what he commands or forbids us to do, there is no difficulty in understanding it, if we honestly and in good faith endeavor to do so. Whenever we do not do so, but set our reasoning powers to work to see, not only whether God's law says so, but whether it is consistent with other things God has said, that is, in the particular command, whether God means what he says, or does he not say one thing and mean another, because, in our judgment, what he says here is inconsistent with what he said somewhere else; or, whether the command under consideration is right and proper; or, whether we can not, by argument, and a series of syllogisms from other portions of the word of God, arrive at conclusions contradictory of the particular command of God that we are examining; or, whether our intuitions "above and before all logical reasonings,"[2] assert something contradictory of the commands of God under consideration; or, in any other way we get to work to shield ourselves from performing the particular command of God under consideration, we, in so doing, ARE APOSTATIZING FROM GOD. Whenever we undertake, by argument or inference, to ascertain what our acts should be, either of commission or omission—what we should do, or what we should not do—we are exalting our reasoning powers and our judgments "against the knowledge of God," instead of doing what the knowledge of God instructs us to do; for it says: "For though we walk in the flesh, we do not war after the flesh; (for the weapons of our warfare are not carnal, but mighty through God to the throwing down of strongholds;) destroying *reasonings* and every high thing

---

(1) Rom. x, 2, 3. *For they being ignorant of the righteousness of God*—Of the method God has established for the justification of the sinner, *and seeking to establish their own righteousness*—Their own method of acceptance with God, *have not submitted to the righteousness of God*—The way of justification which he hath fixed.—*Wesley's Note on the Passage.*

(2) Ante, p. 99.

which exalteth itself against *the knowledge of God;* and bringing every thought into captivity to the obedience of Christ."[1] Mr. Wesley says in his note on this passage, that by bringing every thought into captivity to the obedience to Christ, "reasonings are destroyed." This is true. If we yield our thoughts in obedience to Christ's commands, without cavil as to their propriety or impropriety, "their moral character," or anything else, we cast down or destroy reasoning on that branch of the inquiry, and apply our reason to the only proper use we can make of it in an inquiry of that kind, which is, Did Christ say so by himself, or his sent apostles, during, or after his incarnation? or, did he, as the Word of God, say so before his incarnation, and, if so, is that saying still in force, or was it taken out of the way and nailed to his Cross? *This is the sole and only proper use that we can make of our reasoning powers as to the commands of God relating to our acts either of commission or of omission.* And whenever we do otherwise, and go to reasoning about his commands, and govern our action by the results and conclusions of our reasonings, it leads to, and if continued in, results in apostacy from God. This has been universally so, continually, from the day that Adam was placed in Eden, down to the present time, including all present modern discussions, and, of course, including this. I will cite a few of the many authenticated instances of the truth of this assertion.

1. The Adversary of our race approached Eve in the garden of Eden, and commenced reasoning and arguing with her; and she listened to his argument. "God doth know," said he, having assumed the form of, or rather, entered into, the serpent, "that in the day ye eat thereof, then your eyes shall be opened; and ye shall be as Gods, knowing good and evil."[2] All this was true. It was the tree of knowledge of good and evil. Partaking of it, would give Adam and Eve that knowledge; and they did not then possess it. Superior intelligences who had "kept not their first estate,"[3] had that knowledge; and Adam and Eve, by acquiring it, would become as they, knowing good and evil. They could not acquire that knowledge any other way; for the only law given to them was the one allowing them everything else upon the earth, and thus within their

---

(1) 2 Cor. x, 3-5, *Wesley's Trans.*   (2) Gen. iii, 5.   (3) Jude 6.

reach, and prohibiting them the fruit of that tree. There could be no transgression of law by them, without violating that prohibition; and notwithstanding they had knowledge of good, they could have no knowledge of evil, without sin. The knowledge of evil was beyond their intellectual capacity, in their state of innocence. They could not know good and evil by contrast. Hence, all the serpent said to them was true, except the one thing, "Ye shall not die." Having told that lie, he commenced the *argument* to prove it; every word of which argument was true. The command was plain; the sanction or penalty for disobeying it was not so plain; "for in the day thou eatest thereof, dying thou shalt die."[1] Eve could have no trouble in understanding the command: "Thou shalt not eat of it." But she listened to, and heeded the argument. She saw that the tree was good for food, was pleasant to the eyes, and a tree to be desired to make one wise; she took and eat—transgressed the direct plain command of God, being drawn off by an argument about the penalty—and acquired the knowledge of evil, to the great woe and misfortune of herself, and all her posterity; became wise enough to know evil, and to know good and evil, in or by contrast.

This fact in the history of our race in its outset, proves that we should not get wise above what is written; and that we should not go to reasoning or arguing about the plain commands of God, or their effects and consequences. All the commands of God are plain. "No man ought to be wiser than the laws," is a maxim of the common law, which is put down by Coke in Latin thus: *Neminem apportet esse sapientiorem legibus*. Co. Lit. 97. The common law adopted the same wise principle that governs in the divine law.

2. God said to Abraham, "Take now thy son, thine only son Isaac, whom thou lovest, and get thee into the land of

---

(1) Gen. ii, 17, The Hebrew reading; see the marginal note. As explained by the knowledge of God as now possessed by our race, one day is as a thousand years with the Lord, 2 Pet. iii, 8, and as verified by the fact of the duration of human life from the creation of man to the present time, we can understand the penalty better than Adam could, but not the command. In the day that thou eatest thereof, thou shalt commence dying, become mortal, and thou shalt die within a thousand years thereafter, and none of thy race shall live a thousand years. So now, we can understand the commands of the Gospel better than we can comprehend the sanctions or penalties denounced in it. Hence, we are in a condition similar to that of Adam as to the law and the penalty. In Eve's case, the devil's argument related to the penalty; this should caution us against those who approach us in the same way, attacking the sanctions of the Gospel.

Moriah; and offer him there for a burnt-offering upon one of the mountains, which I will tell thee of."[1]

Had Abraham been an abolitionist, or had he acted upon the principle that abolitionists act upon in trying to prove slavery sinful by argument, he would have reasoned about thus: God has promised me that my seed coming out of my own bowels, shall be as numerous as the stars in heaven; that in Isaac shall my seed be called; and by his direction, I have sent Ishmael away that Isaac may be my sole heir, and the father of my posterity. "The decrees and commands of God must of necessity be consistent and in harmony with each other. I can not suppose that God would command the sacrifice of Isaac, if obedience to such command would conflict with his before expressed purpose and decree."[2] If I sacrifice Isaac, the promise of God will fail; and I, having sent away Ishmael and sacrificed Isaac, will be left without an heir, and without posterity. Besides, my " moral sensibilities " will not permit me to slay my own and only son; " such a thing is too revolting to my feelings,"[3] and I can not do it.

But Abraham, not being an abolitionist, acted differently. Without any argument or equivocation about it; and without pretending to undertake to comprehend and understand how all these promises, decrees and commands of God could be reconciled and made consistent with each other, and all made to stand and be fulfilled; and though his paternal feelings were strongly wrought upon, without doubt, yet his " moral sensibilities " were not shocked, nor was it " too revolting to his moral feelings," *because God had commanded him to do it;* hence, he " rose up early in the morning, and saddled his ass, and took two of his young men with him, and Isaac, his son, and clave the wood for the burnt-offering, and rose up, and went unto the place of which God had told him, * * * built an altar there, and laid the wood in order; and bound Isaac his son, and laid him on the altar upon the wood." What a trying moment to the old patriarch, " the friend of God " ! " And Abraham stretched forth his hand, and took the knife to slay his son." It was enough. The angel of the Lord called to him out of heaven, and said, "Lay not thine hand upon the lad,

---

(1) Gen. xxii, 2. (3) What brother Goodwin says, ante, p. 87.
(2) What O. B. says, ante, p. 150.

neither do thou anything unto him: for now *I know* that thou fearest God, seeing that thou hast not withheld thy son, *thine only son*, from me."[1]

Abraham "staggered not at the promise of God through unbelief; but was strong in faith, giving glory to God; and being fully persuaded, that what he had promised, he was able also to perform. And, therefore, *it was imputed to him for righteousness*. Now, it was not written for his sake alone, that it was imputed to him; but for us also, to whom it shall be imputed, but if we believe on [or confide in] him that raised up Jesus our Lord from the dead."[2] By faith, or confidence in God, and in unequivocal obedience to his command, Abraham thus "offered up Isaac: and he that had received the promises offered up his only begotten son, of whom it was said, That in Isaac shall thy seed be called: accounting that God was able to raise him up, even from the dead; from whence also he received him in a figure."[3] For thus unequivocally and without question, obeying God, "he was called the friend of God,"[4] and became the father of the faithful.[5]

3. God, by the mouth of the prophet Samuel, commanded Saul to "go and smite Amalek, and utterly destroy all that they have, and spare them not; but slay both man and woman, infant and suckling, ox and sheep, camel and ass."[6]

Saul went to work upon abolition principles, and reasoned and argued with himself, that to leave Agag, the king of Amalek, temporarily alive till he could show him in triumph to Israel, would not be a material variation from the command of God to utterly destroy Amalek; for he destroyed all the Amalekites except Agag. And to save alive the best of the sheep, and the oxen, and the fatlings, and the lambs, and all that was good,[7] would furnish abundant sacrifices for the altar of God, and he could thus abundantly sacrifice to, and honor God. But his action from this fine philosophical course of reasoning, was "*rebellion*, which is as the sin of witchcraft, and *stubbornness* is as iniquity and idolatry."[8] And because he followed his reasonings and conclusion upon the subject, instead of obeying the plain

---

(1) Gen. xxii, 2. (4) James ii, 23. (7) 1 Sam. xv, 9.
(2) Rom. iv, 20–24. (5) Rom. iv, 11. (8) 1 Sam. xv, 23.
(3) Heb. xi, 17–19. (6) 1 Sam. xv, 3.

command of God, he was rejected from being king of Israel, and his house and posterity cut off.

4. David was anointed king of Israel in place of Saul, after Saul's rejection. For that reason Saul sought his life, notwithstanding David had been faithful and true, and was blameless. Saul pursued David with armies to take his life, guiltless as he was. While he was so pursuing David, the Lord delivered him into David's power twice,[1] and David was advised by his followers to slay Saul, they saying that God had delivered him into his hands; which was true. Had David been an abolitionist, he would have followed the advice, reasoning thus: God has rejected Saul from being king of Israel, and anointed me in his place and stead. Saul, without cause or fault on my part, is trying to take my life; and the law of self-defence allows me, in order to save my own life, to strike the first blow, and take his life if I can. God has now delivered him into my hands while pursuing after me to take my life, and has given me the opportunity to save my own life, and rid the throne of the rejected of God, and open the way to my own ascension of it, as promised by God through Samuel, who anointed me to the place now filled by Saul. This is a strong case, had David gone to reasoning upon it; but he did not so go to reasoning and arguing the question. The law of the Lord said: "Touch not mine anointed, and do my prophets no harm;"[2] hence, David would not slay Saul, nor suffer his follower, Abishai, to do so; "for," said he, "who can stretch forth his hand against the Lord's anointed, and be guiltless?"[3] He said furthermore, at the time, "the Lord shall smite him; or his day shall come to die; or he shall descend into battle and perish."[4] This last took place shortly afterwards. David even caused the Amalekite who falsely claimed to have killed Saul, to be slain because he had slain the Lord's anointed, stating to him that his blood was upon his own head, because he had testified against himself, as to the fact of having slain the Lord's anointed.[5] This kind of conduct of David, in strictly observing the law of the Lord, without reasoning as to the propriety or expediency of that course, or whether he could help to bring about the

---

(1) 1 Sam. xxiv, 3, 4; xxvi, 7, 8.
(2) 1 Chron. xvi, 21; Ps. cv, 15; Gen. xx, 2–17; xlii, 17.
(3) 1 Sam. xxvi, 9.
(4) 1 Sam xxvi, 10.
(5) 2 Sam. i, 15, 16.

purposes and decrees of God by violating them, is the reason why he was a man after God's own heart, and was sought out by the Lord, and commanded by him to be captain over his people.[1]

5. When David was bringing the ark of the Lord from Kirjath-jearim, from the house of Abinidab, upon an ox-cart, Uzzah and Ahio, sons of Abinidad, drove the cart. On the way the oxen stumbled and shook the ark; and Uzzah, reasoning that if the ark fell from the cart, it would almost necessarily be broken or injured; and being a pious Jew, anxious to preserve the ark of the testimony from injury or destruction, took hold of it to make it steady and prevent its falling from the cart and receiving injury. For this the Lord struck him dead upon the spot;[2] because, by so doing, he violated that law of the Lord forbidding any but priests to touch the ark when traveling.[3]

Before noting other cases, I will sum up these that I have cited. In the first and third cases, Eve and Saul listened, and yielded to reasoning and argument, one of the serpent, and the other of the people; and the result was apostacy from God, death and all the woes that human flesh is heir to, in the case of Eve; and rejection from the throne of Israel, and the cutting off of his house and posterity, in the case of Saul. Eve's was transgression of law; Saul's was unrighteousness; one doing what was forbidden; the other failing to do what he was commanded to do.

In the second and fourth cases, Abraham and David obeyed the word of the Lord at once, without arguing and reasoning themselves into different conclusions, leading to different action, than the direct and straightforward obedience of God's word; and, for so doing, they occupy the highest places among the servants of God in the whole human race.

Poor Uzzah, out of zeal for God, and for the preservation of his ark, put forth his unhallowed hand, took hold of it, and the penalty of God's law was immediately inflicted upon him. He and Saul both had religious grounds for their acts; the one to preserve the ark from injury; the other to procure sacrifices for God's altar. But their mistaken piety did not shield them from the consequences of

---

(1) 1 Sam. xiii, 14; Acts xiii, 22. (3) Num. iv, 15.
(2) 2 Sam. vi, 1-7; 1 Chron. xiii. 5-10.

the transgression of God's law. God had appointed priests to take care of the ark, and it was their duty to do it, and not Uzzah's. God's righteousness for the protection of the ark was to have it taken care of by the priests, and Uzzah had no right to interfere. God has also appointed means for the preservation of the ark of the new covenant, and christians ought to be careful not to attempt to preserve it otherwise. When they attempt to preserve it by means of civil governments, or political action, or by any other means than by the church, the body of Christ, "fitly joined and compacted together" by the laws of the Lord for that purpose, they are guilty of a sin similar to Uzzah's.

It is proper also to note here, that the Philistines took the ark of God at the time that Hophni and Phineas, the priests, were slain, kept it seven months, traveled it through their country from city to city, and yet none of them were slain for touching it, which, of course, they did.[1] Why were none of them slain for touching the ark? Because the law on that subject was not addressed to them, but to the Israelites alone; and "where there is no law there is no transgression;" and "sin is not imputed when there is no law."[2] Hence, the Philistines did not sin in touching the ark.

Having noticed these cases of action recorded in the Old Testament, I will proceed to the New, and see how the Lord acted and taught on the subject. He never gave a philosophical reason or argument in relation to what should be done; but he did as to truths not relating to action.

6. When tempted of the devil, Christ did not argue any of the questions raised by Satan, but answered with a law of God governing the question. If thou be the Son of God, said Satan, command that these stones be made bread. This was questioning his Sonship, and because he was hungry, using that craving to try to get him to attempt to do something not commanded him of the Father. The Father had not commanded him to work miracles, to convince Satan of his Sonship, but the human family; and not miracles to supply his own wants, but to benefit and supply the wants of the halt, the lame, the blind, the deaf, the dumb, &c., of the human race. The Lord did not answer as to his Sonship, but to his craving, and without arguing as to

---

(1) 1 Sam. iv, 5; and vi, 1.   (2) Rom. iv, 15; v, 13.

that, he only quoted the law of God, "Man shall not live by bread alone, but by every word that proceedeth out of the mouth of God."

When he showed him the kingdoms of the world, and offered them to him if he would worship him, he replied directly with the law of God on that subject, and not with an argument: "Thou shalt worship the Lord thy God, and him only shalt thou serve."

When set upon the pinnacle of the temple, and told to cast himself down, the devil tried Scripture on the Lord, thinking, no doubt, that he might ensnare him there, as the Lord seemed to stick so close to what was written. "For it is written," said the devil with a very pious face put on, as thousands have since put on pious faces when quoting Scripture, and thereby misleading honest souls, "he shall give his angels charge concerning thee: and in their hands they shall bear thee up, lest at any time thou dash thy foot against a stone." This was all true; and abolitionists would have acceeded to it at once, and acted upon it. Or, if they had not acceded to it, they would have gone to arguing about it, to show by argument, that it should not be done. But the Lord took neither of those courses, but answered: "It is written *again*, Thou shalt not tempt, try, or put to the proof, the Lord thy God." Abolitionists, however, have no compunctions about tempting, trying, or putting to the proof. Deeming themselves right in their theory, and that the angels of God will bear up everything else in their hands, and keep them from dashing against the rocks, they drive on recklessly and thoughtlessly of every other consideration. Being wrong, however, in their theory, the angels do not bear things up in their hands, and hence the ruinous dashing against the rocks that is now going on.

Thus the Lord used the word of God directly, without any argument, or reasoning, or philosophizing. The word of God is the sword of the Spirit,[1] to destroy error and falsehood with. It is sharper than a two-edged sword.[2] All who drop it and look to reason, argument, deduction, conclusions, philosophizings, apostatize from God, "become vain in their imaginations, and their foolish hearts become darkened."[3]

Having seen how the Lord acted so far as his own con-

(1) Eph. vi, 17.   (2) Heb. iv, 12.   (3) Rom. i, 21.

duct is concerned, when assailed by the adversary, I will now see how he did when applied to by others to know what they should do.

7. When a certain lawyer stood up and tempted or tried the Lord, saying, "Master, what shall I DO to inherit eternal life?" The Lord did not go into an argument, nor into a philosophical disquisition, like Socrates, or Plato, or Cicrco, or Seneca would have done, to show the beauty and propriety of virtue, as they called it, but promptly, and to the point, he answered, " What is written in the law? How readest thou?"[1]

The Lord reasoned and argued as to matters not pertaining to our conduct—what we are to do, or not to do—but of *things* that it was proper for us to know. When the Sadducees, who put the case of the woman who had been the wife of seven brethren, had been told that they erred not *knowing the Scriptures,* nor the power of God, the Lord *argued* the question thus with them: God spoke to you, saying, I am the God of Abraham, and the God of Isaac, and the God of Jacob. God, said he, is not a God of the dead, but of the living.[2] This was a conclusive *argument* that there is a resurrection of the dead, and that Sadduceeism is untrue. But this is a *thing* proper for us to *know*, that is, that there will be a resurrection both of the just and the unjust; but it is not something that we must do or not do. Upon the question, What are we to do? the Lord did not argue, but said, "It is written," or, "I say to you."

8. As to matters not necessary for the human family to know, the Lord gave no information when applied to. Instances under this head are, when the Pharisees and Sadducees sought a sign: and when his disciples desired to know if the Lord would at that time restore the kingdom. In the first case, he said a wicked and adulterous generation seek a sign, but no sign shall be given them, save the sign of the prophet Jonah; and in the other, he told his disciples that it was not for them to know the times and seasons, which the Father had put in his own power.[3]

These are enough instances to enable us to know the course the Lord pursued in his teaching. Many others could be cited to the same purport.

---

(1) Luke x, 25, 26. (3) Matt. xii, 38, 39; xvi, 1-4; Mark viii, 11, 12; Acts i, 6, 7.
(2) Matt. xxii, 24-32.

9. When God revealed his Son in Paul, that he might preach him among the Gentiles, "immediately he conferred not with flesh and blood," but went and did it.[1] Mr. Wesley, in his note on this passage, says: "Being fully satisfied of the divine will, and determined to obey, I took no counsel with any man, *neither with my own reason or inclinations*, which might have raised numberless objections."

I will cite a few instances from the history of christianity since the apostolic day.

The first great one that did so much injury to christianity, and from the effects of which it has not yet recovered, was the Arian and Athanasian controversy about the Father, Son and Spirit in the Divine Being. Reason and philosophy were invoked to settle matters about the divine existence that were not revealed, because not necessary for us to know, and which the human intellect is wholly incapable of knowing. All the *facts* necessary for us to know, are plainly revealed, and we can understand them; the principal of which are, that there is one God and Father of all; that Jesus Christ is his Son, who is the Word, Wisdom, and Power of God, by whom all things were made that are made; that this Word was made flesh and dwelt among us; that he was the manifestation of God in the flesh; that God so loved the world, that he gave his only begotten son, that whosoever confided in him should not perish, but have everlasting life, &c. That when he ascended on high, the Holy Spirit of God, according to the promise of the Father, descended to his disciples to remain with them till the Lord shall appear again. Instead of being satisfied with the facts revealed, and which were pertinent for them to know, and which they could understand, they set to work with their philosophy, to determine the ESSENCE of the Father and Son, and *how* the Father, Son and Spirit make but one God, &c., matters not revealed, and if revealed, could not be comprehended by them: and for one hundred years and more, all Christendom was shaken by the controversy, and christians were drawn off from obeying the righteousness of God revealed in the Gospel for them TO DO, to bickerings about these speculations, the disputants trying to get wise above what is written, and to supply what God had not revealed of his own being and existence, and resulting in the

---

(1) Gal. i, 15, 16.

great apostacy. The effects of that foolish, not to say wicked, controversy, christianity has not yet got rid of.

Because the Lord told Peter that he would give him the keys of the kingdom of heaven; and whatsoever he bound on earth should be bound in heaven; and whatsoever he loosed on earth should be loosed in heaven;[1] by adopting argument, philosophy, reason, and deduction, as the proper course to pursue, the Man of Sin deduces that this made Peter the chief or prince of the apostles; that Peter went to Rome, and became the first bishop of Rome; that the Popes are his successors in regular line; that he had the keys to open and shut all matters in heaven and on earth, and so have the Popes; that Peter was the vicar of Christ, and the Popes being his successors, are vicars too, and hence they have been styled Lord God the Pope. This came of christians allowing themselves to be spoiled through philosophy and vain deceit as to the existence of God, and the delegation of his power.

And because the Lord, after his resurrection when he appeared to his disciples, and showed them his hands and his side to identify his person, told them, that as his Father had sent him into the world, even so he sent them into the world, "and when he had said this, he breathed on them, and said to them, Receive ye the Holy Spirit: whosesoever sins you remit, they are remitted unto them; and whosesoever sins ye retain, they are retained,"[2] this Man of Sin, by philosophical argument, reason and deduction, draws from this transaction proof of auricular confession to the priest, and the power of pardoning, by that priest, of the sins confessed.

Whereas, the truth of God— the knowledge of God communicated in his inspired word—shows that Peter used the keys of the kingdom of heaven given to him by the Lord, first on the day of Pentecost next after the crucifixion, when he unlocked the kingdom or reign of heaven to the Jewish world, and bound and loosed as to who should come in and who should not; and some eight years afterwards, he was taken to the house of Cornelius by a series of miracles, because he had the keys of the kingdom of heaven, and *was the only one the Lord had authorized to use them*, and he then and there unlocked the kingdom, and threw

(1) Matt. xvi. 19.   (2) John xx, 20*23.

wide open the door to the Gentile world, and bound and loosed for all time to come in earth and heaven as to them, as he had previously done as to the Jews. Those doors thus thrown open by Peter, who really had the keys, can not be either shut or opened by Pope, Prelate, Council, General Assembly, General Conference, Synod, nor by any individual or ecclesiastical body, since the apostles; that matter was given in charge to Peter, and to Peter alone.

And the knowledge of God also shows, that it was the apostles that the Lord breathed on, and told them that whosesoever sins they remitted, should be remitted unto them; and that whosesoever sins they retained, should be retained unto them; and that Peter, on the day of Pentecost, in the presence of the other apostles, and of the whole one hundred and twenty disciples, speaking as the Spirit gave him utterance, laid down the law of remission and retention of sins, specifying whose should be remitted, and whose should be retained. This he bound on earth by the words then and there spoken, and by the word of the Lord, when he promised the keys to Peter, it was immediately bound in heaven.[1] And at the house of Cornelius, he bound and loosed the same way to the Gentile world;[2] which was ratified and confirmed by the college of apostles at Jerusalem, when Peter rehearsed the matter to them.[3] The apostles continued to judge or give laws to the Israel of God, the one new man made by the Lord, of Jews and Gentiles, binding and loosing as to sins, for which see their writings in the New Testament. And the knowledge of God shows us that apostles, prophets, evangelists, pastors and teachers, were given by the Lord *till* his disciples should come to a perfect man in the knowledge of the Son of God;[4] that when the laws of the kingdom were fully developed, when the perfect system came, that which was given by the Lord to the church in part, to-wit, apostles, &c., were to be taken away and cease.[5] The apostles and supernatural gifts were taken away. The apostles have no successors, for they did the whole work they were appointed for. They were sent into the world by the Lord, as the Lord was sent into the world by the Father.[6] If the apostles have successors in their mission on earth, so has the Lord. But

---

(1) Acts ii, 38, 39; Matt. xvi, 19, (3) Acts xi, 18. (5) 1 Cor. xiii, 9, 10.
(2) Acts x. (4) Eph. iv, 11-13. (6) John xx, 21.

neither has successors. The Lord and the apostles both did their mission fully, and have been received up into glory.

I will not go over in detail, but refer in general terms, to the numerous sins and acts of righteousness (penances, &c.) that have, for fifteen centuries, been manufactured by the Mother of Harlots, and her numerous daughters, by argument, inference and deduction, called by the good word of the Lord "philosophy and vain deceit;" or, as translated in the new translation, "deceitful philosophy." As to which, christians are commanded by God, to "beware lest any man make a prey of you through an empty and deceitful philosophy, according to the tradition of men, according to the elements of the world, and not according to Christ. For all the fulness of the Deity resides substantially in him; and you are *complete in him*, who is the head of all government and power."[1] The way to abide, or remain *in the Lord*, is to keep his commandments,[2] and not to be led away by deceitful philosophy. If christians thus abide in him, they become *complete*, lacking nothing. But if they follow deceitful philosophy, they get out of Christ—do not remain in him—apostatize, and go away from God. If we want to avoid apostacy from God, we must avoid running after reason and a deceitful philosophy, as to what his commands are, as to what is sinful, and as to what is righteous. And we should take his word at what it says, without question or gainsaying.

For, sin is the transgression of the law; not a transgression of the argument from the law. All unrighteousness (or failing to do what God requires) is sin. Sin is not imputed when there is no law. Where there is no law, there is no transgression. By the law is the knowledge of sin obtained, and not by argument. I had not known sin but by the law: for I had not known lust (inordinate desire) except the law had said, Thou shalt not covet.

Take these principles that I have elaborated at some length, and apply them to brother Butler's number six, and they show how weak, and how far-fetched is his attempt (deceitful philosophy) to prove slavery sinful by the story of the prodigal son, related by the Lord in the 15th chapter of Luke. Weak as were his efforts to sustain his proposition while I was his respondent, he became still weaker

---
(1) Col. ii, 8-10, *New Trans.* (2) John xv, 10, and 4-7; 1 John ii, 5, 6.

when I was thrust out of the debate. What he says about the prodigal son is too weak to need any further notice.

I will notice the other matters in the article. In the 8th chapter of John, the Lord was talking of bondage or slavery; for bondage was slavery in the Jewish law. He said: "He that committeth sin is the slave of sin: and the slave abideth not in the house forever: but the Son abideth forever. If, therefore, the Son shall make you free, you will be free indeed."[1] Mr. Wesley, on the passage, says: "*And the slave abideth not in the house*—All sinners shall be cast out of God's house, as the slave was out of Abraham's: *but I, the Son, abide therein forever.*" Brother Butler's definition about tenures is made to suit his case, and is not true. A man can be as much a slave for five years, as he can for five hundred years Is he held to service? is the question; not how long is he to be so held?

Now, I say as long as the heir is a minor, he differs nothing from a *bondman*, although he be Lord of all. For he is under tutors and stewards, until the time appointed of his Father. So, also, we, whilst we were minors, were in *bondage* under the elements of the world. But when the fulness of time was come, God sent forth his Son, born of a woman, born under the law, that he might *buy off* those under the law, that we might receive the adoption of sons. And because you are sons, God has sent forth the Spirit of his Son into your hearts, crying, Abba, Father. So you are no more a *bondman*, but a son; and if a son, then an heir of God through Christ.[2]

This quotation is sufficient to answer what he says on the passage. *Servant* in Scripture, says Mr. Webster, means *a slave, a bondman*. This translation has *bondman* throughout. The common version has *bondage* in the 3d and 9th verses, which shows that *bondman* is the proper word in the 1st and 7th verses. What is so often repeated by brother Butler about chattel property, is raising a cob house that he may demolish it. It is not involved in the question of slave or no slave, as applied to an individual; and this question I have sufficiently discussed hereinbefore.

I will now proceed to conclude my discussion of the proposition, *Slavery is sinful.*

"And the Lord said unto her, [Rebecca] Two nations

---

(1) John viii, 34-36, *Wesley's Trans.*   (2) Gal. iv, 1-7, *New Trans.*

are in thy womb, and two manner of people shall be separated from thy bowels: and the one people shall be stronger than the other people; *and the elder shall serve the younger.*"[1] Here God granted property in the posterity of one twin brother, to the posterity of the other twin brother. This grant was reduced to possession by David, the man after God's own heart, more than seven hundred years after it was made.[2]

The tenth commandment reads thus:

"Thou shalt not covet thy neighbor's house, thou shalt not covet thy neighbor's wife, nor his man-servant, nor his maid-servant, nor his ox, nor his ass, nor anything that is thy neighbors."[3]

Here, in the first written law ever given to man, written by the finger of God, property in men-servants and maid-servants is recognized, as property in houses, fields, oxen, and asses is recognized. And property in men-servants and maid-servants is not only placed on the same level with property in animals of the brute creation, but with the very lowest animal of the brute creation—the ass. Had brother Goodwin been there at Mount Sinai when this law was spoken by the Lord out of the smoking and burning mountain, he would, at once, have said this is an unrighteous law; for "I conclude that any law that places human beings on a level with brute property, is an unrighteous law"[4]!! "It is too revolting for my moral feelings"[5]!! Had brother Butler been there, he would have said it is "so abhorrent, and so offensive to the moral sense, that I confess I am not able to look steadily and calmly at it;" it "is a thought too revolting for calm consideration"[6]!! But they were not there to correct the Lord; and they are now laboring, and have been for years, to rectify the error!

Query: Was this part of the Decalogue taken out of the way and nailed to the Cross by the Lord? I apprehend not. If not, the abolitionists have been violating it ever since they sprang up; for they have been coveting—inordinately desiring—the men-servants and maid-servants of their slaveholding neighbors; and they have been so inordinately desiring them, that they have been enticing them

---

(1) Gen. xxv, 23.
(2) 2 Sam. viii, 14; 1 Chron. xviii, 13.
(3) Ex. xx, 17; Deut. v, 21.
(4) Ante, p. 79.
(5) Ante, p. 87.
(6) Ante, p. 69.

away, and running them off for years; and have established lines called underground railroads to run them off upon, and boast of the fact, and of the business.

Brother Butler contended in his fifth article, that the slaves granted by the Lord to Israel, of the heathen round about them, were to go free at the jubilee.[1] Brother Goodwin took the same ground in two articles in the *Record* of March 3d and 10th, 1863, in reply to a request from brother Wm. H. Winchell. They all seemed to be troubled, too, about the power to sell slaves. That need not trouble any one. For if one is a slave for life, it would be no worse for the slave, if the master had power to sell; and it might be better, if he had a bad master, that that master had the power to sell him to a good one. I will examine these matters some.

The grant is recorded in the twenty-fifth chapter of Leviticus, from the 44th to the 46th verse inclusive. To say that it does not grant an estate of inheritance in perpetuity to the Israelites and their posterity, is to contradict the plain language of the grant. And to take the ground that it only granted estates from jubilee to jubilee, is to take the ground assumed by Universalists, that *forever* does not mean *always*, but only to the next jubilee, or to the destruction of Jerusalem, or to some other vague time. But this statute of the Lord, recorded in that chapter, is self-expounding, so far as *forever* and *to the jubilee* are concerned, which I will proceed to show.

It sets out with the establishment of the Sabbatic weeks, ending with the jubilee, at which time they were to "proclaim liberty throughout all the lands unto all the inhabitants thereof: it shall be a jubilee unto you; and ye shall return every man unto his family."[2] "In this jubilee ye shall return every man to his possession."[3] It provides that "the land shall not be sold *forever*; for the land is mine; for ye were strangers and sojourners with me. And in all the land of your possession ye shall grant a redemption for the land."[4] It then provides how lands that are sold are to be redeemed, and goes on: "But if he be not able to restore it to him, then that which is sold shall remain in the hand of him that bought it, until the year of jubilee: and in the jubilee it shall go out, and he shall re-

---

(1) Ante, pp. 162, 163.   (2) Verse 10.   (3) Verse 13.   (4) Verses 23, 24.

turn unto his possession."¹ But it goes on to provide, that a dwelling house in a walled city, must be redeemed within a year after it is sold; and if not redeemed within that space of time, "then the house that is in the walled city shall be established *forever* to him that bought it, throughout his generations: *it shall not go out in the jubilee.*"²

Here, *forever* and *in the jubilee* are put down as two distinct things, and not the same thing. And here it is said that some land shall not go out, and the former owner return to it, notwithstanding in the 10th and 13th verses, it is said *every man* shall return *to his possession* at the jubilee, as it is said that *liberty* shall then be proclaimed *to all the inhabitants* of the land. But the statute goes on and makes an exception to the houses of the Levites in their cities.³

Then commences the provisions as to servants and slaves. "If thy brother by thee be waxen poor, and be sold unto thee, [as provided in this and other laws]; thou shalt not compel him to serve as a bond-servant [slave]: but as an hired servant, and as a sojourner, he shall be with thee, and shall serve thee *unto the year of jubilee*: and then he shall depart from thee, both he and his children with him, and shall return unto his family, and unto *the possession* of his fathers shall he return. For they are my servants, which I brought out of the land of Egypt: they shall not be sold as bondmen [are sold]. Thou shalt not rule over him with rigor, but shalt fear thy God. Both thy bondmen and thy bondmaids, [slaves] which thou shalt have, shall be of the heathen that are round about you; of them shall ye buy bondmen and bondmaids. Moreover, of the children of the strangers that do sojourn among you, of them shall ye buy, and of their families that are with you, which they begat in your land: and they shall be your possession. And ye shall take them as an inheritance for your children after you, to inherit them for a possession; they shall be your bondmen *forever*: but over your brethren, the children of Israel, ye shall not rule one over another with rigor."⁴

The statute then goes on to provide that if a sojourner or stranger wax rich, and an Israelite become poor, and sell himself to the stranger or sojourner, he may be redeemed by the brother or kindred of the Israelite, prescribing the manner in which the price shall be reckoned

---
(1) Verse 28.   (2) Verse 30.   (3) Verses 32–34.   (4) Lev. xxv, 39–41.

up to the next jubilee, according to the time of a hired servant, and that as a yearly hired servant he shall remain with him, and that if he be not redeemed in these years, *then he shall go out in the year of jubilee*, both he and his children with him; the same reason being given for this provision as to Israelites sold to strangers or sojourners, that was before given for the provision. as to Israelites sold to Israelites, to-wit, "For unto me the children of Israel are servants; they are my servants, whom I brought forth out of the land of Egypt: I am the Lord your God."[1]

Here is an estate of inheritance granted in bondmen or slaves, to the Israelites and their children, *forever;* and a clear distinction is drawn between the tenure by which they were held, and the tenure by which servants who were of the children of Israel were held, whether they were held by Israelites or by strangers or sojourners. The bondmen were to be *a possession;* they were to be taken *as an inheritance for their children*, to inherit it as a possession; and to be bondmen *forever*. Why was it provided that they were to be an estate of inheritance, and bondmen forever, immediately after and before estates in other servants were granted that were limited to terminate at the jubilee in any event, if the estate in these bondmen was to terminate at the jubilee too? It would be trifling in the divine law-giver, to describe the tenure of the services of three different kinds of servants, Israelites to Israelites, Israelites to strangers and sojourners, and heathen to Israelites, providing that the first two should go out at the jubilee, and that the other should be an estate of inheritance forever to them and their children for a possession forever, when he actually meant that they should go out at the jubilee too, and that the estate in them extended only to the jubilee. The divine law-giver did not so trifle in framing the statute. The estate given by the statute, in bondmen, is an estate in perpetuity to the slave and his children.

But they say that this statute does not give power to sell the bondmen or slaves. Brother Goodwin says: "The Jewish master had no authority given him to sell such servants to third persons. 'You shall take them as an inheritance for your children after you, to inherit them for a possession,' says the law; not as an article of commerce—a

---

(1) Lev. xxv, 47-55.

mere chattel—to be traded and driven from land to land, by speculators in human flesh."[1]

This thing of chattelizing and selling slaves, is a great trouble to the abolitionists. I have had private conversations on the subject with many excellent brethren, who made the fact that the slaves are assignable and transferrable, the principal ground, and some of them made it the only ground, for saying that slavery is sinful. The objection is an objection against the law of the institution, and not an objection against the institution itself; and really does not arise in the inquiry, *Is slavery sinful?* When brother Butler raised the objection, we were discussing the question whether God had granted property in man. In that discussion, it was immaterial whether the grant God gave to Israel of property in the heathen for slaves, included the grant of power to alienate that property, or not. Entailed property is as much property as is property which is alienable. So brother Goodwin's decision above cited, if it is correct, simply shows that the statute made the bondmen entailed property to the Israelite and his children; and the bondmen and their children were both property and slaves, and were granted by the divine law-giver, and were held by virtue of a divine grant.

But brother Goodwin was answering an inquiry from brother Winchell, who wanted to know from him "if any law, which God ever gave to man, authorized or justified the buying or selling of men, women and children." And brother Goodwin, in the above quoted passage, decided the question, that he did not; and all his authority for the decision, is given in what is above quoted from him.

As many are, honestly I have no doubt, stumbling on this question, I will proceed to show that brother Goodwin's decision is not correct.

The part of the statute that he quotes as proof that bondmen were entailed property—to be be kept in the family of the owner—simply creates an estate of inheritance in perpetuity in the bondmen and their posterity. It is not a limitation creating an estate tail, but an expression to create an estate of inheritance in perpetuity. Our common deeds read "to him and his heirs forever," and no one supposes that that creates an estate tail, and prevents the

---

[1] Christian Record, March 3d, 1863.

grantee from alienating the estate the next day, if he chooses. And so of this grant. It was to the Israelites and their children forever: creating an estate in perpetuity, to be alienated or not, at the will of the holder.

When God gave the animal creation to Noah and his sons, he did not add, "you may buy and sell them," because that was implied in the grant itself. If the grant of the heathen to the Israelites for slaves, did not include the power to buy and sell them, but entailed them upon the owner and his children, the grant of the animal creation to Noah and his sons entailed them, and we none of us have a right to sell our horses, cattle and hogs, but must keep them with ourselves and our children. When the animal creation was granted to Adam, the same rule obtained. When Canaan was granted to Israel, God put limitations upon the buying and selling of the land, because he wanted it limited. If he had not put in those limitations, the Israelites would have had unlimited powers of alienation. So as to Israelitish servants. God limited the power of alienation as to them, because he did not want them to be "articles of commerce," as they would have been, if this limitation had not been put into the law. The reason of this is twice given: "For they are my servants which I brought out of the land of Egypt."[1] To prevent the general power of alienation implied from the grant of property in them, God provided, as to them, that "they shall not be sold as bondmen."[2] They were to be kept in the family, and treated as hired servants, and not to be ruled over with rigor, and *should not be sold as bondmen* are sold, and are authorized to be sold by the *unlimited* estate granted in them. This clause prohibiting Israelites to be sold as bondmen, is an expression of the law-giver clearly implying that bondmen were alienable, and "articles of commerce." So the statute itself disproves brother Goodwin's decision given to brother Winchell. Brother Butler did not deny that bondmen were alienable. He is too good a lawyer to take such a position publicly. He placed it upon the ground that they went out at the jubilee.[3]

Again: It was provided that "if a man sell his daughter to be a maid-servant, she shall not go out as the men-servants do. If she please not her master, who hath betrothed

---

(1) Lev. xxv, 42, 55.   (2) Lev. xxv, 42.   (3) Ante, pp. 163, 163.

her to himself, then shall he let her be redeemed: to sell her unto a strange nation he shall have no power, seeing he hath dealt deceitfully with her."[1]

Why put this prohibition into the law, prohibiting the master from selling her to a strange nation, if he had not the power of alienation? The very fact that this prohibition was put in, shows that the power existed under the general grant, and could have been exercised had not this clause, prohibiting it, been put into the law. In the state of facts set out here, the power of alienation was taken away from the master, because he had dealt deceitfully with his maid-servant. As a punishment for that deceit, the law deprived him of a right he had, to sell her *to a strange nation;* which was a right to sell her "as an article of commerce," "to be traded and driven from land to land." Because of that deceit, he was prohibited from selling her as an article of commerce to a strange nation, and required to let her be redeemed by her kins-folks, as provided in the twenty-fifth chapter of Leviticus.

So, also, the clause forbidding Israelitish servants to be sold as bondmen, is a limitation upon a right of alienation possessed. That clause must mean one of two things: either that they should not be sold as bondmen *were sold*, or that they should not be sold *as bondmen*, that is, sold to serve in perpetuity as bondmen have to serve. And either construction shows brother Goodwin's decision wrong.

The play upon the word *chattel*, constantly indulged in by abolitionists, amounts to nothing. If slaves are property, they are either chattel property or real property; and it is no more degrading to be one than the other. Hence, the constant harping by abolitionists, upon the word *chattel*, ringing the changes "human chattel," "his chattel," "their chattels," "chattel property," "chattelized," &c., is as senseless as their theory is groundless. The use of epithets always implies a want of anything better to use, and, either weakness or wickedness in those that use them.

I will now proceed to the New Testament.

The Lord said that the kingdom or reign of heaven is like a man about to travel into a far country, who called his servants and delivered to them his goods. To one he gave five talents, to another two, and to another one talent, and

---
[1] Ex. xxi, 7, 8.

took his journey. After a long time, the lord or master of these servants returned and reckoned with them. The one that had received five, returned ten; and the one that had received two, returned four; and each received from his master the commendation, "Well done, good and faithful servant; thou hast been faithful over a few things, I will make thee ruler over many things: enter thou into the joy of thy Lord." "Then he which had received the one talent came and said, Lord, I knew thee that thou art a hard man, reaping where thou hast not sown, and gathering where thou hast not strewed: and I was afraid, and went and hid thy talent in the earth: lo, there thou hast that is thine. His Lord answered and said unto him, Thou wicked and slothful servant, thou knewest that I reap where I sowed not, and gather where I have not strewed: Thou oughtest, therefore, to have put my money to the exchangers, and then at my coming I should have received mine own with usury. Take, therefore, the talent from him, and give it unto him that hath ten talents. For unto every one that hath shall be given, and he shall have abundance; but from him that hath not, shall be taken away even that he hath. And cast ye the unprofitable servant into outer darkness: there shall be weeping and gnashing of teeth."[1]

Here the man who had the one talent, if he was not an abolitionist, he at least used the argument used by abolitionists, to prove the sinfulness and wickedness of slavery. How much have we heard from abolitionists about unrequited labor—living on other people's labor, system of oppression, &c. This man's language, modernized and turned or translated into the abolition dialect, would run about thus: You reap where you do not sow; you gather where you do not strew; I have brought you your own; take it, but you have no right to my labor; and, because you claim it and want it, you are sinful, guilty of a collossal crime, a monster iniquity, which is the sum of all villianies, and a modern Moloch.

But the Lord said that for thus talking and acting, he was a wicked and slothful servant; and punished him for it by casting him into outer darkness, where shall be wailing and gnashing of teeth.

And the Lord tells us that the kingdom of heaven, which

(1) Matt. xxv, 14-30.

is the christian kingdom, is like this. Is it sinful? Is it wicked? Is it a monster iniquity? Had not abolitionists better quit using the argument which the man with the one talent did, lest his fate be awarded to them?

This part of the parable, as recorded by Luke, reads thus: " For I feared thee, because thou art an austere man: thou takest up that thou layest not down, and reapest that thou didst not sow. And he saith unto him, Out of thine own mouth will I judge thee, thou wicked servant. Thou knewest that I was an austere man, taking up that I laid not down, and reaping that I did not sow:[1] Wherefore," &c.

The Lord judged him out of his own mouth, and pronounced him *wicked*, because he knew that his master was an austere man, taking up what he had not laid down, and reaping what he had not sown, and yet did not put the money to use and make gain for his master.

As recorded by both Matthew and Luke, the two slaves (for that is what Webster says *servant* means in the Scriptures) who had been faithful and diligent, were highly commended and rewarded for that diligent service of their master, and doubling of his goods during his absence. The Lord notes it as something greatly praiseworthy in them, that they had so acted, and conducted, and demeaned themselves, in their master's service, during his absence. Whereas, on the other hand, the slave who had done nothing for his master, but had wholly neglected his master's interest, and his master's service—strictly honest, however, with his master's money, had hid it and kept it securely, and brought it safely to the master when he returned—was condemned by the Lord for being slothful, lazy, and negligent of his master's interest, and of his master's service; which conduct in that slave was pronounced by the Lord WICKED, and he was condemned to very severe punishment for it.

Again, the Lord, speaking to his disciples, said: " But which of you, having a servant plowing or feeding cattle, will say to him as soon as he cometh from the field, Come and sit down to table? And will not rather say to him, Make ready wherewith I may sup, and gird thyself and serve me till I have eaten, and afterward thou shalt eat and drink? Doth he thank that servant because he did the

---
(1) Luke xix, 21, 22.

things that were commanded of him? I think not. So likewise ye, when ye have done all the things that are commanded you, say, We are unprofitable servants: we have done what it was our duty to do."[1]

Here the Lord recognized, as proper and right, the authority of the master over the slave, and that the master should not set the slave down at once to his meal, when he came from the field; but that, instead of so doing, he should command the slave to make ready the master's supper, to gird himself and serve his master till he had eaten; and then afterwards, to eat and drink himself. And he said the master would not thank the slave because he had obeyed his commands, for the reason *that he had only done that which it was his duty to do.*

That the Lord taught that it was the duty of the slave to do so, and that he was not entitled to thanks for so doing, is clear; because he, from the conduct of the master to the slave, enjoins it upon his disciples, to whom he was speaking, when they had done all things commanded them, to say they had but done that which it was their duty to do, and were unprofitable slaves. He could enforce it upon his disciples to say that they had but done their duty from the statement he had made as to the conduct of the master and slave, only on the ground that the slave had but done his duty in the case stated, and was not entitled to thanks.

Here the Lord recognized the relation of master and slave, and the institution of slavery, as it existed all around him, and all over the Roman empire in which he was teaching, and recognized the authority and rights of the master to the slave's labor, and to precedence over the slave, and that it was the duty of the slave to be faithful and obedient to his master, without being entitled to thanks for being so; and from these facts, he impressed it upon his disciples, that his right and their duty to him were similar; that it was their duty to obey his commands, because he was their Master.

As the Lord recognized the right of the master and the duty of the slave, and used the fact of the existence of that right and duty, to impress upon his disciples his right over them and their duty to him, is it worth while to inquire whether the relation of master and slave—the institution

---
(1) Luke xvii, 7-10, *Wesley's Translation.*

of slavery—is sinful? Or, rather, is it not more proper to inquire whether there are any who really love the Lord, and revere his word and teaching, who will affirm that it is sinful? Would he use the rights and duties created by, and existing under, a sinful institution, to inculcate and enforce rights and duties in his kingdom? Let christians, particularly those inclined to abolitionism, think of and reflect upon these things.

The Lord, upon several other occasions, taught matters pertaining to his kingdom, by reference to the relation of master and slave, and the power of the one and the duty of the other. I shall not refer to the particular instances, and note the cases separately. The reader can look them up as cited in the foot-note.[1] I make these general remarks upon them.

The system of slavery established by the Jewish law, existed in the country and among the people where he taught; and also the Roman system of slavery, which was a most severe one, the master having even the power of life and death over his slaves. These two systems or institutions of slavery existed among, and were well understood by the people. The Lord used them to exemplify and elucidate the principles of his approaching kingdom, upon repeated occasions. Now, is it rational to suppose that he would so refer to an institution, to its laws and usages, to the rights and liabilities of masters and slaves, created by, existing in, and recognized under the institution, *if it was sinful?* Is it not most irrational to suppose that he would? In all his references to it, he always commended the faithful and obedient slave, and denounced disobedience and unfaithfulness in slaves. Hence Paul, in writing to Timothy upon this subject, referred to this teaching of the Lord as being "wholesome words, even the words of our Lord Jesus Christ, and the doctrine which is according to godliness;"[2] which I shall have occasion to observe upon at length, when I shall reach it; and which my dear brother Wiley so often referred to in our friendly discussion, and which I did not reach for comment upon, before that discussion ended.

"But as God has distributed to every one, and as the Lord has called every one, so let him walk; and so, in all the congregations, I ordain. Has any circumcised been

---

(1) Matt. xviii, 23-35; xxiv, 45-51; Luke xii, 37, 38, 42-48.   (2) 1 Tim. vi, 3.

called? Let him not be uncircumcised. Has any one been called in uncircumcision? Let him not be circumcised. Circumcision is nothing, and uncircumcision nothing, but the keeping of the commandments of God. Let every one remain in the same calling in which he was called. Were you called being a bondman? Be not careful to be made free. Yet, if you can be made free, prefer it. For a bondman who is called by the Lord, is the Lord's freedman. In like manner, also, a freedman who is called, is Christ's bondman. You were bought with a price: become not the slaves of men. Brethren, in what state each one was called, in that let him remain with God."[1]

I will first give some of Mr. Wesley's notes and comments upon this passage.

"17. *But as God hath distributed*—The various *stations* of life, and the various *relations* to every one, let him take care to discharge his duty therein. The Gospel disannuls *none* of these: *and thus I ordain in all the churches*—As a point of the highest concern.

"20. *In the calling*—The outward state wherein he is when God calls him. Let him not seek to change this without a clear direction of Providence.

"21. *Care not for it*—Do not anxiously seek liberty, *but if thou canst be free, use it rather*—Embrace the opportunity.

"23. *Ye are bought with a price*—Ye belong to God: therefore, where it can be avoided, *do not become the bondslaves of men*—which may expose you to many temptations.

"24. *Therein abide with God*—Doing all things as unto God, and as in his immediate presence. They who thus abide with God, preserve a holy indifference *with regard to outward things.*"

This was ordained in all the churches, "as a point of the highest concern," said Mr. Wesley, and, of course, is a standing statute for all the churches now. And that man or that church that disobeys this ordinance is guilty of unrighteousness, which is sin. If he or they transgress its injunctions, it is sin. The teacher that stands up in the christian congregation, and teaches contrary to this ordinance, transgresses the law of God, and thereby sins; and this is true, and applies to him, whether he be a bishop, pastor, or deacon of a church, or an evangelist, or an editor

---

(1) 1 Cor. vii, 17-24, *New Translation.*

of a newspaper. For the command of God to those who attempt to teach in the Lord's kingdom, is, to hold fast the faithful word as they have been taught by the Lord's inspired apostles, including this ordinance, that they may be able, by sound doctrine, both to exhort and convince the gainsayers.[1] Let abolition bishops, pastors, deacons, evangelists, and editors, think of these things.

This ordinance teaches and enjoins, that if any one is called into the kingdom of Christ, being a slave, he should be not anxious to be made free, that he should not inordinately desire or covet freedom; yet if he can properly be made free, let him prefer it, and thank God for the blessing, being careful not to use his liberty for a cloak of maliciousness or wickedness, but as the servant of God.[2] Abolitionism teaches that slaves should earnestly desire freedom, and may obtain it by any means, even by that of servile insurrection. This ordinance enjoins that every one, including slaves, should remain in the calling, state and condition, in which he was when called into the kingdom of Christ; but abolitionism teaches that they should not; but that they should be freed, even at the fearful and tremendous cost of a civil war, with all its crimes and horrors.

The slave that is called by the Lord is the Lord's freedman; but that does not change his station in this world, nor his relations as to things of this world. Mr. Wesley correctly said, that the Gospel disannuls none of these. The injunction here is, that he should remain in the station in which he is called. The notion that becoming a christian frees a slave, is an abolition phantasy. For in the same manner that a slave's becoming a christian makes him Christ's freedman, the freeman's becoming a christian makes him Christ's bondman or slave. If the station and relations that one holds in this world are changed by his becoming a christian, the station and relations of the other are also changed by his becoming a christian. Will abolitionists, who were free when they became christians, admit that their station in life and their relations in society were changed by their becoming christians, and that they became slaves and subordinates? I apprehend not. Then the slaves' station and relations in society are not changed by their becoming christians.

---

(1) Tit. i, 9.   (2) 1 Pet. ii, 16.

Christians are bought by the Lord with a price, and a great price, no less a price than the blood of the Son of God. For that reason, they should not become the slaves of men. This is the same reason that was twice given in the law of Moses, why the Israelites should not be perpetual bondmen and slaves—because they were the Lord's servants brought or redeemed by him out of Egypt.[1] Christians are bought and brought by the Lord out of the Egyptian darkness, in which the world of mankind are without his illuminating light, and brought into the glorious light and liberty of the Gospel; and for that reason, they are here, prohibited from becoming the slaves of men. By the law of Moses, the six-year Hebrew servant might voluntarily become a slave forever,[2] and Israelites might become slaves till the jubilee,[3] by voluntarily selling themselves, or by being sold for debt: and, by the Roman law of slavery, a man might enslave himself by voluntary mancipation of himself, with or without a consideration, or he might become a slave by being sold for debt. In all these ways, in both laws, the man became a slave directly or indirectly, by his own act. Both of those laws were observed among the people in that day. Hence this injunction to christians that they should not, either directly or indirectly, *by their own act*, become slaves of men. And this was but the first and last injunction in the passage quoted, that every one should remain in the calling, state and condition in which he was when called or converted to christianity. If he was a freeman, he should remain so; whereas, though the slave was enjoined to remain contented in the condition he was, yet if he could properly be made free, he was permitted and directed to accept it. Under the Mosaic dispensation, the Lord allowed his servants to make themselves servants to men; but under the christian dispensation, the command to them, is, that they shall not become slaves to men. And this means as well that they shall not become slaves to their persons and material interests, as that they shall not become slaves to their theories and systems of righteousness. For, as obedience is slavery,[4] the command forbids them to obey human leaders and theorizers, or to suffer such to lead them away from Christ, his teaching and laws. Christians

---

(1) Lev. xxv, 42, 55.
(2) Ex. xxi, 6.
(3) Lev. xxv, 39–43; 47–55.
(4) Ante, pp. 91, 155.

are forbidden to become slaves to human systems, either ethical or ecclesiastical; and as abolitionism is a human system of ethics, it is included in the prohibition. Christians are to remain with God, and serve him, by observing *his system of ethics*, which is "the righteousness of God," and is "revealed in the Gospel."[1] Those who do thus remain with him in deed and in truth, acquire and preserve a holy indifference with regard to outward things—the things of this world.

Would slaves that are converted to christianity be enjoined and commanded by the Lord to remain in that condition, if slavery is sinful? Does not the fact that he so commanded christian slaves, show that he regarded the institution as not sinful?

The apostle Paul, in his letter "to the saints which are at Ephesus, and to the faithful in Christ Jesus," wrote thus:

"Let no man *deceive you with vain words:* for because of these things cometh the wrath of God upon the children of disobedience. Be not therefore partakers with them. * * * Walk as the children of light. * * * * * See then that ye walk circumspectly, not as fools, but as wise, redeeming the time because the days are evil. Wherefore be ye not unwise, but *understanding what the will of the Lord is.* * * * * Submitting yourselves to one another *in the fear of God.*

"Wives, submit yourselves unto your own husbands, as unto the Lord. For the husband is the head of the wife, even as Christ is the head of the church: and he is the Savior of the body. Therefore as the church is subject unto Christ, so let the wives be to their own husbands in everything.

"Husbands, love your wives, even as Christ also loved the church, and gave himself for it; that he might sanctify and cleanse it with the washing of water by the word; that he might present it to himself a glorious church not having spot or wrinkle, or any such thing; but that it might be holy and without blemish. So ought men to love their wives as their own bodies. He that loveth his wife loveth himself. For no man yet hateth his own flesh; but nourisheth and cherisheth it, even as the Lord the church; for we are members of his body, of his flesh, and of his bones.

---

(1) Rom. i, 17.

For this cause shall a man leave his father and mother, and shall be joined unto his wife, and they two shall be one flesh. This is a great mystery: but I speak concerning Christ and the church. Nevertheless, *let every one of you in particular so love his wife even as himself;* and the wife see that *she reverence her husband.*

"Children, obey your parents in the Lord: for this is right. Honor thy father and thy mother; which is the first commandment with a promise; that it may be well with thee, and that thou mayest live long on the earth.

"And, ye fathers, provoke not your children to wrath: but bring them up in the nurture and admonition of the Lord.

"Servants, be obedient to them that are your masters according to the flesh, with fear and trembling, in singleness of your heart, as unto Christ; not with eye-service, as men-pleasers; but as the servants of Christ, doing the will of God from the heart; with good will doing service, as to the Lord, and not to men: knowing that whatsoever good thing a man doeth, the same shall he receive of the Lord, whether he be bond or free.

"And, ye masters, do the same things unto them, forbearing threatening: knowing that your Master also is in heaven; neither is there respect of persons with him."[1]

And in writing "to the saints and faithful brethren in Christ, which are at Colosse," he wrote thus:

"And whatsoever ye do in word or deed, do all in the name of the Lord Jesus, giving thanks to God and the Father by him.

Wives, submit yourselves unto your own husbands, as it is fit in the Lord.

"Husbands, love your wives, and be not bitter against them.

"Children, obey your parents in all things: for this is well pleasing unto the Lord.

"Fathers, provoke not your children to anger, lest they be discouraged.

"Servants, obey in all things your masters according to the flesh; not with eye-service, as men-pleasers; but in singleness of heart, fearing God: and whatsoever ye do, do it heartily, as to the Lord, and not unto men; knowing that

---

(1) Eph. v, 6-32; vi, 1-9.

of the Lord ye shall receive the reward of the inheritance: for ye serve the Lord Christ. But he that doeth wrong, shall receive for the wrong he hath done; and there is no respect of persons.

"Masters, give unto your servants that which is just and equal; knowing that ye also have a master in heaven."[1]

I quote together these two extracts from the inspired writings of the great apostle of the Gentiles, because they are very similar, and each of them embraces and combines together all the domestic relations of society. Those domestic relations are the relations of husband and wife, parent and child, and master and servant. They have existed in human society from its origin; or, at least, we have authentic information of their existence as far back as the days of Abraham, some three thousand and eight hundred years ago: and they still exist in the society of at least one half of the human race. Abraham's day is the period at which the relation of master and slave is first noticed in the divine record; and the period at which the two epistles from which the above extracts are taken, were written, is about the period at which the writing of books of inspiration ceased. Those two periods, then, are the two points of time at which revelation first and last notices the relation of master and slave. And the last is to continue and be in force during, and to the end, of the christian age or dispensation. At the first point or period, the Lord blessed Abraham, and *gave* him flocks, and herds, and silver, and gold, and *men-servants*, and *maid-servants*, and camels, and asses;[2] and he directed the slave Hagar, and her son Ishmael to be cast out and sent away, that he should not be heir with Isaac, the free son of Abraham.[3]

And it may not be inappropriate to remark here, before I proceed to comment upon those two extracts from Paul's writings, that the inspired record of the *gifts* of the Lord to Abraham " places human beings on a level with brute property "[4]—with flocks and herds, and camels and *asses*. Yet I hope that brother Goodwin, and all abolitionists of similar sensitiveness, will not be seriously injured by the "shock" it will give to his and their "moral feelings" to learn it, notwithstanding he may still "conclude" that it

---

(1) Col. iii, 17–25; iv, 1.
(2) Gen. xxiv, 35.
(3) Gen. xxi, 10–12; Gal. iv, 30.
(4) Ante, p. 79.

was very "unrighteous" in the Lord to so give, and to have it so recorded. And that though Paul, on these two different occasions, in writing by inspiration letters to the saints of two different churches, in different localities, "associated" the "divine institution of marriage" with the institution of slavery, and gave laws and directions very similar, if not "parallel," as to the duties of wives to husbands, and of slaves to masters, as well as of the duties of husbands to wives, and of masters to slaves; yet I hope that brother Butler's "moral sense" has sufficiently strengthened itself, that he may be now "able to look steadily and calmly at it," without serious injury. As he was wholly unable to bear it in June, 1862, I spared him then; but now I must declare "all the counsel of God:"[1] I can shun it no longer. It is true that Paul, by inspiration of the Lord, gave laws as to the institutions of marriage and slavery in the two extracts above quoted, from which it seems that he "reasoned in effect, that the one is entitled to equal protection and respect with the other." But brother Butler and abolitionists generally, have been, and are, correcting these sad errors into which Paul and the Lord, and even Peter too, as we shall see hereafter, fell. "This view," says brother Butler, "is so monstrous, so abhorrent, and so offensive to the moral sense, that I confess that I am not yet able to look steadily and calmly at it. The divine institution of marriage, paralleled and associated with the diabolical institution of chattel slavery, is a thought too revolting for calm consideration. But they are so presented by" Paul, "and the consideration is thus forced upon me."[2] And he is "pegging away," abolition-like, to correct these monstrous errors of Paul, and of the Spirit of inspiration that spoke through him.

But irony aside. Does not the fanaticism of abolitionism begin to be visible? Aye, to "appear to all men"?[3]

Preceding and prefatory to the injunctions, as to the domestic relations, copied from the letter to the Ephesians, we are commanded to let no man *deceive us with vain words;* for because of our so doing, comes the wrath of God upon the children of disobedience. We become disobedient when we follow the philosophy and vain deceit, (the vain words in this passage,) of those who teach otherwise as to the

---

(1) Acts xx. 27.   (2) Ante, p. 69.   (3) Tit. ii, 11.

domestic relations of society, than is taught and enjoined in the extracts quoted. Therefore, we should not be partakers with them who so teach, nor follow their teaching.

Is it not time for us, as a nation and people, to reflect and consider, that because we have allowed ourselves to be deceived with the vain words of abolitionists, with their philosophy and vain deceit, as to the sin of slavery, the wrath of God is now upon us in this terrible civil war.

Hence, we should cease being deceived by them, and walk as children of light, of the light which came down from heaven, and which is exhibited to us in the revelation of God in the Scriptures of truth; and not walk in the darkness of abolition theories. We should " have no fellowship with the unfruitful works of darkness, but rather reprove them,"[1] as I am humbly trying to do. We should see then, and take heed, " that we walk circumspectly, not as fools, [fanatics] but as wise, redeeming the time, because the days are" truly and lamentably "evil." For these reasons we should not be unwise, foolish or fanatic, but should go to work in good faith, to *understand* what the will of the Lord is, upon this question of the sinfulness of an institution that has existed among us as a people ever since we became a people; and submit ourselves to one another in the fear of God, by using the light he has given us in his revelation, to ascertain his will, and then following and obeying that light, let it lead where it may.

The apostle, having given us these directions, and this warning against being deceived with the vain words of theorizers establishing their own human systems of righteousness, they being themselves ignorant of the righteousness of God on the subject;[2] or, if not ignorant, trying, like the serpent in Eden, to lead us away from the righteousness of God, goes on to direct us as to our duty in these three domestic relations of human society—the relations of husband and wife, parent and child, and master and slave. He does not tell us to rip up, veto, or abolish any of these relations, or that we must abolish the last relation, though the doing of it produce civil war, internecine strife, anarchy, a reign of terror, the overthrow of the best government God ever gave to man, and the destruction of our own liberties, and the establishment of military despotism;

---
(1) Eph. v, 11.   (2) Rom. x, 3.

all of which our modern abolition preachers, by *word* or *action,* directly or indirectly, tell us to do.

But instead of that, wives are commanded to submit themselves unto their own husbands as unto the Lord; for, in obeying this injunction, they obey the Lord; and in submitting to obey it, they submit to the Lord; for he gave the injunction through his inspired apostle. They are told in the letter to the Colossians, that to do so, is "fit in the Lord." But many of these infidel "humanitarians" teach that man is not the head of the woman, as Christ is of the church, like Paul taught, but they have set up their own righteousness, that is to say, a "woman's rights" system, teaching that women should not be in subjection to their "husbands, as unto the Lord," "as it is fit in the Lord" that they should be. All of whom, so teaching, are abolitionists, and teach the same as to the relation of master and slave, that they teach as to the relation of husband and wife. Being infidel as to one regulation of the Lord, no wonder that they are infidel as to another—yes, as to all regulations of the Lord—which regulations of the Lord constitute the righteousness of God for us to govern ourselves by, and to conform our conduct to.

So the righteousness of God, as written out by Paul in the extracts I am considering, written under the direction, and by the inspiration of the Holy Spirit of God, directs slaves to be obedient to them that are their masters according to the flesh, that is, according to the regulations of the kingdoms of this world, which includes the regulations of the slave States of the heretofore Union of this our heretofore happy country: and to be obedient to them with fear and trembling, in singleness of heart, "as unto Christ; not with eye-service, as men-pleasers, [that is, as abolition-pleasers] but as the servants of Christ, doing the [this] will of God from the heart, with good will doing service, *as to the Lord,* and not to men; knowing that whatsoever good thing a man doeth, [and obeying these injunctions is doing a good thing] the same shall he receive of the Lord, whether he be bond or free;" and knowing also, that when they so act, and do in word and deed, they do it "in the name," under the direction, and by the authority of the Lord, thus giving thanks to God and the Father, by thus obeying the Lord's directions and injunctions to them. And knowing that of the Lord they shall receive the reward of the inheritance, because they serve the Lord Jesus Christ in thus doing; and that he that doeth wrong by disobeying these directions of the Lord, shall receive for the wrong he hath done; and that there is no respect of persons with him, in settling up these matters, even though one is an abolitionist, and the other is a "contraband" deceived and enticed away by the abolitionist, by his "vain words."

Children are also commanded to obey their parents in all things: for this is right. Honor thy father and thy mother, is the first commandment that the Lord gave with a promise; which promise was, that it may be well with them, and that they may live long in the earth. Here the command is repeated, so there can be no doubt that this command of the Decalogue is continued in force, and was not nailed to the Cross by the Lord.

We have now seen, and I have examined, what the Lord commanded the subordinates in these three domestic relations; and we see that wives, children and slaves, are placed by the Lord, in his christian code, in subordinate positions, in those relations, and commanded as to what their duty is in those positions. And there is seen to be a similarity between the duties of wives and slaves; but that the wife occupies the higher, and the nearer, and the dearer position, is also very evident. Wives are only to submit themselves to their husbands; but slaves are not only to be obedient to their masters in all things, but they are to serve their masters, not with pretended eye-service, but with singleness of heart, in good faith, as if they were doing the service to the Lord himself, and not to men. For, in so doing, they "serve the Lord Jesus Christ."

The duties of wife and servant, and their respective positions in the domestic relations of society, are paralleled and associated together here, by the inspired writer; and in bringing to the attention of the reader the whole counsel of God upon the subject I am examining, I am compelled to thus present them, notwithstanding the doing so may throw my abolition friends and brethren into convulsions; but I hope if it does, it will produce no serious injury either to the physical, mental, or moral powers and faculties of my abolition friends and *quondam* brethren.

I will now look at those who stand upon the other side in these three domestic relations of human society.

Husbands are to love their wives as Christ loved the church. How did he love the church? Why, he loved it well enough to give himself for it. That is the kind of love that husbands are commanded to have for their wives; love enough to give themselves for their wives. He that loves his wife loves himself. No man, let him be as bad as he may, ever yet hated his own flesh, but nourished it and cherished it, as the Lord nourishes and cherishes the church. The man and his wife are one flesh by the divine law; and every christian *in particular* is commanded to so love his wife even as he loves himself, and the wife is commanded to reverence her husband, because every christian and every christian church reverences the Lord and all his commandments, including these commandments as to the domestic relations of society.

Fathers are not to provoke their children to wrath.

Masters are commanded to do the same things to their slaves, that is, as Mr. Wesley says in his note, "act towards them from the same principle," the principles just inculcated for the slave to act from to the master; which principles are, that the master act in good faith from the heart, as to the Lord; that he give his slave that which is just and equal between them in their respective positions in the relation they hold to each other; knowing that he also has a Master in heaven, the Lord Jesus Christ, to whom he is amenable as a slave, as his slave is amenable to him: and that the measure he metes to his slave, his Master the Lord, will measure to him again;[1] which is impressively taught by the Lord himself, in the parable recorded in Matthew xviii, 23–35.

This is the Lord's code as to the domestic relations, established for the christian kingdom, and now in force therein; and it is to continue in force during the christian dispensation. When a man occupies the position of husband, father, and master, filling one position in each of the three relations, and he, his wife, children and slaves, all live in the strict observance of these laws, a domestic circle exists similar to that of Abraham, the father of the faithful.

Brother Butler and abolitionists truly say that marriage

---

(1) Matt. vii, 2.

is a divine ordinance, and that the relation of husband and wife is a holy relation. Would the Lord, in giving laws to govern that holy relation, connect with them laws to govern a sinful institution, a diabolical institution, a modern Moloch? Let abolitionists "stop and think" upon this, "ere they farther go."

Marriage is a divine ordinance, while slavery is a human institution. The one is commanded of God; the other is neither commanded nor prohibited. Hence, to enter into the marriage relation is doing righteousness, because it is commanded; but to become a slaveholder is neither doing righteousness nor committing sin, because it is neither commanded nor forbidden; and is like thousands of other human actions, neither righteous nor sinful—but indifferent. But when a man enters the relation of master and slave, then the commands of God reach him, and he does righteousness or commits sin according as he demeans himself. On the other hand, should a person who is in the relation, be properly and lawfully rid of it, then the commands of God pertaining to him in the relation no longer apply to him, and he is not bound by them. Those who do not stand in the relation of master and slave have none of the responsibilities of the relation resting upon them; and are not bound by the laws of the Lord relating to it. The laws of the Lord relating to the institution only apply to, and are only obligatory upon, those who hold the relation of master or slave to some other human being. Hence, there being no law as to others who do not hold that relation, there can be no transgression by them, unless by impertinent interference, they make themselves busy-bodies in other men's matters, when they become accountable—not for "the sin of slavery"—but for being busy-bodies.[1] By the laws of the Lord's kingdom, every one is accountable for his own conduct, and his own actions; and not for the conduct and actions of others. "So then every one shall give an account *of himself* to God;"[2] and not of other people. But more of this hereafter.

The apostle Paul, in his first letter to Timothy, wrote thus:

Let as many servants as are under the yoke count their own masters worthy of all honor, that the name of God

---

(1) 1 Pet. iv, 15; 2 Thes. iii, 11; 1 Tim. v, 13.   (2) Rom. xiv, 12.

and his doctrine be not blasphemed. And they that have believing masters, let them not despise them, because they are brethren; but rather do them service, because they are faithful (or believers) and beloved, partakers of [who receive] the benefit. *These things teach and exhort.* If any man teach otherwise, and consent not to wholesome words, even the words of our Lord Jesus Christ, and to the doctrine which is according to godliness, he is proud, knowing nothing, but doting about questions and strifes of words, whereof cometh envy, strife, railings, evil-surmisings, perverse disputings of men of corrupt minds, [wholly corrupt in mind], and destitute of the truth, supposing that gain is godliness: from such withdraw thyself.[1]

I note first, that the persons spoken of here, were slaves under the yoke of Roman bondage—a much worse system of slavery than any that ever existed in any State of this Union. They were commanded to count their masters worthy of all honor. This is what Paul taught in his letter to the Romans: "Render therefore to all their *dues:* tribute to whom tribute is due; custom to whom custom: fear to whom fear; *honor to whom honor.*"[2] Slaves are here commanded to count their masters worthy of all honor. Honor, then, by the law of the Lord, is due the master from the slave; and the slave, in rendering it, renders only what is due the master. And this is enjoined by Paul that the name of God and his doctrine be not blasphemed, or defamed, as it reads in the New Translation. The doctrine of God, then, is, that slaves render to their masters all honor as their due; and when christian slaves fail to do so, of their own motion, or by advice of abolitionists, they thereby give occasion for the name and doctrine of God to be defamed or blasphemed. And christian slaves that have believing masters, that is, christian masters, are commanded to not despise them because they are brethren in Christ; but that they serve them the more, because they are believers and beloved who receive the benefit of their services and labor.

And these things Paul enjoined it upon his beloved Timothy to teach and exhort. This is the divine command in the premises. Those who so teach and so exhort, do righteousness, because they do the command of God. Those

---
(1) 1 Tim. vi, 1-5.   (2) Rom. xiii, 7.

teachers who fail to so teach, are guilty of unrighteousness, which is failing to do the commands of God; and being guilty of unrighteousness, they sin, for all unrighteousness is sin.[1] And those teachers who teach the contrary of what Paul here enjoined Timothy to teach and exhort, transgress the law, and thereby sin.[2] And Paul went on immediately, after enjoining Timothy to so teach and exhort, to describe this last named class, and "the effects and consequences" of their teaching; which description is an exact one of the preachers and teachers of abolitionism, and of the effects and consequences of their work, as I will now show.

1. "If any man teach otherwise." Abolitionists do teach otherwise. So far the description fits.

2. If they "consent not to wholesome words." Abolition teachers do not consent to wholesome words, as what they have said in the preceding pages abundantly shows. I will not specify in detail, but only make general reference to the many instances where I have had to combat their improper use of words in the preceding pages. In this particular, they fit the description.

3. If they do not consent to "the words of our Lord Jesus Christ, and to the doctrine which is according to godliness"—God-like-ness. The words of the Lord Jesus Christ upon the subject of the duties of slaves to their masters, that being the subject upon which Paul was teaching here, I have referred to in the preceding pages, which the reader will please to look back to and examine.[3] These are the words of our blessed Lord as to the relation, rights and duties of masters and slaves. And the Lord said that the kingdom of heaven, or God's government, was like them. Hence, this doctrine he taught is godliness or God-like-ness on the subject. The Savior was God manifest in the flesh.[4] His conduct while here, was godliness, God-like-ness, or acting God-like. He took upon him the form of a slave, and was made in the likeness of men: and being found in fashion as a man, he humbled himself, and became obedient, that is, he became a slave, for obedience is slavery. He became obedient unto death, the Roman system of slavery requiring the slaves to obey their masters even unto death; and the Lord became obedient unto death, even to

---

(1) 1 John v, 17.   (2) 1 John iii, 4.   (3) Ante, pp. 291-295.   (4) 1 Tim. iii, 16.

the death of the Cross, which mode of death, by the Roman law, could be inflicted only on slaves and malefactors. This was the "mind" that was in Christ, and that christians are commanded to have in them, as is evident from the whole passage cited in the foot-note.¹ And I have also noted in the preceding pages (including this passage that I am now considering, and what Paul said to Titus,² and what the apostle Peter said,³ both of which will be hereafter noticed,) what the inspired apostles of the Lord taught on the subject by his commands; all of which are wholesome or healthy words, even the words of the Lord Jesus through or by his apostles who had plenary power from him to bind and loose on the subject; and they teach the doctrine which is according to godliness. Abolitionists do not consent to these words, nor to this doctrine; neither to the words actually used by the Lord himself, and the doctrine he taught, nor to the words used by the apostles, and the doctrine they taught. They repudiate the whole of it, and make unrelenting war upon it, calling it all the hard names they can think of or invent—and they have great inventive powers in detraction and defamation.

4. The description goes on to say that those who teach otherwise, and do not consent to those words, and to this doctrine, are "proud, knowing nothing; but are doting about questions and strifes of words." Are not abolitionists proud, puffed up, with their super-piety? This book shows how "vain in their *imaginations*"⁴ *reasonings*, as it reads in the New Translation, they are, to try to make out and sustain their theory by their reasoning, independent of the knowledge of God upon the subject. They "walk in the vanity of their mind,"⁵ that is, have their minds lifted up and exalted with the vain notions of their wisdom, learning, and smartness, "above and before" the wisdom that is from above, "and cometh down from the Father of lights;"⁶ the result of which really is, that thereby their "understanding" becomes "darkened" and "alienated from the life of God through the ignorance that is in them, because of the blindness of their heart."⁷ Yet "they speak great swelling words of vanity," and thereby "allure through the lusts of the flesh [for power, place, and popu-

---

(1) Phil. ii, 5–8.   (4) Rom. i, 21.   (7) Eph. iv, 18.
(2) Tit. ii, 9 10.   (5) Eph. iv, 17, 18.
(3) 1 Pet. ii, 13–25; iii, 1–7.   (6) James i, 17.

larity], through much wantonness [as to the public welfare, either of church or State,] those that were clean escaped from them who live in error."[1] And Paul says, in the passage that I am considering, that, because they do as there described, which I have shown that abolitionists do, they are *proud*, puffed up, and high-minded, but really *know nothing*, because they reject the knowledge of God, will not consent to the wholesome words of the Lord Jesus Christ and his doctrine, and attempt, by their own reasoning, to make a better system. Paul denounces those who do so as proud and knowing nothing; abolition preachers and teachers do so: therefore, abolition preachers and teachers are *proud* and *know nothing;* that is, proud and ignorant of the true knowledge of God on the subject. And more than that, Paul says that they dote upon, love, and have excessive fondness for questions and strifes of words. Wordy strife is but the way of doing what the abolition leaders and founders of the sect commanded them to do long ago; that is, agitate! agitate!! agitate!!! which, being translated into the Hoosier vernacular, is, keep up a fuss! keep up a fuss!! keep up a fuss!!! which they have assiduously done from the birth of their sect, and still are doing, with more energy, if possible, than ever.

5. The description further says, that of or from this doting about questions and strifes of words of those men, come "envy, strife, railings, evil-surmisings, perverse disputings of men of corrupt minds and destitute of the truth." How exactly this fits and describes "the effects and consequences" of abolitionism! Of it has come envy; of it has come strife, even to the strife of a terrible and gigantic civil war now raging in our unhappy country. Abolitionism railed all the time, from the time it was born till now, and is now railing at everything and every body that will not worship at its shrine; evil-surmizing has been its daily work all its life, and still is; and perverse disputings of men of corrupt mind and wholly destitute of the truth of God upon the subject of slavery, such as now exists in our unhappy country, caps the climax of its wickedness.

This is an inspired description of abolition preachers and teachers, and of the effects and consequences of abolitionism. The Spirit that spoke through Paul saw the picture

---

(1) 2 Pet. ii, 18.

as it exists and has existed for thirty years, and described it accurately. If any think that I am speaking too strongly, let them look back and see that Paul was speaking of those who teach otherwise than he there enjoined upon Timothy to teach; and then reflect that abolitionists do teach otherwise, and will not consent to the wholesome words of the Lord, and to the doctrine that is according to godliness upon this subject, and they will see clearly that Paul was speaking of, and denouncing, abolition preachers and abolitionism.

6. And Paul closes with this command to Timothy: "From such withdraw thyself" Hence, christians are here commanded to withdraw from, or excommunicate—not abolitionists who entertain their notions as private opinions of their own, and keep them as such—but those who teach abolitionism, which is teaching otherwise than as Paul enjoined it upon Timothy to teach, and who will not consent to the wholesome words of the Lord Jesus Christ upon the subject, and the doctrine which is according to godliness, as taught by the Lord and his apostles. The command of the Lord, through the apostle Paul, is, that such *teachers* be excommunicated. And how much better it would have been for christianity and for our country, if this command of the Lord had been faithfully obeyed from the birth of abolitionism until now.

Thus obeying this command, would have also obeyed another command given by the Lord, through the same apostle, in his letter to Titus. In that letter, he said that bishops of churches should hold fast *the faithful word* as they *had been taught*, that they might be able, *by sound doctrine*, both to exhort the christians to faithfully discharge their duties, which would of course include their duties as to the domestic relations of society, and to convince or confute the gain-sayers. For, said he, there are many unruly and vain talkers and deceivers, *whose mouths must be stopped*, who subvert whole houses, teaching things which they ought not, for filthy lucre's sake. Wherefore rebuke them sharply, that they may be sound in the faith.[1]

These abolition teachers are unruly and vain talkers, as I have shown above. They reject the word of the Lord, and the doctrine which is according to godliness. They

---

(1) Tit. i, 9-13.

subvert, not only whole houses, but whole communities, teaching things which they ought not; and they have done, and are now doing, a world of mischief. Their mouths must be stopped: first by confuting their gainsaying, and rebuking them sharply, that they may be sound in the faith. My humble part in this work I am now trying to perform. And, secondly, if they do not stand reproved and reform, and abandon their unruly course, then, by excommunicating them—withdrawing from them—after a first and second admonition. That will stop their mouths in christian congregations, and *as christian teachers*. If they still persist in their unruly talk after having been expelled from the christian congregation—the assembly of the saints, in which place God is greatly feared,[1] and as a necessary consequence, his commands strictly obeyed—christianity will not be amenable for it; for they will then stand as disowned apostates. This is the Lord's method of stopping the mouths of unruly, vain talkers and deceivers, as prescribed in his laws.[2] If bishops of churches would hold fast the faithful word, and by sound doctrine confute these abolition gainsayers; and if christian congregations would obey the divine injunction to withdraw from the unruly and vain talkers and deceivers that persisted in their course of teaching otherwise than Paul commanded Timothy to teach, after having been rebuked sharply for it, they would but obey the Lord, and would be blessed by him for their obedience. And then neither individual christians, nor whole houses, much less whole communities, would be subverted by their so teaching things which they ought not to teach, and which I have shown that they ought not to teach.

I have now proved the fourth proposition that I proposed to discuss with brother Boggs.[3] I have shown that these abolition preachers, and the teachers of abolitionism in the pulpit and through the press, are "heretical, schismatical and anti-christian." They reject the wholesome words of the Lord, and his doctrine. That position, which they assume and hold, is anti-Christ, or against Christ; for *anti* is *against*. "Whosoever transgresseth, and abideth not *in the doctrine of Christ*, hath not God. He that abideth in

---
(1) Ps. lxxxix, 7.
(2) The abolition method of doing it, as exemplified by the present abolition administration of the general government, is by illegal military arrests, bastiles, &c.
(3) Ante, p. 25.

the doctrine of Christ, he hath both the Father and the
Son. If there come any unto you, and bring not this doctrine [of Christ], receive him not into your house, neither
bid him God speed; for he that biddeth him God speed, is
partaker of his evil deeds."[1] These teachers of abolitionism, in the language of brother Boggs, "persistently refuse" to stand rebuked, and to reform and become sound
in the faith. But instead of that, they labor hard to make
an abolition sect in the body of christians. Hence, they
are heretical and schismatical; for heresy is simply making
a sect; and schism, in christianity, is but rending the
church, the body of Christ. And the Lord commanded
thus: "A factionist, after a first and second admonition,
reject; knowing that such a person is *perverted*, and *sins*,
being self-condemned."[2] Christian churches should therefore rid themselves of those abolition teachers who, either
in the pulpit or through the press, "teach otherwise, and
will not consent to wholesome words, even the words of our
Lord Jesus Christ, and to the doctrine that is according to
godliness;" and who, after being "rebuked sharply that
they may be sound in the faith," "persistently" continue
to be vain talkers and deceivers, by rejecting them as factionists, after a first and second admonition. By so doing,
they will be " walking in the fear of the Lord, and the admonition or instruction of the Holy Spirit, and will be
multiplied"[3] exceedingly, in this our day, when nearly all
the other Protestant denominations of christians have become simply propagandists of abolitionism. Go to their
churches and you hear little said about the Lord and his
kingdom, but much about abolitionism and " the kingdoms
of this world," in our now divided, distracted and unhappy
country. They "mind earthly things," and hence are
" the enemies of the Cross of Christ."[4] But, on the other
hand, if they allow those teachers to continue their nefarious work, teaching "otherwise," the christian body will
go the way of all the other professedly christian denominations, and be swallowed up, body and soul, in abolitionism;
and but add another to the now numerous progeny of the
Mother of Harlots. From which fate may the good Lord
deliver us.

I will now proceed to notice the two other passages in

---
(1) 2 John 9-11. (3) Acts ix, 31, New Translation.
(2) Tit. iii, 10, 11. New Translation. (4) Phil. iii, 18, 19.

the apostolic writings, relating to slavery, that I have not yet noticed.

Paul, in writing to Titus, commands him to speak *the things* that become *sound doctrine*. And among the things following that become sound doctrine, that Paul commanded Titus to teach, was this: "Exhort servants to be subject to their own masters, and in all things to be careful to please, not answering again, not secretly stealing, but showing all good fidelity, *that they may adorn the doctrine of God our Savior* in all things."[1] It is sound doctrine to so teach the slaves; and for the slaves to obey the teaching, is to adorn the doctrine of God our Savior. Abolition teachers disobey the command to so teach, and teach "otherwise," that the slaves should not be subject to their own masters, and should not in all things be careful to please them; but to steal away from them whenever they can, and to show no good faith towards them. Thus disobeying the plain command of God, they sin.

The apostle Peter, in writing to the christians scattered throughout Pontus, Galatia, Cappadocia, Asia and Bithynia, wrote thus:

"Ye are a chosen generation [race], a royal priesthood, a holy nation, a peculiar [purchased] people; that ye should show forth the praises of him who hath called you out of darkness into his marvellous light; which [who] in time past were not a people, but are now the people of God: which [who] had not obtained mercy, but now have obtained mercy. Dearly beloved, I beseech you as strangers and pilgrims, abstain from fleshy lusts, which war against the soul; having your conversation [behavior] honest among the Gentiles: that whereas [wherein] they speak against you as evil-doers, they may by your good works, which they shall behold, glorify God in the day of visitation. Submit yourselves to every ordinance of man for the Lord's sake: whether it be to the king as supreme; or unto governors, as unto them that are sent by him for the punishment of evil-doers, and for the praise of them that do well. For so is the will of God, that with well doing ye may put to silence the ignorance of foolish men: as free, yet not using your liberty for a cloak of maliciousness, but as the servants of God. Honor all men. Love the brotherhood.

---

(1) Tit. ii, 9, 10, New Translation.

Fear God. Honor the king. Servants, be subject to your masters with all fear; not only to the good and gentle, but also to the froward. For this is thank-worthy, if a man for conscience toward God endure grief, suffering wrongfully. For what glory is it, if, when ye be buffetted for your faults, ye shall take it patiently? but if, when ye do well, and suffer for it, ye take it patiently, this is acceptable with God. For even hereunto were ye called: because Christ also suffered for us, leaving us an example that ye should follow his steps: who did no sin, neither was guile found in his mouth: who, when he was reviled, reviled not again; when he suffered, he threatened not; but committed himself to him that judgeth righteously: who in his own self bear our sins in his own body on the tree, that we, being dead to sins, should live unto righteousness: by whose stripes ye were healed. For ye were as sheep going astray: but are now returned unto the Shepherd and Bishop of your souls.

"Likewise, ye wives, be in subjection to your own husbands; that, if any obey not the word, they also may without the word be won by the conversation [behavior, deportment] of the wives; while they behold your chaste behavior coupled with fear: whose adorning let it not be that outward adorning of plaiting the hair, and of wearing of gold, or of putting on apparel; but let it be the hidden man of the heart, in that which is not corruptible, even the ornament of a meek and quiet spirit, which is in the sight of God of great price. For after this manner in the old time holy women also, who trusted in God, adorned themselves, being in subjection unto their own husbands: even as Sarah obeyed Abraham, calling him lord; whose daughters ye are, as long as ye do well, and are not afraid with any amazement.

"Likewise, ye husbands, dwell with them according to knowledge, giving honor unto the wife, as unto the weaker vessel, and as being heirs together of the grace [favor] of life; that your prayers be not hindered."[1]

There can be no doubt of the binding obligation of this teaching upon us; for the Lord gave Peter the keys of the kingdom of heaven, and said that whatsoever he bound on earth should be bound in heaven.[2]

---

(1) 1 Pet. ii, 9-25; iii, 1-7.   (2) Matt. xvi, 19.

I have quoted thus much from Peter's first letter, that I might lay it all before the reader as it stands in the Scriptures. A good portion of it applies to the next general head of which I shall treat, which is, the duty of christians in and to civil governments, or the kingdoms of this world. Upon that branch of the extract, I will now only note briefly, that christians are a chosen, purchased nation, which before Peter wrote had not been a people, but were then, when he wrote, a people. Their mission in this world is to show forth the praises, as it reads in the common version, but, as it reads in the New Translation, to declare the perfections of the Lord, who called them from the darkness in which man is without the knowledge of God, into the marvellous light of the Lord's revelations to our race. They are simply sojourners and pilgrims or travelers in this world, and in the kingdoms of this world. Here they "have no continuing city."[1] They are commanded to submit to every ordinance of man for the Lord's sake—not for their own sakes. The king or civil government is put down as an ordinance of man. It is to be submitted to as such, and submitted to for the Lord's sake, that his kingdom, government, and doctrine be not blasphemed or defamed in the kingdoms of this world. It is similar to a citizen or subject of one civil government residing in another. He submits to every ordinance of the government in which he resides for the sake of his government at home, that it be not scandalized or defamed by his conduct.

All men are to be honored or respected, but the brotherhood are to be loved. This is one proof of what I stated in my debate with brother Wiley, that the Lord has different laws for the conduct of christians, as to those that are christians, and as to those that are not.[2]

Speaking of the duties of christians as to the ordinances of man, Peter speaks of the duties of the servants to their masters. This shows that the institution of slavery is an ordinance of man; and it is also to be submitted to for the Lord's sake. Abolitionists take issue with Peter, and say that it should not be submitted to. As Peter spoke for the Lord, and had authority from him to bind on earth, abolitionists, by taking issue with Peter, take issue with the Lord, and thus are against Christ, or *anti*-christian. Ser-

---

(1) Heb. xiii, 14. (2) Ante, p 239.

vants are commanded to be subject not only to good and gentle masters, but also to the froward, peevish, ungovernable, perverse masters; because it is thank-worthy if a man for conscience towards God, rather than disobey his commands and laws, endure grief suffering wrongfully. And the example of Christ's conduct and suffering is cited by Peter, to show the propriety of the commands he gave the servants. Mr. Wesley, in his note on verses 22 and 23, says: "In all these instances the example of Christ is peculiarly adapted to the state of servants." The Lord, in the condition of a servant, as in every other condition, was PERFECT.

"In like manner," as translated by Mr. Wesley, and in the New Translation, wives are commanded to be in subjection to their own husbands; for it was so "in the old time," even as far back as Sarah's and Abraham's day. They had no infidel or unfaithful that is disobedient, abolition or women's rights theories, and systems of righteousness, in either Abraham's or Peter's day, nor for nearly eighteen centuries afterwards. Peter commanded that wives be in subjection to their husbands in like manner, as servants were just before commanded by him to be subject to their masters. Hence, he not only fell into the grievous error that Paul did in paralleling, and associating the institutions of marriage and slavery, but he commanded that the wife be subject to the husband, as the servant to the master.

I have now noticed all the passages in the New Testament that treat of the institution of slavery, except the letter to Philemon, which is sufficiently noticed in the debates. They show that the Lord did not preach deliverance to the captives in the sense of abolitionism, that is, he did not preach freedom to the slaves. Both brother Butler and brother Wiley failed to show that he did preach so, though repeatedly requested to do so. On the contrary, the Scriptures I have noticed, show that he preached that the slaves should remain in the condition they were, and serve their masters. The deliverance to the captives that the Lord was anointed to preach, and that he actually did preach, was deliverance from mental and moral captivity; deliverance from sin, and death, and the grave; deliverance from the snare of the devil, who had taken the world of mankind captive at his will. The freedom that the Lord preached, was freedom from sin and all its consequences; from death, hell, and the grave; and not freedom from the institution of slavery, an ordinance of man existing in the kingdoms of this world. His command was to submit to every ordinance of man, including that ordinance, for his sake.

As I did not have space to reply fully to brother Wiley's sixth argument, at pages 217 and 218, I will do so now. He took the ground that the passage quoted there, clearly established the general principle, "that as we treat the Lord's disciple, so we treat him." Upon that I took issue, *ante*, p. 224.

This shows how easily we are led astray when we undertake to draw general rules from particular transactions. Here the Lord blest and rewarded those on his right hand, because, in doing certain specified things to his disciples, he accounted them as having been done to himself; and he punished those on his left hand, because, in failing to do those same specified things that the righteous had done to his disciples, he accounted them as having failed to do them to him. From this brother Wiley drew the general proposition, and asserted it to be true, as to everything else, that might be done or not done to a disciple, as being done or not done to the Lord. That is, that because at the final account, the Lord will *impute* us as having been done or not done *to himself*, what we may have done or not have done *to his disciples*, as to six things, that is, as to giving his disciples food, drink, lodging, and apparel, and as to visiting them in sickness, and in prison, that he will impute *every thing else* also, as having been done or not done *to him*, which we shall have done or not have done to his disciples; and as brother Wiley applied it, if a master of a christian slave shall have sold him, it will be imputed that he sold the Lord!

I gave one instance at page 239, "that worshipping the Lord's disciple is not worshipping him," to show that brother Wiley's general rule is not general. One exception is enough to show that his general deduction is untrue, and breaks all its force. I will, however, now give a few others, and could give more. Teaching a disciple, is not teaching the Lord. Obeying a disciple's theory, system, or dogma, is not obeying the Lord. Working for a disciple for wages, is not working for the Lord for wages. And hiring a disciple to work for you, is not hiring the Lord to work for you. By the same parity of reasoning, may we not say, that notwithstanding that by the laws of a State, we own a disciple as a slave, we do not own the Lord as a slave? and that selling that slave is not selling the Lord? If one's owning a disciple by the laws of a State makes him the owner of the Lord by imputation, will not a disciple's being in debt to one, make the Lord in debt to him by imputation?

But let us get closer up. The charge was: I was in prison and ye came not unto me. The blame was for not coming to him in prison. According to abolitionism, the blame is, because they did not release him from prison—free him—break his fetters—open his prison doors. The Lord, however, did not blame those on his left hand, for not releasing either him or his disciples. That was not the sin. The sin was, not coming to him—not visiting him in the condition in which he was;—not for not changing that condition and taking him out of it. And this is in strict accordance with all the teaching of the Lord, as to slaves, as is abundantly shown in the preceding pages. According to abolition teaching and conduct, the Lord should have said to those on his left hand: I was in prison, and the Golden Rule requiring you to do as you would be done by, required that you should have disregarded the laws and ordinances of man by which I was imprisoned, and "agitated" action upon a "higher law" till you got up a party sufficiently powerful to tear down the jail and take me out, though it led to war and bloodshed, devastation, fire and sword; and because you did not do it, depart, &c.

This shows the impropriety and danger of going to reasoning, and drawing deductions and inferences, in ascertaining what is sinful or righteous, instead of looking to the direct commands of the Lord upon the particular subject. I have shown the many commands of the Lord to the master and slave; and yet brother Wiley, instead of looking to them to ascertain the Lord's will in the premises, reasoned from this passage, and the Golden Rule, &c., to find out that slavery is sinful.

During all the three years and a half of the Lord's ministry, he ministered only to the moral, mental and physical wants of the people. He never ministered, in any way, to their political wants, nor as to their condition in life, as to bond or free, high or low, rich or poor. This 'any one can fully and clearly see, who will carefully read the four Gospels.

What more I have to say under brother Wiley's fifth head, will properly come up under the general head I shall next consider—the duty of christians in the civil government.

I have now fully discussed the proposition, *Slavery is sinful.* Brethren Wiley and Butler both undertook to sustain and prove the proposition by the good word of the Lord. They both failed, and both desisted from the further prosecution of the discussion, midway of it. I ask the reader's careful attention to, and consideration of, what has been said in the preceding pages; and that they " search the Scriptures daily whether these things are so,"[1] as the noble Bereans did. We are all equally interested in ascertaining and knowing what the truth is on this now momentous and absorbing question, in our now divided, distracted, and unhappy country. It will do none of us any harm to carefully and calmly look at and consider what is said in the inspired volume, the only true source of light and knowledge, on this now terrible question. It is time for us all to carefully re-examine the ground we occupy, and see whether or not we are, or have been in error. We should do this dispassionately; we should not let our party feelings, either religious or political, sway us from so doing; but, as far as it is possible for human nature to do, we should approach the careful and honest examination of God's word upon the subject, as if we had no opinions of our own, in good faith resolving to follow God's truth, let it lead wherever it may. If we do that, we are certain to come to the light; for " he that doeth [obeys or follows] truth cometh to the light."[2] God has communicated his knowledge to us: it is our duty to examine, ascertain, and acquire it. Let us do so, in good faith, on this subject, at this time. If we do, our errors may be ascertained, and our ways amended, in time to yet save our country and people from utter ruin and destruction. But, if we do not, and are wrong in the assumption that slavery is sinful, as I think I have abundantly shown that we are, and still persist on that false as-

(1) Acts xvii, 11.   (2) John iii, 21.

sumption, to prosecute the present unhappy civil war with the demoniacal zeal of the Saracens, to exterminate the sin of slavery, who can tell or estimate the amount of responsibility, present and prospective, now and in history, in time and in eternity, that such a course of conduct will impose upon us?

May the good Lord enable us all to come to THE KNOWLEDGE OF THE TRUTH, and having come to it, to obey it cheerfully, and with willing mind, is my devout prayer.

As supplementary to this department of my subject, I copy the following article from the *Religious Herald*, of May 31st, 1860. The writer is a graduate of the Virginia University; and his article shows his scholarship and ability. I copy it principally on the account of the information it will give the reader on the terms, slave, servants, &c.; but there are other valuable facts bearing on the subject well stated in the article:

PAUL ON ABOLITIONISM.

NEW ENGLAND.—The following statement has appeared in religious journals published at Boston, Chicago, New York and Pittsburg: "My strong conviction is, that unless there shall soon be a mighty outpouring of the Holy Spirit, the day is not distant which will witness a more extensive and appalling apostacy in New England than we have ever yet seen—and that apostacy will be into Universalism. Is this the whirlwind to be reaped from sowing the wind of ultra anti-slaveryism? Abolitionism seems to us a very direct path to apostacy."

Now, it does seem to me that this remark of the editor scarcely does full justice to abolitionism. Let us look for a moment at the real facts of the case, and see if we can not discover wherein lies the apostacy of abolitionism itself; for I contend that it is not only the *path* to apostacy, but that it is *the thing itself*. This might seem to be a bold assertion to make, in the face of so many wise and reverend men, whose names have adorned the times in which they lived. But the writer believes that he has counted the cost in making such a statement. Look at the authority, and then speak your mind. Just about 1800 years ago, there was a young minister, who had just been sent forth to preach the Gospel. He was remarkably well read in the Scriptures, having been trained in them from his childhood. His object in preaching the Gospel was to teach men their duty, in order that they might be saved. But he was young and inexperienced in the work, and though he understood very well the *general* character of his great work, and was familiar with the great central truths of the Gospel, yet there were many particular points in the *application* of the teachings of the Gospel to every day life, on which he needed advice and instruction. Besides, he needed advice from an older preacher, as to how he should withstand the opposers of the Gospel, and how he should manage those still more dangerous opponents, who, professing to preach the Gospel of the Lord Jesus Christ, should, in fact, preach "*another Gospel.*" The name of this young preacher was Timothy. Now it so happened that Timothy had just such a friend and adviser as he needed in the person of the apostle Paul. This man was not only a very great preacher and distinguished orator, (see Longinus,) but he had been preaching about from place to place among all classes of people. He had met with all sorts of infidels, heathen, pagans, Sadducees, and worshippers of the "Unknown God." He had refuted the philosophical dogmas of the Epicureans and the Stoics. He had condemned heresy and apostacy wherever he had seen it. He had been through all sorts of tribulation and affliction, and had confronted all sorts of opposition. He had, moreover, been the means of Timothy's conversion. Now, these reasons made it very proper that Paul should give Timothy the benefit of his experience, and accordingly he writes a letter to the young preacher. In the midst of this letter, he gives him the following directions: 1 Tim. vi, 1—"Let as many servants as are under the yoke, count their own masters worthy of all honor, that the name of God and his doctrine be not blasphemed." Let us pause here a moment and see what this means. In the first place, what is the exact meaning of the term *servants?* In the original it is "Douloi." This word is used in various places in the New Testament. Let us seek an illustration by comparing this passage with another, also penned by Paul himself. In Romans i, 1, we find the following: "Paul, a servant of Jesus Christ, called to be an apostle," &c. Now, the word "doulos" used in this place to mean servant, is the singular number of precisely the same words which is used in the quotation from Timothy. If we can find out its meaning here, we can know what meaning to give to it there. Now, what does Paul mean by the term *servant* in this first chapter of Romans? The term seems capable of bearing but two interpretations. It either means a hireling, or it means that the person to whom the term applies is the property of the master. Now, it can not mean a hireling here. Paul did not mean to say that he was a hireling. Why, we know what an account Jesus himself gives of the hireling. He tells us (John x, 13,) that "the hireling fleeth because he is an hireling, and careth not for the sheep." This was not the character of Paul. His heart's desire and prayer to God for Israel was, that they might be saved. Besides, the word translated *hireling*, in John x, 13, is totally different from the word *servant* in Rom. i, 1, and in 1 Tim. vi, 1. In the first case, it is the word "misthotos," or one who is paid for services rendered; in the other two cases, as we have seen, it is "doulos."

But we can easily settle this question in a positive manner, by showing from Paul's other writings, in what sense he considered himself the servant of Jesus Christ. Let us turn to 1 Cor. vi, 19, 20, and we find Paul telling the servants of Jesus Christ that they are not their own. And why? Is it because their *time is hired*? No, but it is because they are *bought with a price*. Paul then means to say that he is a servant who is not his own, but is bought with a price; and when expressing the relation in which he, a servant of Jesus Christ, stands to Christ, who *bought* him with a price, he uses the word "doulos." This would seem to be a marvellously plain case to require any proof at all, were it not for the fact that abolition writers have tried to make it appear, to abolitionized ignorance, that the word "doulos" meant only a hireling, or a hired servant. This is certainly either perverting the right ways of the Lord, or else it is darkening counsel by words without knowledge. But, after having settled the meaning of this term, let us look into the meaning of the rest of this verse. The apostle says that these servants are to give all honor to their masters. Now, who are these masters? Are they simply the *employers* of the servants? Are they the undertakers, and the others the *laborers for pay*, as the abolition scholars would have us believe? This would be incompatible with our settled meaning of the word "doulos;" for it is evident that the words are correlative; and that, if "doulos" means *servant*, in the sense of slave, and *not* hireling, then the word "despotes," or *master*, would not supply the proper correlative idea, if it merely meant an undertaker. This interpretation would give Paul as valid a claim to nonsensical writing, as some of the abolition commentators on him have established for themselves.

But, lest there should be any mistake in our reasoning, let us again consult the original, to get the true force and intent of the word. The Greek word "despotes" is used here. This is the very same as our word *despot*. The only difference is in the termination. Now, we should hardly suppose that abolitionism itself could believe that the English word *despot* meant simply a master-workman or undertaker. What do we mean when we speak of a despotic government? Everybody knows that we mean a government in which the will of one man is the law. It would be absurd to talk of an undertaker or master-workman here. And so every Greek scholar knows that it is just as absurd to say that the Greek word "despotes" means a master-workman. Now, it would seem that this case was made out without a possibility of error. There seems to be no other rational interpretation for the passage than the one which is here given. But I am aware that there are those who are not guided by reasoning and argument. Some are blinded by prejudice; some are deceived by the bold and utterly groundless statements of pretended scholars. For the benefit of those, as well as for his own satisfaction, the writer has been at some pains to find authority for what he holds to be the truth. The result of his investigation is as follows: Says Calepin: "Doulos—Latin, *servus; i. e., qui sui juris non est, sed alieno domino subjicitur.*" The English of this is as follows: A slave; that is, one who of his own right possesses no existence, but is subjected to another as his master. This looks pretty plain. But hear him further. The Gallic of this word, he tells us, is *serf.* The French is *esclave;* Italian, *servitore;* Spanish, *siervo;* Anglo-Saxon, a man-servant. Says Schrevelii: "Doulos"—*servus.* "Suidas Lexicon Kusteri" says: "Doulos"—*servus.*

Jones' Lexicon: "Doulos"—a slave a servant; "doule"—a female slave. Damn: "Doule"—Latin, *ancilla, serva*—a female slave. Stephano: "Doulos"—*servus*, correlative "despotes," opposite "eleutheros." Now, "despotes" means a master, and is the correlative term to "doulos;" and "eleutheros" means a freeman, and is opposed to "doulos." Du Fresne says: "Doule"—*ancilla*. Now, *ancilla* means a female slave, a handmaid. Donnegan tells us that "doulos" means a slave, a servant. Grove: "Doulous"—a slave, a servant. Pickering: "Doulos"—a slave, a servant. Diddell and Scott: "Doulos"—a slave, a bondman, strictly one born so; opposed to "andrapodon"—a slave taken captive in war, from the idea of the captive falling at the feet of the conqueror; "doulous," from "deo," to bind. This derivation of the word is put down by the lexicographer as only probable; and in this idea, he seems to be sustained by Professor Gildersleeve, of the University of Virginia, who is decidedly the highest authority I know, and who holds that the origin of the word is not settled. The Persian word is *bendet*, probably akin to our word bondman.

Now, "doulos" is not the only Greek word which means a servant or slave. On the contrary, the Greek language is exceedingly rich in its variety, and most critically nice in its distinctions. This is a marked peculiarity of the language in general; and seldom does this peculiarity show itself more plainly, than in the various words with which the Greeks provided themselves for expressing the various modifications of the idea contained in the word servant. For example: "Andropodon"—a slave taken captive; "doulos"—one born so; "douleuma"—one bought with money; "doulosunos"—one enslaved; "doularion"—a little slave; "pais"—a slave, and in general a servant maid; "paidion"—a young slave, lad; "paidarion"—a young slave; "ktema"—property in slaves; "paidiske"—a young female slave. Now, here were evidently words enough to choose from, (and we have not exhausted them,) so that we are not to suppose that the word "doulo," is used because it came pretty *near* the idea, and there was no word to express it exactly. This supposition is too violent even for an abolitionist, if he has any pretensions to Greek scholarship. But lest it may be supposed that the meaning of this word is different in the New Testament from what it is anywhere else, we may cite the following passages from the classic Greek authors, and any one who feels disposed, and has the opportunity, may compare the passages. The word "doulos," or some modification or synonym of it, occurs, I believe, in the following places: Thucydides viii, 28, iv, 34, ii, 61, and i, 18; Euripides Hecuba 865; Ibid Ion 556; Herodotus vii, 7, i, 27, i, 94, 174; Homer's Odyssey 22, 423. "But if Paul had desired to express the idea of a hired servant in this place," says some man, "could he have found any other word to use?" We answer, in the first place, that whether he could or not, he could *not* use *this* word "doulous." Words, like facts, are stubborn things. After their meaning has been settled by universal use for centuries, we can not take them up and give them an entirely new meaning, without giving any sort of intimation of the fact, that we mean by the words, not what others mean, but something totally different from anything which the words ever meant before. Now, the word "doulous" *never* means a hireling or a hired servant. There is not a single authenticated case in the whole range of Greek literature, where the word has that meaning. And, therefore, even if there had been as great a dearth of words as there actually is an abundance in the Greek language for the expression of this idea, still Paul could not have used this word for it, without giving us some intimation of the liberty he was taking. But just see how very ridiculous this abolition idea of hireling becomes, when we compare it with other passages in the Bible, where the same or cognate idea is to be expressed. I have found the expression "hired servant" in nine different passages of our version of the Bible. Exodus xii, 45—"A hired servant shall not eat thereof," &c. Here the Greek word of the Septuagint is *not* "doulos," but "misthotos"—one who is paid for services rendered. Lev. xxii, 10, "misthotos" is the word. In Lev. xxv, 6, the term "hired servant" occurs under such circumstances as to bring out the difference on which we are insisting. Our version has it, "And the Sabbath of the land shall be meat for you; for thee, and for thy servant, and for thy maid, and for thy *hired servant*," &c. In the Septuagint, the Greek word used here for servant is "pais;" for maid-servant, or maid, "paidiske;" but for *hired servant*, the same old word, "misthotos." Lev. xxv, 40, our version has hired servant—Septuagint, "misthotos." Lev. xxv, 53, our version has hired servant—Septuagint, "misthotos." Deut. xv, 18, our version, hired servant—Septuagint, "misthotos." Deut. xxiv, 14, our version, hired servant—Septuagint, "misthou." Mark i, 20, our version, hired servant—Greek, "misthotos." Luke xv, 18, our version, hired servant—Greek Testament, "misthotos."

Now let us see if any better foundation can be found for abolitionism, if we give them the word *hireling* instead of hired servant. This word is found eight times in the Bible. Job vii, 1, our version has hireling—Septuagint, "misthotos." Job vii, 2, our version, hireling—Septuagint, "therapon." Job xiv, 16, our version, hireling—Septuagint, "misthotos." Isaiah xvi, 14, our version, hireling—Septuagint, "misthotos." Isaiah xxi, 16, our version, hireling—Septuagint, "misthotos." Malachi iii, 5, our version, hireling—Septuagint, "misthotos." John x, 12, our version, hireling—Greek Testament, "misthotos." John x, 13, our version, hireling—Greek Testament, "misthotos." Now, here are some seventeen or eighteen cases, in which the word hireling (or the term hired servant) is used in our English version, and not once do we find the word "doulos" to answer to it. Really, it does seem that the learning of abolitionism must be exceedingly stupid, if it can not see that the word "doulos" means a slave, and *not* a hireling. But let us examine one more extract from Liddell & Scott's Lexicon. Under the word "despotes," which is translated *master* in 1 Tim. vi, 1, we find the following: " A master, lord, *strictly in respect of slaves;* so that the address of a slave to his master was, 'o despot anax:' hence a despot, absolute ruler, whose subjects are slaves." The reader may find further light by consulting Herodotus i, 11, 111; iii, 89—Thucydides vi, 77—Eurip. Hypp. 88—Xenophon Anab. viii, 2, 13; vii, 4, 10.

Now, I hold that abolitionism leads to apostacy, because it makes abolition commentators pervert the right ways of the Lord, and attempt to deceive the unsuspecting and ignorant, by making them believe that when Paul writes on the relative duties of master and slave, he does not *mean* master and slave, but he means something else, which something else the *words* never did or could mean. But we promised to show not only that abolitionism led to apostacy, but that it was apostacy itself. Now, we can do this, if Paul is authority. What is his reason for exhorting servants to honor their masters? Why, "that the name of God and his doctrine be not blasphemed." The idea here is evidently this: "If there are servants among you christians, and they pretend to belong to the Lord, and at the same time do not attend to their duties as servants, and do not honor their masters, the unbelieving world around you will make light of and blaspheme the doctrine which produces such fruits." Compare Rom. ii, 24; Titus ii, 5. Now, I contend that those who withstand the doctrine that Paul here teaches, are not only on the road to apostacy, but have already reached it. For, look further on in this chapter, (1 Tim. vi.) and we find Paul directing Timothy to teach and exhort the people in the doctrine of obedience of servants to masters. "These things teach and exhort." Brethren of the Southern pulpit, have we done our duty? Have we been teaching and exhorting these things? Or have we let a fear of being thought to meddle with politics, keep us back from declaring the whole counsel of God? Remember, that before Columbus was born, before this continent was dreamed of, even when the Jews were traveling through the wilderness, God saw fit to legislate upon this subject; and amidst the dense smoke and vollied thunders of Sinai's awful scenes, there came forth the table of stone, written by the finger of the Lord God Omnipotent, and declaring to the race of men that they should not covet their neighbor's house, nor his wife, nor his man-servant, nor his maid-servant, nor anything that was *their neighbors*. Slavery had its religious importance for thousands of years before New England was known. And shall we, ministers of the Most High, suffer our mouths to be stopped by a few puny politicians? No! let us do our duty, and declare God's truth on this subject, as on all others, without fear of anything that man can do unto us. But Paul goes on to say, that "if any man teach otherwise, and consent not to wholesome words, even the words of our Lord Jesus Christ, and to the doctrine which is according to godliness, he is proud, knowing nothing, but doting about questions and strifes of words, whereof cometh envy, strife, railings, evil-surmisings, perverse disputings of men of corrupt minds and destitute of the truth, supposing that gain is godliness; from such withdraw thyself!" There is the finest picture of modern abolitionism in the language. Paul must have been acquainted with some abolitionist, or else he looked forward to the abolition rant and hubbub of the 19th century. Paul knew very well that the words which he had been writing, (namely, that servants were to honor their masters) were "wholesome words, even the words of our Lord Jesus Christ." And of course he knew how to describe those who should teach otherwise. He practised his own doctrine, too, sending Onesimus, the runaway slave, back to his master, Philemon. See how fully his description of the abolitionist coincides with the character of those same fanatics of the present day. "Proud," says Paul. "Yes," says Henry Ward Beecher himself, "so proud are you, that there is more sympathy for the negro even among the slaveholders themselves, than among you." "Knowing nothing," says Paul; and sure enough, they do not even know enough to be aware of the fact, the open, palpable, staring *fact*, that a negro is a *negro*, and *not* a blackened white man. "Doting about questions and strifes of words;" just exactly so. For instance, discussing the various "isms" and such like. "Envy, railings, evil-surmisings, perverse disputings of men of corrupt minds," &c. For example, calling for an anti-slavery Bible, an anti-slavery Constitution, and an anti-slavery God; saying, as they have said, that the Constitution of their country is "a league with hell;" that "such a God as is described in the Bible, they would put him upon a block and sell him;" and to clap the climax, proclaiming to the world that it is now old fogyism to trust for salvation in Jesus Christ and him crucified, and that henceforth the faith of the people is to rest on "John Brown and him hanged." "From such," says Paul, "withdraw thyself;" and from such, say I, good Lord deliver us.

J. C. HIDEN.

Orange County, Va.

THE DUTY OF CHRISTIANS IN CIVIL GOVERNMENTS.

CHRISTIANS, as such, though in the world, are not of the world. While in this state of existence, they necessarily have to remain upon this globe, which God prepared for the habitation of man before he created him.

Man, consisting of body, soul and spirit, is partly matter and partly spirit. He is the connecting link in God's creation, between matter and spirit. The globe was prepared for him, and he was created and placed upon it. The fruits of the earth were given to him for food,[1] which were sufficient to sustain his animal or physical system; and the fruit of the tree of life was provided and given to him, to rejuvenate and revivify his animal system, and make its existence perpetual. Everything upon the earth, and within his reach was given to him, excepting the fruit of one tree, of which he was prohibited from partaking, on pain of death.[2] He transgressed that command, was driven from the tree of life, and death ensued from it; and the earth was cursed for his sake. In this state of affairs, without redemption, the race was cut off and destroyed, and could not have perpetuated its existence.

But God "so loved the world as to give his only begotten Son, that whosoever believes on him, may not perish, but obtain eternal life."[3] Those who believe on him, and confide in him as the Captain of their salvation and their King, may not perish, but may obtain eternal life, from which the race was cut off by the transgression of Adam. He is "the Lamb of God that takes away the sin of the world,"[4] "that the world may be saved by him."[5]

Other orders of intelligences sinned against the God of heaven, but no provision was made for their redemption. God "hath reserved them in everlasting chains under darkness unto the judgment of the great day."[6] But redemption was provided for the race of man, that his body may be redeemed from the bars of death, and raised a spiritual and immortal body—not animal and earthly as it was before—and his spirit cleansed and purified from sin, the re-

---
(1) Gen. I, 29.
(2) Gen. ii, 16, 17.
(3) John iii, 16, New Trans.
(4) John i, 29, New Trans.
(5) John iii, 17, New Trans.
(6) Jude 6; 2 Pet. ii, 4.

deemed and resuscitated man may dwell in the presence of the Lord, in whose presence he was before he sinned; but with this difference, that he will be wholly spiritual in his redeemed and resuscitated state, whereas, he was partly earthly and partly spiritual, in his primeval state. Hence, those who so conduct themselves as to obtain this "inheritance incorruptible, undefiled, and that fadeth not away,"[1] will hold a much higher position in the scale of existence, than Adam held in Eden.

In the Lord's government of the race after it sinned, as well as before, he used moral power or motive only, till near the flood. He did not inflict physical punishment upon Cain, the first murderer, but set a mark upon him, lest any finding him should slay him.[2] The result of this system was, that in fourteen centuries "the earth was filled with violence."[3] The Lord then laid down a new law: "My spirit [by moral power, persuasion,] shall not always *strive with man*, for he also is flesh: yet his days shall be an hundred and twenty years."[4] That was the probation given them in which to turn to God, and Noah was appointed a preacher of righteousness,[5] to reclaim them to the commands of God without God's having to inflict physical punishment. But God said to Noah, "the end of all flesh is come before me; for the earth is filled with violence through them: and behold I will destroy them with the earth."[6] They did not repent at the preaching of Noah, and God, in his own proper person, inflicted the first legal, physical, capital punishment, that was inflicted upon the earth, by destroying the race, except Noah and his family; to whom he prescribed physical punishment for crime and violence, as the law of the postdiluvian world:

"And surely your blood of your lives will I require; at the hand of every beast will I require it, and at the hand of man; at the hand of every man's brother will I require the life of man. Whoso sheddeth man's blood, by man shall his blood be shed: for in the image of God made he man."[7]

Here he invested man with governmental powers to punish crime, and made it his duty, as stated in the law of

---

(1) 1 Pet. 1, 4.
(2) Gen. iv, 15.
(3) Gen. vi, 11, 13.
(4) Gen. vi, 3.
(5) 2 Pet. ii, 5.
(6) Gen. vi, 13.
(7) Gen. ix, 5, 6.

Moses afterwards, to cleanse the land of the blood of murder by the blood of the murderer;[1] thus making man his minister on earth for governmental purposes. But he was made his minister for wrath or punishment, "a revenger to execute wrath upon him that doeth evil."[2] The Lord was still the minister of mercy, moral power, or motive, in the government of man, as he had been before the flood; and by the Spirit, he continued to strive with man, and still does continue to strive.

In the wrath department, or physical punishment department, of God's government of man on earth, from Noah's day forward, God made use of some of the worst monsters of human government, as well as some of the best, to execute his wrath upon the children of disobedience. The Babylonian and Roman powers, who were made ministers of wrath against the Jewish nation at two different periods of time, are specimens of the former; while Israel under Joshua, and Cyrus the Great, are specimens of the latter. Hence, to be God's minister of wrath, does not imply that the power which is that minister, whether it be a people or a sovereign, is righteous, or even praiseworthy or desirable. It is simply to be an executioner or hangman, which is not a very desirable calling.

For reasons not revealed, and hence unknown to us, God permitted things to go on thus after the flood, century after century. And these kingdoms of this world, monsters though many of them were, were made ministers of the wrath of God to execute his vengeance upon the ungodly; for vengeance belongs to him, and not to man.[3] He would use one nation as a minster of vengeance on another, and shortly after bring another to take vengeance on his first minister; all of which the history of the Bible, as well as profane history, abundantly proves.

In the fulness of time, however, the Lord himself became incarnate and dwelt among us, to re-establish his kingdom on earth, as it existed before the flood, (so far as governmental matters are concerned,) and to supersede human governments as ministers of God's wrath, by remodelling society, so that moral power alone will govern it, terminating in bringing his followers back to the tree of life,

---

(1) Num. xxxv, 33.　　(3) Deut. xxxii, 35, 43; Rom. xii, 19; Heb. x, 30.
(2) Rom. xiii, 4.

whence sin expelled them; having effected which, he will then have put all things under his feet, and will then surrender the kingdom to God.[1] His kingdom, however, was not set up on earth, until after his humiliation, his death, his burial, his resurrection, and his ascension, when God "exalted him with his right hand a Prince and Savior, to grant repentance to Israel, and forgiveness of sins;"[2] when he was crowned Lord of all, and sent forth the Spirit according to the promise of the Father, to his apostles, who set up his kingdom on the day of Pentecost. That kingdom is his body, and he is its head.[3]

Though his kingdom was not set up till after his ascension, yet, during his ministry, he taught its principles; and after his ascension, his apostles fully developed its laws.

At the beginning of his ministry, he chose his twelve apostles. They then became the germ of his kingdom. He told them that they were not of this world, but that he had chosen them out of the world.[4] He prayed to the Father for them "because they are not of the world;" not that he should "take them out of the world," but that he should "keep them from evil. They are not of the world, even as I am not of the world. Sanctify them through thy truth: thy word is truth. As thou has sent me into the world, even so have I also sent them into the world. And for their sakes I sanctify myself, that they also might be sanctified through the truth."[5]

Hence, christians, as such, as the body of Christ, as his kingdom, though in the world, are not of the world. They are chosen by the Lord out of the world, though while in this life they remain in this world. They are a holy nation, a purchased people, who in times past were not a people, but are now the people of God. As christians, they are sojourners in this world, and travelers or pilgrims through it.[6]

When Pilate asked the Lord if he was the King of the Jews, he testified the truth, and said that he was *a King*; but informed Pilate, who was the representative of the Roman majesty, that his kingdom was not of this world: "if," said he, " my kingdom were of this world, then would my

---

(1) 1 Cor. xv, 24-28.
(2) Acts v, 31.
(3) 1 Cor. xii, 27; Eph. iii, 6; iv, 12; v, 23; Col. i, 18.
(4) John xv, 19.
(5) John xvii, 13-19.
(6) 1 Pet. ii, 6-11, N. T.

servants fight, that I should not be delivered to the Jews: but now is my kingdom not from hence."[1]

Here the two kingdoms were brought face to face. The kingdom of this world, the Roman power, represented by Pilate, and the kingdom of the Lord, represented by the King himself. The Lord informed the representative of the former, that his kingdom was not of this world. Pilate knew that the kingdom he represented, was of this world. But as the Lord's kingdom was not of this world, there was no conflict of the jurisdictions of the two kingdoms. The Lord, though King himself, prospectively, while in this world, submitted to the kingdom of this world, and there was no conflict between the two powers. In this he left "us an example, that we should follow his steps."[2]

But the Lord said if his kingdom were of this world, then would his servants fight that he should not be delivered to the Jews. When he was arrested, Peter drew his sword, and struck off the ear of the high Priest's servant. The Lord healed the wound and said to Peter, "Put up again thy sword into his place: for all they that take the sword, shall perish with the sword. Thinkest thou that I can not now pray to my Father, and he shall presently give me more than twelve legions of angels?"[3]

There are some things to be noted here.

The kingdoms of this world operate through *physical power*, because the servants of those kingdoms fight. For the Lord said that his servants would have fought had his kingdom been of this world. And he could have had an army of twelve legions of angels instantly, to physically overcome the Jewish and Roman powers, if physical force could have been lawfully used in his kingdom, as it was in the kingdoms of this world. But it could not be so lawfully used. "For the wrath [or physical power] of man worketh not the righteousness of God."[4] The righteousness of God, or what God has prescribed should be done, is not to be wrought out or brought about by physical force, the wrath or punishment of man. Hence, the folly and sinfulness of all persecution in religious matters, down even to the fanatical folly of "wiping out the sin of slavery" by civil war.

---

(1) John xviii, 33–36. (3) Matt. xxvi, 51–53.
(2) 1 Pet. ii, 21. (4) James i, 20.

"All that take the sword shall perish with the sword." The sword is the emblem of the power of the kingdoms of this world; and it is physical power, force. Physical power can not be used in the Lord's kingdom. Moral power alone, motive, the power put forth in the Gospel, which is the power of God,[1] is the only power that can be used in the kingdom of the Lord, which is "far above all principality, and power, and might, and dominion, and every name that is named, not only in this world, but also that which is to come;"[2] and it wrestles "not against flesh and blood, [physical wrestling] but against principalities, against powers, against the rulers of the darkness of this world, against spiritual wickedness in high [heavenly, ecclesiastical] places;"[3] and the Lord, the head of the christian kingdom, "is the head of all principality and power,"[4] and will finally overthrow all those principalities and powers, when "the kingdoms of this world will become the kingdoms of our Lord and of his Christ."[5] But all this will be done by moral power alone. Physical power has not been used, and will not be used by the Lord, to effect this. He "healed all their sick, enjoining them not to make him known. Thus the word of the prophet Isaiah was verified, 'Behold my servant whom I have chosen, my beloved in whom my soul delights; I will cause my spirit to abide upon him, and he shall give laws to the nations; he will not contend, nor clamor, nor cause his voice to be heard in the streets. A bruised reed he will not break; and a dimly burning taper he will not quench, till he render his laws victorious. Nations shall trust in his name.'"[6] As the kingdoms of this world are all thus to perish by the tri-

---

(1) Rom. i, 16, 17. (3) Eph. vi, 12. (5) Rev. xi, 15.
(2) Eph. i, 21. (4) Col. ii,10.

(6) Matt. xii, 15-21, New Translation. The kingly conquests and triumphant victories of the Messiah, are the subject on which Isaiah dwells in that part of his prophecy from which this quotation is made. The emblems introduced by the prophet are designed to show the ease with which these victories shall be obtained. No trumpets, spears, or torches, shall be employed in making his laws victorious. He will not employ such weapons in subduing the nations under him; not even a bruised reed will be broken as a substitute for a spear or lance; not a spark of fire, not even an expiring wick will be consumed or extinguished, in bringing nations under his yoke. How unlike his conquests are to those obtained by fire and sword! The spear and the torch of ancient warriors, and the clangor of trumpets, are alluded to in these representations of Messiah's regal achievements. * * * With these remarks we introduce Bishop Lowth's translation of Isaiah xlii, 1-5:

Behold my servant, whom I will uphold;
My chosen, in whom my soul delights;
I will make my spirit rest upon him;
And he shall publish judgment to the nations.
He shall not cry aloud, nor raise a clamor,

umphs of the Lord's kingdom obtained without *contention*, or *clamor*, or the exertion of physical power even to the breaking of a bruised reed as a spear, the sword the power of the kingdoms of this world, will perish with those kingdoms. And the Lord says in the passage under consideration, that all that take the sword shall perish with it; shall perish when it perishes. Hence, christians who desire to survive the sword, and not to perish when it perishes, had better not *voluntarily* take the sword. Those who desire to survive the law of force had better not *voluntarily* resort to it. They who take and rely upon physical power, will perish when that power perishes; while they who take, adhere to, and rely upon the Lord, and the principles of his kingdom, will stand in *his* kingdom, which endures forever, and shall not perish.

The Lord taught his disciples to pray "thy will be done on earth as it is in heaven;"[1] as recorded by Luke: "Thy will be done, as in heaven, so in earth."[2] How is his will done in heaven? "Ye his angels, that excel in [mighty in] strength, that do his commandments, hearkening unto the voice of his word."[3] In heaven his commands are hearkened to and done because they are his commands. No disobedience: and no coercion, force or physical power, used to compel obedience. The Lord taught us to pray for that state of affairs on the earth. When it shall have come, human governments, the ministers of God's wrath, his avengers to execute his vengeance upon the ungodly and the disobedient, will no longer be needed on earth—their occupation will be gone, and the kingdoms of this world will have become the kingdoms of our Lord Jesus Christ, and the Millennium will have set in. Hence, the Psalmist sang, "Thy people shall be willing in the day of thy power."[4] They shall need no coercion, wrath, or vengeance.

The kingdoms of this world have jurisdiction of *things* pertaining to this world, life, liberty, and property. The Lord's kingdom is not of this world; hence, he, in all his

---

Nor cause his voice to be heard in the public places;
The bruised reed he shall not break;
And the dimly burning flax he shall not quench:
He shall publish judgment so as to establish it perfectly.
His force shall not be abated, nor broken,
Until he has firmly seated judgment in the earth:
And the distant nations shall earnestly wait for his law.
—*A. Campbell's Note on the Passage.*

(1) Matt. vi, 10.   (2) Luke xi, 2.   (3) Ps. ciii, 20.   (4) Ps. cx. 3.

ministry, refrained, upon all occasions, from interfering with matters pertaining to this world, or with the affairs of the kingdoms of this world, and what pertained to them. After he had fed the five thousand with five loaves and two fishes, when he "perceived that they would come and take him by force, and make him a [political] king, he departed again into a mountain himself alone,"[1] to prevent them from doing it. When "one of the company said unto him, Master, speak to my brother, that he divide the inheritance with me," he said, "Man, who made me a judge or a divider over you?"[2] That was a question to be settled, and a duty to be performed by the civil government, the kingdom of this world having jurisdiction of the property and of the parties; and the Lord would not act in it—it did not belong to his kingdom. His course was the same in the case of the woman taken in adultery. He refused to give judgment in the case, because he had no jurisdiction of the cause. He did not set in Moses' seat to give judgment under the laws of Moses.

The next transaction and act of the Lord that I shall note and observe upon, has so great a bearing upon the subject under consideration, and is so exact a daguereotype of many persons now existing, and of so many things now transpiring, that I shall quote it at length from each of the three inspired writers that record it, Matthew, Mark and Luke. I quote from the New Translation. The reader will have the common version, and can read them as they stand in that version.

"'Then the Pharisees retired, and having consulted *how they might entrap him in his words*, sent him some of their disciples, and some Herodians, who, being *instructed by them*, said, Rabbi, we know that you are sincere, and faithfully teach the way of God, without partiality, for you respect not the person of men. Tell us, therefore, *your opinion:* Is it lawful to give tribute to Cæsar, or not? Jesus perceiving *their malice*, said, Dissemblers, why would you entangle me? Show me the tribute money. And they reached him a denarius. He asked them, Whose image and inscription is this? They answered, Cesar's. He re-replied, *Render, then, to Cesar that which is Cesar's*, and to

---

(1) John vi, 15.   (2) Luke xii, 13, 14.

God that which is God's. And admiring his answer, they left him and went away."¹

"And *they desired to have seized him,* but were afraid of the multitude; for *they knew that he spoke the parable against them.* Then the *chief priests,* the scribes, and the elders, leaving Jesus, went away, and sent to him certain Pharisees and Herodians, *to catch him in his words.* These coming up, said to him, Rabbi, we know that you are upright, and stand in awe of none; for you respect not the person of men, but teach the ways of God faithfully. Is it lawful to give tribute to Cesar, or not? Shall we give, or shall we not give? He, perceiving their artifice, answered, Why would you entangle me? Bring me a denarius, that I may see it. When they had brought it, he asked them, Whose is this image and inscription? They answered, Cesar's. Jesus replied, *Render to Cesar that which is Cesar's, and to God that which is God's.* And they wondered at him."²

"At that time, the *chief priests* and scribes, *knowing that he had spoken this parable against them,* would have laid hands on *him,* but feared the people. And they *watched* him, and set *spies* upon him, *instructing* them to personate *conscientious* men, and surprise him in his words, *that they might consign him to the power and authority of the procurator.* These accosted him with this question: Rabbi, we know that you speak and teach uprightly, and that, without respect of persons, you faithfully recommend the way of God. Is it lawful for us to pay taxes to Cesar, or not? He, perceiving their subtlety, answered, Why would you entangle me? Show me a denarius. Whose image and inscription has it? They answered, Cesar's. He replied, *Render, therefore, to Cesar that which is Cesar's,* and *to God that which is God's.* Thus they could not surprise him in his discourse before the people; wherefore, admiring his answer, they kept silence."³

1. The chief priests were at the head of this conspiracy against the immaculate founder of christianity. They have been at the head of all conspiracies against his immaculate religion, and of all persecutions of those who follow the teaching and example of the Lord, from the day of this conspiracy until the present time, and now are.

(1) Matt. xxii, 15-22. (2) Mark xii, 12-17. (3) Luke xx, 19-26.

2. But they had with them in this conspiracy the scribes and Pharisees. The scribes were the writers and expounders of the Mosaic law. They were the administrators of that law as a civil government among the people, and represented the civil authority in this conspiracy. The Pharisees were the super-pious among the Jews, giving equal weight, however, to tradition (inference, philosophy, reason, argument) than they did to the written word itself. The reader's mind can easily fix upon those who now occupy their position.

3. The chief priests, scribes and Pharisees desired to seize the Lord that they might consign him to the military despotism then in Judea, because he spoke a parable against them that exposed their abominable character and conduct. Who are doing so now? The reader's mind can easily suggest the answer.

4. They "were afraid of the multitude," they "feared the people." Who is afraid of the multitude now? Who now fear the people? Who tries to crush down the multitude of the people? Answer: The chief priests, the super-pious, and those who are now unfortunately holding the places in our government that the scribes did in the Jewish polity.

5. The Pharisees (the super-pious) retired, and consulted how they might entrap the Lord in his words, *upon a political question.*

6. The chief priests and scribes watched him, and set spies upon him. They are now at the same work, only that it is the Lord's disciples—those who follow the Lord's example and teaching—that they are watching and setting spies upon, instead of the Lord himself.

7. The chief priests, scribes and Pharisees instructed their spies and emissaries. Yes, they instructed them to "personate conscientious men," to "feign themselves just men." That was pretty work for the chief-priests and super-pious to be engaged in; but they engaged in such business then, and still do. They were instructed to personate and feign themselves such men, and surprise him in his words, that they might consign him to the power and authority of the satrap of the Roman despot. It is not lawful to enquire whether that satrap was a Burnside or not; but it lies in our way to enquire whether our chief

priests, scribes, and Pharisees, are not now acting as the same classes of gentlemen did in the Lord's day?

8. The emissaries approached the Lord with great apparent respect and deference, hypocritical though it all was. We know, said they, that you are sincere, and faithfully teach the way of God without partiality, and do not care for any man. We know that you are upright, and stand in awe of none; for you respect not the person of men, but teach the way of God faithfully; and without respect of persons, you faithfully recommend the way of God. This was laying on flattery tolerably thick. I suppose, too, that they had on very long, pious faces. Having thus laid so good a foundation, they proceeded: "Tell us, therefore, your opinion: Is it lawful to give tribute to Cesar, or not?" "Shall we give, or shall we not give?" "Is it lawful for us [the chosen people of God] to pay taxes to Cesar or not?"

Part of the emissaries sent were Herodians, a set of men peculiarly attached to Herod, and consequently zealous for the interests of the Roman government, which was the main support of the dignity of the royal family of Herod— they were the "intensely loyal." They held that it was lawful to pay tribute to Cesar, or to the Romans, who had conquered and then governed Judea. The Pharisees, who had sent some of their disciples among the emissaries, held that it was not lawful to pay tribute or taxes to the Roman government, that it was contrary to the divine law to do so, and hence a sin; and they had more proof for that dogma of theirs, than abolitionists have for their dogma, that to pay the services and labor due to the masters by the slaves is sinful, as can be seen by examining Deuteronomy xvii, 14–20, which comes much nearer proving the Pharisaic dogma, than any Scripture that abolitionists can produce, comes to proving their dogma: and yet the Pharisaic dogma is not proved by the above cited passage relied on by them. Hence, there was some apparent pretext for this application to the Lord to settle this question between the Herodians and Pharisees. But their application was really hypocritical; because both parties rejected the authority of the Lord, and despised him, and, of course, would not be bound by, nor submit to, his decision of the question. They asked *his opinion* for ulterior, base, and unworthy purposes, and not that they might obtain an authoritative settlement of the question. They thought that they had cast the toils around him, and so laid the snare, that he could not escape them. If he should say that it was not lawful, the Herodians would accuse him to the Roman governor for "disloyalty," "disloyal practices," treason against Cesar. If he should say it was lawful, the Pharisees, the Praise-God-Barebones class of that day, would denounce him to the Jewish people, as the betrayer of the liberties of their country, and as opposed to the law of God; as pro-Roman in sentiment, as a Roman sympathizer, and in favor of the monster iniquity of the desecration of the holy city by the Roman "power." A very nicely concocted scheme indeed it was, and devised and put into excoution by *very patriotic* and *very pious* gentlemen. We have an abundance of just such pious patriots now-a-days.[1]

9. But the Lord perceived their malice. Their cunning, artifice, and subtlety, could not deceive him. "He knowing their hypocrisy," told them that they were "dissemblers," "hypocrites," and asked them why they sought to entangle him? How pertinent that question now is to be asked of the many similar pretentious, pious patriots we have! He asked them to "show him a denarius." He asked them whose image and inscription it had. They told him, Cesar's. He then gave his answer: RENDER, THEREFORE, TO CESAR THAT WHICH IS CESAR'S, and TO GOD THAT WHICH IS GOD'S.

This was not dodging the question upon his part, to avoid committing himself; but it was the TRUTH OF GOD upon the subject. It was the same answer that would have been given if his interrogators had been as sincere, honest and candid as they pretended to be. Their malice, chicanery and hypocrisy, did not cause him to give a cunningly devised answer to avoid responsibility. He came into the

---

(1) As one among the many thousand proofs that could be cited to sustain this assertion, I quote the following:

"If the Bible teaches that the christian owes no duty to his government in such times as these, let us tell the people so. If it teach that a christian does owe a duty to his government, let us also tell the people so. Neutrality is duplicity, and is unworthy any man, much less a christian man, and a leader and teacher of the people. It is either right or wrong to sustain our government in this struggle. Will Bro. Campbell ask Bro. Franklin which it is, and let us have his reply?"—*Christian Record, Aug 25th,* 1863.

A very nice plan (and exactly similar to that of old) to entangle and destroy brother Franklin, because he is following the example of the Lord. But it is really complimentary to him to have the malice of such men thus exhibited as to him, as it was exhibited as to the Lord.

world to bear witness to the truth,[1] and he did so upon this occasion, as upon all other occasions. Never "was guile found in his mouth."[2] His answer dumfounded his interrogators. They admired it, wondered at it, kept silence, and went away and left him. The truth always discomfits chicanery, cunning, knavery, and hypocrisy, if brought to bear directly upon them.

Let us now ascertain what this answer of the Lord teaches.

The first thing to note is, that the answer clearly shows that there is no conflict of claim between Cesar and God. All that was Cesar's could be rendered to Cesar, and still all that God required could be rendered to him, notwithstanding Cesar had got all that was his, from the same person or persons. The command is, to render to Cesar the things that are Cesar's, and to God the things that are God's; and this command applies to all of us now, as well as it did to those to whom the Lord addressed it. Hence, to discharge our duty under it, we must ascertain what *things* are Cesar's, and what *things* are God's. For much of the trouble that has existed, and still does exist, and many of the calamities that have come upon mankind, and still are upon us, have been produced by the usurpation by Cesar of things that do not belong to him, or by the sinful intermeddling by those who claim to be acting for God, with things that are not God's, but Cesar's.

All admit and take Cesar as standing for, and representing, the kingdoms of this world. The coins of a country designate the sovereignty of a country. Coining money has always been, and still is, a sovereign act, in all human governments. The fact that the Roman coins were the coins of the land of Judea, showed that the Romans held the sovereignty in Judea; and the Pharisees, by their admission that the Roman empire had imposed their coins upon them as the coin of their country, acknowledged that they were under the Roman government. And as money is the measure and representative of value and property, and has been in all ages of the world, from the day that Abraham "weighed four hundred shekels of silver current money with the merchant" to Ephron for his field and the cave of Machpelah,[3] to the present time; and as the Lord,

---
(1) John xviii, 37.   (2) 1 Pet. ii, 22.   (3) Gen. xxiii, 16.

after having had brought to him the coin, the tribute money, and had had his interrogators to say that it was Cesar's, told them to render to Cesar the things that were Cesar's, he thereby taught that money, and all it represents, are things of Cesar. And as money represents all property, and all that relates or pertains to property, to the possession, management, enjoyment, and disposition of it, they all are things that are Cesar's. Hence, the Lord, when applied to, to divide an inheritance between two brothers, declined,[1] because it was Cesar's and not God's kingdom that that work lay in. Hence, too, that apostolic injunction to render tribute to whom tribute is due.[2]

When the mother of Zebedee's children wanted the Lord to grant that her sons might set at his right hand, and at his left hand in his kingdom, and the other ten apostles were moved with indignation against James and John on account of that request, the Lord called them to him and said: "Ye know that the princes of the Gentiles [nations] *exercise dominion over them*, and they that are great *exercise authority upon them*."[3] Hence, the exercise of dominion over the people, and of authority upon them, are *things* that are Cesar's.

When Pilate asked the Lord if he did not know that he had power to crucify him, and power to release him? the Lord did not controvert the fact, but told him that he could not have the power unless it were given to him from above.[4] Hence, the power over life and liberty, are things that are Cesar's, and are given to him from above. But he has only power to kill the body, and is not able to kill the soul. When he kills the body, he has no more that he can do. Hence, the Lord tells christians not to fear him, but to fear him who is able to destroy both soul and body in hell.[5] Hence, also, as Cesar has no power over the soul, he has no right to interfere with matters pertaining to the soul; and whenever he does, he is guilty of usurpation of the *things* that are God's. Hence, all interference by the civil power with matters pertaining to the welfare of the soul—to religious matters—is usurpation.

I have now produced enough (and I must be concise, and

---

(1) Luke xii, 13, 14.
(2) Rom. xiii, 7.
(3) Matt. xx, 20-25; Mark x, 35-42; Luke xxii, 24, 25.
(4) John xix, 10, 11.
(5) Matt. x, 28; Luke xii, 4, 5.

not prolix) to show that dominion and authority over the people, extending to their lives, liberty and property, in all its ramifications, *are things of Cesar*,[1] given to him of God. For the due and faithful discharge of this trust committed to him, God holds Cesar, or nationalities, accountable, and not christians, either individually or collectively. But as this branch does not lay within my present inquiry, I shall only state the fact. The duty of christians in or to Cesar, or the civil government, is what I am now investigating.

I will now briefly examine and ascertain what are the *things* that are God's, that we are required to render to him, as contra-distinguished from things that we must render to Cesar.

"Jesus said unto him, Thou shalt love the Lord thy God with all thy heart, and with all thy soul, and with all thy mind. This is the first and great commandment. And the second is like unto it, Thou shalt love thy neighbor as thyself. On these two commandments hang all the law and the prophets."[2]

"A new commandment I give unto you, That ye love one another; as I have loved you, that ye also love one another. By this shall all men *know* that ye are my disciples, *if ye have love one to another.*"[3]

"This is my commandment, That ye love one another, as I have loved you. Greater love hath no man than this, that a man lay down his life for his friends."[4]

The *things* that are God's, then, that we are to render to him, are, that we love him with all our heart, soul and mind; and our neighbors as ourselves. These things include the law given by Moses, and the prophets. In addition to them, christians are to love one another as the Lord loved them, that is, love one another enough to lay their lives down for each other, as the Lord laid down his life for them. And this love to God, to neighbors, and to christians, is to be manifested by acts. Love to God, to neighbors, (the human family) and to christians, manifested by acts, does not intrude upon the things that are Cesar's. Hence, rendering to God the *things* that are God's, does not conflict with our duty to render to Cesar all that is his. The things of this world, life, liberty, property, are things

---
(1) *Cesar* is used as synonymous with *the civil government.* (3) John xiii, 34, 35.
(2) Matt. xxii, 37–40; see, also, Luke x, 25–28. (4) John xv, 12, 13.

that are Cesar's; the things preparatory for, and looking to, another and a better world, are God's.

The *power* and the *glory* of the kingdoms of the world are delivered to the devil, and to whomsoever *he* will give it, at least, he said so in the presence of the Lord, uncontradicted by him.[1] He did not say the *kingdoms* of the world, as is commonly stated; but the power and the glory of them. It is not material, however, to settle that question. The *glory* of an Alexander, a Cesar, and a Napoleon, I am inclined to think, was derived from the devil rather than from God.

Shortly before the Lord was arrested, he said, "The prince of this world cometh, and hath nothing in me."[2] He had committed no crime against the Roman law, and hence was not amenable to it; he had not forfeited his life, nor his liberty to it, nor to any law of any kingdom of this world. He had neither money nor property. Hence he said the prince of this world had nothing in him. And his expression goes further. The prince of this world, the kingdoms of this world, have nothing in him or his kingdom, that is, they have no jurisdiction or right, to interfere with either him or his kingdom. When they do interfere, it is usurpation; and the interference of the kingdoms of this world with the kingdom of the Lord, always has been injurious or deleterious to it.

The kings of this world exercise dominion and authority over their subjects, but the Lord directed that it should not be so in his kingdom; that whosoever would be great in his kingdom, should be a servant, and whosoever would be chief, should be a slave, as He came not to be served, but to serve.[3] The elders or bishops in his kingdom are commanded to take the oversight of the flock, not by constraint, but willingly, *not for filthy lucre*, but of a ready mind, neither *as being lord's* over God's heritage, but being examples to the flock.[4] Christ expressly taught, that in his kingdom there was no Pope or Father but God; no lord or Master but himself; and that all his disciples were brethren.[5]

Hence, the Lord's kingdom is the exact converse of the

---

(1) Luke iv, 5, 6.
(2) John xiv, 30.
(3) Matt. xx, 25-28; Mark x, 42-45; Luke xxii, 25-28; New Trans.
(4) 1 Pet. v, 1-3.
(5) Matt. xxiii, 8-10.

kingdoms of this world. In the kingdoms of this world, there are kings, and princes, and lords, who have "dominion" and "authority" over life, liberty, and property, and "honor" and "fear" are "due" them. They are founded upon, act and exist by force, physical power, the sword. Thou shalt, or shalt not, do this, with the sword raised to enforce the command, is their manner of acting in discharge of their office. They rule by force and fear, and by them alone. And God makes them his avengers to execute his wrath upon them that do evil.[1] In the Lord's kingdom, there is no Lord but Christ, and all of his subjects are brethren. They all stand upon a democratic equality, in his kingdom. The Lord exercises no dominion or authority over life, liberty or property; and no coercion, no physical power whatever is used, even to the breaking of a bruised reed as a spear, in making conquests to his kingdom, nor in governing his subjects when conquered and brought under his sway. Love is the supreme controlling power by which he conquors, and by which he governs. All the tribute his subjects render him, whether of their services or their property, are free gifts, given "not grudgingly or of necessity; for God loves a cheerful giver."[2] He freely gave himself for them; and they must freely give themselves to him. When they cease to do so, coercion is not used by him to compel them to do their duty, but excision from his body, expulsion from his kingdom, is the penalty. He governs by "the consent of the governed;" when they withdraw their consent, he withdraws from them the benefits and blessings of his government.

We have seen that the two classes of government exist in this world. And we have seen that their jurisdictions do really not conflict. The Lord's people, though in the world, are not of it. But they are expressly commanded by the Lord, to be subject to the powers that exist in this world; that they are ordained of God, and whosoever resisteth them, resisteth the ordinance of God. They are informed, however, that they are not a terror to good works, but to the evil; that if they do that which is good, they shall have praise of the powers that be, which has always proved to be true when fairly tested, ever since it was uttered. Christians are therefore commanded to pay tribute or taxes

---
(1) Rom. xiii, 4.   (2) 2 Cor. ix, 7.

to these powers that be; to render to all their dues of tribute, custom, fear and honor.¹ They are also commanded by the Lord to submit to every ordinance of man for his sake; whether it be to the king as supreme, or unto governors or subordinate magistrates, as unto them that are sent by the supreme power for the *punishment* of evil-doers, and for the *praise* of them that do well. For so is the will of God, that with *well-doing* christians may *put to silence* the ignorance of foolish men. To honor all men: to love the brotherhood: to fear God: and to honor the king, or supreme power.² And to render to Cesar all the things that are Cesar's, which, we have seen, are life, liberty and property.

The Lord also commands his people to "abstain from fleshy lusts,"³ which, he informs us, produce the following, among other works of the flesh: hatred, variance, emulations, wrath, strife, seditions, heresies, envyings, murder, drunkenness, revelings, and such like.⁴ And that if they have bitter envying and strife in their hearts, about abolitionism or anything else, to glory not, and lie not against the truth. For that wisdom descends not from above, but is earthly, sensual, and devilish, or devil-like. For where envying and strife is, there is confusion and every evil work.⁵

The law of liberty in and by which the christian kingdom is governed, is perfect, as all the Lord's works are perfect. It is as well adapted to one form of government of the kingdoms of this world as to another. There are various forms of human governments—kingdoms of this world—as despotisms, limited or constitutional monarchies, aristocracies, oligarchies, republics, and democracies. The christian kingdom is as well adapted to one form as to another, and can exist as well in one as in another. It submits alike to all, and leaves to all the control and management *of all the things of this world*, and interferes with the control of none. Whenever it does, it is guilty of usurpation, and the history of eighteen hundred years has proved, that whenever and wherever it did, it has received injury by it. Whenever it does so, it becomes anti-Christ. We have been in the habit of calling one great religious body anti-

---

(1) Rom. xiii, 1-7.   (3) 1 Pet. ii, 11.   (5) James iii, 14-16.
(2) 1 Pet. ii, 13-17.   (4) Gal. v. 17-21.

Christ; but all others who interfere with the affairs of State, with the control of the kingdoms of this world, are anti-Christs too. The "mystery of iniquity" is ambition, pride and love of power. They have been the foundation and prime cause of all iniquity from the period of Satan's fall till now. That mystery, or secret source of iniquity, began to work in Paul's day, and only the pagan power of Rome then hindered it, and he said would continue to hinder it till it was taken out of the way; and then that lawless and wicked one would be revealed.[1] History proves this to be true. But because one great anti-Christ was thus built up, and has existed ever since, it does not prove that others, who, from ambition, pride, and love of power, acquire and exercise control of the things of the kingdoms of this world, are not anti-Christs too. On the contrary, it proves that they are anti-Christs. John told christians not to believe every spirit, but to try them, whether they be from God. Every spirit, he says, "that does not confess Jesus," acknowledge *him* and obey *his* laws, "is not from God: and this is that spirit of anti-Christ, which you have heard that it comes, *and now is* in the world already. * * * They are of the world; therefore they *speak from the world,*" from that stand-point, "and the world hearkens to them. We [apostles] are of God: he who knows God, hearkens *to us;* he who is not of God, hearkens not to us. By this we know the spirit of truth, and the spirit of error,"[2] which he had just before said was the spirit of anti-Christ. And wherever we have that spirit now, it is the spirit of anti-Christ, whether it be found in the great anti-christian body, or in a small one.

And whenever a kingdom of this world interferes with religious matters—with matters pertaining to the kingdom of the Lord—it is guilty of usurpation, and becomes a dragon or a beast, great or small, as the case may be, such as are described in the Apocalypse. Hence, if the abolition theory was true, (which it is not) that slavery is a sin, the administration now in power in our Government, and that has control of our Government, by undertaking (as it has undertaken, and is now prosecuting the undertaking,) to eradicate that sin by the war now being prosecuted, thereby becomes, for the time being, a dragon or a beast of

---

(1) 2 Thes. ii, 6-8,   (2) 1 John iv, 1-6, New Translation.

the Apocalypse, small as yet, it is true, but it may grow into "a great dragon" for all we know, if we allow it to grow. It has no right or authority, from the christian Scriptures, to prosecute such a work; but, on the contrary, they teach that it has not. The Constitution of the United States does not give it such power, but expressly reserves the slavery question, and all other domestic questions, to the States respectively, or to the people of the States.[1]

On the other hand, as slavery is not a sin, and is purely a political question, and hence belongs exclusively to the kingdoms of this world to control, manage and settle, the States respectively in our form of government being the kingdoms that have control of it, the various religious denominations that have, by the action of their ecclesiastical bodies, assumed to control the question, and the various *very wise* and *very pious* preachers, and editors, and societies, and corporations, religious and educational, among us of the free States, where slavery does not exist, that have assumed, and are assuming, to interfere with, control, and manage the question, are all thereby usurping what belongs to Cesar, and violating the express commands of the Lord to them, and hence are anti-Christs. John, the harbinger of the Lord, said, that "he that is of the earth is earthly, and *speaketh of the earth.*"[2] They speak of the earth, and hence, according to the harbinger, they are earthly, from which the slide is very easy into becoming "sensual and devilish."[3] Were Paul here now, he would tell us of them, as he did the ancient christians, that "I have often told you, and *now tell you even weeping*, that many walk as the enemies of the cross of Christ; whose end is destruction, whose god is their appetites, whose glory is in their shame, *who mind earthly things.*"[4] He would also say that "they that are after the flesh, do *mind* the *things* of the flesh."[5] And he would say to those preachers and editors, that "the world is crucified unto me, and I unto the world";[6] "be followers together of me,"[7] if you assume to be preachers and teachers in the kingdom of Christ, and "set your affections on things above, *not* on *things* on the earth."[8] Were John, the beloved disciple, here, he would say: "Love not

---
(1) Const. art. x, amendments.
(2) John iii, 31.
(3) James iii, 15.
(4) Phil. iii, 18, 19, New Translation.
(5) Rom. viii, 5.
(6) Gal. vi, 14.
(7) Phil. iii, 17.
(8) Col. iii, 2.

the world, neither *the things* that are in the world. If any man love the world, the love of the Father *is not in him.* For all that is in the world, * * * * is of the world."[1] But Paul and John are both here in the inspired writings they left us, and now say these things, and these men hearken not to them, because they are not of God.

I will give a few specimens of the many thousand proofs that could be adduced, of the way and manner in which these bodies and these men usurp "the things that are Cesar's." I cite some of those that have transpired among our denomination—the Christian—simply because I have those at hand, and it is more convenient to me to cite them than others. Similar ones could easily be furnished, however, as to other denominations of christians; and hence I hope that none of them will feel slighted and take umbrage, because I do not cite instances from them.

The Indiana Christian Missionary Society met in semi-annual meeting, at Rushville, Indiana, May 20th, 1862; Elder E. Goodwin, President, in the chair. Ovid Butler and B. F. Reeve, the majority of the committee having the matter in charge, reported the following resolutions, which were adopted by the Society, the first after some debate, and with one dissenting voice; the others *mem. con.* and unanimously:

"RESOLUTIONS.

"*Resolved*, That in the opinion of this meeting, sympathy to the civil government is a christian duty, subordinate only to sympathy and fidelity to Christ Jesus, the Lord. That loyalty to the civil government involves the obligation to aid and assist in the necessary efforts to protect, sustain and defend it against agressions from without, or treason and rebellion from within.

"*Resolved*, That those of our fellow citizens, and especially our Christian brethren, who have volunteered to defend our Government and Union against treason and rebellion, deserve, and shall receive, our approbation, our sympathy, and our prayers, and that the Board of Managers of this Association be instructed to furnish to them, so far as they may have means and opportunity to do so, such spiritual food and consolation as their circumstances require.

---

(1) 1 John ii, 15, 16.

"*Resolved*, That the exigences of the times, the present and immediately future issues, in this conflict with rebellion, admonish us that we should seek humbly, earnestly, and trustingly, of the great Head of the church for wisdom, to determine, and for strength to do, what God in his providence requires of us, as citizens and as disciples of the Lord Jesus.

"*Resolved*, That the Board of Managers be instructed to push forward the work of the Society, both in procuring means, and in missionary operations, to the full extent that it shall be found practicable to do.

"*Resolved*, That hereafter the name of this association shall be, " The Indiana State Christian Missionary Society."

This does pretty well for a society whose sole *avowed* object, is the promotion of the Lord's cause, and the extension of *his* kingdom; three strong, earnest resolutions for Cesar, and one little weak one for the Lord. " Out of the abundance of the heart the mouth speaketh;"[1] and where our treasure is, there will our heart be also:[2] and, as the treasure of this society is political abolitionism, its heart is there; and out of the abundance of its heart, its mouth spoke as above. While it was changing its name, however, honesty and fair dealing with the public required that it should have taken a more truthful appellation—" The Indiana State Political Missionary Society."

The same society convened again, in semi-annual meeting, at Lafayette, Indiana, on the 14th day of May, 1863. I cut the following from its published proceedings:

"The following preamble and resolutions were offered by Bro. H. Z. Leonard:

"WHEREAS, Our country is involved in the calamities of civil war, inaugurated by the rebellion of a part of the Southern States of our Union, and whereas, God at times uses the sword in the hand of the civil power to maintain equity and justice among the nations of earth, and whereas, man but renders obedience to God when he renders obedience to the legally constituted authorities; therefore,

"*Resolved*, That we, in proper capacity, as a Christian Missionary Society of the State of Indiana, do hereby de-

---
(1) Matt. xii, 34. Luke vi, 45.   (2) Matt. vi, 21.

clare our unwavering allegiance to, and our unqualified support of, 'the government under which we live.

"*Resolved*, That, recognizing our chief ruler as the minister of God, 'a revenger to execute wrath upon him that doeth evil,' we will render him a cheerful support with earnest prayer to the great Head of the church, that he may be guided by that wisdom that cometh from above.

"*Resolved*, That we will cheerfully submit to all legally constituted authorities, both civil and military, to the express intent that we may not only be loyal citizens, but that we may also see the present rebellion crushed speedily, and our government triumph over every foe.

"*Resolved*, That we assure and reassure our brave and noble soldiers in the field, that they have our warmest sympathies and constant prayers, and shall have our material and spiritual aid whenever it is possible to bestow it.

"After some discussion as to the propriety of entertaining such resolutions in a missionary meeting, they were made the order of business for 2 o'clock P. M., when the society took a recess until that hour.

"2 o'clock P. M.

"The society convened and resumed the consideration of Bro. Leonard's resolutions, and after some further discussion, Bro. Bartholomew moved to strike out of the first resolution the words, 'In proper capacity as a Christian Missionary Society of the State of Indiana,' which was done, and the resolutions were then adopted without a dissenting vote."

It seems that there was enough compunction of conscience and regard for truth then in the society, to prevent it from saying that this was done "in proper capacity as a christian missionary society;" and they struck that falsehood out; and then they gulped it down "without a dissenting vote," though their previous vote striking it out, had said that it was not *proper* in a *christian* society.

I also copy the following from the official proceedings:

"On call for members, the following brethren became annual members by the payment of one dollar each:

O. A. Burgess, Indianapolis, Ind...................,... $1 00

J. M. Tilford, Indianapolis, Ind........................... 1 00
Wm. Brothers, Illinois.................................... 1 00
B. Crist, Pleasant Grove, Ind 1 00
C. G. Bartholomew, Rockville, Ind..................... 1 00
H. Z. Leonard, Lafayette, Ind........................... 1 00
James Hadsell, Spencerville, Ind....................... 1 00
George Campbell, Groves, Ind.......................... 1 00
John Campbell, Oxford, Ind............................. 1 00
Lizza Sims, Laporte, Ind................................. 1 00
Frank Closser, Laporte, Ind............................. 1 00
D. J. McPeak, Culver's Station, Ind................... 1 00
R. Faurot, Newville, Ind................................. 1 00
Wm. Grigsby, Logansport, Ind......................... 1 00
H. Z. Leonard presented a communication from Bro.
Jont. H. Henry, containing $16 55, contributed
as follows:
By the Church in Martinsville........................... 7 30
   "   Lower Liberty 3 90
   "   Major's School-house............... 4 35
By C. Davidson, for annual membership.............. 1 00
A communication was received from the Church in
Indianapolis, with a contribution of................. 30 00

      Total............. ....$61 55

Which also recommend a number of brethren as Messengers to the meeting, of whom brethren J. B. New, O. Butler, J. M. Tilford, E. Goodwin, O. A. Burgess, appeared and took seats in the meeting."

There are more than 50,000 members of the Christian Church in Indiana; and yet this is the beggarly number taking part in this Society, in May last. Sixty-one dollars contributed, and thirty-two of it from Indianapolis, with men sent to manage the Society. These facts furnish food for reflection. Does converting a christian missionary society into a political conclave of abolitionists, benefit or injure the cause of Christ? is a question that each one must reflect upon and answer for himself. The above facts and figures show that it has pretty much destroyed that Society. How much that has injured the cause of the Lord every one must decide for himself.

The Ohio Christian Missionary Society had not been

troubled with these factionists; but having conquered the Indiana Society, and by conquering it had destroyed it, they attacked the Ohio Society in its annual meeting convened at Shelby, Ohio, on the 26th of May, 1863. A brother Lamphere introduced the same resolutions introduced and passed at Lafayette, and copied above, with the false clause "in proper capacity as a Christian Missionary Society of the State of Ohio," retained in them. After some debate they were passed, with the false clause above quoted in them. Our esteemed friend, brother Goodwin, in his publication of the transaction, in his *Record* of June 9th, 1863, said: "Bro. Frame remarked that if they would convert the meeting into a *mass meeting*, he would go for the resolutions. *To this no attention was paid*,[1] the question was put and the resolutions passed, without a single negative vote. I could but notice how a few persons kept their eyes on Bro. Franklin. Before the vote was taken, he made a few remarks, stating that he was opposed to introducing such resolutions into a missionary meeting, but since they were to be voted on, he would vote for them, for they expressed the sentiments of his heart, and he did vote for them."

The stragetic tactics by which they took the Ohio Missionary Society by assault, greatly gratified them; and particularly, the adroit manner in which they caught brother Franklin in their toils, and, as they thought, took him captive at their will, gave them as much joy as those who endeavored to ensnare the Lord about paying tribute to Cesar would have felt, had they succeeded. "A few persons kept their eyes on Bro. Franklin," and brother Goodwin " could but notice " it. What set them to watching Franklin? and how came brother Goodwin to be so observant of the watching? Were they the conspirators? There were but "few" of them, it seems, which I have no doubt is strictly true. Had they been told, as they should have been, that the Lord's command was to render to Cesar the things that are Cesar's, and to God the things that are God's; that Cesar had no rights there; but that that body and its action and services, belonged to God and not to Cesar at all, they would have been foiled as the Lord foiled those similar pious patriots who attempted to ensnare him, and inviegle

---

(1) These italics are mine.

him *into the expression of an opinion upon a political question*,[1] which he did not then do, nor never did.

I must spare space here for what brother Franklin said in his *American Christian Review*, of July 7th, 1863, about this transaction, and reserve what I have to say further till I shall have cited another case or two:

"The propriety of introducing worldly questions—mere worldly questions of any sort—into the pulpit, into the church, missionary meetings, and religious literature, no matter how important, is now a matter of no small magnitude, and by no means settled with many good people. Our mind is made up on this matter. Our course is settled. We are satisfied, too, that the course of a large proportion of the christian brotherhood is also settled. When we can not preach without dragging into our preaching the issues of the world, *we shall not preach at all*. When we can not publish a *religious* paper, devoted *exclusively to religion*, without making it a worldly engine, to advocate the issues of the world, we shall not publish a *religious paper at all*. When we can not belong to a church, or a missionary society, and attend the meetings without the issues of the world being forced in, no matter how great they are, nor how momentous, we shall consider the church or the society so carnalized, perverted from its gracious and benevolent purpose, if it can not be reformed, unworthy of support or advocacy. We mean what we are saying. We know that we are right in this matter, that the kingdom of Christ is not of this world; that it must be kept distinct from the world, and attend to its own affairs. Let the ministry be devoted to its great work, the church to the work to which the Lord has sanctified it, and the missionary society to its own work, and all will go well; but whoever attempts to pervert them, to turn them aside from their *professed purpose*, and make them engines of the world, no matter how great nor how important the worldly cause, will destroy the cause of the Lord to the extent of his influence. Nothing has saved us from disruption, in almost all sections of the country, only our keeping the issues of the world out of church, and nothing will do this in the future. There will be constantly questions of the world arising, issues forming

---

(1) Ante, pp. 339, 340, 341.

and complications, which will take their course in the world, but which, if dragged into the church, would keep up perpetual schism, strife and worldly discussions.

"If any man in this country has become such a fanatic that he thinks a man can not be loyal to the civil government, in the highest and fullest sense, a Union man of the first order, and a true friend to the law and the executives of the law, without introducing the issues of the country into the pulpit, religious publications, the church, and the missionary society, he needs enlightenment to make him a sound *Union man,* in the church or anywhere else. The masons meet from time to time, in their different meetings, pass no resolutions, discuss no questions, and have no action touching the troubles of the country. What man of intelligence charges them with disloyalty, simply because, in their *Masonic meetings,* they attend simply to *Masonry?* What mason thinks of such a thing as that he jeopardizes his loyalty simply because he spent a few hours in a masonic meeting, without saying anything about the great issues of the country? All we ask is, that when christians meet in their capacity, as christians, to attend to religious matters, that they, for the time being, dismiss from their minds the affairs of the world, and attend to things of the kingdom of God and the name of Jesus Christ.

"The brethren in Indiana, or *a few of them,* have been passing resolutions touching the worldly upheavings of the country, because other denominations have been doing so, to popularize the State Missionary Society. They did this a year ago, and have lately done so again, but the almost entire absence of all account of missionary work, *through their Society,* and of money for the work, furnish an unfavorable commentary on the success and popularity gained through this means. At our late meeting in Shelby, Ohio, we were bored all one afternoon with a string of resolutions touching the troubles of the country, and some gassy, fulsome, and weak speeches. We had no objection to the sentiment, so far as there was any, in these speeches, nor to the resolutions. The resolutions were good enough, any where proper for them, but had certainly no business in that meeting The speeches were *out of place,* and *too weak* to have been interesting in a political meeting or a war meeting. All in all, it was a very flat affair—a great letting down for such a meeting—and will do a vast amount of harm to the State Missionary Society.

"We were well satisfied before the resolutions came to a vote, that a majority would have been in favor of throwing the whole affair out of the meeting, though probably none had any objection to the sentiment contained in the resolutions. Of this we now have no doubt. But we were not present when the resolutions were introduced, and saw that there was no excitement about the matter, or interest in it any way, only to gain a point in getting it into the meeting, and we explained to the audience that we considered it letting down, and entirely aside from our work, but that as it was now introduced, and as the sentiments in the resolutions were good, we thought it best to pass the resolutions, and let the world know that the movers in the little affair were *loyal men*. The question was put, and the resolutions were passed without any dissent.

"If the present trouble were the only thing of the kind that would be likely to rise, we would let it pass unnoticed. But, knowing the mischief that must result from such a precedent, we now give notice, that if anything of the kind shall be introduced into the General Missionary Meeting, or the State Missionary Society, again, when we are present, we shall make an effort to have it thrown out. We deem it useless to give our money and influence for these societies, if they are to be carnalized, made worldly engines, and turned aside *from religious purposes.* When we want political resolutions, we will attend political meetings; when we want to hear a political speech, we will go and hear some of the regular political speakers, who *can* make a political speech; when we want to hear a war speech, we prefer to hear some of the generals, or great war men, who *can* make a war speech, and not the spouting of preachers, who generally keep out of the reach of bullets; and when we want the secular news, we go to the *Commercial* or *Gazette,* and not to starved religious papers, containing a little budget of war and secular news, rehashed and sent out *ten or fifteen days after it had appeared in the secular papers,* and everybody had seen it."

The same men ran the North-western Christian University into party politics too. At the annual meeting of the

Board of Directors in July, 1862, after a preamble and preliminary resolution, to prepare the way, came this, which was passed, myself and one other member voting against it :

"*Resolved*, That while we deny that any action of this board, or the faculty of the institution, has been either religiously or politically partizan in its character, we rejoice to be able to state, and for the first time we now state, that the members of this board and of the faculty of the institution, are true and loyal to the constitution and government of the United States, and warmly and deeply sympathize with the soldiers of the Union who are engaged in the suppression of the present wicked rebellion."

The University is limited in its charter to teaching literature, the sciences, and the morals of the bible; prohibiting sectarian tenets and dogmas from being taught; and though most of its Directory and Faculty were abolitionists from its organization, and were inculcating their tenets as it is their nature to do, yet there had been no *corporate act* favoring any party or party tenets, political or religious, up to the time of the passage of that resolution. I know this to be so, because I was a member of the Board from the time of the incorporation of the Institution. This resolution, after stating this fact, says that now "for the first time," the corporation breaks over the boundary, and commits the Institution to the party politics of the day.

There is not more than one-fifth of the stock owned by abolitionists; and yet they have had entire control of the Board from the organization of the Institution, and still have. There is not more than ten per cent. of the brotherhood in the State abolitionized; and hence nine-tenths of them are kept from taking an interest in, and sustaining the Institution, because it is abolitionized.

A few remarks now upon these matters; and first of *loyalty.*

Loyalty is not a proper word to use among us while we are a free people, and while our free government, formed by the fathers of the revolution, remains to us. But as they change the free government we had, into a despotism, they change the terms used.

Loyalty, is, " firm and faithful adherence *to a prince.*"
Loyal, is, " obedient, true *to the prince.*"

Loyally, is, "with fidelity, with true adherence *to a king.*"
Loyalist, is, "one who professes uncommon adherence *to his king.*"

Hence the term applies *to a person*, and not *to a free constitutional government*. Hence the recent constant use of the term *loyal* with its variations, by those who claim that the President and his administration, are *the government*. And they all agree and insist that they are loyal to the government, meaning the President, and insist that all must be so. Mr. Jefferson, the great father and expounder of our free government, gave the true phrase, which expresses the idea, and performs the office in our free government, as we had it, that loyal and its variations do in monarchies. That phrase is *a friend to the constitution.* That is the appropriate term in our free government, as we had it. Our allegiance is due to *the constitution;* not to *the President.* Our official oaths are to support *the constitution;* not to support *the President* nor *the government.* We can not be loyal in the literal sense of the term, and remain free; for loyalty is fealty, allegiance to a person, a prince: but we can be friends to the constitution, and support the constitution, and still be free. For by the constitution, the sovereignty is vested in the people, who retained the power in it to modify it or change it.

Words are *things.* The term *loyal* is used to accustom the public mind to the *thing* it represents, fealty, fidelity to a person. See the oaths that have been framed and enforced *to support the government*, &c.

In the Rushville resolutions, "loyalty to the civil government" is the phrase; not to the constitution. In the Lafayette resolutions, "we do hereby declare unwavering allegiance to, and our unqualified support of, *the government*," not of the constitution, is what they say. In the Ohio resolutions, they made the Christian Missionary Society of the State of Ohio declare unwavering allegiance to, and unqualified support of, the government, not allegiance to, and support of, the constitution. I doubt very much whether the men who concocted these resolutions, and engineered them through, would publicly solemnly pledge their unwavering allegiance to, and unqualified support of, *the constitution;* for they have denounced it as a league with hell and a covenant with death, for years. And by the sophistry of the term *government* for the *constitution*, and *loyalty*, which means fidelity *to a person* instead of fidelity *to the constitution*, they are trying to make the impression that they really are patriots; and not only that, but that all who see their sophistry and will not be caught with their guile, are traitors!

The Ohio Christian Missionary Society, if it was a christian body, owed no allegiance to Cesar at all; but to the Lord, and to the Lord alone. The men who composed the body, as men, owed allegiance to their respective constitutions, State and National. But the society owed no allegiance to Cesar at all; and any interference by Cesar with the society, or its affairs, would have been a usurpation by him. But when the society, *in proper capacity as a society*, declared its unwavering allegiance to Cesar, and its unqualified support of Cesar, it changed its allegiance from the Lord to Cesar, rebelled against the Lord, "seceded" from his kingdom, and "annexed" itself to "the kingdoms of this world"—to Cesar and his fortunes. For the Lord expressly says they can not serve two masters—God and Cesar.[1] For which may the good Lord have mercy upon it, and bring it to repentance and reformation—which would be a change again of its allegiance.

In the University, resolutions, which were the first they got up, the word *constitution* was retained, but *loyalty* and *government* were also put in. But ever afterwards the constitution was left out entirely.

The Lafayette and the Ohio resolutions recognize the chief ruler, to wit, Lincoln, as the minister of God, a revenger to execute wrath, and *tender* their cheerful support to him in that work. Christians, and a christian society, tendering their services as hangmen! Is not that a pretty spectacle?

Because the Lord commands christians to be subject to the higher powers, to rulers, to kings, to every ordinance of man, these men affect now to be extremely patriotic; but being subject to rulers, and submitting to the powers that be, is a very different thing from thrusting themselves in, and tendering their services as the executioners of these avengers. And their conduct shows that vengeance impels their action rather than patriotism; and much more than

(1) Matt. vi, 24.

the love of all men, that dwells in every *christian* heart, impels them. Submitting to rulers, and being the willing active instruments of rulers, are very different things; and more so, when rulers are engaged in a bad cause, and endeavoring to affect an improper object. Subjection and obedience is one thing; active participation is another and a different thing.

The only divinely authorized mention of kings, and rulers, and men in authority, in the christian bodies and congregations, is the authority and direction given to pray for them in common with all men, that *christians* may lead a quiet and *peaceable* life in all godliness and honesty.[1] We are commanded to pray for them as men, and not for their measures as rulers; but that they may be God-fearing men, which, if they be, they will rule in righteousness, and if they do so rule, christians subject to them, can lead a *quiet* and *peaceable* life. As christians are commanded to pray for them for that object, it clearly indicates what kind of prayers are to be made for them. But abolitionists pray, not for the rulers as men; that they may be God-fearing and rule in righteousness; but for the measures of the rulers, for their abolition programme to be carried out, and tender their services as avengers and executioners. "Now the *fruit* of *righteousness* is *sown* in *peace*, by them who practice peace."[2] "Blessed are the *meek;* for they shall *inherit the earth*. Blessed are the *merciful;* [not those who want to be avengers]; for they shall *obtain mercy*." How will it be with the unmerciful? "Blessed are the *peacemakers;* for they shall be called THE CHILDREN OF GOD."[3] Peace men, according to these pious abolitionists, are traitors. The Lord says, however, that they are the children of God. "Doubtless," says brother Goodwin, "many will be much pleased on reading brother Lucas' declaration in favor of our National Union; still their joy would have been considerably increased, had he said he was in favor of prosecuting the war, with all the means and forces at the command of the government, until the rebellion is effectually and forever subdued."[4] How merciful! Of course brother Goodwin will obtain mercy. How meek, mild, soft and gentle! Of course he will inherit the earth.

(1) 1 Tim. ii, 1, 2.
(2) James iii, 18, New Trans.
(3) Matt. v, 5, 7, 9.
(4) Christian Record, May 12th, 1863.

As to the peacemaker part, I express no opinion. But being in favor of the National Union is not the thing; that will not do. The prosecution of this civil war is the essential ingredient in abolition piety and morals, and without which *loyalty* can not exist! Here is abolition morals, piety, and loyalty, all in a nutshell. The war must be prosecuted to free the negroes and take *vengeance* on their masters, their wives, and children; and the National Union is immaterial. These scribes and Pharisees ought to be told, as the Lord told those scribes and Pharisees of his day, who brought to him a woman taken in adultery, in the very act, " He that is without sin among you, let him first cast a stone at her;"[1] and if their consciences are not "seared with a hot iron,"[2] as I fear they are, they would sneak away one by one, as those ancient ones did from the presence of the Lord. " But if ye forgive not men their trespasses, neither will your Father forgive your trespasses;"[3] and as I am anxious to have my trespasses forgiven, I freely forgive the great wrongs that the rebels of the South have done, as well as those that the abolitionists have done, and shall " follow after the things that make for' peace;"[4] " follow peace with all men,"[5] and " seek peace and pursue it;"[6] hence, I can not work up to the abolition programme, either of morality, piety, or loyalty. " For he that will love life, and see good days, let him *refrain his tongue* from evil, and *his lips* that they *speak no guile:* let him eschew evil and do good: let him seek peace and pursue it."[7] Had abolitionists obeyed this passage, we would not have had our present troubles. Were they now to commence obeying it, it would greatly help to save us from the wreck and ruin into which our people and government are plunging deeper and deeper every day. May the good Lord have mercy upon us, and turn his wrath from us. Amen.

I have, up to this point, considered christians as being the governed. In our heretofore free country, (alas! not so any longer; at least abolitionists are trying hard to prevent its being so any longer,) christians, as citizens, exercised their equal portion of the sovereignty; hence it is

---

(1) John viii, 3–9.
(2) 1 Tim. iv, 2.
(3) Matt. vi, 15.
(4) Rom. xiv, 19.
(5) Heb. xii, 14.
(6) 1 Pet. iii, 11.
(7) 1 Pet. iii, 10, 11

proper that I consider their rights and duties as christians, and as citizens of a free government.

In this position, in exercising their franchises as free American citizens at the ballot box, and in the discussion and determination of public measures, they are properly exercising the functions of Cesar. They each stand as a sovereign, and they are accountable to God for their conduct, as all Cesars are accountable to God. If they rule in righteousness, they will be blessed of God; if they rule in unrighteousness, he will surely visit them, as he has heretofore visited all unrighteous Cesars. They occupy the position here, that christian kings occupy in monarchies. They are limited sovereigns, limited in their powers by the constitutions, State and National; and to discharge their functions as Cesars, righteously, they must be guilty of no usurpations of *things* beyond their chartered rights, privileges and franchises. As our States are sovereignties, and have retained to themselves and their people, all the sovereign powers not delegated to the United States by the Constitution of the United States, the people of the States, respectively, have no right to interfere with the business and affairs of other States any more than they have, of other nations; and when they do, they are guilty of usurpation, and of governing unrighteously. The Golden Rule is the proper rule for the people of the States to govern their political conduct by, as to the other States and the people thereof; and certainly *christians*, when acting as Cesars, can cheerfully govern their political conduct towards their co-States, by that rule. And applying that to the question of domestic slavery, we in Indiana desire to settle and determine that question for ourselves, and do not want Kentuckians or Tennesseeans to settle it for us; hence we should cheerfully yield to Kentuckians and Tennesseeans what we would that they should yield to us, and let them settle and determine the question of domestic slavery for themselves, and not attempt to settle it for them. The control of the question whether the States shall or shall not have the domestic institution of slavery, is not delegated to the United States Government; and hence, all attempts by that government to control it, is sheer usurpation, and political iniquity. And christian Cesars who perpetrate that iniquity, will be held accountable by God, as he holds all Cesars accountable; that is, by visiting his *wrath* and *vengeance* upon them in this world. All Cesars are punished in this world; while the Lord's punishment, for those who reject his kingdom, and sin against him, is in a future state of existence.

I have not space to cite from the Bible the proofs of this, and to show how God deals with Cesars; with the governments of this world; and it does not lay particularly within my field in the present inquiry. Hence, I shall not go into it. A portion of the people, both in the slave States and in the free States, originally a very small portion in each, made use of slavery as a lever and pretext to bring about a dissolution of our Union. Falsehood and misrepresentation, in each portion of the Union, of the people, their institutions, habits, and intentions, in the other portion of the Union, were the means used to sever the ties of fraternal feeling, and sow hatred and variance in their place. As they succeeded in their work, they increased in strength, and in intensity of action. For the last six or eight or ten years, torrents of falsehoods and misrepresentations have been poured out in both sections against the other, a dissolution of the Union has been effected, and a most gigantic and horrible civil war has raged for more than two years. I have in this book treated of the errors we have been guilty of in the free States, and have not spoken of the great and grievous errors that have been committed by the people of the slave States, because that did not lie in my field of inquiry. I can not sum up and close this branch of my subject better than to quote from my namesake, the prophet Jeremiah, what he spoke by inspiration, to and of the Jewish people, when they were in the terrible condition that we are now in, and have been for four or five years. It is equally true of us as a people, both North and South, (for I can not bear to think of, or contemplate ourselves any otherwise than as one people,) as it was of the Jewish people at the time Jeremiah spoke it. And it is also one of the proofs of the manner in which God deals with Cesars:

"Oh that my head were waters, and mine eyes a fountain of tears, that I might weep day and night for the slain of the daughter of my people! Oh that I had in the wilderness a lodging-place of wayfaring men, that I might leave my people, and go from them! For they be all adulterers, an assembly of treacherous men. And they bend *their tongue* like they bow for *lies;* but they are not valiant *for the truth* upon the earth; for they proceed from *evil* to *evil*, and they know not me, saith the Lord. Take ye heed every one of his neighbor, and trust ye not in any brother; for every brother will *utterly supplant*, and every neighbor *will walk with slanders.* And they will *deceive* every one his *neighbor*, and *will not speak the truth:* they have *taught* their tongue *to speak lies*, and weary themselves *to commit iniquity.* Thine habitation is in the midst of deceit; through deceit they refuse to know me, saith the Lord. Therefore thus saith the LORD of hosts, Behold, I will *melt* them, and *try* them; [alas! we are being melted and tried now] for how shall I do for the daughter of my people? Their tongue is as an arrow shot out; *it speaketh deceit;* one speaketh peaceably to his neighbor with his mouth, *but in heart he layeth his wait.* Shall I not visit them for *these things?* saith the LORD : Shall not my soul be *avenged* on *such a nation as this?*"[1]

O Lord! give us repentance and reformation, that thy avenging hand may be stayed, and thy wrath withdrawn om us.

PREJUDICE OF COLOR.

Abolitionists have, for years, talked much about the prejudice of color, and insist that it must be broken down and eradicated, and that whites must mingle and associate with blacks as they do with whites, socially and politically.

This, like almost every other abolition tenet, is untrue. There is no *prejudice* of color between the whites and blacks, and never was. Prejudice is literally pre-judgment, a judgment before hand, before examination. But it is not pre-judgment that makes the whites and blacks disinclined to associate with each other; and the feeling exists as strongly in one class as in the other. The negroes are as much disinclined to associate with the whites, as the whites are disinclined to associate with the negroes. But it is not prejudice that causes this. It is INSTINCT.

Instinct is defined to be the power which determines the will of brutes; a desire or aversion in the mind not determined by reason or deliberation. Though thus defined by

(1) Jer. ix, 1-9.

lexicographers, it is really the fiat of God. The fiat of God places instincts upon all the animal creation, including man. The fear of man and the dread of man was placed upon all the brute creation by the fiat of God, immediately after the flood,[1] and they have existed ever since, and still exist. That the young seizes the teat of the mother and sucks the milk, is the result of instinct, not of reason or judgment, though some very nice mechanical laws are brought into action thereby.

The same instinct, placed by the fiat of God upon the races, white and black, causes them not to desire to commingle and associate. Whether the curse pronounced by Noah, is the fiat that placed it there, it is not necessary to have authoritatively decided; but I am of opinion that it was that that did it. That fiat debased the race that it applied to, let it be whatever race it may, to the position of *a slave of slaves*, which necessarily made a large chasm between it and the free races; and the whole negro, physical and mental, shows him debased to that position. And the difference of color between the negroes and whites, made an equally large chasm; and there can be no question but that God placed that distinction between the races. Yet we have no revelation of when or how it was done, and hence we do not know. But the fact is there, patent to all. It must have been placed there by the word or fiat of God; for by it the worlds were made, and without it was not anything made that was made.

Hence, to call the instincts thus placed upon the races, prejudice, and to attempt to eradicate those instincts, and to override and close up the great chasms placed between the races by the fiat of God, is folly, not to say impiety, such as abolitionists only can be guilty of.

The negroes are wholly incapable of elevation. I thought otherwise formerly; but thirty or forty years of observation and reflection upon the subject, have conclusively satisfied my mind that the curse of Noah, or some other fiat of God, has debased them; and that they can not be elevated until another fiat of God makes them capable of elevation. That is with Him, and not with me. I will try and do my duty to them as fellow human beings; but I will not try to eradicate the instincts placed upon their race and mine, by

---

(1) Gen. ix, 2.

the fiat of God, nor will I scold and abuse any one for obeying those instincts.

I will close this branch of my subject, and with it my book, by copying in a letter from Professor S. F. B. Morse, the inventor of the telegraph, who says some things proper to be said in this book, so much better than I can say them, that I take the liberty of using his labors. That it may be properly understood, the letter from Mr. Edward N. Crosby, of Poughkeepsie, New York, to which it is an answer, is nserted also. I hope the reader will give the Professor's etter a careful reading, and ponder well what he says.

LETTER FROM EDWARD N. CROSBY, ESQ.

TROY, February 25th, 1863.

PROFESSOR S. F. B. MORSE—*My Dear and Respected Sir:*—I have read with deep interest the letter in the New York *Evening Post*, of the 19th inst., addressed to you by Mr. D. D. Field. Its general tenor harmonizes with views which I have long coveted the privilege of expressing to you, but which have been repressed by a constitutional feeling of respect for eminence and seniority, and a fear of even seeming officiously to intrude. But, as Mr. Field suggests, your fame has become a national inheritance, and this alike is a motive and an apology for a jealous care on the part of your fellow-citizens as to aught that may impair its luster. It is the omissions, however, rather than the contents, of Mr. Field's sensible and temperate letter, that prompts me to speak. While appealing to you on many high grounds, still he fails to reach the highest from which the subject is to be viewed. And I trust it is not assuming too much for one who is not only an admiring fellow-countryman and a near neighbor, but also a christian friend, to discuss this matter with you from the christian's standpoint. And what, may I ask, appears to you the sufficient reason for a christian citizen to ally himself with others, for the extreme and radical purpose of undermining or paralyzing the power of the government at a crisis when unanimity of support is so plainly essential, not only to the welfare, but to the very life of the nation?

There are many, alas! who, from ignorance or passion,

persistently confound all the immense party, which came into being and into power only on the grand purpose of resisting Southern aggression, with the extremest radicalism and infidelity of the Garrison stamp. They would thus justify themselves in an indiscriminate and reckless hostility to the policy of the government. I can, of course, find in this fact no explanation of the deliberate action of one of your principles and intelligence. Some may say that "the war on our part is unrighteous, and therefore unworthy of support." But the rebels began it. To this it may be said: "The provocations offered them were such as greatly to diminish, if not remove, their criminality in thus beginning it." These assertions, though easily refuted, might require a discussion both long and foreign somewhat to my purpose. But it may be said that "the war, though righteous, is waged by unrighteous methods, such as confiscation, and more particularly, emancipation." If, however, it is a legitimate function of our government to destroy the fabric of the Southern Confederacy, *a fortiori*, is it not justified in removing that which their own highest authorities pronounce to be the *corner stone* of that fabric? Moreover, though this position is as palpably untenable as the two previously stated, yet supposing it to be a sincere christian conviction, inasmuch as these methods must be objected to rather as inexpedient than as morally and legally unjustifiable, should not another christian conviction, that of duty to the "powers that are ordained of God," prevent any disposition to resist or thwart the government? But I would fain suppose that rather than either of the above, the grounds of your political views and action have been an earnest desire for peace, and an abomination of war and its attendant horrors. In both of these feelings I claim the fullest sympathy with you, and yet I can not possibly construct upon them a fulcrum for unfriendly action against our government.

I have seen in the progress of events much to criticise and regret in the administration, but I feel assured that as far at least as our President is concerned, the errors have been those of the judgment, and are compatible with a pure integrity, and a high-toned patriotism. Horrible too as war is, we are to remember that it may yet be a worthy means to a worthy end. God has certainly in his word more directly and repeatedly given his sanction to it, than he has to slavery. But what is the legitimate, the inevitable tendency of such unfriendly demonstrations as those to which you were persuaded to give countenance at Delmonico's, and which have had a fuller but natural development in Connecticut and elsewhere? We are not left to theories for a reply. Facts show that while the rebel leaders insultingly spurn all pusillanimous overtures of conciliation, they also exult over them as evidences of divided counsels and increasing feebleness at the North. They are thereby emboldened to declare themselves utterly implacable, except by success in their own ruinous plans. What, then, should be our necessary logic, our irresistible inference? Certainly patriotism, and a wise appreciation of the worthy and the abundant means committed to us, would decide at once. Let us, by united and couragous effort, show the rebels that their success is perfectly hopeless. May I venture to speak a word also as to the *personnel* in these matters? Mr. Field says that he knows personally nearly all of those who were associated with you at Delmonico's, and implies very plainly that they borrowed from your presence a respectability for which they could make no becoming return. It was on a previous public occasion, that I saw, with no slight regret, your good name published, as appearing on the same platform with the characterless ———, the infamous ———, and the pitiable ———. Can it be that the purest and most patriotic measures draw to their advocacy such persons, while they fail to attract the innumerable host who dissent, and whose patriotism and probity you can not but heartily commend?

The high estimate I have formed of your christian character, confirmed and increased by my intercourse with ———, has encouraged me to speak with the more freedom, and with the hope that it will be received in the same kindly spirit which has prompted it.

Yours most sincerely and respectfully,
EDWARD N. CROSBY.

PROFESSOR MORSE'S REPLY.

New York, March 2, 1863.

My Dear Sir:—Yours of the 25th of February is received, and I take in good part what you say, written, however, wholly under misconception of my opinions, my position, and the objects for which the society for the diffusion of political knowledge has been organized. I know from your estimable character, that your intention and motives were of the most benevolent kind in addressing me, and in reply, I shall make a few remarks, I trust in the same kindly spirit, while on the subjects you introduce I use perfect plainness of speech.

Your letter touches on many topics, upon some of which, I have, for years, bestowed much study; and it may be, that a frank discussion of them at a time when the public mind is alive to such discussions, may be useful in eliciting truth. Fundamental difference of opinion is often more seeming than real, perhaps from the inherent imperfections of language itself, in conveying our real thoughts to another's mind, or through some defect of intellect or education in not using perspicuous language. If due weight were given to a consideration of this kind, there would be less of that asperity of remark upon other's misconceptions, which, in this day of excitement, deforms the popular style. Mere difference of opinion, honestly entertained, is entitled to that forbearance which is denied to brazen-faced, persistent falsehood.

I can account for your misconceptions of the purpose of our society, as well as of many other topics upon which you have written, only on the presumption that you ground your remarks on the assumed truth of the egregiously false and impudent representations of an unprincipled reporter of the *Evening Post*. If this was the source of your information, you might as well look for truth respecting Bible doctrine from Voltaire or Thomas Paine. Are you not aware that the pretended report of the incipient meeting at Delmonico's, which led to the formation of our society, is a tissue of falsehoods from beginning to end, exposed and refuted in numerous journals? Of how many falsehoods, persistently repeated, must a journal be convicted, before its statement of facts shall be received with suspicion?

I need not say to you that the admission into the *Evening Post* of such a grossly abusive report, while entertaining, as I have hitherto, for its senior editor, so much personal respect, (however much I may differ from him politically,) is a source of deep mortification to me.

MR. FIELD'S LETTER.

Mr. Field's letter, addressed to me, was probably indited under the influence of impressions made by that same infamous report; and while I have no complaint of want of courtesy on his part toward me personally, I saw nothing in its general tenor of sufficient importance to require any answer from me. Though addressed to me, it was evidently addressed to the public through me, and I was used only as a convenient mode of addressing the public. So far as anything he said required notice, that notice was taken of it by several journals. I inslose you clippings from two which happen to be at hand. Whatever personal regard I have for Mr. Field, and for his highly respectable family connections, the state of the country compels me to waive all considerations of social relations, in treating of its political condition. His views and mine, on the subject of the policy of the administration, are anti podal; and in view of his reported action in the Peace Congress, in connection with some of his radical associates, to which action can be traced the present awful conditions of the country, since it was in their power (if I have been rightly advised) to have averted the war, I can not but look upon his and their political course as laying upon them a weight of responsibility which I would not have upon my conscience for a thousand worlds.

CHRISTIAN STAND-POINT.

You desire "to discuss the subject from the christian's stand-point." I accede to this the more readily since that is precisely the stand-point from which I have always endeavored to view the whole field of controversy. On Bible truth, therefore, I am ready to plant every position I take.

Did it not lead me into too long a discussion for a letter like this, a discussion starting from a point too far back, even from fundamental theological principles, I should like to establish with you this stand-point impregnably on the Bible. This will have to be done ere the perverted christian mind of the country can be disabused of the ruinous fallacies which have turned aside the incumbents of so many pulpits from their legitimate duty of allaying the fierce passions of men, through the tranquilizing influences of the Gospel of peace, and changed them into impassioned political orators, whose exasperating harrangues have added fuel to the already raging fires of a ferocious and desolating fanaticism.[1] Such a discussion, important as it is, must be in abeyance.

I proceed to answer your question, "What appears to you the sufficient reason for a christian citizen to ally himself with others for the extreme and radical purpose of undermining or paralyzing the power of the government at a crisis when unanimity of support is so plainly essential, not only to the welfare, but to the very life of the nation?"

GOVERNMENT AND ADMINISTRATION.

I will analyze the component parts of your question. You assume, without any warrant, that my purpose is to "undermine and paralyze the power of the government." You appear to have fallen into the prevalent error of confounding the government with the administration of the government. You are too sensible not to see that they are not the same. The word government has indeed two meanings; and in order to rescue the subject from ambiguity, allow me to say that the ordinary meaning of government, in free countries, is, that form of fundamental rules and principles by which a nation or State is governed, or by which individual members of a body politic are to regulate their action. Government is in fact a constitution by which the rights and duties both of citizens and public officers are prescribed and defined. If the word sometimes has a sec-

---

(1) "*Politics* and the *pulpit* are terms that have little agreement. No sound ought to be heard in the church but the healing voice of christian charity The cause of civil liberty and civil government gains as little as that of religion, by this confusion of duties. Those who quit their proper character to assume what does not belong to them, are, for the greater part, ignorant both of the character they leave, and of the character they assume. Wholly unacquainted with the world in which they are so fond of meddling, and inexperienced in all its affairs, on which they pronounce with so much confidence, they have nothing of politics but the passions they excite. Surely the church is a place where one day's truce ought to be allowed to the dissensions and animosities of mankind."—BURKE: *Reflections on French Revolution,* vol i, p. 460.

"I have something also to the *divines*, though brief, to what were needful, not to be disturbers of the civil affairs; but in hands better able, and more belonging, to manage them; but to study harder, and to attend the office of good pastors, knowing that he whose flock is least among them, has a dreadful burden, not performed by mounting twice into the pulpit with a formal preachment huddled up at the odd hours of a whole lazy week, but by incessant pains and watching, in season and out of season, from house to house, over the souls whom they have to feed. Which, if they well considered, how little leisure would they find to be the most pragmatical sidesmen of every popular tumult and sedition."
—MILTON: *Treatise on Tenure of Kings, &c.*

ondary or more limited meaning synonymous with administration of public affairs, then "the government" is metonymically used for administration, and should not be confounded with the original and true signification of the term administration, which means the persons collectively who are intrusted with the execution of the laws, and with the superintendence of public affairs.

Opposition to the administration, then, is not opposition to the government; the former may not only be utterly destroyed without affecting the health of the government, but it may be, and constantly is, thought to be necessary, in the opinion of the supreme power, the people, to destroy the administration in order to preserve the life of the government. This is in accordance not only with the theory of our institutions, but with the daily practice of the people. Every change of administration, at every election, Federal, State, or municipal, great or small, exemplifies this great truth. The government remains intact, unscathed, while the administration is swept out of existence.

In the light of this explication, you must perceive, that so far from "allying myself with others for the purpose of undermining and paralyzing the power of the government," the very purpose of our society is to uphold and strengthen the government, by diffusing among the people such a knowledge of the principles upon which it is founded, that it shall not be in the power of any administration, whether weak or wicked, to work its injury.

I yield to no man in hearty loyalty to the government, nor in obedience also to the administration in all its constitutional measures, whatever may be my private opinion of their wisdom. You mistake me, if you suppose I have any "radical purpose of undermining or paralyzing" any of its legal measures. If I think them unwise, I shall use my constitutional liberty to say so; and if the administration transcends the power intrusted to it by the people, I shall endeavor to point out their error, not in a contumacious or unkind spirit, but nevertheless firmly. To the standard of the constitution, and the Union under it, of all the United States, I shall cling as the only political hope of the country, our only defense against anarchy and despotism.

WHAT MUST WE SUPPORT?

But you say "unanimity of support is essential to the

very life of the nation." Support of what? Laws and acts subversive of the government? Laws and acts in direct and palpable contravention of the constitution? Laws and acts outside of the constitution? Where, in the fundamental law of the government, the constitution, does the President, one of the administrators of the supreme law, find his authority for his emancipation proclamation? Where for his usurpation of the power to suspend the *habeas corpus?* Where for the confiscation acts? Where for his authority to arrest and incarcerate citizens? These are all acts of the *administration*, not of the *government;* they are acts subversive of the government; acts that are "paralyzing and undermining" the government; acts that are dividing the people of the North, alarming them for the safety of the constitution, the government, and arousing them to call their servants, the administrators, to account.

It is on such a confounding of terms as this, of *government* and *administration*, that you charge "extreme and radical purposes" upon those who rally in support of the government.

NECESSITY FOR OUR SOCIETY.

You must excuse me, dear sir, if I say that your letter, to so great an extent based upon the popular fallacies of the day, is itself a proof of the necessity of just such a society as we have formed; because, if minds like yours, intelligent, reflective, ingenuous, and conscientious, are so much at fault on the fundamental principles of our institutions, what must be inferred of the minds of others less intelligent, who imbibe their opinions, and mold their actions, from the prejudiced and befogged intellects controlling the fanatical avenues to public opinion?

CHARACTER OF ABOLITIONISM.

By the manner in which you allude to the "extreme radicalism and infidelity of the Garrison stamp," I am glad to find we have a common stand-point from which to view a portion of the field. Look at that dark conclave of conspirators, freedom-shriekers, Bible spurners, fierce, implacable, head-strong, denunciatory, constitution and Union haters, noisy, factious, breathing forth threatenings and slaughter against all who venture a difference of opinion from them, murderous, passionate advocates of imprisonments and hangings, bloodthirsty; and if there is any other epithet of atrocity found in the vocabulary of wickedness, do they not every one fitly designate some phase of radical abolitionism?

DISTINCTION BETWEEN ABOLITIONISTS AND REPUBLICANS IMPOSSIBLE.

But you would have us make a distinction between these " radicals and infidels of the Garrison stamp," and the " immense party which," as you say, " came into being and into power only on the grand purpose of resisting Southern aggression."

Waiving the question you raise of the existence of any Southern aggression, (previous to the last Presidential election,) making resistance necessary on the part of the North, I ask you how can any distinction be made between parties in close alliance, carrying out together and sustaining the same policy? Did not the Republican party, (in whose ranks I recognize many excellent, intelligent, conscientious men,) did not, I say, that party, in full consciousness of the diabolical character of that "radical and infidel" faction, form a political alliance with it for the purpose of obtaining the power which they now hold? The expectation in forming the coaliation was doubtless that you would be able to control the numerically smaller wing of the alliance. You thought this possible; I did not. So soon as it was apparent that such an alliance had been formed, I predicted that the abolition wing would control the whole; and if the party thus formed were successful, the hopes of the country for peace and Union would be wrecked; for it is the very nature of fanaticism to leaven the whole lump. Was I not right? I ask you now to look at the state of the country. Is it not true that the abolition element has acquired the control of that "immense party" of which you speak? Are you not advocating and supporting the abolition policy of the administration? Is it not true that these very "radicals and infidels of the Garrison stamp," whom you justly loathe, have framed and passed the most offensive abolition measures that tinge the whole policy of the administration? So notorious is this fact, that to ask is to answer the question. These, then, are the men with whom I find you affiliated. May I not appropriately quote your own question, and ask: "Can it be that the purest and most patriotic measures draw to their advocacy such persons, while they fail to attract the innumerable host who dissent," &c? But I will not do you the injustice thus to judge you by the standard by which you would judge me, for your standard is defective. Every one of any experience in political movements is aware, that on both sides, in party excitements, there is every possible variety of character associating together, not because of other or general affinities, but for the single purpose of carrying a common measure, in which all feel more or less interest. Their several interests in that common measure may be as diverse as possible; some from high principle, some for the triumph of an opinion, some to obtain office, some to obtain money. It is not, therefore, safe to characterize a cause by the character of some few who may be loud and forward in advocating it. Bad men may promote a good cause for bad ends. It is safest to judge of a cause on its own merits.

EMANCIPATION PROCLAMATION AND THE CORNER STONE.

I am sorry to find you defending the President's emancipation proclamation. It is a measure which I have considered from the moment of its promulgation unwise, unconstitutional and calamitous, productive of evil and only evil; a measure that, more than any other, has tended to divide the counsels of the North, and unite the South, and render restoration of the National Union next to hopeless. Your defense of it rests on a fallacy. You say "if it is a legitimate function of our government to destroy the fabric of the Southern Confederacy, *a fortiori*, is it not justified in removing that which their own highest authorities pronounce to be its corner-stone?" To answer your question intelligently, it is necessary to know the nature of that corner stone, before we can pronounce whether the government would be justified in removing or attempting to remove it. If the stone should happen to be a providential fixture, unalterable in its very nature by anything that man can do, a condition of a physical character, not to be affected by any act of man, you will agree with me, that the government would not be justified in making any such necessarily abortive and quixotic attempt. I presume from your question, you have adopted the prevalent misunderstanding of a passage in Mr. Stephens' speech at Savannah, in which he speaks of the corner stone of the Confederate Government. You assume that this corner stone is slavery, and so our government is justified in its measures to destroy slavery. Although a great multitude, both in Europe and America, entertain this stereotyped error, and it has, within a few days, been twice reiterated in the late non-intervention report of the Senate Committee of Foreign relations, yet it is none the less an egregious misapprehension of Mr. Stephens' remark, and a false assumption that the Confederate Government have adopted any such corner stone. In the first place, if Mr. Stephens had made such an announcement in his speech, (which he has not,) that would not constitute law for the government. We do not look for the authority of the fundamental law of a government in a casual speech of any members of its administration, not even from the President, but in the fundamental law itself, in its written officially accepted constitution. Now, there is not one word in the Constitution of the Confederacy that gives color to any such idea as slavery being the corner stone of the government. On the contrary, sec. ix, art. 1, clearly repudiates it. For if slavery is the adopted corner stone of their government, common sense suggests that, in their fundamental law, they would and should use every effort to strengthen and support it; and yet they forbid in that section and article that very policy, which would give strength and permanency to such a corner stone. Mr. Stephens, however, has made no such declaration, yet he is quoted everywhere as the source when this wide-spread erroneous apothegm has proceeded. It may be well to ventilate this matter more thoroughly.

THE CORNER STONE IS THE INEQUALITY OF THE TWO RACES.

Let us learn what Mr. Stephens actually did say. His language is this: "The foundations of our new government are laid, its corner stone rests upon "—what? slavery? no— "upon the great truth that the negro is not equal to the white man;" that slavery, which he then defines to be " subordination to the superior race, is his natural and moral condition. This, our new government, is the first in the history of the world based upon this great physical, philosophical and moral truth." This language could not be applied to slavery. It would be a strange misapplication of terms to call slavery a physical, philosophical and moral truth. He had just been stating to his hearers that the ideas prevalent at the time our Federal Constitution was formed "rested upon the assumption of the equality of the races." This proposition he declares to be unsound, and that the new government was founded upon exactly the opposite idea. The error on one side, which he combats, is the assumed equality of the races. The opposite truth which he propounds, is the physical, philosophical and moral truth, that the two races are not equal; and the inference he draws from this truth is, that this physical difference determines the *status* of the inferior race. I confess I can not see how to escape that conclusion, except by denying the inequality of the races; by denying that there is this physical difference between them; for, if there is this difference, then one race, of necessity, is superior, and the other inferior; and if the two physically unequal races are compelled to live together in the same community, the superior race must govern the inferior. Can you avoid this conclusion?

THE CORNER STONE CAN NOT BE REMOVED.

What prospect of success, then, is there of any attempt to remove such a corner stone? Who has constituted the two races physically different? There can be but one answer—it is God. To attempt, therefore, a removal of this corner stone, which infinite wisdom has laid in the fabric of human society, is of so presumptious a character, that few should be rash enough to undertake it. The physical inequality of the races, then, is this corner stone, and not slavery. Slavery, which is a government, must be, in some form, the necessary resultant of this fact; and if you can remove the corner-stone, to-wit, the physical inequality of the races, you may thus destroy slavery; but since the "Ethiopian can not change his skin," nor can any earthly power do it for him, so long as the two races exist together in the same community—you may change the master, or the relative position of the races, but one or the other will still be dominant. Slavery in America can only be abolished by separating the races. Is it worth while to attempt to remove a corner stone which God has laid?

The reasoning of Mr. Stephens has an apposite parallel in the reasoning of the elder Adams, on the theory of government, as given in his "Life by his grandson," C. F. Adams, the accomplished representative of our government to the Court of St. James.

"Unlike most speculators on the theory of governments, Mr. Adams begins by assuming the imperfections of man's nature, and introducing it at once as an element with which to compose his edifice.

"He finds the human race impelled by their passions as often as guided by their reason, sometimes led to good actions by scarcely corresponding motives, and sometimes to bad ones rather from inability to resist temptation than from natural propensity to evil. This is the corner stone of his system."

Let us put Mr. Adams' theory in the language of Mr. Stephens. "The foundations of civil government are laid, its corner stone rests upon the great truth that man has an imperfect nature; that the human race is impelled by their passions; that, therefore, subordination of the inferior to the superior, inherent in the very nature of government, is man's natural and moral condition. Civil government is based upon this great physical, philosophical and moral truth." Would it be just to accuse Mr. Adams of basing government on slavery as the corner-stone, because he admits the necessity of the subordination of the inferior to the superior? In other words, to make him utter the absurdity that "government is the corner stone of government."

PRESIDENT LINCOLN AND MR. STEPHENS PROCLAIM THE SAME CORNER STONE.

Perhaps you may think I have adopted Southern views on this point, and that the inequality and physical differerence of the two races are altogether Southern dogmas. I need not cross the Potomac to find the same great truth proclaimed in a quarter entitled to respect, and by one who politically outranks the Vice-President of the Confederacy, to-wit, the President of the United States.

You will recollect the interview, on August 14, 1862, between a committee of colored men and President Lincoln, invited by him, to hear what he had to say to them. His object in summoning them before him was to persuade them to emigrate; and he bases his argument to them on the very corner stone declared by Mr. Stephens, to-wit, the physical difference or inequality of the two races. President Lincoln's plan was to separate the races.

"You and we," said he to them, "are different races. We have between us a broader difference than exists between almost any other two races. Whether it is right or wrong, I need not discuss, but this physical difference is a great disadvantage to us both, as I think. Your race is suffering, in my judgment, the greatest wrong inflicted on any people. But even when you cease to be slaves, you are far from being placed on an equality with the white race. On this broad continent not a single man of your race is made the equal of a single man of ours. Go where you are treated the best, and the ban is still upon you. I do not propose to discuss this, but to present it as a fact with which we have to deal. I can not altar it if I would. It is a fact about which we all feel and think alike, I and you."

THEIR DIFFERENT MODES OF DEALING WITH THE CORNER STONE.

Thus you perceive that both President Lincoln and Mr. Stephens are in perfect accord in accepting and acting upon the same great truth. President Lincoln accepts the physical inequality of the two races as completely as Mr. Stephens, for where there is a broader difference than exists between almost any other two races, it would be absurd to say they are equal, especially when the President justly adds that this difference is physical, that is, grounded in the original constitution of each race. The only difference between the President of the United States and Mr. Stephens, is in the use to which they put this physical, philosophical and moral truth, this corner stone. Mr. Stephens proposes it in his Savannah speech as the basis of the new government; Mr. Lincoln adopts it as the basis of his plan of separating the races, because of this physical difference. Mr. Stephens takes the stone, as a whole, upon which he would construct a government; Mr. Lincoln would split the stone, and drag the parts asunder. Mr. Stephens accepts the fact, and adjusts his fabric to it. Mr. Lincoln also accepts the fact, and is perplexed with inextricable difficulties in his attempts to dispose of the two portions of the common corner stone.

THE PRESIDENT'S PERPLEXITIES IN DEALING WITH THE CORNER STONE.

It is well to notice these perplexities of the President's mind as they are manifested in his singular interview with this colored delegation. The great truth of the physical difference of the two races is so palpable that he can not controvert it, and he frankly declines to make the attempt; yet, while accepting the fact, he more than doubts the wisdom of the fact itself, by raising the singular question of right and wrong upon its existence, and thus (no doubt unconsciously) impugns the wisdom of the Creator, for who but God could ordain a physical difference in the two races? The raising of the question, therefore, whether a physical fact is "right or wrong," as if there were two sides to such a question, directly implicates the wisdom of the Creator. The President, too, while declining to discuss this question of right and wrong, actually decides it to be wrong, by declaring it to be a "disadvantage to both" races, in his opinion. The plain good sense of most of the remarks of the President in this interview, and the collisions of thought in his own breast, which he discloses, where truths and doubts come into constant conflict, point to some great radical disturbing error, not in the President's mind alone, but pervading the popular mind on the subject of African slavery everywhere.

THE GREAT ERROR OF THE WORLD ON SLAVERY.

The great fallacy, so rife everywhere throughout the world, that slavery is the cause of our national troubles, rests on the almost universal persistent closing of the eyes to this fact of the physical difference between the two races. Slavery is not the cause of the sectional war, but a blind and mad resistance to a physical condition which God has ordained, and which man is in vain attempting to subvert.

THE CORNER STONE DULY ACKNOWLEDGED, SOLVES THE VEXED QUESTION OF SLAVERY.

Take your stand on this great acknowledged fact, that the African and white races are physically different, follow out this truth to its logical result, and the question of slavery, or subordination of the inferior to the superior race, is clearly solved in all its phases.

Do you ask how?

First: We must accept as a fixed fact that ordinance of God which he has decreed, that the two races are physically different, and not complicate the fact, with any modifications, drawn from the prevalent visionary, infidel notions of an equality which has no existence, nor make any vain attempt to fix upon the mere relation of superior and inferior, or of rulers and ruled, moral or religious qualities which God in his word has not fixed to the relation.

Second: We must leave to each and every State in the Union, where the two races exist together, whether in larger or smaller proportions, unmolested control over any adjustment of their relations to each other.

Third: In the kindly spirit of the fathers of 1787, which they brought to the construction of our priceless constitution, we should refrain from embittering the relations of the two races by an irritating busy-bodyism, a meddlesome interference with the manner in which the duties belonging to their relation to each other are or are not fulfilled, and taking the apostle's counsel " to be quiet and mind our own business."

These three directions carried out in a christian spirit faithfully, would restore the Union on the only basis on which it can ever be restored. Whether enlightened reason can make its voice heard in this din of warring passions and interests, so that its "peace be still" can calm the storm that is desolating us, is a question I will not pretend to answer. It is to the true, sober, christian sentiment of the country, when disenthralled from its entanglement with the delusive socialistic and infidel theories of the day, that we look with any hope for our national salvation.

I have dwelt at some length on this one point, because of its paramount importance. It is a noticeable and gratifying circumstance, that our President and the Vice-President of the Southern Government, are in accord on a fundamental principle. Union of opinion on one point, especially if that point be fundamental, is hopeful, and prophetic of further conciliation, perhaps pacification, in the future. The great physical fact of the broad difference of the Afri-

can and white races, which the President so justly and
openly recognizes, lies at the root of the whole controversy
respecting slavery. Let us, then, study the condition of
things resulting from this truth in the light of an intelligent christian philosophy, not viewing it through the dis-
torted medium of abolition spectacles, but with the clear
vision of an eye spiritually enlightened, and a temper of
heart which accepts a providential fact with humility, recognizing the highest wisdom in all God's ordinances, however mysterious to us, endeavoring to adapt our ways to
his facts, not his facts to our ways. In that temper of
heart, you will clearly discern that this providential arrangement of conditions in human society, has for its end a purpose of infinite and eternal good to both races—a purpose
clearly discerned in the light of Gospel truth, but wholly
obscured in the smoke with which a proud but shallow infidel philosophy, a false christianity, and pretentious human-
itarianism, have enshrouded the whole subject.

PROBABLE ENGLISH INTRIGUE TO PREVENT RE-UNION.

One word on your remark, that the South "spurns all
overtures of conciliation." When, where, and by whom
have any overtures been made? When, where, and by
whom have they been spurned? If you take the intemper-
ate speeches, the passionate flings in editorial and anonymous articles, in the Southern journals, as the exponents of
the real sentiments of the Southern masses, are these the
safe bases upon which to found 'your remarks? If so, by
parity of reasoning, the Southern masses should take the
"radical and infidel" ravings of the "Garrison stamp,"
which are their counterpart in the speeches, editorials and
anonymous articles of our newspapers. We have been ac-
customed to condemn the South for its false judgment of
Northern sentiment, because formed from just such radical
sources. These are very unsafe sources of information on
each side in exciting times like these, on which to found in-
tersectional sentiment. Let me hint at one danger from
relying on such undiplomatic sources of information. Glance
for a moment at the attitude of England toward the United
States. We there see two well-defined parties, neither of
them friendly to us as a nation; one the cotton interest
siding with the South; and the other her abolition coteries

siding with the North; and so, England, balancing herself adroitly between these two parties in her own island, safe from any dangerous collision between them, harmful to herself, through her administration can give aid in our deplorable strife to the one section or to the other, or to both, to prevent conciliation, as best may serve the great political purpose of England—the permanent division of the United States. Keeping within the bounds of a quasi-neutrality, England can, on the one hand, furnish the South with munitions of war, and privateers to prey on Northern commerce; and, on the other, can get up abolition demonstrations at Exeter Hall and elsewhere, to strengthen and encourage the fanatical element of the North, as the vicissitudes of our unnatural war manifest, in one or the other section, any abatement of that ferocity of hate which she has for so long a period engendered and seduously promoted as the sure means of accomplishing her political purpose of *permanent separation*.[1]

---

(1) Let me ask your attentive reflection upon such indications of English designs and desires as the following: In an able article on the American Revolution, in the *Edinburgh Review*, of October, 1862, the reviewer says: "We therefore say, without hesitation, that we wish the war to cease, and the independence of the South to be established." Lord Campbell, in the House of Lords, on the 4th of August, 1862, said: "It is not too much to say that no class or party in the country any longer desires to see the reconquest of the South, and the reconstruction of the Union." The reviewer says: "At the outset of the struggle, the tendency was strong in England to side with the North. On the other hand, many felt undoubted satisfaction at the breaking up of that great democratic government, whose institutions had been held up to them by their own reformers as a model of perfection," &c. The reviewer puts the question: "Is it the interest of the civilized world, and especially of our own country, (England,) that the American Union should be restored?" And he answers it by saying: "It can scarcely be said that the relations of the American Union to Europe, and to England in particular, have been so satisfactory as to make us anxious for its continuance."

Further on he says: "The feeling in England is not founded on a desire of vengeance or personal retribution on any one, for insults which we have received. It rests on a much more calm and rational basis—that is to say, on the conviction that the unity of the government at Washington alone made the blow tell; it is hoped that when that unity is gone, all insults of the kind, if not so impolitic to be avoided altogether, will at least be harmless, and of no consequence to England." In another place: "The independence of the South would open new markets for our manufactures, without the previous restrictions of Federal tariffs."

These extracts, from the most intelligent exponents of public opinion in England, could be multiplied to any extent. I give one or two only from the *North British Review*, of February, 1862: "Most Englishmen, and ourselves among the number, have arrived at the conclusion, not only that the secessionists will succeed in their enterprise, but that this success will, eventually, be of the most signal service to humanity, to civilization, and to the cause of universal and enduring peace."

Again: "We entertain, then, no doubt that the dissolution of the Union is an accomplished and irreversible fact, and one of the very greatest facts of our day. We can see no grounds on which the continuance of that Union should be desired by any wise or good man."

Again: "That the independence of the South and the dissolution of the great republic are accomplished and irreversible facts, seems to us undeniable. The nation founded by Washington is severed—the Union contrived by his wisdom, and consecrated by his name, is at an end. We have now to ask what beauty there was in it that we should have longed for its continuance? What sacred purpose did it serve that we should deplore its end?"

These are specimens only indicating the bias of English sentiment, and showing that the English Government looks with exultation on the success of its plot of dividing our Union. Is this, then, the time for persistence in unconstitutional acts, which must inevitably create further rendings and divisions?

It is not an unreasonable supposition, that English emissaries at the South, supported from the "secret service fund," are the authors of those assumed spurnings of conciliatory overtures which you look upon as coming from the Southern heart? While this supposition, natural in the light of her past history, is not only *possible*, but *probable*, I need better evidence than has yet appeared, that the Southern masses, the great conservative body of the Southern people, are really disunionists. There is evidence on the contrary, that Union sentiment exists in the South, and would show its existence and activity, were it not stifled by the *unconstitutional* means which Northern, in alliance with English abolitionism, have brought to bear, to kill it.

I stop rather abruptly, possibly to my disadvantage, for I am compelled to leave untouched points perhaps necessary to prevent misapprehension. There is, however, a sentence in your letter, which I can not pass unnoticed, grounded, it appears, upon a remark of Mr. Field, casting an imputation upon the respectability and purity of intention of those associated with me in the effort to diffuse political knowledge. What Mr. Field may have said under the influence of that mendacious report of the *Post*, or what he may think of their characters, becomes of consequence only through your reiteration of his opinion. I notice it, therefore, (since you are in actual ignorance as well of the persons who were present, as of their social and moral position,) to say that neither could their respectability be enhanced, nor my own diminished, by my association with them. I can not close without thanking you for your frank letter and expressions of neighborly and friendly interest, which I cordially reciprocate.

Truly, with respect and high personal esteem, your friend and neighbor,

SAMUEL F. B. MORSE.

Edward N. Crosby, Esq.

THE END.

APPENDIX.

NUMBER I.

Pleas before the Hon. Jehu T. Elliott, Judge of the 13th Judicial Circuit, in the State of Indiana, on Thursday, the 16th day of October, A. D. 1862, held at the court house, in and for the county of Jay, in the State of Indiana.

Jay County, } Heretofore, to-wit, on the 8th day of September, A. D. to-wit. } 1862, Jeremah Smith filed in the clerk's office, of our said Jay Circuit Court, in the State of Indiana, his complaint in the words and figures following, to-wit:

State of Indiana, Jay county. In the Jay Circuit Court, October Term, A. D. 1862. Jeremiah Smith, the plaintiff in this suit, complains of John F. Bowden, the defendant in this suit, and says: Paragraph 1st. That heretofore, to-wit, on the 12th day of March, A. D. 1859, the plaintiff contracted with, and sold to the defendant, the west half of the southeast quarter of section number nineteen, in township number twenty-four, of range fourteen, east, containing eighty acres, and lying in the county of Jay aforesaid, at and for the price and sum of sixteen hundred dollars, out of which the defendant agreed to, and then and there was to pay $166 50, for which the said land was then mortgaged to the school fund of said county, and for the remainder of which purchase-money he gave the plaintiff his four several promissory notes of that date: one for $233 50, and due December 1st, 1859, and the other three for $400 each, and due on the 1st day of August, 1860, 1861, and 1862, respectively, all of said notes bearing interest from date, and collectable without any relief whatever from valuation or appraisement laws; and the defendant also agreed, and was to pay the taxes of the current and subsequent years of said lands, and was put in possession of the said lands and premises by the plaintiff, and has remained in possession thereof from thence hitherto, and at the time of making said contract, the plaintiff executed and delivered to the said defendant a title-bond reciting said contract and sale, and binding and obligating the plaintiff to convey the said lands to the defendant, his heirs or assigns within a reasonable time after the said purchase-money should be fully paid; and the said plaintiff says, that on the 15th day of October, 1861, by the judgment and consideration of this honorable court, he recovered against the said defendant the sum of $1086 92 for the balance of the principal and interest then due and unpaid of the three notes first falling due of the said notes so given for said land, and also his costs in that behalf expended, taxed $———; on which judgment, he afterwards sued out execution, and which execution was returned by the sheriff "no property found whereon to levy," all of which fully and at large appears by the records of this court herein remaining; and the plaintiff further says that the last of said notes with its interest, is now due, and is unpaid, and every part thereof, and he files a copy thereof herewith, and makes it a part of this complaint: WHEREFORE, the plaintiff prays judgment for five hundred dollars, the amount of said note and interest, together with the costs of this suit, all collectable without any relief whatever from valuation or appraisement laws; and the plaintiff also prays that this court will, by its order and decree, direct the said defendant to specifically perform his said contract, and pay into this court, for the use of the plaintiff, the amount of the said first named judgment, with all the interest and costs that have accrued thereon, and also the judgment now prayed for on the said last named note, with all the interest and costs accrued thereon, within a short day, to be fixed by this court; and in default of his so paying the same, that this court, by its order and decree, direct the sheriff of Jay county to sell the said lands and premises, to-wit, the west half of the southeast quarter of section nineteen, in township twenty-four, of range fourteen, east, lying in Jay county, Indiana, or so much thereof as may be necessary, as lands are sold on execution, without valuation or appraisement, to make the said judgments, with the interest and costs, and accruing costs, and upon the sale and payment of the purchase-money by the purchaser, the sheriff to execute to him a deed for the premises sold, and to put the purchaser into immediate possession thereof; and in case the said premises shall not sell for sufficient to fully satisfy all of said sums of money, that the sheriff be directed to levy the residue of any other property of the defendant subject to execution, without relief from valuation or appraisement laws, and grant to the plaintiff other necessary and proper relief in the premises. Jer. Smith, plaintiff. [Copy of the note omitted.] And on the day and year first aforesaid, now come the said parties, and the said defendant files his demurrer to the said complaint, in the following words and figures, to-wit: The defendant, John F. Bowden, demurs to the plaintiff's complaint, and for cause sets down the following: 1. Said complaint does not state facts sufficient to constitute a cause of action. 2, That said complaint contains several causes of action improperly united therein. John F. Bowden, defendant. And the said demurrer is submitted to the court, and the court having heard the argument of counsel, and mature deliberation being thereon had, overrule said demurrer, and said defendant having wholly failed to file and [any] further and other answer in discharge of the rule heretofore taken against him, the court therefore render the following judgment: It is therefore considered by the court, that the said plaintiff recover from the said defendant the sum of four hundred and eighty-six dollars and — cents, ($486 00) the full amount of the said last mentioned promissory note set out in said cause of action, and interest thereon, and also the sum of —— dollars, the costs paid, laid out, and expended by the said plaintiff in the prosecution of said action, collectable without any relief from valuation or appraisement laws. And it is further decreed by the court, that the said plaintiff execute and acknowledge a good and sufficient deed in fee-simple for the real estate described in said complaint, as required by said title-bond, with the proper covenants of warranty, excepting out of the operations of such warranty the incumbrance of a certain mortgage to the sinking fund, existing on said land at the time of the sale of said land to the defendant, and also the taxes on said land at the time of said sale, and subsequently accruing; and that said deed, when so executed and acknowledged, be placed in the hands of the clerk of this court, to be by him handed to the said defendant whenever he shall fully pay the balance of the said purchase-money due on said land described in the cause of action; and it is further decreed that said defendant, on or before the 4th day of July, 1863, pay into the clerk's office of this court, for the use of said plaintiff, the full and entire residue of the purchase money due on said lands, including the said amount of sixteen hundred and thirty-eight dollars and 13 cents, the amount of the judgment set forth on the last mentioned promissory note mentioned in said complaint, as also the amount remaining unpaid of the judgment heretofore rendered by this court on the three first promissory notes given to secure a portion of the purchase-money for said real estate, rendered October 15th, 1861, for ten hundred and eighty-six dollars and ninety-two cents—interest to October 15th, 1862—and on the full payment of said ,purchase-money as above said by said defendant, the said defendant shall be entitled to the deed of conveyance for said lands directed as aforesaid to be deposited with said clerk of this court. And on the failure of the said defendant to pay the full amount of the purchase-money remaining unpaid as aforesaid, by the 4th day of July, 1863, then, in that case, it shall be the duty of the sheriff of said county to sell said lands on a certified copy of this decree, if the same can be sold for an amount sufficient to pay the full residue of the purchase-money, and the costs of this suit; and if the same can not be sold for said amount, then said real estate shall be struck off and transferred to the said plaintiff in full discharge of his said judgments, interest and costs, and the same shall be accepted and received by him in full satisfaction for the full amount of said purchase-money remaining due and unpaid, and said defendant shall be acquitted and discharged from the payment of the same

I have inserted this complete record of my case against Bowden, pending when the outrage, noticed at pages 183 and 184 of the book, was perpetrated on me, that all may come to the light. Any lawyer will at once see how grossly my rights were outraged by the decree of the court. For the benefit of others, I note the following things:

1. The demurrer admitted my complaint to be true, and the court decreed upon the state of facts set out in my complaint. It was the duty of the court to enforce the contract, not to vary the contract, or make a new one; yet it required that I should execute and deliver a deed into court *before* the money was paid, when by the contract it was to have been made *after* the money was paid.

2. All the money was due and overdue; and yet the court extended the time of payment nearly nine months. The law allowed a stay of six months upon good security being put in, but prohibited the court from giving time for the payment of the money; 2 R. S. 123, § 378; and yet the court gave nine months without any security whatever.

3. If not paid, the costs of a sale had to be incurred as decreed by the court, for Bowden's benefit; for if it sold for more than the debt and costs, he would get the overplus, and if it would not bring the debt and costs, I was decreed to take it in full discharge of the debt and costs. By the contract it was to be sold without valuation; the law said the court should so adjudge and decree; it so adjudged, and then decreed that I must take it, not at two-thirds of its value, nor at its full value, but in full discharge of my claim, with the costs of a sheriff's sale added on, for Bowden's benefit.

This was public justice in October, 1862. It is worse now, and is getting worse every day. Alas! what is our country coming to! The land was offered, and no bid for it. I sold it afterwards, at a loss of over $600. I give this to the public in sorrow for the condition it shows our country to be in, and not in sorrow for the loss of the money.

NUMBER II.

We had a moot Legislature in Winchester, in the winter of 1860-61. It honored me with the office of Governor, and I delivered the annual message on the 4th of January, 1861. The following is the portion of the message relating to our national troubles, which shows what my views and opinions were then, and I have seen no reason to change them. My fears then expressed, are being realized, alas, too truly! Internecine strife will now soon be upon us, unless we stop in our mad career.

[From the Daily Indiana State Sentinel, January 7, 1861.]

But while we have been in the reception and enjoyment of these manifold blessings from the Giver of all good, and while we have inherited from our revolutionary ancestors the freest and best government and political institutions ever given to man, and are in the full enjoyment and fruition of its incalculable blessings and advantages, the fell spirit of discord and disunion has been constantly, steadily and rapidly shedding its baneful influence among us, severing the ties of fraternity, harmony and good feeling, and sowing the seeds of hatred and ill-will broadcast over our heaven-favored land, till we are now in the midst of a dissolution of our National Union, and in imminent danger of being precipitated into all the horrors of civil, servile and internecine wars. One of the original thirteen States of this Union, in her sovereign capacity, in solemn convention of her people, has, so far as she can by her individual act, severed herself from the Union, and dissolved the political connection hitherto existing between her and the United States of America. Other States are making rapid preparations to take the same action, and there is great probability, if not absolute certainty, that in a short time, fifteen of the thirty-three States of this Union will have withdrawn from it, and declared themselves out of it.

The dire effects of this state of the political atmosphere is beginning to be felt already. Panic and alarm have seized upon the public mind from one end of the country to the other. Property of all kinds has depreciated in value millions and millions of dollars. Our own beloved State lost $2,000,000 in four weeks by depreciation in the price of pork and wheat, two of her great staples. Commerce has become almost entirely prostrated, sinking with it the millions invested in ships, steamboats and railroads, and throwing out of employment thousands of employees, engaged in those industrial pursuits, and thereby depriving them and their families of the means of sustenance. Manufacturers are suffering a like prostration. Banks and the monetary affairs of the country have also felt the shock. It would swell this communication to too great a length to give specifications as to all, hence I will give one as to the railroad interests of the country, as a specimen of all. I take it from the *American Railroad Journal*, the organ of that interest for the United States:

"Commerce flourishes only in times of quiet. As far as our railroads are concerned, consequently, the effect of the present political agitation is simply disastrous, and to a degree that can hardly be estimated. The construction of these works in the newer States has already been thrown back five years. Is there any compensatory advantage gained on the other side? Nothing. Everything that tends to alienate the two sections, tends to the same extent to destroy the traffic of our public works Is it not then the duty of all parties interested in their construction, or in their securities, to lend a hand to place the material interests of the country in harmonious relations? These transcend all of a political character. So long as they are maintained or preserved, the other can not possibly go wrong. Political obligations should be deduced from, and always subordinate to, considerations of personal or material advantage. The moment these are disregarded, a course is entered upon which, sooner or later, must be abandoned, though not, perhaps, until mischief is done that can hardly be repaired."

These disasters, dire as they are, are but the results of the incipient steps to, and the apprehensions of, the breaking up of our National Government, and the dissolution of this Union; and they are but as a drop to the ocean of overwhelming calamities that will surely attend the full consummation of those dire events, should God in his wrath allow them to come upon us. May He, in his infinite mercy, prevent their consummation!

A peaceful dissolution of this Government is an impossibility. Were it possible, and the slave and free States separated peaceably, and organized into separate republics, how long would they remain at peace? The discordant elements that have been operating for years to array these sections of the Union one against the other, and that have had them in *quasi* civil war for some years past, with the Constitution and the General Government in existence, would, when those restraints are taken away, at once plunge us into war. The pent up ill feeling and hatred that they have been so long creating and building up between these two sections of our Union, would spontaneously burst forth into the most bitter and relentless war, the results of which it is horrible to think of or contemplate.

But if the Union can not be peaceably dissolved, and inasmuch as if could it would at once result in disastrous and ruinous warfare between the dissevered sections, let us contemplate a forcible dissolution of this, the best government ever given to man.

A forcible dissolution is a dissolution in and by civil war. Civil wars are the most vindictive, cruel and ferocious of all wars. The institution of slavery being the pretext if not the cause of the troubles, efforts would soon successfully be made to make it not only a civil but a servile war. There being differences of opinions and views all over the Union, as to the questions out of which these wars were brought about and prosecuted, these differences will soon bring about internecine strife. Thirty millions of the most enterprising, enlightened and powerful people on the globe will then be engaged in civil, servile and internecine wars, a combination of the three most horrid forms of war known to the human family. Once so engaged, the blood will become hot, and all the fiendish passions of which the human heart is capable will be called into action, and they will not cease to fight till perfect exhaustion compels them to. Strong and powerful as this people are, it will take ten or fifteen years to so exhaust them. In the meantime military men—Captains, Colonels and Generals—will have been manufactured, and when the country becomes depopulated and the besom of destruction of ten or fifteen years of devastating wars shall have overrun it, these military men will parcel out our territory, and the remnants of our people, into petty military despotisms. We once had a Washington to return our country, exhausted and prostrate from seven years of devastating war, to civil life and to the building up of free institutions; but we will never have another one. For more than five thousand years from its creation, the human family produced but one Washington. We need not expect another one soon, if ever. Hence, civil war and a forcible dissolution of this Government will be the death knell of free institutions all over the present territory of the United States; blight the cause of free institutions throughout the world; and prove what despots have always insisted was true, *that man is incapable of self-government.* For if we, enlightened, wise and wealthy as we are, can not preserve the civil and religious liberty inherited by us from our revolutionary fathers, and the glorious form of government they framed to secure the enjoyment of that liberty, and govern ourselves thereunder, can we expect to ever find another people that can govern themselves? It is futile to think we can. If we, surrounded with the blessings and immunities that we have, can not preserve our institutions and govern ourselves under them, the world need not look for another people that can.

Washington himself said that the preservation of our Union was essential to the preservation of our liberties. In his Farewell Address, he said: "The unity of the Government, which constitutes you one people, is also now dear to you. It is justly so; for it is the main pillar in the edifice of your independence, the support of your tranquility at home, your peace abroad; of your safety; of your prosperity; *of that very liberty* which you so highly prize."

It becomes our duty then, and the duty of every lover of his country, of every lover of the cause of liberty and free institutions among mankind, to look the danger that is now at our door, fully in the face. As a dissolution of this Government will result in the loss of our liberty and the destruction of the hopes of free institutions throughout the world of mankind, and as that dissolution is now imminent, it behooves us all to cast about and see if any plan can be devised to avert the threatened danger.

Can the union of these States be preserved by force?

When comparatively small portions of our fellow-citizens disobey the laws, or resist the due and proper execution of the trusts and duties confided to the Government, the strong arm of the Government can properly crush out such resistance, and restore order and obedience to the laws of the country. But when whole States, or a large combination of States, resort to the revolutionary right inherent in all mankind, and place themselves in resistance to the constituted authorities of the Government, the question assumes a different aspect, and requires a different mode of treatment.

Ours is a union of free States, constituted of free men, who have the right to govern themselves. The real ligament of our union is fraternity of feeling and a common desire to promote the welfare of each and all; while each State, in the original compact, reserved to itself the right to judge and determine for itself what municipal and social regulations and institutions would best subserve its interests. Can we preserve this fraternity of feeling by force and compulsion? Can we prove our common desire to promote the welfare of any State or States by garrisoning our armies among them and filling their ports with our navies? Do we honor and respect their reserved right to establish and enjoy their own municipal regulations and institutions when we go to war with them about one of them, and that a vital one that effects their whole social organization and material wealth? All of these questions must be answered in the negative. It is a contradiction in terms to say that a free people can be held in durance, and governed by compulsion, and still be a free people.

Coercion, then, being incompetent to preserve union and harmony among free and independent States, composed of free people, and as the union of these States is absolutely essential to the preservation of our own liberties as well as of the hopes of mankind for ultimate free government throughout the world, we must find some other means to preserve what is so essential to ourselves, as well as to "the rest of mankind."

With great respect for the opinions of others, and diffidence in my own judgment, I venture respectfully to say that a return to that fraternal feeling that existed among the fathers who formed our Government, and an exercise of the same spirit of conciliation and forbearance that actuated them, can again cement us in union, in fact as well as in name, and dispel the gloomy clouds that now lower over us. Whatever any of us may have done, or may now be doing, to alienate us one from another, let us all promptly abandon. Let us promptly correct our own faults or faulty conduct, if we have any, and not set ourselves up as the censors or conscience-keepers of our fellow-citizens of any of our sister States, for any faults, real or supposed, that we may conceive they have. Each State is accountable itself only for its municipal regulations, and we for ours. Neither is accountable for those of any of the others. While some of our citizens incorrectly think differently, and conceive that they are *morally* responsible for the political institutions of other States, they should remember that, even in the moral code, each is to give an account for himself and not for another; and that we will all have enough to do to attend to the making up of our own account without attending to those of our fellow citizens of other States of this Union. But our duties and obligations, as citizens of this great confederacy, are constitutional and political, and not moral nor religious; and the faithful discharge of our constitutional duties and obligations will not conflict with any moral or religious one; and the divine obligation is, that we discharge our political duties and obligations faithfully, "that we may lead a quiet and peaceable life in all godliness and honesty."

I am happy to be able to say that our own beloved Indiana has, in in her legislative, executive and judicial departments, faithfully discharged all her constitutional duties and obligations to her sister States; but truth and justice require that I should confess, in this official paper, (which I do with much mortification) that some of our citizens have not. Under a mistaken notion of their constitutional right to liberty of speech, they have freely used licentiousness of speech against some of our sister States and their institutions. While freedom of speech is an invaluable right, dear to every American citizen, our own constitution makes every person responsible for the abuse of that right. There is as marked a distinction between liberty of speech and licentiousness of speech, as there is between liberty of action and uncontrolled or reckless action. While we all enjoy liberty of action, that does not authorize us to interfere with, molest or disturb the persons, families or property of any of our fellow citizens. So, while we all enjoy liberty of speech, that does not authorize us, by our speech, to interfere with, molest, disturb or endanger the persons, families or property of any of our fellow citizens. Whatever, in word or action, disturbs or endangers the public peace and tranquility, is illegal at common law, as against public policy and the public peace. So let us not deceive ourselves, and claim and do what is illegal and unconstitutional, under that inestimable constitutional right of liberty of speech.

But it is said in defence of this course, that Washington and the fathers of the Revolution opposed bad laws and improper claims of authority by the British Crown with speech, the press, and the sword So they did. But that course and conduct of theirs was revolutionary, and resulted in the overturning of the government and existing order of things. The argument is an argument for revolutionizing and upturning our government—the very thing that now so fearfully threatens us. It is not an argument or an example to show us how we should act to maintain our government and the existing order of things, but is an argument and example for dissolution of our government and revolution—the very thing we profess to be anxious to avoid. Those who quote the Declaration of Independence, and examples and precedents from the Revolution, are (though, in charity, I think, unwittingly,) arguing for the dissolution and revolution of this government, as the revolutionary fathers were arguing for the dissolution and revolution of the then existing government. Washington and the fathers were then dissolutionists and revolutionists. By quoting them and their action during that struggle, we thereby avow ourselves dissolutionists and revolutionists. By taking their conduct in that struggle for exemplars for us, we place ourselves in the category of revolutionists. The right of revolution, and of recurrence to the natural rights of man, exists when a proper case arises for the exercise of that right. But the maxims and principles proper to recur to in the exercise of that right, are not the proper maxims and principles to recur to in sustaining and maintaining an existing order of government. The constitution and principles of the government are the proper things to recur to for that end. As well might the law and precedents in burglary cases be cited in an action of covenant (for the constitution is a covenant) as revolutionary principles and precedents be cited to determine rights and duties under the existing Government of the United States.

Let us then recur to the constitution, and not to revolutionary principles or precedents, to determine what we shall do to preserve this Union. Let us see what is in the bond, and then faithfully and honestly perform all the obligations it imposes upon us. Let us conciliate our brethren who think that the case is made that entitles them to exercise the right of revolution, in the true spirit of fraternity and affection. Let us approach them in the same spirit of compromise and concession that the constitution itself was made in. Hear what the Father of his country said of it: "The constitution which we now present, is the result of a spirit of amity and mutual deference and concession, which the peculiarity of our political situation rendered indispensable." Whatever the peculiarity of our political situation at this time, renders indispensible to restore harmony and unity among us, let us, in the spirit of amity, at once concede it. Let us implicitly follow the advice of the Father of his country in his Farewell Address, and hereafter "indignantly frown upon every attempt to alienate any portion of our country from the rest, or to enfeeble the sacred ties which link together the various parts." Let us not "characterize parties by geographical discriminations, *Northern and Southern, Atlantic and Western;* whence designing men may endeavor to excite a belief that there is a real difference of local interests and views. One of the expedients of party to acquire influence, within particular districts, is to misrepresent the opinions and aims of other districts. You can not shield yourselves too much against the jealousies and heart-burnings, which spring from these misrepresentations; they tend to render alien to each other those who ought to be bound by fraternal affection." Thus said Washington in his last political will and testament to this nation. Though we may not have followed his advice heretofore, let us resolutely do it hereafter, for all time to come. The failure to obey these injunctions has brought us to where we are, as Washington said it would; a return to the obedience of them may bring us out of our present difficulties.

* * * * * *

The importance of preserving this Union, and the imminency of the danger which threatens it, makes it the first and principal duty of all of us to save it if possible. Should you, in your wisdom, be able to accomplish so glorious a work, it will be enough for one session of the Legislature; and the country will cheerfully wait for two years for any minor correction of existing laws that may be needed, if you can secure for them the continuance of our glorious Union. And my whole heart is so thoroughly enlisted in this work, that I extend my hand to all of you in the spirit of political and patriotic fraternity, as members of one and the same great and glorious Union, one and inseparable now and forever.

JER. SMITH.

January 4, 1861.

NUMBER III.

The abolitionists have been resisting for years the *constitution*, which really constitutes and creates *the government*. And yet they are now claiming to be the exclusive Union men, the exclusive loyal men; yes, the "intensely loyal." They have for years rested the "powers that be," to wit, the constitutional covenant to return fugitive slaves; and now they are croaking in every church, on every Lord's day, about the 13th chapter of Romans, and the duty of christians to support *the government* meaning that they must be in subjection to abolitionism; for that with them is *the government*.

The American Anti-Slavery Society long ago passed these resolutions, and have ever since been acting upon them:

"*Resolved*, That *secession* from the *United States Government* is the duty of every abolitionist, since no one can take office, or deposit his vote under its constitution, without violating his anti-slavery principles, and rendering himself an abettor to the slaveholder in his sin.

"*Resolved*, That years of warfare against the slave power have convinced us that every act done in support of the *American Union* rivets the chain of the slave—that the only exodus of the slave to freedom unless it be one of blood, *must be over the remains of the present American Church, and the grave of the present Union.*

"*Resolved*, That the *abolitionists* of this country should make it one of the *primary* objects of *this agitation* to *dissolve the American Union*."

In 1856, William L. Garrison truly said:

"The Republican party is moulding public sentiment in the right direction for the specific work the abolitionists are striving to accomplish, viz: *The dissolution of the Union, and the abolition of slavery throughout the land.*"

In 1850, the New York *Tribune* said:

"THE AMERICAN FLAG.
"Tear down the flaunting lie!
Half mast the starry flag!
Insult no sunny sky
With hate's polluted rag!
Destroy it, ye who can!
Deep sink it in the waves!
It bears a fellow man
To groan with fellow slaves."

Are not these and their followers pretty Union men? and have not they a full right to brand those who have always been for the Union, and "friends to the constitution," as "disloyal?"

They pretend to be great friends of "freedom." Yet they passed in the last Congress an illegal and unconstitutional act, and in August, 1863, provost marshals, illegally and unconstitutionally exercising authority under the President, published circulars, copying in the 24th section of that act, making it a penal offence to harbor, conceal or give employment to a conscripted citizen, who did not answer the call of conscription, and thereby, by the terms of that act, became *a deserter;* and warning free American citizens that it would be strictly enforced. For the last twenty-five years, when fugitive slaves were thus harbored and employed *in violation of a constitutional law of Congress*, these abolitionists wholly disregarded the 13th of Romans, and their christian duty "to support the government," and made resistance and sedition upon repeated occasions.

The result of all this is, that, in September, 1863, white conscripts who were chained together in couples, were marched more than a mile publicly along Broadway, New York, guarded by armed soldiers. White men dragged in chains from their families, their homes, and their States, to aid in freeing negroes at the South!

Similar sights were seen in Philadelphia, as reported by the Philadelphia *Age*, which said:

"Over the iron manacles that bound the wrists of several, were thrown handkerchiefs, and the downcast look and sorrowing eye of the conscripts told how deeply they felt the degradation they were compelled to suffer. These men had committed no crime. Their names had been drawn from the fatal wheel; and, in the agony of doubt, whether they should remain with their loved ones in these sore times of want and trial, or eagerly march to fill the ranks of the army in this "war for the African and his race," they had not promptly reported to the Provost Marshal's office, and were called deserters. This sight, we are informed, is no extraordinary one. It is of frequent and almost hourly occurrence. Compelled to suffer the grossest indignities, thousands are daily tortured with the galling thought, that in this land of freedom, they must meet the fate of slaves."

Unless these monomaniacs are soon put out of power, we will be irretrievably ruined and destroyed as a people, when our proper epitaph will be:

HERE LIE A PEOPLE,
WHO, IN A VAIN ATTEMPT TO FREE SLAVES,
LOST THEIR OWN LIBERTIES.

www.ingramcontent.com/pod-product-compliance
Lightning Source LLC
Chambersburg PA
CBHW032010220426
43664CB00006B/194